CANADIAN
FOREIGN POLICY

CANADIAN FOREIGN POLICY
DEFINING THE NATIONAL INTEREST

STEVEN KENDALL HOLLOWAY

broadview press

Library and Archives Canada Cataloguing in Publication

Holloway, Steven Kendall, 1951-
    Canadian foreign policy : defining the national interest / Steven Kendall Holloway.

Includes bibliographical references and index.
ISBN 1-55111-816-5

    1. Canada—Foreign relations—1945–. 2. National interest—Canada. I. Title.

FC242.H63 2006   327.71   C2006-904061-3

Broadview Press is an independent, international publishing house, incorporated in 1985. Broadview believes in shared ownership, both with its employees and with the general public; since the year 2000 Broadview shares have traded publicly on the Toronto Venture Exchange under the symbol BDP.

We welcome comments and suggestions regarding any aspect of our publications—please feel free to contact us at the addresses below or at broadview@broadviewpress.com.

North America
PO Box 1243, Peterborough, Ontario, Canada K9J 7H5
PO Box 1015, 3576 California Road, Orchard Park, NY, USA 14127
Tel: (705) 743-8990; Fax: (705) 743-8353
email: customerservice@broadviewpress.com

UK, Ireland, and continental Europe
NBN International, Estover Road, Plymouth, UK PL6 7PY
Tel: 44 (0) 1752 202300; Fax: 44 (0) 1752 202330
email: enquiries@nbninternational.com

Australia and New Zealand
UNIREPS, University of New South Wales
Sydney, NSW, Australia 2052
Tel: 61 2 9664 0999; Fax: 61 2 9664 5420
email: info.press@unsw.edu.au

www.broadviewpress.com

Broadview Press gratefully acknowledges the financial support of the Government of Canada through the Book Publishing Industry Development Program for our publishing activities.

Designed by Chris Rowat Design, Daiva Villa

PRINTED IN CANADA

Contents

List of Tables and Figures

TABLES

FIGURES

CANADA

Yukon
Territory

• Whitehorse

Northwest Territories

Nunavut

• Yellowknife

• Iqaluit

British
Columbia

Newfoundland

Alberta

• St. John's

• Edmonton

Saskatchewan

Manitoba

Quebec

• Vancouver

Victoria •

• Calgary

• Saskatoon

Ontario

• Regina

Winnipeg •

P.E.I.

Quebec •

• Charlottetown

Fredericton •

• Halifax

Montreal •

New
Brunswick

Nova Scotia

OTTAWA ◎

• Toronto

Introduction to the National Interest Perspective

Canadians seem at times obsessed about whether they are obsessed about their role and place in the world. Much of this preoccupation focuses on some unique and virtuous qualities that allegedly guide our foreign policy. These qualities include multilateralism, peacekeeping, model global citizenship, multicultural harmony, and generosity in foreign aid. Since our actual performance on many of these principles falls short of the popular image, the above list might better be labelled "the myths of Canadian foreign policy."

This book on Canadian foreign policy might well have been subtitled "Canada as an ordinary country" — one that pursues more or less the same national objectives as any other state. All states want to be secure and prosperous. To the best of their abilities, they each defend their borders and try to preserve their independence and domestic unity. Even the desire to be unique is not unique, as many countries expend much effort showing off how their cultures, values, and principles distinguish them. A National Interest Perspective (NIP) allows us to see the commonalities between national foreign policies by showing us that all states share similar requirements. What make foreign policies different from each other is the unique strategies adopted by each state to attain these common goals, given their different contexts (geographical situations, histories, and resource allocations).

A National Interest Perspective is not exactly equivalent to a Statist approach, but for many purposes they are complementary. National interests are implemented by states, so we can naturally link them to a Statist paradigm (see Chapter 1). However, defining the national interest can also be thought of as a broad public discourse involving many societal actors. The Canadian nuclear weapons controversy of the early 1960s shows how state leadership that is weak and divided can open the policy debate to a wide range of people, becoming a major campaign issue in a national election. Similarly, national interests are often associated with the Realist paradigm in international relations, which emphasizes the lack of global government and the role of individual state power and diverse state interests in global politics. Indeed, Chapter 1 shows how a National Interest Perspective might be grounded in the assumptions of Realism for theoretical rigour. But a public discourse definition of national interest could argue for collective security, peacekeeping, and foreign aid, items not usually found on the Realist's agenda. Hence, this study will embrace both broad and narrow conceptualizations of the national interest.

What gives coherence to all definitions is the focus on policy: national interest puts the "policy" back into foreign policy. The National Interest Perspective forces Canadians to think explicitly about the goals of government actions and the assumptions that underlie them. It requires us to plan ahead and prioritize our objectives rather than just react to events as they arise. It demands that we set aside our preoccupation with the interests of our own societal group, province, or region and think about what is to the benefit of all Canadians.

Even when we use the "broad public debate" definition, and no matter how cacophonous that debate may be, the National Interest Perspective suggests we will find general, large-scale interests that unite our national political community. These enduring interests can best be observed by adopting a long, historical time frame. We cannot talk about the challenge of Quebec separatism without tracing its historical roots. Nor can we fully comprehend Canada's current concerns about loss of political independence to the United States without knowing how we gained it from Britain. An historical approach is a natural accompaniment to defining national interests.

For the student, the National Interest Perspective organizes and simplifies the various threads of Canada's foreign relations by concentrating them into a handful of enduring themes or national interests. Chapter 1 enumerates them as the following:

1. National security (including territorial sovereignty)
2. Political autonomy
3. National unity
4. Economic prosperity
5. Principled self-image (identity)

The rest of the book shows how these five national interests encompass the vast range and diversity of Canada's past, current, and future foreign policy. Chapter 2, on territorial sovereignty, discusses Canada's major jurisdictional conflicts on land and sea, past and present, including current conflicts over the Grand Banks and Hans Island. Chapter 3 discusses how national security defines the threat or the enemy and how Canada has historically adopted the enemies of its major partners, the United Kingdom and the United States. A schema for assessing potential enemy threats is presented, including its relevance (and possible misuses) in 1914, 1940, and 1946.

Chapter 4 brings national security up to date. It begins with the cold war period, important in part for the creation of Canada's two current alliances, NORAD and NATO, which receive extensive attention. The terrorist attacks of 9/11 and those that followed have fundamentally refocused attention on basic national security and homeland defence and thus receive detailed scrutiny here, along with a case study of Canada in Afghanistan.

Chapter 5 expands the definition of national security to include the alternatives of neutrality and disarmament, and the possibility of United Nations-directed collective security and peacekeeping. A taxonomy of neutrality is presented to analyze its potential relevance as a policy option for Canada. Disarmament, arms control, and the banning of certain weapons are discussed through UN resolutions and treaties, from non-proliferation to land mines. The League of Nations and the UN's role in collective security, and the successes, failures, and crucial assumptions of that mode of security, are laid out. In particular, Canada's role in the Ethiopian crisis in 1935, Korea in 1950, and Kuwait in 1990 demonstrates the limitations of this approach. The chapter moves to examine the more passive activity of "classic peacekeeping" and shows through a variety of such missions how Canada became identified with it. The ending of the cold war has resulted in a proliferation of new peacekeeping forms, as shown in a case study on the Balkan conflict and the genocide in Rwanda. Finally Canada's role in promoting security reform and human security at the United Nations is discussed.

Some commentators have claimed that Canada is a semi-colony or dependent of the United States. The subject of political autonomy is broadly covered in the next three chapters. Chapter 6 sets up the basic analytic tools necessary to bring clarity to this contentious subject and briefly traces the history of Canada's progression from colony to protectorate to independence from the United Kingdom. This history demonstrates the analytical categories of dependence, which still have relevance today and might serve as a road map for Quebec secession. Chapter 7 examines the state of Canadian political autonomy for each government since 1945. The chapter argues that the common perception that Prime Minister Diefenbaker was a strong nationalist and champion of independence must be re-evaluated, as shown in a case study of the nuclear weapons controversy. Political autonomy is linked to economic and cultural autonomy in Chapter 8. This chapter traces the rise and partial decline of Statist measures in these fields through the stories of the Foreign Investment Review Agency (FIRA), the broadcasting industry, and the split-run magazine controversy.

Chapter 9 focuses on the third national interest, national unity, and specifically on the issue of Quebec separatism. It briefly traces the history of contention between Canada's "two solitudes" through the Lesage Quiet Revolution, de Gaulle's visit, the FLQ crisis, and the two sovereignty referendums. The main concerns here are external factors, such as France's role in the "War of the Conferences" and the effects of an independent Quebec on foreign policy. The latter is analyzed in terms of security interests, economic factors, and territorial and constitutional questions. The story is brought up to date with the Canada-Quebec Accord on immigration, Premier Charest's proposals on overseas representation, and the rise of pro-sovereignty sentiment that has accompanied the investigations of the recent sponsorship scandal by the Gomery Commission.

Chapter 10 returns to economic matters and the state's pursuit of economic prosperity. It begins with a short primer on economic problems and policy tools facing any government, and then shifts to the external aspect of this quest for growth and stability. Free trade and mercantilism are presented as opposing approaches for producing growth through trade. The history of Canada's trade policy is traced through the Navigation Acts, Reciprocity, the National Policy, Imperial Preference, and Bretton Woods, showing how Canada has always been dependent on foreign markets. The Free Trade Agreement and NAFTA are examined in detail. The unresolved problem of trade remedy measures is presented along with a case study of the perennial softwood lumber dispute. Canada's broader role in regional and global trade negotiations is discussed before ending the chapter with an analysis of the economic impact of NAFTA so far.

The final national interest, projecting Canada's identity abroad, is dealt with in Chapter 11. Using the 1995 foreign policy review report *Canada in the World*, the chapter begins with a thorough examination of the image of Canada that the Department of Foreign Affairs projects overseas. This broad spectrum of attributes is narrowed to a lengthy discussion of Canada's foreign aid policies. The reasons for aid in general are explored, and the history of the ideas behind development assistance is traced. How these ideas and trends have impacted Canada's own aid policy is shown and the success and failures of Canada's policies are evaluated.

The concluding chapter provides an assessment of the National Interest perspective. It begins with a short description of the process for making foreign policy in Canada, explaining the roles of the major governmental and societal players. Then the main issues of the book are reviewed and shown to be intricately interconnected as in a finely balanced mobile.

* * *

I would like to thank Donna Huffman, Marcy Baker, Ozeas Costa, and Aubrey Whittle for their contributions in the preparation of this book.

Chapter One
Defining the National Interest

The modern state appears besieged on all fronts. On the international front, environmentalists and globalists tell us that the state is an obsolete and irrelevant institution for managing the growing crises of ecological collapse, economic restructuring, international drug cartels, and nuclear proliferation. The technological explosion represented by the Internet, fax, and satellite communications is eroding the regulatory powers of traditional national governments. Non-governmental Organizations (NGOs) and civil society are rapidly filling the vacuum of services no longer provided by the state.

On the domestic front, the national consensus in Canada for the past decade appears to be that the state should be downsized. Ballooning deficits, taxpayer fatigue, and government bureaucracy perceived as bloated and generally ineffective in solving societal problems have all generated a strong anti-state atmosphere. Even nominally socialist governments today mouth the buzzwords of *deregulation*, *efficiency*, and *global competition*.

Yet the premise of this book, to paraphrase Mark Twain, is that reports of the state's death have been greatly exaggerated. On the international side, since the end of the cold war the state system has actually expanded from 159 to over 190 United Nations (UN) members. Where states have collapsed, as in the Soviet Union, their territory has been replaced by nationalistic successor states. Where international organizations, such as the UN, appear to have been revitalized, they have only been so with the permission and approval of their member states.

Likewise, in the domestic arena, as one author has observed, we must not confuse state control with state authority: "state control has waxed and waned enormously over time, regions, and issue-areas, while the state's claim to ultimate political authority has persisted for more than three centuries."[1] At any time, states may choose different policies, empower different private institutions, or delegate partial authority to other agents without calling into question their ultimate authority (or "meta-authority") to determine what is political, what is public, and what is open to the state's control. What has been deregulated may be re-regulated by the state; what has been privatized may be re-nationalized.

We also must not confuse the demise of one particular state or government with the death generally of states. Revolution, conquest, and civil war are all features of our current state system and they do involve contesting state authority and state power. But the ultimate victors so far have usually been states. To argue that the state is waning as an institution, one must demonstrate that its authority or right to rule is being transferred to some other institution.

For any political community, the question of what constitutes the purpose or ends of good governance can be raised. A strength of the Statist model is that it highlights the question of the objectives of state authority, usually in the form of debates about the *public good* or the *national interest*. Both of these terms suggest a higher order of interests or benefits to society than mere private, individual, or group concerns and demands. The Statist model gives to the state the important role of determining and implementing those general societal goals. The term *national interest* has tended to fall in and out of fashion, paralleling the fortunes of the term *the state*.

Both terms are often seen as particularly relevant to Canada. The building of a strong Canadian state was seen as crucial, given this country's harsh environment, cultural diversity and centrifugal tendencies, and geographic proximity to a superpower. Yet in the study of Canadian foreign policy since World War II, most commentators have tended to use the discourse of internationalism and multilateralism. Despite former prime minister Trudeau's attempts to adopt a more nationalist stance, the phrase *national interest* has gone relatively unused in academic discussions of Canadian foreign policy.

This purpose of this book is to demonstrate the continuing relevance of both the state and the national interest as important analytical concepts, especially in the study of Canadian foreign policy. A National Interest Perspective (NIP) will be used to structure a comprehensive historical guide to the main issues of Canadian external affairs. The rest of this chapter will be spent sorting out the various conceptualizations of the state, sovereignty, and national interests. A deductivist model of the national interest will be described, and its particular relevance to Canada will be demonstrated.

STATE, NATION, AND GOVERNMENT

Considerable confusion exists in use of the terms *state*, *government*, and *nation*. The different perspectives (or "levels of analysis") from which one can view the state are, in part, responsible for this ambiguity. For example, we could look at the state from the international level and see a system of interacting sovereign states negotiating, trading, and sometimes making war with each other. We could also look from the level of domestic politics and see the state interacting with its society: making, implementing, and policing laws and regulations with its own citizens.

From the standpoint of international law, states are viewed as possessing four things: 1) a territory; 2) a population (citizens); and 3) one national government that is 4) sovereign over the people and territory. The key concept of sovereignty denotes the legal authority or "right to rule" that the government possesses and includes both an internal and external aspect. Sovereignty at home means the government has no rivals as the ultimate source of political authority and is at least tacitly accepted by its people. This latter aspect of authority, originating from the community it governs, is usually called *legitimacy* or the sense of a people that they are properly ruled. Sovereignty also has an international aspect in that the state seeks recognition from other states. Usually, foreign states will grant formal diplomatic recognition and exchange ambassadors with the representatives of one government per state. Civil wars demonstrate how a given government can lose sovereignty internally, when citizens shift their loyalties to the rebel cause, and externally, when other states shift their recognition and support to the new government.

The term *nation* is used to designate a large community of people who share certain characteristics. As Anthony Smith has suggested,[2] the list of these shared characteristics depends on how exclusive or inclusive a nationalist you are. Some nationalities share only a common territory and certain political or civic rights, duties, and symbols. Canada and the United States, with their large immigrant citizenries, are examples of this type of nationality. A more restrictive use of the term *nation* would require a shared ethnicity, implying that all members of the nation might be distant cousins, related by blood. States in which one nation of common ethnicity makes up most of the citizenry, such as Japan, are relatively rare and, in fact, every "nation" does not have it own "state," as witness the Kurds and Palestinians in the Middle East. In the early twentieth century, US president Wilson, among others, argued for a "principle of national self-determination" by which each nation should in practice have its own state in the international sense given above. This principle was employed to some extent at the Versailles Peace Conference following World War I to redraw the boundaries of Eastern Europe along ethnic or national lines. The result was a Hungarian "nation-state," a Polish "nation-state," and so on. Likewise today, the Chechens are fighting for a nation-state of their own. But should this principle be applied to redrawing boundaries of existing states? Are the Québécois a distinct nationality deserving, under the principle of self-determination, a separate nation-state of Quebec? Some have suggested that a nation is any community that defines itself as one.

In 2003 this very issue arose in the Canadian House of Commons when the Bloc Québécois motion calling Quebec a nation was defeated. Nonetheless the federalist premier of Quebec, Jean Charest, felt compelled to respond with a motion in the provincial assembly stating that "the Quebec National Assembly reaffirms that the Quebec people constitute a nation." This motion passed unanimously, though there were different interpretations as to how exclusively the concept applied.[3]

Another problem lies in distinguishing states and governments. The term *state* usually implies more than just the institutions of government. The international legal definition given above adds territory and citizenry to the concept. Indeed, from the international perspective, only states (and not individuals) are the subject of most international laws.

Writers who compare national political systems are inclined to separate the state from the society it rules. Patrick Dunleavy and Brendan O'Leary make the distinction by classifying the state as a "recognizably separate institution or set of institutions, so differentiated from the rest of its society as to create identifiable public and private spheres."[4] But this sounds like what international relations specialists would take to be the definition of government. Dunleavy and O'Leary go on to separate the terms *state* and *government* by making the state a special type of government: government exists in any society where there are rules and decisions, whereas the state is a recent formation dating from seventeenth-century Europe.

Sometimes the distinction seems to lie in the term *government* referring merely to the institutions, while *state* refers more to a theoretical or conceptual label. This is the case when particular *functions* are assigned to the state. Authors have attributed various functions to the state, including such things as maintaining law and order, pursuing social justice, and protecting private property. Critics have attacked such functional definitions for their tendency to reify and anthropomorphize the concept of the state.

Despite these criticisms, academic writers in the 1980s began to "bring the state back in" as an important theoretical concept and created a distinctive Statist approach or school. Thus, Theda Skocpol defines states as "organizations through which official collectivities may pursue distinctive goals, realizing them more or less effectively given the availability of state resources in relation to social settings."[5] In a similar vein Stephen Krasner sees the state as a unified and autonomous actor pursuing aims understood in terms of the national interest.[6] What these definitions share first and foremost is an emphasis on the relative independence of the state in drawing up and pursuing its goals and policies.

Living in a liberal democracy, it is difficult to think of the state as anything but a servant of the various political parties and interest groups that control or influence it. In other words, government policy starts from the political platform of the party that won the last election, conditioned by the lobbying efforts of special interest groups. Demands arise from society and the state responds with policy and decisions.

The Statist approach puts the emphasis back on the state or government itself as the main source of policy. It sees the state as autonomously formulating it goals and then planning how best to "sell" its policies to domestic and foreign audiences. The state may in fact meet considerable resistance from large segments of its society towards unpopular policies or laws. Even in democracies, some acts of government may be implemented despite a large measure of public hostility, for example tax increases, seat belt or smoking regulations, cuts in public services, and budget cuts. Likewise, in foreign affairs, the state must plot its strategy for handling external hostility to its policies. Two examples of states under strong external pressure are Israel, in its handling of the Palestinian question, and Sudan, over its treatment of citizens in the Darfur region.

This book adopts the Statist approach, using Krasner's version of the state. First of all, like the comparative approaches, it distinguishes state from society by emphasizing the state's relative autonomy from societal pressures. At the same time, the state is linked to society through the concept of sovereignty, which implies societal recognition or legitimacy. The definition used here is a hybrid one: *The state is a generally unified and relatively autonomous institution that claims sovereignty over a given territory and people and pursues on their behalf objectives understood in terms of the national interest, though this may involve internal and external resistance.* Though it defines the national government as the organization of the state, it distinguishes the state from generic governments by giving it the function of pursuing the national interest.

NATIONAL INTEREST

What, then, is this "national interest" that Krasner says is the state's goal or objective? This simple phrase has had a long and controversial history in the study of foreign affairs. It usually denotes a general public interest as opposed to a merely private one. Joseph Frankel suggests that in general terms, the national interests of all states are "broadly similar" and "centred upon the welfare of the nation and the preservation of its political doctrine and national style of life."[7] But in practice, what constitutes the "public good" is a matter of heated political debate.

Considering the diversity of groups within modern society, it is easy to see how different groups would possess different images of the national interest. Political parties across the spectrum try to sell us unique visions of the public good. Neo-conservatives believe deregulation will strengthen the country, while radical socialist parties want large businesses nationalized. Green parties stress environmental concerns; labour unions push for social policies supportive of the workers' interests; and business has its own definition of welfare. Even among business leaders, steelmakers might believe that protectionism is in the national interest, whereas export industries argue for free trade.

Nonetheless, even with this fragmented, competitive, pluralistic view of society, we can still make the Statist case for a broader view of the public good. The Statist argues the need for an autonomous actor or judge overriding these multiple, private views, not unlike the "benevolent prince" of European history. Such a prince was supposed to determine the interest of the society as a whole and not be swayed by the petty corporate interests of any group or coalitions of groups. While a benevolent ruler might be hard to find, the Statist nonetheless argues that the general public good is not to be found in the free competition of interests presented by the liberal model.

There are at least two ways of making this case. First, Krasner points out the nineteenth-century-economist Vilfredo Pareto's distinction between utility *for* the community and utility *of* the community.[8] Utility *for* the community is arrived at by summing up the individual preferences of all members of the community. This process would be something similar to the philosopher Jeremy Bentham's "greatest good for the greatest number." We would try to determine what is good for our state merely on the basis of what is good for each individual. This process sounds quite reasonable and democratic, and leaves the definition of what is best for the individual or group up to the judgment of that individual or group. It is quite consistent with liberal democratic visions of the good political system. On the other hand, utility *of* the community involves making judgments about the welfare of the community as a whole. What is good for the community as a whole may not be found by looking at the individual preferences alone. Consider the business community, for example. Since each businessperson might prefer unregulated profit-making, utility *for* the community might suggest a totally unregulated economy. But utility *of* the community shows that unrestricted capitalism might well result in monopoly or revolution, surely not in any particular business's interest.

A second argument for making the Statist case is to distinguish between private and public goods. Private goods and services are provided for us in the marketplace every day. The merchant selling us a newspaper, a haircut, or cable TV expects to receive the going rate or payment for the good or service provided. If we refuse to pay for this type of private good, the merchant will refuse to offer it or will cut off service, as in the case of the cable company. Public goods cannot be selectively offered or denied in this manner. The classic example is defence. We all want to live in a state protected from attack or invasion by other states. The size of this task rules out its provision by a private individual or company. National defence is a service usually provided by national armies. But in providing this service, the state cannot selectively withhold it from people who refuse to pay for it. It would be absurd to imagine a government marking the houses on a given street that have not paid their taxes so that in wartime it will know which houses to defend. Once the public good is provided, it is available to all, contributors and "free-riders" alike. Other public goods include radio and TV transmission (if unscrambled), clean air and water, and domestic law and order.

The Statist would argue that in the absence of the state, most such public goods would not be offered by the private marketplace. Since such goods cannot be selectively denied to those who do not pay for it, private businesses will earn no revenue from providing it. The liberal or market paradigm is inadequate for providing them. We can buy an education from a private tutor; we cannot buy an educated society unless the state steps in and demands compulsory education. We might well agree with the Statist that these public goods are in the public or national interest and should be provided. This, then, is the unique and necessary role of the state.

PROBLEMS WITH THE STATIST APPROACH

Some authors attack the basic concept of the state as used by the Statist paradigm. Pluralists and transnationalists agree that the paradigm overemphasizes the role of the state in world politics or else uses the term *state* too ambiguously. Popular usage overworks the concept in phrases such as "Russia wants a warm-water port" or "for reasons of state" invoked to justify a controversial act of the government. They claim we must avoid the anthropomorphic fallacy of attributing human characteristics to a non-human object. This happens when we hear someone say that a given state "needs" or "wants" something, as demonstrated in the first example above. Technically only humans need or want things. Likewise they claim we must try to avoid reifying the state; that is, we must be careful not to give it vague, transcendental, or mystical powers in the way that the Nazis glorified the "German nation." In less extreme usage, the charge of reification is used on a person who has given a term an overblown status.

Objections also exist to the use of the words *national interests*. Even if we grant that the state might have a use in providing goods not available privately, we still might be skeptical as to how or why a given state would always act strictly in the public interest. Such skepticism is healthy and necessary for the functioning of democracy. We should always ask whether our political leadership is really pursuing the interests of the community or advancing their own private interests when they wrap a policy in phrase "the national interest." Thus, we may grant that national interests exist, but that states are too corruptible to implement them. Corruption and self-serving interests are a problem for any state. Vigorous enforcement of antibribery laws is part of the solution, but the political culture of the country is also an important aspect. To what extent have all office-holders internalized the impartial and public role of the state? To what extent have they grown up in a culture where *public service* and *national duty* were terms taken seriously?[9]

But even if we solve the problem of individual interest, there may still be group or institutional interests that cloud the state's ability to find the national interest. Even merit-based bureaucracies have interests that may bias the definition of the national interest.[10] An official may not even be aware of this institutional "conflict of interest." A civil servant who has spent most of his or her life working in a particular ministry tends to adopt the values of that bureaucracy. Military officers see the world in terms of security problems; finance officials in terms of dollars and cents. Office politics leads to a form of bureaucratic imperialism with each agency trying to expand its budget and attract more attention from cabinet ministers. In the extreme form, this critique asks whether we would trust any state to decide whether its own abolition would be in the public interest.

NATIONAL INTERESTS AS A NORMATIVE CONCEPT

One way out of this predicament (defining or determining national interest) is to suggest that the national interest is also a normative concept, a prescription for "what ought to be" rather than just "what is." As an ideal or normative concept, the national interest can serve in two ways. As a code for politicians, bureaucrats, and all public figures, it operates as an antidote to the disease of corruption discussed above. Indeed, corruption itself may be thought of as placing alternative loyalties ahead of the state. Bribery and graft result from putting one's own interests first. Looking after family interests is nepotism. Patronage and sectarian favouritism are the result of placing societal or group loyalties and interests first. Statism as a normative prescription calls on the public servant to set aside these other interests and loyalties to serve the greater public or national interest.

Second, the national interest can serve as a forum for a public policy debate on the just purposes of state authority. In every democracy today, regardless of the academic or theoretical status of the phrase "the national interest," there is a public discussion taking place that often uses those words to debate key policy concerns. As issues come and go, and media and public attention waxes and wanes, the size of the discussion correspondingly contracts and expands. At times, it appears restricted to elite foreign affairs journals, newspaper editorials, and university classrooms; at other times, it becomes the top story on the national TV news broadcasts. If ideas count, then the substance of these debates have an important conditioning influence on the state's definition of the national interest, both directly as state agents themselves are recruited from the elite debaters and indirectly through the amorphous legitimizing consensus of what we call "public opinion."

SPECIFYING THE NATIONAL INTEREST PERSPECTIVE

Our goal now is to determine whether with all these differing conceptions, we can specify a set of national interests around which something resembling a public consensus can emerge. To limit the scope of this study, we will remove all domestic public interests from consideration and concentrate on foreign affairs. This is not to deny the linkage that inevitably exists between domestic affairs and foreign policy. As we will see, domestic problems have a way of spilling over national boundaries, as witness the Ottawa-Quebec-Paris triangle of the 1960s and 1970s (see Chapter 11).

Joseph Frankel provides us with one definition of national interest in his book *National Interest.*

> If foreign policy is defined as 'a formulation of desired outcomes which are intended (or expected) to be consequent upon decisions adopted (or made) by those who have authority (or ability) to commit the machinery of the state and a significant fraction of national resources to that end,' national interest describes the desired outcomes.[11]

This definition explicitly links the national interest to foreign policy. As such, it makes any major decision by a state an attempt to realize a national interest. This broad definition seems to open the door to a very large and contentious set of national interests. The only limitation here is that the decision-makers intend a particular policy to have a desired end, which does not, Frankel admits, even rule out "vagueness of aspiration" or "incomplete knowledge." There is nothing here to suggest that these objectives do not change with time or regime. National interest is whatever the state pursues at a given point in time! Clearly this definition is much too broad.

In a book titled *Defining the National Interest,* Stephen Krasner offers us another method for determining a state's national interest. He suggests we can find it inductively by examining the government's preferences over time. Specifically, his definition of national interests has three components:

1. They are objectives related to general societal goals.
2. They persist over time.
3. They have a consistent ranking of importance.

In other words, if we see a state pursuing a certain goal or policy over a long period of time, despite changes in leadership, and if that goal can be justified as being in the interest of society as a whole, then we have found a national interest. This definition satisfies our problem about partisan politics and competing goals. If we see parties of very different ideological backgrounds pursuing the same goal, it suggests that something very fundamental to the state is involved. For example, if both czarist and Bolshevik Russia sought to obtain the same objective, then a national interest would have been at stake. Krasner argues that the importance or salience of the goal is so clear as to not only transcend ideology but to allow it to consistently rank in the national interests for any government.

However, it is difficult to see how on a purely inductive basis one can argue for a consistent ranking.

Both Frankel's and Krasner's definitions of public interest share an inductive or empirical approach to the problem. In Frankel's case, any incident of goal-seeking behaviour by a state indicates the presence of national interest. Krasner is somewhat stricter in laying down conditions to delimit the concept. Nonetheless, both determine the national interest by examining the actual behaviour of states. One immediate problem with such an approach is that we are left with no way to test their assertion that any particular goal is a national interest. Instead we have a tautology: national interest is what states have done, and to prove it, look at what states have done.

Both infer national interest from observed behaviour. A stronger case can be made for reversing the process and working deductively. A rationalist approach to national interest would first posit basic principles of the international state system and then derive specific national interests from those principles. Any given candidate for "national interest" status could then be checked against the historical record of the given state.

Table 1.1 summarizes a rationalist method used by the National Interest Perspective. We begin by stating initial assumptions about states in a state system. Parsimony demands that we keep this set of suppositions to the smallest number possible, but that are required to be complete. From this set of givens, we deduce generalized principles that are national interests that might apply to all states. To determine the vital interests of a given state, we translate those principles to a given geographical, political, historical, and economic context.

Table 1.1 Derivation of Canadian National Interests

Initial Assumptions	→	Nature of Current States System
↓		
Generalized Principles	→	National Interests
↓		
Specific Applications	→	Canadian Interests

Rationalist methods can be found in some previous works on the subject. Hans Morgenthau's famous and parsimonious dictum that national interest is power is a case in point. Given an initial set of assumptions about the world, he argues that it is the vital interest of every state to maintain or increase its power. Each state will do this in the context of its own geopolitical situation. The main problem with Morgenthau's approach lies in the difficulty with defining the key concept of power. Realist theorists frequently argue about its definition and uses. Therefore, we will seek a more specific definition of national interest here.

For the purposes of this book, let us make the following assumptions about the nature of the international state system. First, let us agree that at present we are dealing with a *states system*; that is, a system made up of states or nation-states, and not city-states or a world government. This assumption does not rule out transnational actors, but it does give relatively less importance to them. This assumption also entails the previously given definition of the state as an autonomous institution.

Second, given the absence of world government or effective international dispensers and enforcers of justice, our states system is *anarchic* in the sense Realists use the term. This assumption is rich in consequences. Some Realists see it as inevitably leading to an ongoing state of war or preparedness for war. A more flexible approach views the system oscillating between periods of peace and stability and periods of open conflict. At its worst, such as system can be characterized as a "self-help" or vendetta system. The latter label describes a situation where states return "hits" for "hits," tit-for-tat, in the style of clan or mafia warfare. Examples of a vendetta system in world politics would include Somalian clans (in the absence of a national government) and the Israelis and Palestinians in the Middle East. At its best, peace may be maintained by alliance and the negative golden rule: I won't hit you, if you don't hit me. Long periods of peace for some sub-regions of the system are quite possible, so long as major clashes of interest do not arise and custom partially restrains resort to arms. In fact, this Realist approach to anarchy is broad enough to include the existence of norms of behaviour and even a form of international society. But in the back of each statesman's mind is the realization that without world government, there is ultimately nothing to prevent the system from crashing down to the level of vendetta and the lowest common denominator.

The third assumption about our system formally affirms the key Statist position that states seek to maximize their own welfare; that is, they *maximize utility of the community*. Among other things, this assumption rules out suicidal states. It also complicates but does not rule out cooperation with other states. States are seen as more self-interested and concerned with their own citizens than as altruistic or concerned with non-citizens.

From these three basic assumptions, the following general principles are derived (the term *states seek* refers to the preferences of government officials who make up the state):

1. All states seek to survive and be secure from attack.
2. All states seek to be as autonomous as possible.
3. All states seek to maintain their domestic unity or cohesion.
4. All states seek to be as economically prosperous as possible.
5. All states seek principled self-justifications and prestige in the international system.

The first principle seems to be the most important and draws on all three assumptions about the nature of out political system. Priority for this principle is derived from assumption two about the anarchical system. Given that resort to arms might still be the final arbiter in any conflict, security needs must be looked to first. Furthermore, the desire to maximize societal goals would lead in itself to securing the population against the devastation of military attack. As we have seen, defence is a public good that only the state can provide.

The second principle grows out of the first assumption that the nature of the state is an autonomous organization. Large organizations seek to maintain their freedom to act. This autonomy is expressed not only by domestic actors but also in foreign terms. In a sovereign state system, states come in different sizes with different capabilities vis-à-vis each other. This disparity in relative strength opens the door to more subtle modes of influence and dependency than outright military assault. Historically, some states may have been colonies or satellites of other stronger states. The principle of autonomy affirms that once the basic security need is fulfilled, all states will next try to maximize their freedom to act. Thus, a subtle tension may exist between the first and second principle. A small state may be driven by security needs to depend on a larger state for protection, yet within that alliance, the small state will still try to preserve as much autonomy as possible.

The third principle, domestic cohesion, relates to the first two principles. Division of a state into smaller subunits represents an internal threat to its survival. Usually the state is protected from domestic challengers by its monopoly or pre-eminence in the possession of arms. But democracies face severe restrictions in using force against domestic political movements, even when they threaten the coherence of the state. As long as separatist movements employ political and legal means to seek their goals, the state can employ little direct coercion. This includes situations in which other states are involved as supporters of a separatist group, despite the conflict being a "domestic matter." Such states are only engaged in the time-honoured activity of "fishing in troubled waters." Likewise, federal states may face challenges from their subunits seeking a greater role in world affairs. Again, international activity dilutes the claim to sovereignty of the state and international recognition of a subunit may foretell dismemberment of the state.

The fourth principle, economic prosperity, is based on the second and third assumptions (that our system is anarchic and states seek to maximize their welfare). Security demands a strong economy to produce the weapons of defence: to reverse an old Japanese slogan, "rich country, strong army." Likewise, the economic well-being of its citizens is a main concern of most states as witness the extensive regulatory activities vis-à-vis their domestic economy. Crucial areas of public policy revolve around the economic arenas of employment, inflation, and investment. In this book, the external factors affecting domestic prosperity — trade and investment policy — will be considered.

Finally, status and image (the final principle) are important though less vital aspects of state foreign behaviour. Having a strong self-image or identity helps in binding the citizenry to the state for security, domestic cohesion, and other purposes. There are many aspects to a state's self-image and prestige, which may range from principled behaviour derived from an official religion or ideology to merely the sentiment that the state's foreign policy is just. Prestige or influence in the international community can expedite other state goals in the security and economic arenas. On a "higher plain," legitimacy is an important element of sovereignty. A just or principled national interest is therefore an element in gaining domestic and international legitimacy.

To say that all states share the same general national interests is not to say that their foreign policies will be at all similar. Each state faces a very different context in which to implement these goals. Security needs will depend on geopolitical factors and the "neighbourhood" as well as diplomatic history. Due to limitations of the local economy, some states (for example, Holland, Japan, or Canada) will be more dependent on foreign trade than others (the United States or China). Domestic ethnic fragmentation or homogeneity will affect the cohesiveness of the state. This book will present an historical examination of the implementation of these five national interests in view of Canada's unique situation.

THE QUESTION OF PRIORITIES

Krasner's definition of national interest raised the idea of a consistent ranking. Clearly it is ridiculous to worry about international prestige or prosperity if a state is about to be dismembered by its neighbours. If we think of states' desires as needs, we can make the analogy to Abraham Maslow's hierarchy of needs. This psychologist argued that human needs and desires can be ranked by the order in which they must be fulfilled: food, shelter, clothing, sex, self-esteem, and so on. Priority in this system is obviously given according to survival value. Applied to states, survival interests would likewise come first. Thus, the listing of general national interests given above can be seen as ranked on the basis of survival value. Since self-image is only indirectly related to survival, it comes late in the ranking.

Maslow's ranking also suggests that the stages of needs may overlap and multi-tasking, or multiple goal-seeking, can occur. Thus, some basic food is required before progressing to shelter, but not all food needs are necessarily fulfilled before getting at least some shelter. In our example of states, at least some security is demanded first, but other security problems may be addressed after at least some autonomy, unity, and prosperity needs are attained. In other words, a state need not complete all its security concerns before moving on to its second or third priorities.

As with all human needs, it is not clear that there is an upper limit to the fulfillment of needs by the state. When does a state know it has "enough" security? If the economic law of diminishing returns applies, then above some floor or minimum threshold for survival, satisfaction with additional amounts of the need should fall off. To use the example of hunger and food, at the bottom there is a floor level necessary for human survival, and at the top a diminishing satisfaction if not illness that comes from overindulgence. The parallel to security-seeking by states is intriguing.

Examining of the priority of needs also serves to point out the difficulty of inferring national interests from state behaviour alone. The fact that Canada does not seem to be seeking security as its primary foreign policy priority at a given date does not belittle the value of security as an interest. The importance of security to the survival of the Canadian state has varied with time and circumstance; compare, for example, its needs in 1812, 1940, and 1950 to the present. Likewise, Canadian citizens are reminded from time to time of the importance of national unity when, for example, Quebec threatens to hold a referendum on separation. A relatively privileged state such as Canada may focus much of its energies, most of the time, on category number five because it has previously achieved satisfaction in the four other categories of national interest.

DEFINING THE CANADIAN NATIONAL INTEREST

One of the clear strengths of the National Interest Perspective is its immediate relevance to the actual formulation of Canadian foreign policy goals. The Department of Foreign Affairs publishes an annual review that includes an effort to specify and prioritize Canada's major foreign interests in a manner very consistent with the NIP. What is striking in this effort is that over the past decades the same goals turn up time and again. Governments change and the rankings vary somewhat, but consistent goals do appear to persist over time.

Some historians will no doubt claim that this is merely an artifact of the managerial revolution introduced in late 1960s by Prime Minister Trudeau. He believed in formulating Canadian foreign policy by requiring state bureaucrats to specify long-term goals and to ensure that those goals served the Canadian national interests. Trudeau was reacting to the alleged deficiencies of the previous Pearson government, which he viewed as too ad hoc in policy-making and too internationalist in substance. Instead his government's 1970 reassessment, *Foreign Policy for Canadians*, suggested the following six areas of national interest:

1. Peace and security
2. Sovereignty and independence
3. Economic growth
4. Social justice
5. Quality of life
6. Harmonious natural environment

We can see similarities to our list of five principles or national interests once we note that the last three items above can be identified as further specification of our fifth principle, which includes self-image and identity. Only national unity (the third principle) is missing, an omission soon to be corrected by the events of the October Crisis.

The Clark/Mulroney Green Paper of 1985 made no such mistake. Quebec separatism appeared at the top of its list of six foreign policy priorities:

1. National unity
2. Sovereignty and independence
3. Justice and democracy
4. Peace and security
5. Economic prosperity
6. Integrity of the natural environment

Again, this list fits clearly into our original list of five principles or national interests. "Sovereignty and independence" translate into political autonomy (number two). Justice and democracy, along with the environment, again are part of principled self-justifications and self-image (number five). The apparent difference in the order in which the interests appear on both lists can be explained by the difference in short-term versus long-term concerns. In the short term, national unity rose as a concern with the timing of Parti Québécois (PQ) governments and referendums, and other transient events.

This process of listing priorities defined as the national interest continues today in the Department of Foreign Affairs (DFA). Even the disorganized Paul Martin foreign policy review of 2005 used the phrase "national interest" over seven times. One might be tempted to claim that Trudeau started something new and that there was no Canadian national interest before him. Such a conclusion would be unwarranted. It is a gross simplification to claim that the Pearson government had no sense of a Canadian national interest or any foreign policy because it did not specify those goals in a government document. Canadian national interests had been discussed in and out of governments for a long time. If one examines the actual practice of foreign policy, one sees the same problems reappearing again and again in Canadian history.

CONCLUSION

The National Interest Perspective claims that there is a set of logical national interests that should apply in the long term to all states in a states system. These interests have been grouped into five generalized principles or national interest areas. Specific Canadian national interests can be determined by translating these general principles into the specific geographic, historical, and cultural context of Canada.

For example, geography creates specific dilemmas and opportunities for the Canadian state. Canada's vast territory with most of the population heavily concentrated along the border of a great power (the United States) has posed a major security problem for all Canadian governments. Unlike Russia, Canada has only one contiguous neighbour by land, and, while not an island like the United Kingdom or Japan, it has three bordering oceans. It was this geography that led the Canadian politician Raoul Dandurand to say, "Canada is a fire-proof house, far from inflammable materials." History and culture have assured that the two most powerful nations in Canada's region, the UK and US, share many similarities and are therefore unlikely to be major enemies. Geographic, historic, and cultural factors condition the fulfillment of other interests in addition to security: unity, autonomy, prosperity, and so on.

This book applies the Statist/National Interest model to Canadian foreign policy. While it is difficult to prove the existence of the ranking given, we should nonetheless discover the same five general interests have persisted over time. To do this, I will adopt a broad historic approach, tracking Canadian foreign relations and interests back even before Confederation. In the concluding chapter, I will assess the validity of the NIP. Throughout the book, the reader will be reminded that the discussion of the national interest also serves the normative function of opening a debate over the correctness of Canada's foreign policy. In reading my version of Canada's national interest, the reader may disagree completely and wish to assert an alternative set of Canadian national interests. Either way, the importance of the concept of national interest will have been demonstrated.

Notes

1. Thomson (1995), p. 214.
2. Smith, Anthony (1991).
3. Séguin (2003), A8.
4. Dunleavy and O'Leary (1987), p. 2.
5. Evans, Rueschemeyer, and Skocpol (1985), p. 28.
6. Krasner (1978), p. 5-6.
7. Frankel (1970), p. 19.
8. *Utility* is an economist's term that can be roughly translated as a *benefit* or *a useful good*.
9. In many Western democracies, this problem historically has led to "clean government" or reform movements that introduced the concepts of replacing patronage and nepotism with a merit-based civil service and civil service examination. Today, we see ongoing attempts to deal with this problem in the use of audits, oversight and "watchdogs," and rewards for "whistle-blowers."
10. This proposition is the basis of the bureaucratic politics approach in public policy. For example, public bureaucracies rarely like to advocate cutting their own budgets, reducing staff, or seeing their authority diminished, even if it is in the public interest to do so.
11. Frankel (1970), p. 18. Frankel quotes here the definition of foreign policy found in Vital (1968), p. 11.

Chapter Two
Sovereignty and Secure Borders

To judge from the numerous wars of the past century, security has been the main preoccupation of states. For various Canadian governments over the past few decades, security has been one foreign policy area where objectives have been clearly enunciated and even given priority. Beginning with the Defence White Paper of 1964, the government of Lester Pearson implied three major security objectives, roughly ranked as 1) peacekeeping, 2) the NATO (European) commitment, and 3) the NORAD (North American) commitment. Trudeau's 1971 White Paper gave an even clearer listing of goals and priorities:

1. Sovereignty protection
2. NORAD commitment
3. NATO commitment
4. Peacekeeping

By downgrading peacekeeping and NATO, Trudeau had reversed the ranking from Pearson, though in practice Trudeau's policies and weapons procurement by the late seventies seemed to suggest a return to Pearson's ranking.

The Mulroney government made its first major statement on defence priorities in September 1985, when external affairs minister Joe Clark spelled out measures to strengthen Arctic sovereignty. Shortly thereafter, the Department of External Affairs (DEA) issued the Green Paper Competitiveness and Security, which discussed the same four priorities in the same order as the 1971 White Paper.

The government of Jean Chrétien produced its own ranking of defence priorities in its 1994 Defence White Paper. The goals were simplified down to three basics:

1. Protect Canada
2. Defend North America (with the United States)
3. Peacekeeping and other multilateral operations

Assuming sovereignty protection is included under "protecting Canada" and that NATO, in the post-cold war era, has been combined with "peacekeeping" as "other multilateral operations," then this list reflects Trudeau's previous ordering of priorities from "home to globe." The Martin government's 2004 defence policy review basically reaffirmed this ordering with a new post-9/11 urgency.

Thus, while the rankings have varied somewhat, we see evidence of consistent objectives across different governments. This evidence supports even Krasner's minimalist definition of national interests as "enduring goals." In this study, we will subdivide national security into three component interests: 1) sovereignty and secure borders, 2) defence against threat of direct attack (also known as national defence), and 3) international security. Care will be taken to distinguish means such as "the NORAD commitment" from ends such as "defence against attack." With this distinction in mind, the connection between means and ends for the 1971 priorities becomes evident: "sovereignty protection" is the means to "securing borders," the "NORAD and NATO commitments" are the vehicles for traditional defence against attack from a common enemy (the USSR until 1991), and "peacekeeping" demonstrates Canada's attempt to realize a more global solution to its security problem. In this chapter, we deal with the first goal (as ranked number one by the Trudeau government) — sovereignty and secure borders.

ESTABLISHING SECURE BOUNDARIES

"Nothing is more fundamental to statehood than the ability to exert control over sovereign territory." So spoke the 1985 Green Paper, re-emphasizing the role of sovereignty protection as a vital Canadian interest. Historically, sovereignty has been defined as 1) international recognition of a state's right to supreme and unchallenged law-making authority over a territory and its people, and 2) effective occupation or use of the claimed territory.

We will examine boundary issues both on land and at sea. In recent years, Canada has had active boundary disputes with Denmark, France, and the United States. Of course, one might argue whether sovereignty deserves treatment ahead of threats of attack. As many wars have been caused by border disputes, the two are clearly related. Sovereignty is discussed first here because for Canada such disputes arose from the moment of the creation of British North America (BNA). Historically, most of Canada's sovereignty conflicts have been with the US.

Canada's long boundary with the US has its origin in the peace treaty ending the American Rebellion of 1776-83. The Treaty of Paris effectively partitioned BNA between 13 independent American colonies, soon to be federated into the United States of America, and the "loyal" British colonies of Nova Scotia, New Brunswick, Newfoundland, Prince Edward Island (PEI), and Upper and Lower Canada, the latter two including parts of the present provinces of Ontario and Quebec. As with later global partitions, a mass movement of population occurred as about 35,000 Loyalists moved northward.

The former combatants had widely different views about where the partition boundary should be drawn. In theory, the border began in the east with the Saint Croix River. The northern boundary of Maine was left only vaguely defined as the height of land between the Saint Lawrence and Atlantic basins. The issue of the Great Lake basin was decided by splitting all the lakes, except Lake Michigan, and then extending an ill-defined line from Grand Portage on Lake Superior to the Lake of the Woods. This British concession on the Great Lakes basin was a particular blow to the Montreal fur trading interests, since most of the Great Lakes region had been part of Quebec since 1774, and this deal gave nearly all the important trading posts to the Americans. The Montreal merchants had good reason to suspect that Britain was pursuing the strategic interest of sundering the American and French alliance with generosity toward the US at Canada's expense. This pattern of the British appeasing the US with Canadian concessions was to develop as a recurring theme in later border negotiations.

Such negotiations were soon needed. The informal nineteenth-century doctrine of Manifest Destiny proclaimed that the US should fill the continent from sea to sea. Thus the need to place clear limits on American expansion, and after the US acquired land from France in the 1803 Louisiana Purchase, border negotiations resumed between 1814 and 1818. In the Convention of 1818, the boundary was extended along the 49th Parallel to the Rocky Mountains. Beyond the Rockies, Britain and the US agreed to joint occupation of the Oregon territory up to 54° 40', as Russian and Spanish claims on the West Coast had yet to be sorted out.

Negotiations over the Maine border proved to be quite contentious, resulting in the failed arbitration attempt by the king of Holland in 1833. The dispute flared into open conflict in the brief Aroostook War of 1839 between rival lumber interests. This lead to the Ashburton-Webster Treaty of 1842, which basically split the two disputed areas: the northern Maine and Minnesota/Ontario borders (see Figure 2.1). John Brebner calls the treaty "a remarkably fair compromise."[1]

Figure 2.1 The Maine Border Dispute

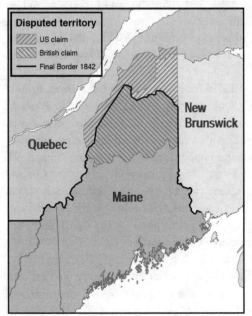

No sooner was the Maine border resolved than the Oregon border issue flared up. "Oregon fever," generated by a popular American book of 1836, so increased American settlement in the region that they soon outnumbered British subjects. Though President James K. Polk had used "54° 40' or Fight!" as a slogan in his election campaign, he soon compromised on the 49th parallel. The treaty of 1846 extended that previously chosen latitude to the straits of Georgia and Juan de Fuca. Vancouver Island was granted to Britain, but the status of the San Juan Islands, located between Vancouver Island and the mainland, remained in dispute until the Treaty of Washington, where it was agreed that the new German emperor would decide their ownership.

Canadians had some reason to feel let down by Britain's agreement to these terms. The Hudson's Bay Company had staked its claim to the Columbia River long before the Americans began arriving and, as to the San Juan Islands, there was no reason to believe the emperor of Germany, as Britain's chief rival in Europe, would do her any favours. He did not: he promptly turned over all the islands to the Americans.

With the southern land boundary now established, Britain had only to fix the northern limits of its territories. Between partition and Confederation, most of this land was claimed by the Hudson's Bay Company. In 1849, as a result of the division of the Oregon territory with the US, the British government granted Vancouver Island to the company as a colony. But the gold rush of 1856 required that the British government intervene and repurchase Vancouver Island, and create a second colony on the mainland. Ten years later, Britain merged the two to form the colony of British Columbia. The new Dominion of Canada acquired the rest of the company's land (also known as Rupert's Land) through negotiations with the British government beginning in 1865. This vast territory, which included the future provinces of Manitoba, Saskatchewan, and Alberta, as well as the northern territories, was given up by the company in return for a loan guarantee from the British government. As the British Parliament did not pass the enabling legislation until July 1868 — after Confederation — the deal can be seen as a tremendous birthday present for the new dominion.

Confederation itself began on July 1, 1867 with the creation of the Dominion of Canada, including the provinces of Ontario, Quebec, Nova Scotia, and New Brunswick. By offering to pay debts and build railroads, the dominion induced British Columbia to join in 1871 and PEI in 1873. While independent on many internal matters, the dominion government was not sovereign in its foreign policy, and thus it was something more than a colony but less than an independent state. It was not until 1931 that Canada achieved full legal control over her foreign affairs (see Chapter 6). The boundary in the Arctic expanded in 1880, when the Canadian state gained title to the Arctic Islands, and in 1925, when it laid claim to a wedge-shaped piece of the polar ice cap up to the North Pole. Newfoundland became the tenth province in Confederation on March 1949, completing the process of land acquisition.

The Alaskan Panhandle presented the last major land-based boundary dispute with the US. As early as the 1830s, George Simpson of the Hudson's Bay Company recognized the strategic value of the Panhandle, the northwestern coast of what was to become British Columbia, as an access way into the northern interior of the continent. In the Hamburg agreement of 1839 with Russia, which then owned Alaska, he secured a lease for the Panhandle for the Company between 1840 and 1850. But ultimately the US was to gain control by purchasing of all of Alaska in 1867 from the Russians.

Historically, the Panhandle was defined as a line north from 54° 40' to follow the summits of the mountains parallel to the coast up to the main body of Alaska itself. As Figure 2.2 shows, such instructions were virtually worthless with so irregular and inlet-riddled a coast. Particularly contentious was the large inlet at Skagway.

Figure 2.2 The Alaskan Border Dispute

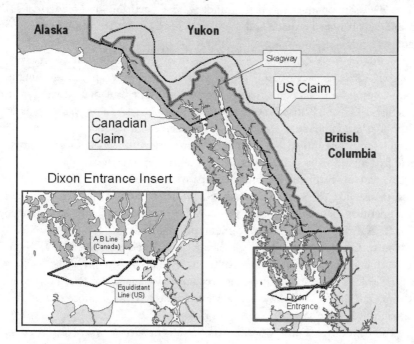

The dispute came to a head with the Klondike gold rush of 1896-1903, when the region of Skagway and the Lynn Canal became the access route to the Canadian gold fields. Hence, Skagway became a vital point of interest for Canada in the negotiations: without it the Yukon became landlocked and remote. While Canada's legal case was not strong and amounted to what one historian called a "major revision" in the boundary,[2] there was hope in Ottawa that Britain would demand it in exchange for the concessions it was so easily making to the Americans in Central America at that time. Instead, by the Hay-Herbert Convention of 1903, the matter was to be decided judicially by a tribunal of six "impartial jurists of repute" with three appointed from each side. What particularly rankled

Canadian opinion was the outrageous behaviour of the American president Theodore Roosevelt, who appointed as his "impartial jurists" his secretary of war and two senators from Washington, a state with a strong commercial interest in the outcome. Furthermore, he directly involved himself in the judicial considerations, in effect threatening war and flaunting his victory when, later in 1903, the British jurist on the tribunal voted with the Americans against Canada. From the Canadian viewpoint, this dispute again raised the question of how far the British would go in sacrificing Canadian interests to appease the United States. It also showed the Americans to be self-interested (if not unprincipled) bargainers unwilling to do their Canadian neighbours any favours, even when stronger Canadian interests were at stake. In fact, a US delegate at the Paris Peace Conference of 1919 offered to trade the Panhandle away for more rapid British decolonization in the Caribbean.

With this decision on the Alaskan boundary, the partition of northern North America's landmass between Canada and the US was nearly complete. It might well seem that Canada was implicitly pursuing a "Manifest Destiny" policy of its own. Though perhaps a reaction to American expansion, by the twentieth century Canada itself had expanded "from sea to sea" across North America. Nor were leaders beyond seeking territorial compensation for Canadian efforts in World War I. The Canadian delegation to a London meeting discussing British Empire terms for peace brought along a shopping list, including the Alaskan Panhandle, Greenland, Saint-Pierre and Miquelon, and the West Indies as "war spoils" of interest to the Dominion. Unfortunately, as these territories were all held by Canada's allies in the war, this list produced only ill will.[3]

But Canada had one further avenue for the expansion of sovereignty: Newfoundland. Nonetheless, the island's entry into Confederation with Canada was not a forgone conclusion. Competition between Canadian and American interests intensified during World War II. A British-Canadian agreement of August 1940 left the defence of Newfoundland to Canada, but a month later a strong American presence was established when Britain granted the US several bases on the island as a result of the "destroyers-for-bases" deal. A subsequent agreement recognized Canada's special concerns in Newfoundland, and for the rest of the war, Ottawa made sure it had more troops and a higher-ranking officer there than the Americans did.

With the end of the war, Ottawa began negotiations in earnest with Newfoundland for terms of Confederation. These negotiations where at times rancorous because a large minority of islanders distrusted Ottawa and believed that Canada and Britain were pressuring the island into a deal harmful to its economic interests. Ultimately a referendum decided the matter, though sentiment was so divided that a runoff was necessary.

Canadian governments since Mackenzie King have also been sensitive to potential threats to sovereignty. The concern grows out of the vast amounts of territory, especially in the North, where "effective occupation" is virtually non-existent. In this day and age of carefully drawn maps and respect for national boundaries, it is difficult to imagine a scenario whereby the United States or some other power might lay claim on Canadian territory. The only actual northern territorial dispute today is with Denmark over the tiny Hans Island, between Greenland and Ellesmere Island. In August 1984, Ottawa officially protested a visit to the island by the Danish cabinet member in charge of Greenland, during which he planted a Danish flag. In 2005, this dispute flared up again, ending only with an agreement to avoid future provocations.

Mackenzie King's main concern over the North was that in the event of a long-term foreign occupation, a territory might become alienated from previously accepted Canadian control. In the early days of British Columbia, such a gradual alienation was a possibility, given the massive influx of Americans during the Fraser gold rush. This concern was also at the root of Prime Minister King's World War II policy that refused to allow foreign bases on Canadian soil. The practice of allowing foreign bases is not unknown among Canada's allies as witness the numerous American bases in Britain and the Federal Republic of Germany. But quite often, especially in the Third World, foreign bases are perceived as proof of dependency, as seen in the long dispute over American bases in the Philippines.

Prime Minister King worried about the presence of American troops in the Canadian northwest during World War II.[4] The American government was seeking to defend Alaska (part of which was briefly occupied by Japan) and possibly use it as a staging area to attack Japan. To further this goal, the United States constructed the Alaskan Highway and Canol pipeline, which brought 33,000 American troops into northwest Canada, leading King to fear they might peacefully take "possession [...] with a welcome of the people of BC, Alberta, and Saskatchewan."[5] After the war, the Canol pipeline was closed down, and the Alaskan Highway was acquired by Canada in April of 1946.

Tougher questions arose over American military installations growing out of the World War II alliance between the UK, the US, and Canada and later from NORAD commitments. With Canadian permission, the United States began constructing weather stations in the far North during World War II. Fort Churchill, in northern Manitoba, was operated as a joint experimental station. In 1946, it became a joint training base for fighting in extreme Arctic conditions. However, Ottawa limited American forces to one hundred soldiers. During the 1950s, as we will see in the next chapter, Soviet bombers posed a direct threat to North America. As a result, three radar warning-systems were built on Canadian territory, with only the mid-Canada line initially built and operated solely by Canadians. Sovereignty concerns were negotiated into the building of the Distant Early Warning (DEW) radar line in 1955. Canada kept the title and legal authority over these DEW stations, and from 1959, ensured the presence of at least one Canadian officer. Finally, in the mid-1980s, in negotiating a replacement for the DEW line, Ottawa ensured that the new Northern Warning System radar, while funded in part by the US, would be Canadian owned and operated.

Even more serious and surprisingly unexamined was the "back door" entry of American bases into Newfoundland when it joined Confederation in 1949. The "destroyers-for-bases" deal in 1940 gave the United States 99-year leases on bases at Argentia and Stephenville. In 1942, Canada and Britain built an air base at Goose Bay in Labrador, and in 1944, the United States joined the project, building five hangers of its own. In the early years of the cold war, the US was particularly interested in Goose Bay because it was the only point in North America from which B-47 bombers with nuclear warheads could reach the western USSR and return. The base remained an American strategic air command (SAC) base until June 30, 1976. Ottawa's solution to the American presence has been to multilateralize the base, making it more of a NATO base by allowing the West Germans facilities there in 1981. The Pentagon closed the Harmon USAF base at Stephenville in June of 1966, and Fort McAndrew naval base at Argentia was reduced in 1974 due to US-government cutbacks, and finally closed in 1994.[6] European use of Goose Bay appears to be coming to an end: the German and Dutch military forces withdrew in 2003, and the British Royal Air Force announced its intention to leave.[7] Threats to Canadian sovereignty could potentially arise from domestic plebiscites or direct annexation. Prime Minister King had an exaggerated concern about a possible massive defection of western Canadians to the United States. Fear of annexation was a consequence of war threats with the US in the nineteenth century and will be treated in Chapter 3. The remaining territorial disputes have all been at sea.

TERRITORIAL WATERS

Until the 1970s, the international law pertaining to oceans appeared quite clear on two matters. By tradition, coastal states exercised direct sovereignty over three miles of territorial sea (extending from the coast), as this distance was for many years the effective range of coastal artillery. Secondly, all seafaring states enjoyed the right of "innocent passage" through straits, even if this took them through the territorial waters of adjacent states. No prior warning or permission was required. Straits were defined as water routes that gave sole access from one body of open sea to another. In practice, a very liberal definition of strait has been accepted, as seen in the Corfu Channel case between Britain and Albania.[8] For the British and all great maritime powers since, an important principle — freedom of the high seas — was upheld.

International law tends to be conservative because its source is historical custom. Unfortunately for Canada, most historical practice in the Atlantic fishery has been contrary to its economic interests. Fishers of Britain, France, Spain, and Portugal knew of the rich fisheries of the Grand Banks long before the shores of Atlantic Canada were settled by Europeans. Traditionally, annual summer voyages in search of cod brought huge fleets to Grand Banks, Sable Island, and other places. Furthermore, it was common practice for fleets to put into shore for supplies, such as fresh water, and to dry the cod. As the New England colonies were settled, American fishers joined the others. Though Britain eventually established control over the lands of Atlantic Canada, except for the French islands of Saint-Pierre and Miquelon, it recognized the historic rights of other states to the fishery. It even went so far as to grant American and French "shores" on Newfoundland, recognizing the rights of those countries' fishermen to come ashore. Fully sovereign states are deemed to have full rights over their inshore fisheries (those within their territorial waters), to regulate, to sell licences to foreign ships, or to dispose of the resources as they wish. Unfortunately for Canada, the British colonies of Atlantic Canada were not fully sovereign and their treaties were made by Britain in Westminster.

Beginning in the 1950s, international conferences have slowly become more important as a source of international law on the sea, in addition to practice and treaty. Canada has been a leading nation in the use of these Law of the Sea (LOS) conferences to revise maritime practices. In the first major LOS conference of 1958, the Canadian delegate, George Drew, supported Canadian maritime interests by proposing a "6-plus-6 system." This proposal would have extended territorial waters to 6 miles and added a further 6 miles as an exclusive fishing zone, but it was not adopted. Nevertheless, the next two decades witnessed a series of unilateral measures taken by smaller coastal states against the great maritime powers. The general trend of these actions was to bring more and more of the "open sea" under individual state control, and hence was opposed by states with historic fishing rights (Portugal and Spain), large navies (US, UK, and USSR), or large commercial fleets (Germany and Japan).

One practice increasingly used by these revisionist states was the use of "baselines" to determine territorial waters. Norway successfully argued that it had the right to close off its fjords using straight baselines. The implication for Canada, with its jagged coastline, was immediately obvious. The Pearson government began to consider whether the Gulf of Saint Lawrence could be enclosed using baselines: after all, it was geographically enclosed by the shores of Nova Scotia and Newfoundland. In 1964, Pearson introduced legislation to begin using straight baselines on the Canadian coast and to extend fishing jurisdiction to nine miles. International reaction forced the government to water down its plans, and so in 1967 baselines were introduced on parts of the East Coast only. They were not used to close the Gulf of Saint Lawrence, and the government continued to seek bilateral agreements, leaving the problem for the subsequent Trudeau government.

The next major Canadian extension of territorial waters resulted from a crisis over the notion of innocent passage. By the late 1960s, the United States had discovered large reserves of oil on the north coast of Alaska. The question became how to get this oil to the large markets on the American East Coast, and the answer seemed to be to use the Northwest Passage through Canada's Arctic archipelago. Accordingly, in early 1970, the American government sent the oil tanker *Manhattan* through the passage on an experimental run. The action caused great consternation in Ottawa, both because the Americans had not given prior notice and because the recent *Arrow* oil spill off Nova Scotia had alerted the Canadian public to the dangers of oil shipping. Ecologists argued that an oil spill would be particularly damaging in the fragile Arctic environment.

As a result, the Trudeau government brought in the Arctic Waters Act of 1970, which unilaterally extended Canadian sovereignty over 12 miles of territorial sea and established a 100-mile pollution-control zone in the Arctic. The implication was that through its right to regulate the environment, the Canadian state could demand that other states using the passage obtain permission. At the same time, in an amendment to the Pearson Fishing Zones Act of 1964, baselines were brought in to close off the fisheries in the Gulf of Saint Lawrence, the Bay of Fundy, Queen Charlotte Sound, and the Dixon Entrance on the West Coast. In these two steps, the Canadian state had massively expanded its territorial jurisdiction.

The American government protested the Canadian action. The United States claimed that the Barrow Strait (also known as the Northwest Passage) was an international strait, in that it connects the Beaufort Sea to the North Atlantic Ocean, and invoked the right of innocent passage. Indeed, the Nixon government demanded that the matter be taken to the World Court. When Trudeau refused and attached reservations to the act denying World Court jurisdiction, Nixon retaliated by reducing the American import quota on Canadian oil.

The *Manhattan* affair thus began a major and ongoing dispute with the US. In conjunction with the "Nixon shock" surcharge of 1971 (see Chapter 8 and 10), it was a major factor in changing Trudeau's continentalist orientation to a more internationalist outlook. Though the Americans found an alternative route for their North Slope oil in the Alaskan Pipeline, they have continued to press their claim, and in 1985 sent the *Polar Sea* icebreaker through the passage without official notification.

On the Canadian side, international legal scholars have criticized Trudeau's action. They claim that Canada built a reputation of being a strong supporter of international law, and that by reserving the *Arctic Waters Act of 1970* and refusing to recognize the jurisdiction of the World Court, that reputation was tarnished. Of course, if Canada had gone to the World Court with the matter in 1970, it probably would have lost.

In September 1985, in response to the *Polar Sea* incident, external affairs minister Joe Clark announced a strengthening of Canadian sovereignty in the Arctic by

- clarifying Canada's claims to waters in the Arctic archipelago using straight baselines;
- planning to build a $500-million polar-class icebreaker;
- increasing surveillance flights by long-range patrol aircraft;
- introducing legislation extending the jurisdiction of Canadian laws to the offshore;
- increasing Canadian naval operations in the eastern Arctic;
- initiating new talks with the United States concerning the use of the Northwest Passage; and
- deciding to drop the reservation on any World Court ruling on Arctic waters.

The last item suggested Ottawa believed that international legal opinion had changed sufficiently to block an American challenge. In any case, the Bush (Sr.) administration agreed in January 1988 to seek prior permission from Ottawa for any future use of the Northwest Passage.

Dramatic advances on the issue of the territorial sea came in the 1970s. The question of using baselines to close the Gulf of the Saint Lawrence fisheries was soon overtaken by more dramatic developments at the LOS conferences. Clearly now identified with the countries who wanted change at the LOS, Canada put a special emphasis on change in the ocean regime by sending a large delegation to the Stockholm Conference of 1972 on protection of the ocean environment, and played a major role at the LOS conferences in 1973 and 1974. By the late 1970s, the LOS had moved toward recognition of a 200-mile jurisdiction, as even the US began to see the advantages of a 200-mile Exclusive Economic Zone (EEZ) on its extensive coasts. Thus, when Canada adopted the 200-mile zone on January 1, 1977, the American Carter administration was not far behind.

However, extending national jurisdiction over a 200-mile EEZ created new boundary disputes. With the rich fishery of Georges Bank at stake, a new boundary between territorial waters of Maine and New Brunswick was needed. The World Court eventually settled the dispute in October 1984, with a division of the Georges Banks between the two countries (see Figure 2.3).

Figure 2.3 The Georges Bank Settlement

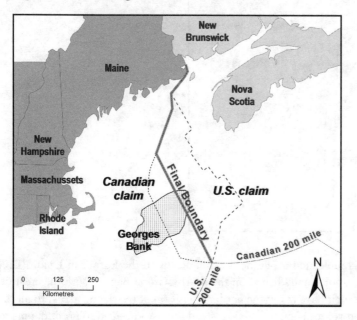

Still unresolved is a West Coast dispute with the US over the offshore boundary in the Dixon Entrance between Alaska and Queen Charlotte Island.[9] Here, Canada argues that the boundary was set by custom from 1803 as the 54° 40' N latitude line, whereas the US says the boundary should be set farther south, according to the more recent practice of drawing such lines equidistant from the two shores (see Figure 2.2 again). Thus, in this case, the roles are reversed with Canada arguing for custom and the United States for LOS principles.

More difficult was the claim by France for a 200-mile EEZ for its islands of Saint-Pierre and Miquelon, which lie near Newfoundland in the middle of Canada's own EEZ. The small size of the islands compared to Newfoundland suggested that France's claim would ultimately be greatly reduced. Nonetheless, in August 1983, France sent a gunboat, *Le Henaff*, and a seismic ship, *Lucien Beaufort*, to explore the continental shelf for oil in the disputed zone. In addition to traditional fishing grounds and potential oil reserves, a $75 million scallop fishery was at stake in the dispute. In June 1992, the dispute was resolved by a five-person international court of arbitration that awarded France a 10.5-mile corridor due south from the islands for 200 miles (see Figure 2.4).

Figure 2.4 The Saint-Pierre and Miquelon Islands Dispute

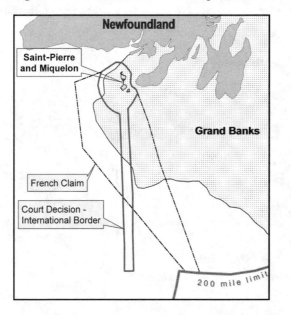

The matter was complicated by France's affiliation with the European Union (EU), whose members had traditionally fished on the nearby Grand Banks. With the creation of its EEZ, Canada might have taken the hardline position of restricting access to all the fisheries under its control to its own fishers. Instead, Ottawa decided to grant quotas to these traditional users, hoping that by selling rights to fish, Canada would gain access to the European market for its own fish. Due to manoeuvres by the EU, Canada was disappointed with the market access given, and so negotiations over quotas were accompanied by a good deal of acrimony.

The creation of the EEZ in 1977 generated a great expansion, or in hindsight an over-expansion, of the Canadian fishing fleet.[10] Furthermore, Ottawa was required to greatly increase its coastal fleet for surveillance and regulation of the fishery. Regulation increased with attempts to manage the cod stocks to ensure that over-fishing would not destroy the fishery for future generations. In the late 1980s, indications of declining fish stocks began to raise serious concern over the depletion of the fishery. For details of the resulting conflicts over the cod fishery see the case study Fish Wars on the Grand Banks, below.

Figure 2.5 The Grand Banks and Canada's 200-Mile Limit

Another fish-war showdown with Spain occurred in March 1995, when Canadian inspectors seized the Spanish trawler *Estai* on the high seas and brought it into St. John's harbour. The ship was charged with fishing halibut despite a 60-day moratorium, possessing a hidden compartment for the illegal catch, and keeping two sets of books. The Spanish government, backed by other fellow EU members, responded with outrage, calling the Canadian action a violation of international law (which technically it was) and therefore an act of piracy.

Nonetheless, that same year, new negotiations through NAFO resulted in a compromise. Thus far, Ottawa's strategy has been to seek stronger NAFO management and enforcement of the high seas fisheries, punctuated by brief unilateral threats and actions. The 1995 agreement swapped higher EU fish quotas (mainly for Portugal and Spain) for more enforcement mechanisms demanded by Canada. Many European fishers are unhappy with the various quotas set by NAFO, and invariably the quotas are the result of heated political bargaining and remain far above levels recommended by biologists to preserve the fish stocks. By 2003, the Canadian government had the right under NAFO rules to monitor, board, and cite ships fishing on the seas for violations of the cod moratorium and the use of small mesh nets, which capture immature fish. Unfortunately, it is still up to the ship's home state to inspect and lay charges upon the return of the cited ship to its home-port, and such enforcement is often not forthcoming.

Therefore, in May 2004, Ottawa launched another offensive by boarding and citing two Portuguese ships for violations and expanding its right under the 1995 agreement to increase surveillance with $150 million in federal expenditure toward planes and ships, allowing greater numbers of boardings and citations.[12] Though the Portuguese government failed to lay charges against the two cited ships, Ottawa claims that so far its inspection blitz has changed behaviour. Between May and August 2004, Canadian government officials boarded 98 foreign ships, and inspectors targeted suspect trawlers with repeated boardings. This activity has caused foreign ships to withdraw from the shallow cod fisheries and many to cut their fishing seasons short. However, many fishers in Newfoundland and Labrador believe that without full enforcement, only unilateral Canadian enforcement of the terms of the 1995 agreement will save the North Atlantic fishery in the long run.

THE FUTURE OF SOVEREIGNTY

Through the 1970s and 1980s, sovereignty protection was assigned great importance in Canadian defence priorities: both the Trudeau and Mulroney defence reviews gave prominent attention to it. Since then, the sharpest sovereignty disputes of the Chrétien government arose over fisheries jurisdictions. Clearly, sovereignty remains a major preoccupation of the Department of National Defence. Does it deserve the pride of place given it?

The Statist model probably offers the strongest defence for the place of sovereignty, given the key role it assigns to it in statehood. In the long term, failure to exercise effective sovereignty can lead to national disaster (for example, the failure of the North American native peoples to have their sovereign control recognized by the invading Europeans). But claims to sovereignty must be upheld against threats of non-recognition posed both by other states and by foreign individuals. (Indeed, the later pose the more immediate threat today with actions such as smuggling or illegally crossing the border for criminal or terrorist purposes.) The question then is one of appropriate measures.

In recent years, most official boundary disputes have come from Canadian allies. Two authors writing before 9/11 found it "surprising that sovereignty should be an issue at all in defence policy."[13] Furthermore, they cite the difficulty that Department of National Defence (DND) has had in coming up with concrete sovereignty protection actions that do not intrude on the "policing" functions of the RCMP and fisheries patrol boats. They also found a general lack of enthusiasm for it in the Canadian Forces. In dealing with other states, we have seen a "militarization" of the issue of sovereignty since 1971, when the Trudeau government raised it to the status of a top defence concern. Prior to that time, and in practice since, Canada has preferred to use diplomacy and international arbitration to sort out such disputes.

Sovereignty perhaps has taken on special significance in the Canadian context due to the other factors of cultural and economic dependence. We will examine these factors more completely in Chapters 7 and 8. If so, sovereignty concerns may be better handled by specific acts to enhance political autonomy than by "flag showing" expeditions to the Arctic.

Today, we read of violations of Canadian boundaries by American and European fishers in the newspapers. It must be pointed out that these are acts of private individuals not sanctioned by their governments, although the Statist model tends to blur this distinction. On the long, porous US border, Canada's law-enforcement needs can often best be met through joint policing activities. Concerns about illegal immigration and smuggling people led to integrated border enforcement teams on the BC-Washington state border in the late 1990s. Similar problems of drugs, small arms, and smuggling people between Quebec or Ontario and New York or New England stimulated the formation in 1997 of the Canadian Anti-smuggling Working Group and the Northeast Border Working Group to coordinate joint law enforcement. Further to this end, occasional joint raids on smugglers were conducted such as Project Othello (Canadian side) and Operation Over the Rainbow (from the US side) in 1998.

The events of September 11, 2001 and the global threat of al Qaeda-style terrorism has greatly increased the salience of the issue of border security. In particular the United States now casts a wary eye at what it sees as gaps in border surveillance. In this vein, a 2004 Canadian Senate report pointed out the lack of continuous surveillance of the Great Lakes and the inadequacy of Canada's unarmed Coast Guard.[14] Terrorism poses a much broader security threat and therefore serves as a link to our next chapters on the defence of Canada.

Notes

1. Brebner (1960), p. 144.
2. McNaught (1969), p. 208.
3. Hillmer and Granatstein (1994), p. 61.
4. By historian Donald Creighton for one.
5. Quoted in Earys (1972), p. 351.
6. This is according to the *Newfoundland Encyclopedia*. Elsewhere there is a striking lack of information about these bases.
7. Galloway, "Allies Quitting Goose Bay" (2004), A2.
8. Britain claimed the right to passage through Albanian territorial waters near the island of Corfu and was upheld by international jurists. A glance at a map will demonstrate that the British warship could have easily taken the longer route around the Adriatic side of Corfu and avoided Albanian waters.
9. Howard (1986), A8.
10. Jim Meek's article "Nova Scotia 'holding own'" in the *Chronicle-Herald* reported that cod landings for 1977 to 1982 were up 251 per cent.
11. Canadian Press (1988), A1.
12. Cox (2004), A5.
13. Middlemiss and Sokolsky (1989), p. 167.
14. Galloway, "National Security in Peril" (2004), A6.

Chapter Three
Defining the Enemy and National Defence

Once a state has gained international recognition for its boundaries and sovereignty, its next priority would be that traditional preoccupation of armies and defence ministers: national security or national defence. We will begin with the traditional, limited definition of security: policy-planning to deal with threats of attack, whether imminent or potential, from foreign states or actors (such as terrorist groups). Given the anarchical nature of the international system and the absence of an international police force, departments of defence and standing armies have always been a necessary feature of the state. The state's military need has to be judged in the context of the violence of the neighbourhood; compare, for example, Scandinavia since 1945 to the Middle East in the same period.

The use of arms is not the only way of settling disputes. Provided that the states involved are not motivated by empire-seeking and conquest and that there exists some overlap in bargaining positions, then diplomatic negotiation can successfully terminate a conflict, even after a phase of military threats and demonstrations. Even appeasement, a policy of surrendering at the bargaining table to the demands of the opponent, can be successful. For example, British diplomats made concessions to US negotiators on a few Canadian border disputes and in Central America, and for their policy of appeasement the United States rewarded them with peace after the War of 1812 and American support in World War I.

Where an opponent's motives are more expansionist, no amount of appeasement can serve, as was demonstrated by Neville Chamberlain's attempted appeasement of Hitler at Munich in 1938. At such times, states must prepare for war first by self-strengthening, and where that is insufficient, by seeking allies. The underlying logic of national security lies in deterrence of attack and the calculation of the balance of power. The concept of deterrence holds that a rational opponent will attack only if he perceives his forces as stronger than his target. As the size of the armies become evenly matched, success in war becomes difficult to guarantee and attack less likely. Winston Churchill went even further and argued that an extremely aggressive enemy, as he perceived the Soviet Union to be, would only be deterred by absolute inferiority of arms. Thus, in the early 1950s, he advised Western governments to seek military superiority over the Soviets to keep the peace.

Availability of resources for national defence differs between states. Sometimes no amount of internal arms building will balance the size of the enemy's armies. In that case, the state is advised to seek powerful allies to balance the defence equation. Even here, deterrence is contingent on the perceived strength of the alliance and the promises made, as seen by Chamberlain's failed guarantee to Poland to keep that country from being overrun by Germany in 1939.

In this and the following two chapters, we examine defence interests from the Canadian point of view. Geopolitics has hindered and helped Canadian defence planning — hindered in that Canada has too much territory for its modest population to defend, but helped in that it had a non-strategic location until the advent of long-range bombers. Nonetheless, Ottawa has identified a series of potential enemies including the United States, Germany, and the Soviet Union. In the past, Canada viewed the enemies of Great Britain as her own (as in World War II), inviting attack from distant powers. Having insufficient internal resources, Canadian governments have traditionally sought security through reliance on stronger powers, first Great Britain and then the United States (see Chapter 4).

THE AMERICAN THREAT

If we consider Canada's present strategic situation in purely military terms divorced from history, there is no denying that the greatest danger of potential attack is posed by the US. Aside from the United States' status as nuclear superpower, its population and economic power exceed that of Canada tenfold. The US is the only country sharing a land border with Canada, and hence the only nation that could threaten with an immediate tank and infantry invasion. Furthermore, the Canadian population tends to be clustered near the American border, easily reached by American strikes, whereas most American targets are far back from the Canadian border and widely dispersed. In the rubric of nuclear deterrence, a much greater proportion of the Canadian population lies hostage to a potential strike by America.

Even without taking nuclear weapons into account, the United States has historically possessed an overwhelming edge in power since the American Civil War (1861-65.) Luckily, states are rarely motivated by purely military factors, or Canada might well have disappeared in a late-nineteenth-century American invasion. In fact, states are motivated by a complex interplay of ideological, societal, historical, and even moral factors. Nonetheless, given the prevalence of warfare among the great powers before World War II, it is easy to see how a border dispute, commercial misunderstanding, or wave of popular resentment might have led the two countries into a war, to Canada's great disadvantage. The War of 1812 serves as an example. The capture of Canada and British North America was not the initial intention or cause for the war on the American government's side. The Americans went to war over grievances with British maritime practices. Nonetheless, once war had broken out, the occupation of Canada became the obvious military goal of the American armies.

According to deterrence theory, Canada would need alliances or outside forces to balance the power advantage of the United States. Throughout the nineteenth and early twentieth century, this outside balance was provided by the mother country, Great Britain. From the British standpoint, the defence of Canada against American aggression looked extremely tenuous, since the United Kingdom was primarily a naval power. Thus, the failure of the American invasions of the War of 1812 was a pleasant surprise for British strategists; and for Canadians, according to Desmond Morton (1981), it gave rise to a "heroic national myth" that Canada could be defended largely through the efforts of her own militias. Morton suggests, however, that in reality, from 1814 onwards, increased American settlement and development of the Great Lakes region made Canadian defence increasingly impossible (because it shifted the American power base far away from the coastal regions easily attacked by British naval power).

Britain sought to strengthen Canadian security through diplomatic means. The Rush-Bagot Treaty of 1817 demilitarized the Great Lakes and actually led to the destruction of existing US and UK naval forces. Thus, it stands as an early example of disarmament, and through its longevity (lasting formally until World War II) served as the precedent for the "longest undefended border" of the twentieth century.

If the growing entente or cordial relationship were to break down, British North America would be defended, on paper, by the small British garrison (as few as 3,000 men in 1854) and colonial militias (which since 1855 tended to be organized on a local, volunteer basis). While these militias served a political and social function, they were not viewed by British military strategists as sufficient to meet the American threat, particularly as relations declined in the 1860s.

In 1861, the American Civil War erupted, mobilizing huge armies in the Union and the Confederacy. Economic interests pushed Britain to favour the South, and by the summer of 1862, the government was in fact covertly supporting the Confederacy.[1]

Union sentiment was particularly aroused by the building of Confederate warships, such as the *Alabama*, in British shipyards[2] and by Southern raiders using Canadian territory to attack the North at St. Albans, Vermont. As a result of the later incident, the US closed the border with Canada and demanded the use of passports by Canadians for the first time. Even more inflammatory was the Trent Affair of late 1861. When a Union warship forcibly removed two Confederate diplomats en route to Europe from the British mail ship the *Trent*, the British claimed that international law had been violated, and war was barely avoided.

The threat to Canada did not end with the Union victory of 1865. The Fenian Brotherhood, organized in 1857 in New York City by Irish Americans, aimed to end British domination of Ireland by attacking the nearest British target at hand, Canada. In 1866, they launched small invasions of Campobello Island, New Brunswick, and Fort Erie, Ontario. Though the United States army was quick to move on the Fenians once they attacked Canada, capturing some 700 of them, it had taken no steps to prevent their preparations.

CONFEDERATION AND THE BRITISH COMMITMENT

By 1866, there were plenty of grievances between the United States and the British Empire, and the Union had huge armies hardened by a long, bloody struggle. If the US wanted to attempt the conquest of Canada, the time seemed ripe. In 1866, the American

House of Representatives passed legislation to enable Canada to "join" the Union (such legislation would have been blocked by the South before the war).

This American threat played an important role in forging the Dominion of Canada. When the political leaders of the British North American colonies met to discuss Confederation, military considerations were high on the agenda. British military planners complained that individual colonial militias were not being maintained. The resulting agreement between the Canadian Fathers of Confederation and the British government involved two security pledges: the Dominion of Canada promised to do everything in its power to maintain its "connection with the mother country," including a commitment to spend $1 million a year on the militias; in return, Britain "fully acknowledged [...] reciprocal obligation of defending every portion of the Empire with all the resources."[3]

At first, Canada showed signs of serious commitment. The new government's minister of militias brought in a bill in 1868 that standardized the militia system across the Dominion. In 1874, the government began the practice of appointing a senior British officer to command the militias as a way to support the British connection, and in 1876, the Royal Military College was opened in Kingston to train Canadian officers at home. In 1873, Parliament created the North West Mounted Police to assist with internal security, particularly in the West.

But beyond these commitments, Ottawa did very little, and London was soon disillusioned by Canadian efforts. Spending on the militia dropped well below the $1 million pledged, militia recruitment was quite difficult, and quotas went unfulfilled. The rising threat of Germany toward Britain forced a withdrawal of British troops from central Canada in the early 1870s, leaving only small garrisons at Halifax and Esquimalt.

Desmond Morton claims the "century of peace" between the United States and Canada dates from this withdrawal of British forces, for it removed the main source of potential conflict. Also on the positive side, the absence of the army did give Canada the benefit of a lower tax burden and a relatively less militarized society. The removal of the British troops and the failure of the militias to grow meant that the Americans felt less threat from Canada and hence no need to build up defensive forces in response. Unilateral disarmament may have encouraged general North American disarmament in the late nineteenth century, but Morton's thesis goes on to make the more controversial claim that peace existed because Canada was now at the mercy of the United States. This statement implies an ongoing threat of military coercion and subordination based on power relations.

Was there really a serious threat of annexation coming from the US? Lawrence Martin certainly makes this case, based upon the public statements of American presidents of the period. Manifest Destiny and the Monroe Doctrine are also sometimes broadly interpreted to indicate a desire for Canadian annexation. Monroe's doctrine expressed, among other things, ideological hostility towards European colonialism in the Western Hemisphere. Did the fact that Canada represented British colonialism, the very thing the Americans had revolted against, imply an ambition to "liberate" it? The

Spanish-American War at the end of the century seems to show that the American expansionist appetite was not yet sated. (The US acquired Puerto Rico in that war and thought seriously about annexing Cuba.)

First of all, we must make a clear distinction between the American desire for Canada to join the Union of its own will and the use of military means to accomplish that end. Despite the Monroe Doctrine, the United States had taken very little action against European colonies or European interventions in the Western Hemisphere until the Spanish-American War. Likewise, the creation of the Dominion of Canada and the removal of British troops reduced the American perception of Canada as an oppressed colony.

After the gradual demobilization of the Union's Civil War army, evidence of military preparations is difficult to find. The American peacetime standing army, up until World War II, was to remain quite small by European standards, as both Canada and the United States seem to have shared an agriculturally based isolationism in this period. Nonetheless, by the turn of the century, the US seemed more intent on acquiring a colonial empire and had a growing willingness to send the American marines into neighbouring Caribbean states. The Philippines was not asked whether it wanted to become part of the United States.

Undoubtedly, the main reason Canada was treated differently was due to the distinction in how the US perceived Canada compared to other regions. At the time, American president Theodore Roosevelt pointed to the weak and unstable governments in the Western Hemisphere as open invitation to European intervention, justifying his "corollary to the Monroe Doctrine" of preventative intervention to forestall such interference. In 1914, he compared Mexico (where the US was intervening) to Canada in saying "if Mexico governed herself as well as Canada, she would not have any more to fear from us than has Canada."[4]

As to whether a supposed American military predominance cowed or pressured Canadian leaders into appeasement of the US in the late nineteenth century, the reader must judge. That story is more a question of political autonomy than outright invasion and will be told in subsequent chapters.

MILITARISM AND IMPERIALISM IN CANADA

Canada itself was not beyond experiencing in a limited way the imperialist sentiment of the late nineteenth century. Though not directly involved in the competition for colonies, many in the Dominion nonetheless were able to share the imperialist experience through vicarious participation in British expansionism. Organizations such as the Imperial Federation League[5] stressed closer ties with Britain and more direct contributions to British imperial adventures in Africa. The pamphlets of league writers such as Colonel Denison, G.M. Grant, and G.R. Parkin show influences of the general Social Darwinism and racism of the period, emphasizing a British or Anglo-Saxon civilizing mission. Imperial sentiment was concentrated in cities such as Toronto and weakest in French Canada and rural areas in general.

In tandem with imperialism, the turn of the century also saw the emergence of Canadian militarism. Morton defined this militarism as "a state of mind or set of values which supported patriotism, discipline, subordination, order, and a competitive view of human nature."[6] The image of Canada as a peaceable kingdom so dominates our thinking today that it is difficult to comprehend the thinking of the nineteenth-century Canadian militarist. He or she perceived society as increasingly indulgent and materialistic, in tandem with the growth and prosperity of the period. By teaching discipline and strengthening character, military training and war were the best antidotes for this soft life. War taught young men the higher spiritual values of excellence, heroism, and self-sacrifice.

Two institutional forms of this militarism were the Canadian Defence League (1909) and the cadet movement. The defence league called for a strengthening of Canadian defences and universal military training. The cadet movement sought to introduce school-age boys to the rigours of military training and drill; it was introduced into Canadian schools through a federal program in 1908. By 1913, 40,000 boys, three times the number in the Boy Scouts, were cadets.[7]

The natural convergence of imperialism and militarism lay in direct Canadian involvement in British colonial wars. For the British imperialist, Canadian contributions demonstrated loyalty and support for the empire, and allowed the younger generation direct participation in the ostensibly salubrious benefits of war. The empire's enemies were Canada's enemies; Britain's wars were Canada's wars. In 1884, 400 Canadian volunteers were sent to the African Sudan as a result of British expansion there. Likewise, the Boer War of British expansion in South Africa stimulated the imperialists to demand public Canadian contributions (see Chapter 6). Through individual enlistment and semi-official contributions, some 7,000 Canadians saw action there.

Militarism also led to calls for greater defence efforts by the government. After the Conservative Party victory of 1911, defence spending rose rapidly. Abandoning a small Liberal program for a Canadian navy, Borden decreed a $35-million contribution toward three new dreadnoughts for the British navy. Under his active minister of militia, Colonel Sam Hughes, the militia and the cadet movement were expanded.

GERMANY AS THE ENEMY

By the principle that Britain's enemies were Canada's enemies, Canada was immediately involved in the two great wars of the twentieth century. Unlike the long and agonizing debates that preceded American alignment with Britain in World War I, Canada's commitment was fairly automatic. The menace to Britain was geographically close and hence perceived by Canada as much more direct and threatening than any of the previous colonial wars. Nonetheless, and unlike in other dominions such as Australia, the war eventually divided rather than united the nation.

Though historians still debate the German kaiser's true ambitions in Europe, the official British government view was that German expansionism in Europe caused World War I. Specifically, the invasion of neutral Belgium by German troops triggered Britain's, and hence the empire's, involvement.

From the limited viewpoint of military factors, the war was ultimately a success. Canada was relatively well prepared for and able to send a Canadian Expeditionary Force (CEF) of 32,000 to serve in the "Imperial Army" within weeks. The war's length and costs were grossly underestimated, but eventually, with American entry in 1917, the allies prevailed. Canada was lucky in that the war was not fought on her territory, so while the cost of 60,661 dead was high (in fact, higher than that of the US), the economic benefits from supplying wheat and equipment were great. Furthermore, over 600,000 Canadians served and distinguished themselves in such major battles as the Second Battle of the Ypres (1915) and Vimy Ridge (1917). The foundation was laid for British, Canadian, and American military collaboration in World War II and the early cold war years.

From the viewpoint of other Canadian interests, the Great War was less successful. As we will see in the following chapters, the "consultation crisis" raised again the issue of Canadian autonomy within the empire, and the Conscription Crisis damaged the Canadian interest in national unity.

The interwar period saw many important organizational changes within the military. At the end of World War I, the demobilized CEF needed to integrate with the old volunteer militia. As a result of this integration, new regimental titles were adopted, such as Princess Patricia's Canadian Light Infantry for the West. In 1921, the Liberal government created the Department of National Defence, with military authority over all services combined in a single chief of staff. In 1924, a new service was created—the Royal Canadian Air Force—and in 1928 the first fighter planes were ordered. Aside from reorganization however, this period was one of lower military expenditure and the navy almost died of neglect. In the late 1930s, Canada, as with Great Britain, undertook a belated rearmament drive to catch up with the growth of Nazi arms.

Collaboration in World War I had finally ended the Canadian perception of military threat from the US, though the top defence priority, premised on an American invasion, was not officially abandoned until 1931. With the advent of another war in 1939, the calamitous fall of France, and the subsequent isolation of Great Britain as the new frontline, formal alliance with the United States was deemed appropriate. Hence, at the Ogdensburg, New York meeting between Prime Minister King and Franklin D. Roosevelt in August 1940, Canada entered its first defence pact with the United States. The main result of this treaty was the creation of the Permanent Joint Board of Defence (PJBD) to consider plans for joint security. The commission still exists, with combined civilian and military membership and alternating US-Canadian leadership, though its recommendations are not binding.

By 1939, British and Canadian perceptions of the German threat had lagged so far behind reality and their military capabilities had been so neglected that Britain came very close to defeat in the early stages of World War II, particularly in the Battle of Britain air campaign. With supply lines to the Continent severed by German occupation, the ocean links to Canada and the empire became vital lifelines, imperilled by the activity of German U-boats. Hence, for the besieged front line in Britain, naval and air power were all-important, and Canada played a major role in each. Canada's air contribution entailed participating in the British Commonwealth Air Training Plan (BCATP), and in the naval war, Canada shared in defending the North Atlantic and the vital convoys that left from Halifax and St. John's. The later task built up the Royal Canadian Navy (RCN), with 64 corvettes as convoy escorts and submarine hunters. This war was also different from World War I in that the enemy, on a small scale, "invaded" Canadian territory: German U-boats set up temporary meteorological bases in the Canadian Arctic and Japanese submarines shelled a British Columbian lighthouse in June of 1942. The fighting came closest to Canadian shores when the Japanese invaded the Aleutian Islands of Alaska. To some, this appeared to be the first stage of a Pacific Rim campaign that would bring the Japanese down the Alaskan coast to British Columbia and the American Pacific coast. In fact, the invasion appears to have been a move to divert attention from the attack on the Midway Islands in the North Pacific Ocean, but Canadian units were moved into Alaska and eventually fought in the retaking of the Aleutians.

Indeed, Churchill and Mackenzie King perceived America as key to eventual victory in the war. Hence, in the years before the attack on Pearl Harbor (December 1941) and American involvement in the war, King saw Canada's main role as wooing an isolationist US into greater collaboration with Britain. This was then the true period of Canada as "linchpin," linking the United States and Britain: Canada and Newfoundland provided summit venues for the two nations, beginning with a Churchill-Roosevelt meeting in August 1941.

In other aspects, World War II replayed the interests and problems of the first war on a grander scale. Once again, the contribution of Canadian army forces raised issues for Canadian sovereignty and national unity. Prime Minister King approached these concerns with far greater caution than Borden had, seeking to limit the commitment of overseas land forces. The early stages of the war abetted the prime minister's plans, for once Hitler abandoned any further attempt at a British invasion, Canadian troops in England saw little action. But with the entrance of the Americans in the war and defeat of the German armies in the Soviet Union, large-scale operations involving Canadian forces became possible. Beginning in 1943, Canadian infantry participated in the invasions of Sicily and Italy, the Normandy landings, and the liberation of Belgium and Holland. Canadian pilots recruited into the Royal Air Force (RAF) shared in the Anglo-American bombing program that destroyed major German cities and killed over half a million civilians. But on the whole, King's caution helps to explain the relatively light casualties in a very bloody war (about 45,000 soldiers — fewer than in World War I).

ANALYSIS OF THREATS TO CANADA PRE-1945

The main business of security policy is the assessment of threat. Correct assessment of threat involves difficult judgments about power (how strong is my enemy?) and intention (how strong is the hostility?). Power theorists such as Hans Morgenthau have much to say on both of these questions. Given the Realpolitik theorist's belief that power considerations underlie all major interests and intentions, he outlines three broad patterns of intention:

Type 1   **Status quo** is typical of a great power that is content with its present rank and power level. As a result, its motives are largely defensive, though it may feel "forced" into a war to stop a rising challenger. Great Britain in the nineteenth century is often cited as an example of status quo.

Type 2   **Limited expansion** covers a wide range of motivations, from the simple desire for "more respect" or prestige and recognition as a "great power" to concrete acquisition of territory or colonies arising out of economic need or sense of historic grievance. In this last sense, an irredentist nation that believes a part of its home territory has been "stolen" would qualify. France provides an example of the range of motivations under limited expansion: Napoleon III's Second Empire seeking prestige, and the Third Republic demanding the return of Alsace and Lorraine from Germany.

Type 3   **Imperial supremacy** includes only those nations or leaders ultimately seeking an unlimited and global empire. This expansionism seeks the final removal of all rival power centres and may arise from the megalomania of an individual leader or the inspiration of a dogmatic and evangelistic ideology. Napoleon I and Hitler are the clearest examples of recent empire-builders. Though this type of motivation is rare, the extreme nature of the threat requires the greatest vigilance in its detection.

Table 3.1 Intentions and Defence Policy

Intention of Potential Enemy	Recommended Policy
Status Quo	Détente
Limited Expansionist or Status-seeker	Appeasement
Imperial Supremacy or Unlimited Expansionist	Containment

Indeed, Morgenthau has very specific policy recommendations for dealing with each type of potential enemy or rival.[8] Since the status quo power is behaving only defensively, such a nation rarely poses a threat and a cooperative policy can be followed. The real challenge of statesmanship comes in sorting out and responding to the second and third categories of nation.

For the second category, limited expansionists, serious conflict can be avoided through negotiation, diplomacy, and a judicious policy of appeasement. Since the demands are truly limited, concessions can be safely made, particularly where peace, goodwill, and friendship or even alliances are to be gained. A country seeking greater prestige or recognition often can be appeased by largely symbolic or rhetorical gestures. Irredentist demands for territory are trickier, but can often be resolved by negotiation, adjudication, or even outright concession. Such concessions can be made because they will not whet the appetite for more.

However, giving land to the third type or empire-building state, with unlimited territorial ambitions, would not quell demands for more. For this type of state to succeed in its goals, it usually must mask its real intentions to avoid the formation of a grand coalition of all its potential victims. This gives rise to the strategy of divide and conquer, or isolate and defeat your enemies one at a time. Thus Hitler entered a pact with the USSR in 1939, secretly intending the destruction of his "ally" after he had dealt with France and Britain. Another commonly used tactic is "salami diplomacy," which means one should not ask for the whole salami at once but instead take successive, thin slices. Each request for a thin slice seems easy to grant, since not much appears to be at stake. But each concession of a thin slice sets the precedent for future concessions, until the entire salami has been given away. Hitler was a master of this type of diplomacy: he skilfully played to the misperception he was a Type 2 (limited expansionist) by reassuring his victims that each request was his "last territorial demand."

The prescribed counter-strategy for a nation of this third type is a policy of containment and no concessions. Granting concessions would only weaken the conceding nation physically and psychologically, and embolden the ambitious leader of the imperial supremacy to make further demands. To counter his or her aims of unlimited expansion, a grand alliance of all states bordering the aggressor must be forged to contain it and prevent divide and conquer tactics. Even relatively small concessions or annexations must be denied as they may prove to be salami tactics, the "driving wedge" of future expansion. A later variation of this salami tactic was the domino theory: if the first country falls, it weakens the second, causing it to fall and so on down the line. There is good reason to believe that if Hitler had been contained by a firm alliance between Britain, France, the USSR, and all surrounding nations at some early stage in his demands, he could have been blocked from expansion or have even been removed from power by his own military. Thus, World War II and its horrendous casualties might have been avoided.

Hitler's near success in bringing Europe and perhaps the world under Axis domination shows the dire consequences of misperceiving external threats. From the British government's perspective, it is clear that Chamberlain mistook Hitler as the second type of nation and explicitly pursued a doomed policy of appeasement until it was too late to implement a containment policy. The Canadian government under King actively shared in this mistake: King embarked on a personal eleventh-hour mission to Berlin and willingly swallowed Hitler's reassurances.

There are also negative consequences to exaggerating the threat by misclassifying a Type 2 (limited expansionist) nation as a Type 3 (imperial supremacist). Given that the tactics of both involve deception, correct security perception demands a great deal of skepticism, and probing of real intentions and hidden agendas. Depending on the context, this state of mind can be considered either prudent or paranoid!

In the worst case, alarmism can lead to an inappropriate refusal to negotiate and cause unnecessary wars. Many historians believe World War I was such a case; that is, Britain exaggerated the threat Germany posed. Kaiser Wilhelm was classified as an unlimited expansionist rather than a Type 2 leader still seeking recognition and parity with Great Britain (limited expansionist). If true, then a few concessions in the Balkans to Germany's ally might have helped to avoid the terrible destruction of the Great War and preserved British economic and financial power for decades longer. For Canada, 60,000 deaths and the divisive Conscription Crisis might have been avoided.

Under this analysis, British statesmen appeared wiser in the golden years of nine-teenth-century diplomacy. Then, both France and the United States were correctly diagnosed as Type 2 (limited expansionist) states, and appeasing them successfully led to twentieth-century alliances with both countries. Indeed, from the British viewpoint, a few concessions in Canada and Central America swung the US from Anglophobia to Anglo-alliance. The problem for Canada was that most of the bargaining chips, while insignificant to the empire, were of strong interest to her. Thus, while British appease-ment of the United States brought peace in North America, it created a considerable feel-ing that Canadian assets where being bargained away in Whitehall and not Ottawa.

Notes

1. Dimbleby and Reynolds (1988), p. 20.

2. The *Alabama* went on to destroy nearly 60 Northern ships, and US claims for compensation from the UK became a major sticking point in future negotiations.

3. Quoted in Morton (1981), p. 17.

4. Quoted in Martin (1982), p. 65.

5. The Canadian branch of the Imperial Federation League was formed in 1884. In 1896, it became the British Empire League.

6. Morton (1981), p. 49.

7. *Ibid.*

8. Morgenthau in fact categorizes intention slightly differently, so Table 3.1 represents a modi-fication of his ideas. See his book *Politics Among Nations*.

Chapter Four
Defining the New Enemy: From the Cold War to Jihad

All that has been said in the previous chapter about the importance of defining the nature of external threats is crucial to understanding the origins of the cold war. In the post-cold war age, it is difficult to comprehend the intense sense of danger, indeed paranoia, which seemed to have gripped Western leaders vis-à-vis the Soviet Bloc. The perceived threat was based on assessments of Soviet power and its hostile intent. This section will explain the basis for those perceptions and how they influenced Canadian security thinking. Studying the cold war is crucial to understanding Canadian foreign policy because it led to Canada's two important, enduring alliances: the North American Aerospace Defense Command (NORAD) and North Atlantic Treaty Organization (NATO).

It is difficult to define a single point at which the cold war began and the Soviets became the new enemy. Table 4.1 lists some of the major early conflicts.[1] The allies in the defeat of Hitler soon became bitter ideological enemies. In tracing this change in perception on the Western side, government documents and memoirs show a great deal of uncertainty and debate about Soviet intentions in the early years. A classic anecdote demonstrating Washington's rather clumsy attempts to sort out Stalin's intentions tells of a new American ambassador's first audience with Stalin in 1946. Throwing polite diplomatic language to the winds, Bedell Smith reportedly asked Stalin point blank, "How much further is the Soviet Union going to go?" to which Stalin smiled enigmatically and said, "Not much further." It's not clear whether Stalin meant this as a reassurance or a threat.

Table 4.1 The Western View of Soviet Expansionism in the Early Cold War

1945	Gouzenko Affair revelations
1945–1949	Sovietization of Eastern Europe:
	• breaks Yalta agreement
	• leads to Churchill's "Iron Curtain speech" of 1946
1946	Greek Civil War
	• USSR and Yugoslavian arms to the Greek Communists
	Slow Soviet exit from northern Iran
	Diplomatic pressure on Turkey and Norway

1948	Prague coup d'état
	Berlin Blockade (Soviets lay siege to West Berlin)
1949	Chinese Communist victory
	Soviet nuclear test
1950	North Korean invasion of South

By the mid-1960s, American historians had begun a serious debate about the origins of the cold war. Revisionist historians argued that the West, and the United States in particular, deserve most of the blame and that the USSR only responded defensively to Western provocation. Part of the problem has been the absence of open Soviet archives of the sort that have existed for most Western governments. However, the opening of secret Kremlin files since the fall of the Communist regime has shed new light on such crucial controversies as Stalin's involvement in and planning of the North Korean invasion of 1950.

Following that attack and the commencement of the Korean War, a rough consensus emerged in most Western capitals that Stalin clearly did not have Type 1 intentions (status quo) and that, of the remaining two possibilities, the evidence seemed to indicate Type 3 (unlimited expansion). Analogies were frequently drawn to Hitler; the main difference appeared to be that Stalin was more subtle and cautious in his expansionism. But his long-term goal seemed to be the destruction of the Western Capitalist system. Dissenting views tended not to deny Soviet expansionism, but to urge a Type 2 (limited expansion) rather than Type 3 definition of the enemy. However, majority opinion in most Western governments in these early years supported and deemed appropriate the American policy of containment. Indeed, by the end of the Korean War, a more or less common agreement had developed on the following set of six assumptions or perceptions about the Soviet threat:

1. *The Soviets do not believe Capitalism and Communism can coexist in the long run. For them, this belief makes war between the two blocs inevitable.* This perception certainly had some validity while Stalin lived, but even he seemed to believe that there would be another world war among the capitalists before a final showdown of the two camps. A few years after his death, at the Twentieth Congress of the Communist Party of the Soviet Union (1956), this "inevitability of war" doctrine gave way to the notion of peaceful coexistence, though many Western capitals remained skeptical.

2. *The Red Army in Eastern Europe poses a tremendous and immediate threat to Western Europe, which, due to historical, political, economic, and other factors, is the single most important front line of the cold war.* In fact, initial estimates of the size of the Red Army were exaggerated, as Stalin had to withdraw some of his forces from Eastern Europe for his massive reconstruction campaign. Some have argued Stalin purposely misled the West to provide a counter-threat to American nuclear superiority. Nonetheless, while Western governments rapidly demobilized their forces in the late 1940s, Russia

kept large armies in Eastern Europe. This threat looked all the greater because of the political instability and the large pro-Soviet Communist parties in France and Italy. Over the following forty years, the Soviets persisted in maintaining superiority in manpower and tanks, though some have argued this merely offset the technological advantage of the West. Nonetheless, Washington, Ottawa, and Whitehall were in considerable agreement, even during the Korean War, that Europe was the key front line of the cold war.

3. *The Soviets enjoy an important advantage over the West due to the totalitarian nature of their system.* Despite the larger economy of the United States and its temporary nuclear advantage, the USSR's non-democratic political system gave it compensating advantages. Control over media limited the domestic repercussions of dissent, which hindered US government military actions (for example, the Vietnam War). A centralized command economy could gear up for war production much faster. Greater internal security and secrecy made spying more difficult and assessments of Soviet capabilities and intentions more difficult, which led to greater disagreements and divisions about such vital intelligence among Western capitals. Collectively, these Soviet advantages can be summarized by the characterization that Soviet "will-power" and "resolve" were greater than the West's.

In the absence of good information, many exaggerated claims developed about Soviet achievements. The speedy catch-up in nuclear technology, the development of long-range bombers, and the breakthrough of the *Sputnik I* launch in 1957 greatly increased the myth of a Soviet technological advantage. By 1960, many people seriously believed the Soviets were ahead in space exploration (which they were, briefly) and in missile production (which they were not). The collapse of the Soviet economy has shown that while the command economy gave some advantages in the basic "metal-eater" industries, in the long run it created significant problems for the overall economy.

The "totalitarian advantage" also gave the Soviets the benefit of alliance solidarity. With the exception of Romania, the Warsaw Pact allies usually followed Moscow without dissent,[2] while NATO had to accommodate 12 to 16 independent governments. This problem is reflected in France's decision to withdraw from the NATO command structure in 1966, as well as in the divisions among NATO members into either "hawks" or "doves" and the obvious attempts by the USSR to exploit such differences. Yet despite these divisions, NATO has shown remarkable consensus on European security over the years.

4. *The conspiratorial heritage of Lenin's Bolshevik (Communist) Party gives the Soviets untold advantages in espionage, sabotage, and subversion. Hence, an additional threat to the West exists in the presence of "fifth column" Communist parties and sympathizers.* Perhaps no other assumption captures so well the emotional context of the cold war, leading to the near-hysteria of the McCarthy era in the United States. Soviet espionage was seen as directly responsible for the transmission of nuclear secrets to the USSR.[3] In 1945, the Gouzenko Affair in Canada alerted nations that Soviet agents had infiltrated the West, and frequent news reports of spy scandals in Western countries, even until the

1980s, helped to harden Western public attitudes generally. Also, the existence of large Communist parties in Western Europe with divided loyalties led to attempts to exclude them from power. It must be admitted that the loyalty of the French Communist Party toward the Soviets despite the interventions in Hungary, Czechoslovakia, Poland, and Afghanistan was astounding.

On the other hand, espionage activities by American and British spy agencies have led some to charge a double standard. Whether as a response to Soviet actions or as necessary accoutrement to American global power, Truman created the Central Intelligence Agency (CIA) in 1947, and the US spy agency soon was engaging in nasty covert operations of its own.

5. *The conspiratorial advantage can be seen at the global level in Soviet coordinating agencies such as the Comintern (Communist International) and the general solidarity of world Communist parties. Hence there is an international Communist conspiracy and a Communist monolith.* Of all the assumptions, this one seems to have aged most quickly. By the late 1950s, Mao Zedong and Nikita Khrushchev were openly feuding, and all technical, economic, and nuclear ties were soon broken between the two Communist giants. Even before ethnic breakup in Yugoslavia and the USSR, nationalism seemed a stronger force than ideological solidarity.

Yet, despite the evidence of Sino-Soviet schism, President Kennedy created the Green Berets to counteract the perceived unfair advantage that the Soviets had in Third World Communist/Nationalist movements, and President Johnson intervened in Vietnam to halt so-called Chinese Communist expansion. In reality, soon after the withdrawal of the Americans, the Vietnamese were involved in military action against their supposed Cambodian and Chinese allies. Under President Reagan, the American conservative yearning for a counter international movement led to sponsorship of a democratic front of "freedom fighters," such as the Contras in Nicaragua.

6. *Communist governments are particularly dangerous because they view Western Capitalist governments as corrupt, weak-kneed, and incapable of solidarity. Hence the United States was a "paper tiger" (as Mao put it) best handled by aggressive bluffing.* Though Mao and Fidel Castro persisted in this view of Western Capitalist nations into the 1960s, in the doctrine of peaceful coexistence, Khrushchev pointed to the special responsibilities of nuclear powers in preserving peace. He also distinguished between hawkish and sober leaders in the West. He may have initially viewed Kennedy as weak-kneed and thus was encouraged to bully him about the Berlin Wall, but the Cuban Missile Crisis soon changed his assessment and tactics. Of course, Western acceptance of this assumption about how the other side viewed it justified a tough, military response to dispel any "paper tiger" reputation.

Though each of these six assumptions contained flaws or were made somewhat obsolete with time, it took many years for attitudes first formed in 1940s to shift. From time to time, the superpowers found their way to cooperation (for example, Kennedy and Khrushchev's Test Ban Treaty of 1963), but real progress occurred only with West German leader Willy Brandt's openness to the East (Ostpolitik), and the Nixon-Kissinger rapprochement with the Soviets in the early 1970s. Détente, or relaxation in the tense cold war relationship, was delayed on the American side by the prolonged involvement in Vietnam (1964-73) and the continued pressure of an initially small but significant hard-right ideological movement led by senator Barry Goldwater and later Ronald Reagan.

On the Soviet side, the conditions for détente were laid with Khrushchev's peaceful coexistence doctrine, though he blew hot and cold for many years before settling into a true détente policy just prior to his ouster in 1964. Indeed, the irony of Khrushchev's peaceful coexistence was that his successors drew a different lesson from the Cuban Missile Crisis. Rather than perceiving it as a near brush with global disaster requiring an attempt at peaceful resolution, the Leonid Brezhnev regime felt that it was a Soviet humiliation resulting from military weakness and began the Soviet arms and naval build-up of the 1960s and 1970s, which fuelled Western anxiety even through the best détente years. Furthermore, Brezhnev's explicit exclusion of Soviet involvement in the Third World from the détente agenda and the perception of Soviet advances in Africa, Latin America, and Afghanistan laid the foundation for a return to cold war hostilities when Ronald Reagan was elected to the American presidency in 1980. This time around, however, only the government of Margaret Thatcher in Britain showed anything near the same ideological commitment to the old six cold war assumptions as the United States under Reagan. Only Mikhail Gorbachev's reforms and his formal abandonment of Communist ideological goals, followed by the dismantling of the Soviet Bloc and the dissolution of the Soviet Union itself could bring a sudden end to the cold war (1990-91).

In brief, we can roughly date three major periods to the cold war. The first period, from the Berlin Blockade of 1948 to Brandt's Ostpolitik of 1969, was followed by a period of détente, until the Soviet invasion of Afghanistan in 1979. The last phase, or the second round of the cold war (roughly 1979-89), involved a common agreement within NATO that the Soviets still posed a threat, but the nature and assumptions underlying this perception varied greatly among members. We now turn to examine the evolution of Canadian perceptions of Soviet threat and Canada's security policy response.

CANADIAN PERCEPTIONS OF THE SOVIET THREAT

John Holmes cites three major events in the formulation of the Canadian public's perception of the USSR as the new enemy: the Gouzenko Affair, Berlin, and the Korean War. Since the Gouzenko Affair was a Canadian incident, it will be considered in some detail.

Igor Gouzenko was a cipher clerk, a person who translates secret messages, for Soviet military intelligence. On September 6, 1945, he defected from the Soviet embassy in Ottawa, taking with him many of the secret documents he was translating from his embassy. So shocking was his story of an extensive Soviet spy network infiltrating the highest levels of the allied governments that the Mackenzie King administration initially sent him and his documents away. Only after agents of the Soviet embassy broke into his apartment (while Gouzenko was hiding elsewhere) did the RCMP take him into protective custody. Over the next few weeks, the documents Gouzenko had brought with him were translated, substantiating Gouzenko's story and immediately identifying a British scientist, Dr. Alan Nunn May, as having passed information to Soviet agents.

The Western allies were slow to follow up on Gouzenko's leads, due to their desire to continue cooperating with the Soviet government. Nonetheless, Gouzenko's charge of an extensive spying network was verified with the eventual exposure of the British Cambridge spies: Kim Philby, Donald Maclean, Guy Burgess, Anthony Blunt, and John Cairncross. In his excellent account of this period, Anthony Smith concludes that the Gouzenko Affair gave support to the public perception of an international Communist conspiracy and created a new secular faith.

> The anti-Communist faith dominated the North American public consciousness, providing a touchstone of "loyalty," narrowing the range of speculation [...] about Russian intentions and progressively limiting the margins for diplomatic manoeuvre.[4]

Mackenzie King's assessment was pessimistic, as usual: "Now the conflict is whether the US or Russia shall control the world [... which will] inevitably lead to World War III, in which Canada will become the battlefield." His only solace for Canada was that she might hope to play a role in the "self-liberation of the Russian people from their jailers."[5]

There is also the matter of how similar Canadian perceptions were to those in the United States or Britain. Some American revisionists have gone so far as to suggest that American attitudes were all that mattered and that American allies were dragged along into the cold war by American economic domination. As John Holmes has pointed out, such an interpretation is not supported by a detailed examination of the record and may merely reflect again American academics' exaggerated sense of their own nation's self-importance (if even in a negative sense): "These revisionist historians, mostly Americans, are paradoxically guilty of megalomaniac Americanism. They see no other actor on the world scene of any consequence."[6]

In fact, by the summer of 1946, the British government's attitude towards the Soviets was more hawkish than American policy. Though Prime Minister Clement Attlee publicly disavowed Churchill's Iron Curtain speech, he privately supported it. Indeed, the government's main concern was to stop Soviet "economic and ideological infiltration" by "unmasking Soviet intentions to the world." According to Anne Deighton, "Whitehall's major preoccupation was now to alert the Americans of the danger that dealing with the Soviet Union would present to European security."[7] Ernest Bevin, the British foreign minister, skilfully manoeuvred to sabotage American-Soviet agreement on Germany. Likewise, the French government's main preoccupation seems to have been to gain an American security guarantee against the Soviets. If there was manipulation going on between the United States and the Europeans, it certainly appears to have been mutual.

Both Canada and Britain had independent sources of information and analyses on

Soviet intentions, including strong diplomatic representation in Moscow. If much of American official perception was formed by US advisor George Kennan's "Long Telegram" on Soviet expansionist motives and the need for containment, then British and Canadian policy was similarly influenced by long telegrams from their own respective capable ambassadors. Frank Roberts, the British ambassador, at first explained Soviet expansion into Eastern Europe as the limited, historical pursuit of Russian power, but ultimately decided that Marxist-Leninist ideology could not be ignored. The Canadian ambassador Dana Wilgress made perhaps the greatest *volte-face*, swinging from a pre-war sympathy with the Bolsheviks to a more sinister interpretation of Soviet motives. In a cable of March 6, 1946, he stated that "Stalin must have often chuckled to himself over the ease with which he secured the tremendous concessions to his point of view at Teheran, Yalta, and Potsdam,"[8] foreshadowing the US Republican Party's charge of a Roosevelt "sell-out" at the Yalta conference. A later telegram from Wilgress suggested that Moscow had faith in the ultimate triumph of Communism, but both Canadian and British ambassadors saw Soviet imperialism as more cautious, long-term, and subtle than Nazi imperialism had been. Given our earlier analysis for identifying the intentions of potential threats (see Table 3.1, p. 45), it is not surprising that both nations favoured Kennan's containment policy.

More extreme ideological views can by found in both the United States and Canada during this period. John Foster Dulles, who was later to become President Eisenhower's secretary of state, published an influential article that called on the West to take the offensive in "rolling back" Communism by liberating Eastern Europe. Dulles's views grew out of a strong religious commitment and at times gave his policy the rhetoric of a holy crusade. Likewise, this ideological element can be seen in the quote by Mackenzie King on page 54 and in some of the pronouncements of Escott Reid:

> The essence of Western Christian faith is that the individual is eternal and the state and the community are temporal [...] Opposed to this faith is the totalitarian heresy that whatever serves the interests of the state or the community is right [...]
>
> In order that the schism may be ended without in the process destroying the values of civilization, the Western world must convert the Soviet world from its heresy. In order to prevent war, we must launch a war for men's minds.[9]

It is important to bear in mind that these are the words of a prominent Canadian (not American) government official. French Canadian speakers also had a tendency to introduce moral or religious overtones, for example, Prime Minister Louis St. Laurent's clarion call for the creation of NATO. In the early years of the cold war, a spectrum of opinions can be found in each of the major Western capitals.

In fact, other concerns did exist among the allies about American foreign policy. The British feared that if the United States followed the anti-imperialist line of former president Roosevelt, she might turn her back to the colonial powers, Britain and France, or that Congress might force a new retreat into isolationism. Overall, though, the main concern was over inconsistency in American policy. According to Deighton, "Many British policy-makers felt that the Americans wavered between hesitancy and overreaction to events."[10] This concern about an American tendency to oversimplification and extremism was expressed continually through the cold war period. Yet, by far, the pressing concern from official European circles throughout the cold war was to keep the Americans involved in Europe.

This concern over extremism or hawkishness in American views also appears in the memoirs of certain Canadian leaders, such as Lester Pearson. But on the whole, significant differences in perceptions of the Soviet threat do not appear prevalent until the third stage, or second-round cold war of the Reagan years. While Canada and most of Western Europe agreed that the Soviet invasion of Afghanistan in 1979 required a tough Western response and boycotted the 1980 Summer Soviet Olympics, few leaders other than Margaret Thatcher were willing to follow Reagan in returning to the harsh rhetoric of the early cold war. By the 1980s, Canada and most Western allies discounted the ideological factors in Soviet motives and instead accepted a limited expansionist interpretation. Or, to put it in terms of our analysis of intentions, most Western leaders believed that the Soviet leaders were no longer Type 3 (unlimited expansionists) but rather Type 2 (limited expansionist or prestige-seekers). Thus, a major disagreement ensued over policy, with the Reagan government pursuing containment or even "roll back," while Pierre Trudeau and most European governments favoured détente.

A common perception exists among many Canadian foreign policy elites that Americans were more belligerent, militaristic, and hawkish in attitudes toward the USSR than the average Canadian. Listed below are some structural reasons that might explain why, over time, the consensus of the late 1940s disappeared, with the Americans taking a more bellicose line:

1. **Leadership role.** As the largest Western power and "arsenal of democracy," the American government may have sometimes felt the need to "get out front" and take a stronger stand than its allies. American officials seem to interpret leadership as making tough decisions, unilaterally. America's allies would have preferred consultation and multilateralism (see Chapter 7).
2. **The military-industrial complex.** The Korean War represented a major watershed for the United States, marking a new period of high defence spending over the following 40 years. America truly became the arsenal of the West, making twice to six-times the defence effort of its allies, even in periods of peace. By the late 1950s, President Eisenhower himself began to wonder about the effects of such a prolonged military build-up on the American economy and political scene. Certainly "national security" policy was given a higher priority in Washington than in Ottawa and some of the other allied capitals.[11]
3. **The legacy of the McCarthy years.** No other Western country experienced anything quite as extreme. Democrats in particular had been unfairly charged with "losing" China. Both Kennedy and Johnson were to cite fears of being labelled

"soft on Communism" as justifications for tough anti-Communist actions (the Bay of Pigs and Vietnam).

3. **The Vietnam experience.** America's long and misguided involvement in this war tarnished its image and fuelled a radical critique of "American Imperialism." The dissent movement that developed in the United States against the war was paralleled at higher levels in other Western countries. Many Canadians cite that war as the point at which they began to doubt the wisdom of Canada's alliance with the US.

Yet, despite this vast potential for disagreement, Western bloc harmony has been amazingly persistent. Charles de Gaulle may have distanced France from NATO at least in part due to different perceptions of the USSR, but later French governments have virtually rejoined the alliance. Challenges posed by American missteps and hawkish policy decisions were usually resolved by quiet diplomacy. This NATO resilience must in part be seen as the result of a continuing basic consensus on the Soviet threat throughout the cold war and the need for a security alliance with the United States.

DEFENDING AGAINST DIRECT ATTACK

Military planning for the defence of Canada itself had entered a new and extremely unsettling phase after World War II. The old assumption that Canadian territory was too remote to suffer invasion from outside North America was shattered by the development of two new major weapons: nuclear warheads and long-distance bombers. Canada had participated directly in the heavy bombing of Germany and thus had first-hand knowledge of the bombers' destructive capability. Added to this were the awesome new atomic and hydrogen bombs: now only a handful of bombers would be needed to devastate the cities of Canada. Initially, Ottawa and Washington both played down the nuclear threat to North America. But in 1947, the USSR demonstrated that it had intercontinental bombers capable of reaching across the Atlantic. Suddenly the Arctic was no longer an impenetrable shield but the short route to Soviet and American cities.

As we have seen, King had already predicted that Canada would become the battlefield for World War III. Given its geographic location directly between the superpowers, a Canadian declaration of neutrality would have been treated as Belgium's neutrality was in the previous world wars. In any case, politics, economics, and public perception of the Soviet threat all predisposed Ottawa to seek greater military cooperation with the United States.

Cooperation but not formal alliance was the key to the cautious approach Mackenzie King bequeathed to the St. Laurent government. Hence, defence coordination before 1957 developed on a gradual ad hoc basis. The structures for cooperation had been created during the war, and in 1946, at the recommendation of the Permanent Joint Board of Defence (PJBD), a military cooperation committee (MCC) was established. Nonetheless, when Harry Truman and Mackenzie King met in February of 1946, King politely refused any quick moves towards a bilateral alliance. This approach was continued under St. Laurent, manifested as a tendency to multilateralize the defence of North America by tying its military structures to NATO.

Canadian defence strategy had already adopted a two-theatre approach: Western Europe and North America. In the latter arena, the military's main objective was to defend Canadian airspace from incursions by Soviet bombers. Canada's airspace needed defending not just from bombers on their way to American targets: through its cooperation with the United States and Western Europe, Canadian military bases had also become Soviet targets. Likewise, through Newfoundland Confederation, Ottawa was to inherit American bases. As early as 1947, the United States had begun stationing B-47 bombers capable of reaching Soviet targets at Goose Bay, Labrador.

The Soviet threat to North America developed much quicker than either Ottawa or Washington expected. At the Moscow May Day military parade of 1947, Stalin showed off his new Tu-4 bombers to startled Western diplomats. The Tu-4, modelled on the American B-29 bomber, was capable of flying one-way bombing missions to all points in Canada and the United States. By 1949, the US Pentagon estimated the Soviet fleet of Tu-4s at 1000. By September of that year, the Soviets again surprised the West by detonating an atomic bomb, years ahead of Western projections. In 1951, *Maclean's* carried an article titled "If the Russians Attack Canada" in which a Canadian defence expert[12] described a Soviet Tu-4 assault on North America. If the Soviets used the 50 to 60 atomic bombs they were then believed to possess, he predicted 9 would be targeted on the Canadian cities of Vancouver, Edmonton, Winnipeg, Toronto, Sault Ste-Marie, Windsor, Ottawa, Montreal, and Halifax. Such an attack would cripple both the US and Canada, and yet North American skies were virtually undefended.

Part of this defence problem was to have been solved by the development of a Canadian jet fighter. Through the efforts of politician C.D. Howe, A.V. Roe Canada (AVRO) was test-flying the new CF-100 by January 1950. This costly plane used British jet engines, but by 1952, plans had begun for an all-Canadian interceptor, the AVRO CF-105 or AVRO *Arrow*. In the meantime, Canada strengthened its air force by ordering 56 American F-86 jets, with an agreement to produce them under license in Canada. The development of an "all-Canadian" interceptor was seen as a unique Canadian contribution to Western defence, a method of stimulating a high-tech industry for Canada, and a source of Canadian pride.

In order for the jets to find the Soviet bombers, a better radar defence (another new weapon from World War II, along with the jet fighter) was needed. Eventually, in the 1950s, three major radar lines were built. In 1950, Ottawa joined an American plan to build a new radar line along the Canadian-American border. The Pinetree Line extension was built to cover some of Ontario and Quebec and thus push the site of potential air battles between North American and Soviet planes farther north and away from densely populated areas. America supplied two-thirds of the money and personnel for this screen, but in 1954 Ottawa decided on an additional all-Canadian project called the Mid-Canada Line. Public unease at the Soviet detonation of a hydrogen bomb in August of 1953 and headlines such as "Russian Planes are Raiding Canada's Skies" created the stimulus for the project. Thus, the Mid-Canada Line pushed the defended air border north to the 55th parallel. Lastly, in 1955, with Canadian agreement, the Americans undertook the difficult construction of the Distant Early Warning (DEW) line in the high Arctic, paying for it and initially operating it themselves.[13]

Thus, defence of North American airspace also included this key "early warning" component. The Pentagon believed it was vital to give the president and National Security Council ample time to consider their options for responding to an incoming attack. While general civil defence operations such as evacuations were soon abandoned as impractical, at least the DEW would allow for time to put the command structure (including the American president) under cover. It was doubtful that jet interceptors would knock out all the incoming bombers and thus provide a shield against a full attack. Nonetheless, the United States hoped they could handle a small attack at least sufficiently well to deter the Soviets from trying a surprise air strike to disarm American air bases. These initial stratagems eventually evolved into a nuclear doctrine called deterrence theory, which relied on the threat of an unstoppable (hence invulnerable) and devastating retaliatory counter-strike to prevent nuclear war. When the Soviets had clearly demonstrated similar defence capabilities by the 1960s, the doctrine became known specifically as Mutually Assured Destruction (MAD).

NORTH AMERICAN AIR DEFENCE COMMAND (NORAD)

By the mid-1950s, pressure was growing from the air forces of both Canada and the United States for a more integrated defence structure. In 1954, the US Air Force (USAF) created a continental air defence command, which seemed to imply that in time of war American jets would be patrolling all of North America's airspace. The establishment of a joint headquarters and integration of the air forces for this purpose was being recommended by Canadian-American military study groups, the chiefs of staffs, and the American secretary of defence.[14] Not surprisingly, George Pearkes, the defence minister of the newly elected Conservative government of John Diefenbaker, was soon advocating the same. In July of 1957, Diefenbaker claimed Pearkes had told him that Lieutenant General Charles Foulkes and the Canadian military approved of the plan and the previous Liberal government had given all but formal assent. Liberal Party critics denied that such approval had been given. Furthermore, Prime Minister Diefenbaker gave his verbal assent to the plan to the US secretary of state John Foster Dulles in late July, before cabinet and the Department of External Affairs (DEA) had been consulted. Despite that this major step in military integration appears to have taken place with remarkably little discussion in Canada,[15] the House of Commons debate on the NORAD agreement in May and June of 1958 seems to have focused more on criticizing the way the decision was made rather than the decision itself.

The NORAD agreement of May 1958 created an integrated North American air defence command centred in a mountain fortress (Mt. Cheyenne) in Colorado Springs, Colorado. The military staff of this headquarters was led by an American commander, a Canadian deputy, and an alternating Canadian-American chain of command on down the ranks. For defence purposes, North America was subdivided into eleven sub-regions regardless of national boundaries, and the overall American commander reported to the chiefs of staffs of both Canada and the US. Canada's specific contribution to NORAD, aside from headquarters personnel, included nine interceptor squadrons (later reduced to three squadrons of CF-101s), and later the Royal Canadian Navy (RCN) played an anti-submarine role in North American waters.

Given the real Soviet bomber threat of the 1950s, NORAD can be seen as a logical step for enhancing Canadian security. Aside from deterring a large-scale nuclear bomber strike and lessening the possibility of a surprise air strike, collaboration with a super-power greatly improved the technological capabilities and morale of the Royal Canadian Air Force (RCAF) (explaining the persistent popularity of NORAD with that service). Nonetheless, in hindsight, the following questions have been raised:

1. Was the procedure by which Diefenbaker evaluated the agreement extensive enough?
2. Was civilian control over the military adequate, especially given the charges that the military services rushed the agreement past Diefenbaker?
3. Was Canadian autonomy adequately protected? (This very large matter is discussed further in Chapter 7.)

But, unfortunately for Diefenbaker, NORAD was soon to generate even larger contro-versies. Military plans were soon made obsolete by the relentless march of military tech-nology. By 1958, a more efficient method for active defence against incoming Soviet bombers appeared with the development of surface-to-air missiles, such as the Bomarc-B. Armed with a small tactical nuclear warhead, the Bomarc did not actually have to hit the enemy bomber for its detonation to destroy it. Indeed, it was hoped that this small nuclear blast would fuse the larger nuclear bombs on board the Soviet bombers, prevent-ing their detonation when they crashed.

The Bomarc also appeared to be the salvation for the financially troubled AVRO *Arrow* project. Development of the *Arrow*, Canada's main interceptor jet, was consis-tently behind schedule and over its cost estimates. Indeed, the tremendous cost of $8 mil-lion per *Arrow* was not competitive, due to the small Canadian market and a lack of projected foreign sales. In September of 1958, the Diefenbaker government terminated the *Arrow* project, concluding that "the Canadian taxpayer would most likely not have been willing to pay the cost of a truly independent defence industry."[16] Shortly there-after, he ordered 56 Bomarcs, which were duly received in 1961. The United States paid for the Bomarcs; Canada paid for and built the sites for them near North Bay, Ontario. Ironically, by then, the Americans were expressing doubt about the military value of the Bomarc and were dissuaded from dropping the Bomarc program in part by pressure from Diefenbaker to keep it.

The end of the *Arrow* also meant the further integration of the North American defence industry. Having concluded that Canada could not afford to produce its own advanced jet, Diefenbaker decided that an agreement to gain a Canadian share of the American market was preferable to having no Canadian defence production at all. Though his friend President Eisenhower was not initially enthusiastic about a Canadian exemption from national security protectionism due to the domestic political difficulties it raised for him, a US defence department directive of December 1958 allowed it under the title, "Defence Economic Cooperation with Canada." In practice, Canadian firms have experienced difficulty competing for US defence department orders, for a number of reasons, and so most of Canada's share of defence production has come about through specific demands by Ottawa for Canadian content on its own orders. For example, in 1961, the Diefenbaker government ordered 66 F-101 Voodoo interceptors (again with nuclear tipped missiles) from the American McDonnell-Douglas company, and in return the US government agreed that the F-104 Starfighter for Europe would in part be manufactured in Canada.

Thus, in 1962, the Diefenbaker government had on order nuclear Bomarcs, nuclear Voodoos, and nuclear Honest John missiles for deployment in Europe, in addition to the American nuclear weapons at Newfoundland bases. This led to the nuclear weapons controversy, which ultimately helped defeat the Conservative prime minister in the April 1963 election. For a non-nuclear nation, Canada was developing a formidable arsenal of imported nuclear weapons. Diefenbaker weakly claimed he had not been fully informed about it—a claim which has been flatly denied by his own defence minister, Douglas Harkness. More likely, Diefenbaker stumbled into an unforeseen public-opinion crisis through a series of small incremental decisions in the absence of a coherent long-term nuclear policy.

Ultimately, the succeeding Liberal government's policy to accept but gradually phase out the weapons resolved the question of the nuclear arms build-up, abetted by the quick march of technology. Even as the Bomarc sites were being built, the US and USSR were shifting their arsenals towards intercontinental ballistic missiles (ICBMs), against which the Bomarcs were useless. Indeed, most of NORAD seemed useless against the growing arsenal of missiles that fly high above the Canadian air space. During this period of the cold war, early warning of a missile attack required new technology, employed at US Ballistic Missile Early Warning Stations (BMEWS), which were not located in Canada. As a consequence, by the late 1970s, the Bomarcs were gone, the Mid-Canada Line and most of the Pinetree Line dismantled, and Canadian interceptors for NORAD reduced from 200 to 36.[17]

With such high stakes, neither superpower was willing to totally decommission its bomber forces. Prudence suggested keeping redundant systems in case the front-line forces failed in battle. As long as the Soviet bomber force remained, an obvious military justification existed for NORAD, which explains its renewal by Ottawa from 1968 to the present and the Trudeau government's decision to order CF-18 interceptors in 1980.

The 1980s witnessed a renewal of interest in NORAD from both the Canadian and American sides, though for different reasons. Canada was interested in modernizing the radar systems because she relied on them for her own sovereignty protection. Thus, in addition to the larger objective of detecting a Soviet strategic strike, Canada used the radar to detect and challenge violators of her airspace. In the pre-Gorbachev days, the Soviet air force frequently played the game of testing individual Western countries' air defences. By the 1980s, press reports were reporting serious incursions by Soviet aircraft over Quebec and Labrador.

Likewise, the Americans by 1979 were beginning to worry about the possibility of a surprise strike by a cruise missile (CM), which flies lower and slower than ICBMs and could be launched across Canadian airspace from Soviet subs and aircraft. For a time, there was even talk about using jet interceptors to shoot down individual CMs. In this context, Washington was prepared to discuss modernization of the DEW line.

Canada had proposed such a modernization as early as 1975, but it was not until 1981 that the Reagan administration adopted a new air defence plan. At the 1985 Mulroney-Reagan summit, a NORAD modernization plan was signed, which in Canada involved replacing the DEW line with the North Warning System (NWS) radar stations, and new northern airfields for Canadian interceptors and American Airborne Warning and Control Systems (AWACs) with Canadians on board. Though the Americans paid for 60 per cent of the new radar system, it was entirely owned and managed by Canadians when operational in the 1990s. But with the rapid decline in the Soviet and then Russian strategic threat, the main function of this system became Canadian sovereignty protection.

NORAD AND MISSILE DEFENCE

Military technology continued to evolve and pose new issues for Canada in NORAD as can be seen in its name change to North American Aerospace Defence Command in 1981, which might imply extending its authority into space. Some Canadians expressed concern that Canada would be drawn into Reagan's anti-ballistic missile (ABM) defence plans, despite that Mulroney officially declined direct collaboration. Indeed, at the time of the name change and the 1981 renewal, a clause from 1968 specifically exempting Canada from any ABM defence plans disappeared from the treaty. But, in the 1990s, the importance of this issue was reduced by ongoing doubts about the feasibility of the Star Wars program and the rapid progress in US-USSR arms cuts, followed by the US-USSR Strategic Arms Reduction Treaty (START).

However, late in the 1990s, concerns about the proliferation of nuclear weapons and missiles to smaller, aggressive, and vehemently anti-American states reopened the missile defence debate. Later, President George W. Bush famously characterized three of these "rogue states" (Iraq, Iran, and North Korea) as an "axis of evil." Given Canada's historical record of adopting her allies' enemies and her alliance commitments to the United States, one might expect Canadian defence planning to shift accordingly. Indeed, as shown in the next chapter, the Mulroney government joined a US-led coalition to fight Iraq in 1990-91. Weapons of mass destruction (WMD), which include the nuclear, chemical, and biological weapons sought by Iraqi president Saddam Hussein, figured prominently in the ceasefire conditions ending that conflict. More recently, Communist North Korea, a holdover from the cold war, poses the greater threat.

In 1992, shortly after inspectors from the International Atomic Energy Agency (IAEA) (the UN's proliferation watchdog) were admitted, plutonium fuel rods capable of being transformed into nuclear bombs were discovered missing from North Korea's Yongbyon nuclear reactor. Responding in typically choleric fashion, President Kim Il-sung threw out the inspectors, threatened to rip up the Non-Proliferation Treaty that North Korea had signed in 1985, and warned of a war against his South Korean neighbour and its ally, the United States. Eventually, the Bill Clinton administration brokered a deal, the 1994 Framework Agreement, by which North Korea agreed to decommission its plutonium nuclear plant and allow the inspectors to return, in exchange for an alternative energy source[18] in the form of free oil and new "safeguarded" nuclear reactors from the United States, South Korea, and Japan.

Under the leadership of Kim Il-sung's son, Kim Jong-il, North Korea seemed set on a slow but unsteady path towards reform and reconciliation with South Korea and the United States. Then, in October 2002, a US delegation to North Korea confronted Kim's officials with evidence of another clandestine operation to acquire nuclear weapons through the alternative, uranium-enrichment path. North Korea angrily acknowledged that it had nullified the 1994 deal, and the US retaliated by suspending oil shipments until an accounting was made. North Korea escalated by throwing out the IAEA inspectors, suspending the Non-Proliferation Treaty, and resuming production of plutonium and, additionally, nuclear warheads. As a major producer and seller of missiles, North Korea possesses the nightmare combination of nuclear weapons and a delivery system, along with an apparent willingness to sell both to the highest bidder.

The George W. Bush administration had come to power ready to invigorate a new scaled-back version of Reagan's plans for theatre missile defence (short- to medium-range missiles), later developed into Ballistic Missile Defence (BMD), and the North Korean threat bolstered the arguments for its rapid development. In this new version, BMD (not to be confused with WMD, weapons of mass destruction) does not pretend to be a massive shield capable of stopping hundreds of missiles launched by a major nuclear power such as Russia or China. Instead, it aims to shoot down one or a small number of missiles such as might be launched accidentally by a major power or intentionally by a small rogue state (such as North Korea). In 1998, North Korea shocked Japan by launching a ballistic missile through Japan's airspace. The North Koreans coyly stated that the missile test was for scientific purposes, but Japan didn't miss the point that it could have had a nuclear warhead. It is not surprising that Japan has eagerly signed on to Bush's new BMD. In fact, a viable missile defence may be one of the strongest points to counter recently revived Japanese arguments that in the long run Japan needs its own nuclear deterrent.

Thus North Korea's missiles pose an immediate threat to US allies Japan and South Korea, and in the long term a threat to the Canadian and US Pacific Coast. The Bush administration has generalized this threat to justify abandonment of the ABM treaty and deployment of BMD for North America. Since in the view of the US and many Canadian military analysts, the logical organization to oversee the BMD is NORAD, the Canadian government again faced a decision on whether to join in this deployment. The Liberal

Martin government initially gave affirmative indications, but delayed making a decision after being reduced to minority status in the 2004 election, showing the Liberal caucus to be deeply divided. Table 4.2 shows a few of the arguments made on both sides.[19] In addition to ongoing concern that it simply would not work and complaints about its cost (even with the US paying), the main arguments against the BMD centred on abrogation of existing international agreements (such as the ABM treaty) and on potential violation of the ban on weapons in space. Proponents argued that if Canada refused, the United States might retaliate[20] and that since in 2002 the US created the United States Northern Command (USNORTHCOM) as an alternative structure for operating BMD and for defending North America, NORAD would be ignored and bypassed. In response to this latter concern, the NORAD agreement was amended in August 2004 to allow NORAD to share radar and satellite monitoring information with USNORTHCOM's BMD program. This "compromise" then allowed Prime Minister Martin to decline formally President Bush's invitation to join BMD in February 2005 without marginalizing NORAD. But the issue of BMD, as with the issue of further military integration with the United States, is likely to keep coming up in the future, especially given the dramatic events of September 11, 2001, as discussed below.

Table 4.2 Arguments For and Against Missile Defence (2005 Scaled-down Version)

For
1. There is an obvious need for a defence against a single or small number of missiles fired by a desperate or irrational opponent (cases of irrationality where normal MAD would fail) or fired by accident.
2. It is an alternative nuclear deterrent for non-nuclear states. It gives states like Japan or South Korea a defence against small North Korea arsenals without "going nuclear" themselves. It can be an adjunct to non-poliferation.
3. On moral grounds, a shield (defence) is more acceptable than a sword (offence).
4. Given the stakes, a small chance that it may work is better than none. With a missile fired at Los Angeles or Vancouver and a million lives threatened, even a 50 per cent chance of knocking it down is better than no chance.
5. It may be the only credible way to get existing nuclear powers to disarm their offensive weapons and thus achieve a nuclear-free world.
6. Canada should participate because the current US administration wants it and is willing to pay for it. To avoid doing so risks offending our ally and largest market.

Against
1. Missile defence is destabilizing (increases likelihood of war) because
   a) any technological innovation in the field of nuclear weapons stimulates a new arms race;
   b) it breaks existing legal agreements such as the ABM treaty, the weaponization of space; and

    c) it stimulates offensive efforts to defeat/overwhelm it.

2. The distinction between defensive and offensive weapons breaks down, especially when missile defence is combined with offensive nuclear weapons. (Disarming an opponent for one's own strike.)

3. It politically harms Western relations with Russia and China.

4. It is too expensive and won't work. Tests results suggest more research is needed but does not support deployment at this time.

5. Canada should not bend to US pressure.

DEFENDING EUROPE: CANADA AND NATO

At first sight, a national interest approach must question the wisdom of a Canadian commitment to Western Europe. What security interest is served by stationing Canadian troops so far from Canadian soil? In fact, Trudeau asked just such a question in 1969. There are two basic justifications given for Canadian participation in European defence.

The first justification arises from the nature of the threat. If we assume that at least in the early cold war years, the Soviets did represent something like the Nazi threat of the 1930s, then a policy of containment by all the potential victims of that expansionism would be wise. Using something like a domino-theory analysis of Hitler is instructive. The fall of France and most of Western Europe put enormous pressure on Great Britain. Had she fallen, how would Canada and the rest of the Commonwealth have survived? One might still question whether a Nazi invasion of Canada was next on the list (at least after the USSR was conquered), but even if it were not, Canada's security situation would still have been drastically altered by the fall of the UK.

In the immediate 1945 context, the same arguments were made about Soviet domination of Western Europe. It could be argued that Soviet control of Western Europe would have dramatically increased the Soviet naval presence in the North Atlantic and threatened Canada's eastern coast. Canada has done very well in the twentieth century in avoiding war on its own territory; defence in Europe can be seen as part of the strategy to avoid future battlefields in Canada.

Beyond this security justification, most arguments for defence in Europe involve political or economic motives. Indeed, Ottawa frequently has cited these non-military motives as the main justifications for the NATO commitment. Canada belongs to a common North Atlantic or Western community of nations that shares many ties in government, political philosophy, economics, and culture. Defence of Western Europe is justified as protection of a common way of life. In some senses, this argument is also a security argument. To the extent that Canadian military strength depends on economic growth, then access to markets in Great Britain and the other NATO countries is a security asset. Likewise, the psychological effect of the defeat of Western Europe on Canadian public opinion and morale has to be considered. Throughout the cold war, concern was expressed in various NATO capitals over a possible "Finlandization" of parts of Europe: neutralization not through military defeat but through Soviet psychological intimidation. For example, Soviet threats and pressures against Norway and

Turkey might well have resulted in their capitulation or neutralization if they had not had the alternative of NATO membership.

Canada had a major role in founding NATO. The war was scarcely over before Britain, France, and the BENELUX countries (Belgium, Netherlands, and Luxembourg) had perpetuated their wartime alliance in the Brussels Treaty. Britain and France had hoped for an American guarantee of support to give the defence of Europe real muscle, but American isolationism and financial restraint seemed to dampen the possibility.

Louis St. Laurent and the Department of External Affairs (DEA) also desired Canadian and American involvement to avoid North American isolationism and an isolated alliance between the two countries. Thus, Canada participated in "secret" talks[21] in the Pentagon along with the United Kingdom to discuss an Atlantic defence pact in March of 1948. Canadian diplomats also played an important role in changing the minds of important American policy-makers like George Kennan. When talks resumed in December 1948, Canada was able to put a distinctive stamp on two of the main articles of the agreement. The North Atlantic Treaty Organization (NATO) created in 1949 contains the Article 5 "pledge" for a mutual defence treaty rather than a limited, one-way guarantee, which reflected Canada's desires. Likewise, Article 2, the so-called Canadian article, attempts to broaden the alliance into other non-military activities, demonstrating Canada's belief in a larger North Atlantic community. The growth in membership in NATO since 1949 is shown in Table 4.3.

Table 4.3 The Membership of NATO

Original Members of April 1949
- Five Brussels Treaty members: Belgium, France, Luxembourg, the Netherlands, the United Kingdom
- Canada
- Denmark
- Iceland
- Norway
- Italy
- Portugal
- The United States

Joining in 1952
- Greece and Turkey

Joining in 1955
- Federal Republic of Germany (West Germany)

Temporarily leaving in 1967
- France (by the 1980s again informally cooperating)

Joining in 1982
- Spain

Joining in 1999
- Poland, Hungary, and the Czech Republic

Joining in 2004
- Latvia
- Slovenia
- Lithuania
- Slovakia
- Romania
- Bulgaria
- Estonia

At first, NATO was militarily an empty shell, but the Korean War created a sense of urgency, leading to the doubling of Western defence spending and the agreement to station American and Canadian forces in Central Europe. At this time, Canada sent a brigade group to West Germany, pledged a full infantry division in reinforcements, sent an air division to France, and committed much of its navy to the defence of the North Atlantic.

In 1957, NATO made the crucial decision to increase the tactical nuclear component of NATO forces in West Germany. This "fire-power over manpower" policy grew out of an ongoing inability or unwillingness by NATO governments to match the larger Communist Warsaw Pact forces in Central Europe. Hence, to balance the forces, NATO introduced tactical nuclear weapons to be used to stop the advance of an expected Soviet heavy armour breakthrough. As Prime Minister Trudeau later pointed out, this policy in effect committed the West to the "first use" of nuclear weapons in the event of conflict. Nonetheless, it has remained a part of NATO strategy up to the present. In 1957, to implement this policy, the Diefenbaker government agreed to acquire Honest John surface-to-surface missiles with nuclear warheads for the Canadian Forces (CF) in Germany. This decision further inflamed the nuclear weapons controversy, which later crippled his government.

In 1968, the arrival of the Trudeau government seemed to herald dramatic reductions in Canada's commitment to NATO. Trudeau cogently argued against the priority given to NATO on security and national interest grounds. In Germany, he wanted to reduce the size of Canadian forces and change their role from front line to reserve. Such a change for Canada would have allowed for less costly armaments and the removal of tactical nukes. Instead, the Canadian reinforcement brigade to Germany was changed to the Canadian Air-Sea Transportable (CAST) reinforcement, to be sent to a northern NATO ally. This "dual use" reinforcement was also to strengthen defence of Canada by increasing the army's capabilities for Arctic fighting (the so-called "Northern dimension").

Though initial plans for even bigger cuts were scaled back, from 1969 to 1975, defence spending, and the NATO commitment in particular, languished. Then, in 1975,

Trudeau returned NATO to top priority, largely for political and economic reasons. Canada's heavy armour role in Germany was restored with the purchase of 128 Leopard tanks. The Anti-submarine Warfare (ASW) role in the North Atlantic was strengthened by Canada's purchase of 18 CP-140 Auroras and a new class of patrol frigates. CAST was strengthened by the pre-positioning of some equipment in Norway.

In general, the Trudeau governments of the 1970s and 1980s were attacked by the Tory opposition and Canada's allies for not making a larger contribution to European defence. Canada ranked at the bottom of NATO or just ahead of Luxembourg in terms of defence spending as a per cent of GNP. D.W. Middlemiss and J.J. Sokolsky disputed the charge that Canada was not contributing its fair share by pointing out that in terms of total expenditure, Canada ranked sixth, and on a per capita basis, fifth. Nonetheless the public perception of Canada as a free rider in NATO led the Mulroney government of 1984 to pledge increases.

The Tory Defence White Paper of June 1987 spelled out these plans for beefing up the Canadian military and the NATO commitment. The role of ASW, seen as crucial for both NATO and the direct defence of Canada, was to be strengthened by additional frigates, helicopters, and maritime long-range patrol aircraft. The initial pledge to increase support for CAST was soon seen as impractical, and its brigade group and two air squadrons were allocated to Germany instead. The number of troops was increased and a fully mechanized division was created in Germany, supported by an air division. Thus, after 20 years of cuts and experiments, Canada finally seemed to return to a strong position in Central Europe.

But even as this Tory white paper was being penned, it was being made obsolete by Soviet leader Gorbachev, who came to power in 1985. By 1986, he had decided that the old methods did not work and that his country needed drastic reform: economic restructuring (Perestroika) and political openness (Glasnost). In 1988, he abandoned the principle of exporting the socialist revolution to the Third World, pulled Soviet forces out of Afghanistan, and pressured his allies Cuba and Vietnam to withdraw their troops from Angola and Cambodia respectively. But Gorbachev's revolution careened out of his control by late 1989 with the fall of the Berlin Wall. Then, in a reversal of the domino theory, the Warsaw Pact states, one by one, overthrew their Communist governments and began to move out of the Soviet (Russian) orbit. In December 1991, the Soviet Union itself broke up into Russia and other formerly Soviet republics.

Faced with sudden loss of NATO's enemy, the Mulroney government quickly saw the opportunity to cut the ballooning federal budget by announcing plans for what Trudeau had wanted in 1969: a total withdrawal of the Canadian Forces from Germany. As before with Trudeau's plans, Canada's refusal to consult its allies or even leave a token force behind left the Germans in particular very angry. But all the NATO countries, including the United States, were busy trying to cash in on a cold war "peace dividend" by cutting back their military spending. For the Canadian Forces, these cuts made the 1990s an even more impoverished period of neglect.

Indeed, some Canadians were soon wondering why we needed NATO any more at all. With French and German plans to beef up the European Union's (EU) military forces, many in Canada, the US, and Britain worried that a European army would soon take over the role of defending Europe. Then came the ethnic conflict in Bosnia and Kosovo, which opened up divisions about foreign policy among the European states and required US muscle power to enforce the peace in the region. NATO soon developed as a primary adjunct to United Nations peace enforcement in the troubled Balkans (see Chapter 5). By the end of the 1990s, former Warsaw Pact members were queuing up to join (see Table 4.3).

Al Qaeda's 9/11 assault on the US World Trade Center and the Pentagon dramatically revised American perceptions of threat and at once broadened NATO's horizons. The next day, Canada helped instigate the first use of Article 5 in NATO's history: "an attack on one is an attack on all," meaning that NATO itself rallied to the US's defence. The Bush administration preferred to operate its own assault on the Taliban of Afghanistan when that government refused to turn over al Qaeda and Osama bin Laden. Nonetheless, the United States accepted aid from most of its NATO allies, with Canada immediately offering 850 troops to serve alongside American forces. In addition, as part of its contribution to the "War on International Terrorism," Canada dispatched a naval task force and patrol aircraft to the Arabian Sea and Hercules transport aircraft to deliver humanitarian supplies to Afghanistan in what it called Operation Apollo. Knocking the Taliban from power and forcing al Qaeda to abandon its bases was quickly accomplished; creating a stable, democratic government in Kabul to prevent their return has proven in the long term to be much more difficult, as recounted in the following case study, Canada in Afghanistan.

Case Study: Canada in Afghanistan

Canada's commitment of substantial land forces to Afghanistan has come in three major deployments. The first deployment immediately followed the initial response to the al Qaeda attacks of September 11, 2001: the US and NATO's declaration of War on Terrorism and the US and its local Northern Coalition allies' war in Afghanistan against al Qaeda and the Taliban government. As a NATO member and close military ally of the United States, the Chrétien government sought a way to demonstrate its support, and in October 2001 announced the deployment with US forces of some two thousand Canadian Forces personnel, primarily to the Arabian Sea in the form of ships and planes for patrol and surveillance. Despite the offers from its NATO allies, the Bush administration decided to begin its offensive against the Taliban using mainly its own and local Afghan opposition forces. That offensive against the Taliban went so quickly that by December 22, 2001, the UN-supported Karzai government was able to take office in Kabul, the capital. What Canada referred to as Operation Apollo was expanded in January 2002 when Ottawa accepted a US request for aid in the ongoing fighting around Kandahar and soon deployed 750 soldiers, mainly from Princess Patricia's Canadian Light Infantry Battle Group, for combat under US command. With nearly three thousand soldiers deployed in the region, Canada had made the fourth-largest military contribution in the US-led war.[22] On April 17, 2002, four soldiers from the Patricia's died in a "friendly-fire" incident, sparking numerous press accounts and an inquiry into the procedures used by US pilots. For a variety of reasons, including limited military resources and tradeoffs with Canada's Bosnian commitment, the 2002 Kandahar mission was not extended beyond its six-month deadline and the Patricia's were removed by the end of that summer.

The second major wave began in February 2003, while the United States and the United Kingdom were preparing for the invasion of Iraq. Since that military action did not have UN approval, Ottawa decided instead to contribute another force to Afghanistan, this time under the NATO-led International Security Assistance Force (ISAF). The ISAF had been authorized under the United Nations Security Council Resolution 1386 in December 2001 to provide security and to assist state-building initially around Kabul. Ottawa had previously considered joining this UK-led NATO force of 4500 before deciding to join the US force in Kandahar. Now, Canada offered a contribution to ISAF: under Operation Athena, from the summer of 2003 to the fall of 2005, some seven hundred infantry were maintained at Camp Julien near Kabul. They assisted the new Afghan government with security, intelligence, and the National Assembly elections in September 2005.

The third major mission will include a deployment in February 2006 of 1000 new troops for the ISAF mission in Kandahar. At that time, Canada will lead the NATO force assigned to prevent a resurgence of the Taliban in its southern home-land, but the mission goes beyond security. As the United States has refocused its forces on the deteriorating situation in Iraq, it has increasingly sought NATO and allied replacements in Afghanistan. In August 2005, it turned over responsibility for the Provincial Reconstruction Team (PRT) in Kandahar to Canada. Indeed, the Canadian commander training the Canadian Forces for this third mission has dubbed the soldiers "warrior-diplomats."[23] This label is in keeping with the state-building policy spelled out in the Martin government's International Policy State-ment. Under its "3D approach" (defence, diplomacy, and development) the Canadian Forces in Kandahar will be fighting Islamic insurgents, while winning the "hearts and minds" of the local people with reconstruction aid. As further testimony of the 3D approach, the mission in Kandahar includes Canadian government repre-sentatives from Foreign Affairs, the RCMP, and the Canadian International Development Agency (CIDA). This approach is also in line with US attempts since 2002 to create mixed civilian-military teams to aid the government in Kabul by backing up local governments with law and order and reconstruction aid.

Ottawa has also made a covert "fourth" security contribution to Afghanistan of undisclosed size,[24] in the form of a secret commando operation. In October 2001, at the same time as it dispatched ships to the region, it sent the Joint Task

Force 2 (JTF2), a CF special operations unit, to Afghanistan to fight in a multinational US-led effort that seeks to track down al Qaeda and Taliban forces in their remote mountain sanctuaries. In September 2005, a Department of National Defence (DND) official stated in a rare disclosure that the JTF2 was still active in Afghanistan, had recently killed insurgents, and had turned captured soldiers over to US and local authorities with "specific assurances" about their treatment.[25]

What does Afghanistan represent for Canada? Critics worry about a major commitment having been made with little public debate to a distant country with few traditional ties to Canada. What interest does Canada have in a military commitment that may last "at least a decade?"[26] The security official will point to the al Qaeda sanctuaries located there, but so far the best military efforts have failed to capture either bin Laden or the leader of the Taliban.

Critics also worry that it represents a shift in priorities for the Canadian military away from peacekeeping and towards aggressive combat. In fact, this is one of the things that the CF like about it: Afghanistan, Canada's biggest combat mission since Korea, dispels the myth that they are unprepared or unsuited for combat.

The "hearts and minds" strategy of mixing aid and military action troubles other commentators. Non-governmental Organizations (NGOs) in the region especially don't like soldiers being involved in aid efforts. By "politicizing" the aid, military involvement breaks down the boundary between combatant and non-combatant and will make NGOs acceptable targets to the enemy. Military leaders, on the other hand, fret about the deals and concessions NGOs are making with their enemies in order to preserve their neutrality. And perhaps military leaders should be praised for seeing security as a broader humanitarian issue.

Finally, Michael Byers, among others, has criticized the increased integration of Canadian combat units into American forces as a threat to sovereignty and independence. On the other hand, Grant Dawson points out that "interoperability" (for example, the ability of ships like HMCS *Vancouver* to integrate seamlessly into the US Naval Task Force in the Arabian Sea) is what makes Canadian units appealing to the US government. Thus, they are the most cost-efficient way of increasing Ottawa's military clout in Washington. Furthermore, he argues that a case-by-case approach to deciding whether to place units under US command preserves Canadian choice.[27] (See Chapter 7 for more on the autonomy issue.)

TERRORISM AND HOMELAND SECURITY

With the ending of cold war tensions, the rise of ethnic conflicts, and then the spectacular al Qaeda assault on the New York City World Trade Center on September 11, 2001, Canadian public attention has been galvanized by a new major threat: terrorism. On that day, small teams of al Qaeda hijackers (mostly Saudi by origin) slipped through US airport security to board four American planes, which they seized in-flight, turning the well-fuelled Boeings into massive guided bombs. Recorded dramatically by news video, two planes were piloted into the twin towers of the World Trade Center, causing both to collapse. The third plane was crashed into the US Pentagon in Washington. Passengers on the fourth plane acted to destroy it and all on board in a crash in Pennsylvania before it reached its intended target. Responsibility for the defence of North American aerospace of course lay with NORAD, and, interestingly, a Canadian officer happened to be heading up operations at the Colorado headquarters that day. Thus, as a poignant symbol of North American integration, a Canadian oversaw the initial military defence of the United States at this crucial moment. Indeed, Jennifer Welsh describes Canada's response as "nothing short of heroic":

> In an amazing feat of coordination, our air-traffic controllers managed to divert over 250 airplanes (with more than 40,000 passengers) from US airspace to land on Canadian soil. [...] Our communities opened their arms to bewildered and frightened travellers who couldn't get back home. We dispatched hundreds of firefighters and emergency workers to assist in the rescue efforts in Washington and New York. Our own national day of mourning saw 100,000 people gather at Parliament Hill to support the United States in its time of trial.[28]

Almost 3,000 civilians died that day, making it one the largest terrorist tragedies of all time.

But terrorism, to cite only a few examples, has long been a fact of life for Israel in its struggle with the Palestinians, Spain with its Basques, Sri Lanka with the Tamil Tigers, and India with various groups. The salience of this threat for Canadians has been heightened by the adoption of frightening "new" techniques by terrorist groups: the suicide bomber, chemical weapons such as anthrax and sarin gas, and the dramatic use of civilian airliners as guided missiles. Many Canadians and Americans share Samuel Huntington's[29] fear that the United States and its allies are headed for a mega-clash of civilizations with the Islamic world: such a conclusion seems supported by Osama bin Laden's videotaped calls for a global jihad, in the sense of religious war by Islamists against the US and its allies. Canada has already experienced incidents of terrorism by "sideswipe" when immigrants bring their communal grievances with them to Canada, as seen in the 1985 Air India and Air Canada bombings. While Canada has so far not suffered a major Islamist attack, Osama bin Laden has mention Canada as a potential target, and many of the attacks listed on Table 4.4 (see p. 76) involved a "Canadian connection," a fact not missed by United States security authorities.

Defining who is a terrorist has long been a contentious and political act. Recently, UN Secretary General Kofi Annan proposed the following broad definition:

> Any action constitutes terrorism if it is intended to cause death or serious bodily harm to civilians or non-combatants with the purpose of intimidating a population or compelling a government or an international organization to do or abstain from doing any act.[30]

Annan's definition stresses two common features of most descriptions of terrorists: the intentional targeting of civilians and the fostering of a psychological climate of fear and panic. Civilians frequently die in war through state-authorized military actions, but the Geneva accords have long tried to build a "firebreak" between combatants and non-combatants, which most states try to honour most of the time. Indeed, from the state's perspective, terrorism is usually limited to the behaviour of a "non-state" actor. Terrorism is a criminal act in that it is not authorized by a state authority, so some governments treat terrorists as common criminals rather than political prisoners. It could be argued all that separates terrorism from regular criminality is this political motive: one citizen shooting another citizen is a murder, but with a political purpose it becomes an assassination. Since terrorists frequently refuse to recognize the legitimacy of any of the target state's laws, it is not surprising that terrorist organizations sometimes slip easily into criminal activities, such as illegal drug trafficking (the FARC [Fuerzas Armadas Revolucionarias de Colombia] guerillas) or bank robbing (recently the IRA in North Ireland). Under this narrow Statist definition, "state terrorism" could arise only when a government gives aid, harbours, or directly sponsors a private terrorist organization's activity against another state.

Operating outside of the state system further assists most terrorists in that they can easily hide among their intended targets until the moment they choose to strike. This ability to "mix in" heightens the anxiety and paranoia (e.g. that anyone could be carrying a bomb) of their easy civilian targets and greater hampers and limits the countermeasures that a democratic government committed to civil liberties can take to protect its civilians. (This paranoia suggests interesting parallels to the early cold war period.) Given the intense media attention terrorist acts attract, there is a strong incentive for terrorists to outdo themselves with even more spectacular and horrific feats to maintain their shock value. The terror element is thus linked to the other terrorist objectives of gaining publicity and panicking and demoralizing the opponent. The fact that relatively few people actually die in such acts doesn't seem to matter. Terrorist bombings appear to play into a human flaw of cognition that causes us to over-assess the risk of this unusual threat as opposed to the more common and likely risk of dying in an auto accident. Often, the terrorists also count on their government opponent to "overreact" and unfairly crack down on the population, which results in new converts and recruits. Indeed, the non-government aspect of terrorists makes it difficult not only for governments to target them, but also to know with whom to negotiate or who to hold responsible. Terrorist causes are often only loosely organized with small, independent cells, or may attract independent volunteers and "copycats" as emerged immediately after 9/11. The usual state reliance on WMD to deter attack completely breaks down since it is difficult to threaten a devastating retaliation. All of the above suggests to the pessimist that it is only a matter of time before a terrorist group detonates a thermonuclear device in a major world city.

Given that terrorist organizations are often embedded in civilian populations, the best form of response lies not in traditional military action but in patient intelligence and police work. With time, terrorist networks may be tracked and infiltrated. The better-organized networks can have their funding and communications interdicted. Intelligence work also involves non-intrusive surveillance methods and the sharing of information across jurisdictions. In Canada, the primary institution for this domestic intelligence work was the RCMP until 1984. As we saw, the Gouzenko defection and interrogation in the 1940s has handled by the RCMP. However, because the Mounties have many other law enforcement tasks, the federal government decided in 1984 to create a new civilian agency, the Canadian Security Intelligence Service (CSIS), to monitor domestic espionage, sabotage, and terrorism. Unlike the intelligence services of most of Canada's allies, CSIS does not operate overseas and must rely heavily on information-exchange agreements with its allied counterparts. CSIS is the most important of several Canadian agencies involved in counter-terrorism, and as a whole the "intelligence community" has received greater attention and funding since September 11, 2001.

The Canadian Forces now also have a role in counter-terrorism in planning for civilian disaster relief in the event of a major WMD bombing on Canadian soil. There is the danger of overacting due to the tendency to misevaluate the threat. Nonetheless, demands for action by a panicked citizenry after an event on the scale of 9/11 are difficult for any government to ignore. Even when foreign bases or sponsoring governments exist, as in the case of al Qaeda and Afghanistan, completely successful military action can prove elusive. Four years of military deployment have yet failed to capture bin Laden.

The July 2005 London Underground bombings by homegrown British Islamists again demonstrated the threat of domestic terrorist attack, as Canadians asked, "Could it happen here?"

As one Canadian senator pointed out at the time, "Canada is the only country on the al Qaeda list that hasn't been hit yet."[31] To meet just such a concern, the Liberals enacted several domestic security measures since 9/11, such as the creation of a new cabinet minister for Public Safety and Emergency Preparedness and a new government agency, the Communications Security Establishment, to carry out electronic eavesdropping on suspected terrorists. In addition, the government increased security spending by billions of dollars, tightened-up airport security, and hired additional security and intelligence agents. In the spring of 2004, the government released a review of "national security policy," which among other things called for the creation of a "nerve centre" to handle future national crises. However, a Senate report on national security later that year found much yet that needed to be done, including better patrolling of Canadian coastlines. The threat of a bomb assault on the Detroit-Windsor Ambassador Bridge, a vital choke point for Canadian imports and exports, poses an obvious risk to the Canadian economy. Given standard customs practice, cars and trucks sit on the vulnerable bridge before meeting government officials on the opposite bank. One solution would be to put the customs gate of each country before the bridge. But the fact that this would put armed US customs guards on Canadian soil, raising sovereignty concerns, has complicated negotiations.

The creation of the Binational Planning Group early in 2002 acknowledged this interlocking of Canadian and US domestic security concerns. Composed of equal numbers of military authorities from both countries, the group makes proposals and seeks to develop joint responses to terrorist attacks or other emergencies (as demonstrated in

Canada's response to Hurricane Katrina in the fall of 2005), which include the sending of troops across the border with the permission of the host or through prior approval granted in contingency plans. The group also released reports that called for revamping NORAD and increasing maritime surveillance cooperation.

Collaboration is necessary in part because a major challenge for Canada thus far has not been the direct threat of terrorist attack but the indirect threat posed by potential American responses. As we will discuss in Chapter 10, Canada now depends on the US market to buy over 80 per cent of our exports. US security authorities perceive ports of entry on the Canada-US border as vital checkpoints for intercepting terrorists. To Canada, they are the transit points for some $1.5 billion (CAD) in goods each day. Two days after 9/11, the backup of traffic awaiting entry to the United States at the Windsor-Detroit Ambassador Bridge stretched 36 kilometres. Such delays took a heavy toll on highly integrated companies. In the North American auto industry, Ford temporarily closed three plants in Windsor. The estimated loss was 47,000 fewer vehicles produced in the following two-month period.[32] As a proportion of total activity, these losses were harder on the Canadian economy and thus inflamed the existing Canadian complaint about border delays. Nonetheless, border traffic soon returned to normal, and Canadian negotiators have so far managed to meet American security concerns and derail their more draconian proposals that would have harmed Canadian exports.

Christopher Sands suggests this border-reform harmony was facilitated by a history of past cooperation to improve customs and immigration procedures.[33] In fact, the conflict between Canada's desire to speed the movement of goods and the American desire to regulate the movement of people goes back at least to the North American Free Trade Agreement (NAFTA) in 1993. At that time, the US Congress was mainly concerned with the expected increase in illegal Mexican immigration to the United States due to NAFTA's closer economic ties. As this problem grew, Congress (in its Section 110 provision to the 1996 Illegal Immigration Reform Act) ordered the US Immigration and Naturalization Service (INS) to development a massive new system to track foreign entry and exit across all American border crossings.

Canadian officials consistently lobbied against Section 110, arguing that it adding red tape and delay to an already overburdened system. To buttress the campaign, Canada succeeded in negotiating the 1999 Canada-US Partnership Agreement (CUSP), which led to a series of public consultations with "grassroots" stakeholders in the border-crossing situation who spoke up for greater border traffic facilitation. To minimize border red tape, Canada negotiated a series of agreements, including the 1995 Shared Border Accord, the 2000 introduction of the NEXUS card for frequent travellers and shippers, and, soon after 9/11, the 30-point Smart Border Declaration of 2001, which, according to Welsh, adopted Canada's proposals to keep "high-risk cargo and people out, but to make the free flow of low-risk cargo and people even easier."[34] Nonetheless, Canadian travellers to the United States find that boarding security for flights to the US is much more thorough than pre-9/11. The United States even has plans to require passports at ground crossings by 2007.

These changes in customs regulations have taken place in the context of growing US security concerns that Canada could serve as a staging-ground for Islamist terrorist attacks. This concern grows out of the geography of our long and in many places poorly patrolled border and the history of past threats (see Table 4.4), where some of the terrorists either visited Canada or resided here before their attacks. For example, Abu Mezer entered Canada in 1993 on a student visa. He then applied for political refugee status in Canada on the basis that as a member of Hamas (which the Canadian government lists as an Islamist terrorist organization), he was subject to persecution by Israel. Denied a visa to the United States, he was caught three times trying to illegally enter from Canada, each time with no immediate consequence. The Canadian government did eventually begin a deportation process, but by then Mezer had successfully crossed the border and was planning his New York City bombing when he was picked up by US authorities.[35]

Table 4.4 Some Islamist Terror Actions against US Homeland (Planned or Committed before 9/11)

February 1993	First attack on World Trade Center; suspects include Sheikh Abdel Rahman and Ramzi Yousef
July 1996	Downing of TWA flight 800; suspects include Ramzi Yousef
September 1996	Ramzi Yousef convicted for planned bombing of other US flights
July 1997	Arrest of Ibrahim Abu Mezer and Lafi Khali, who were preparing bombs to use on NYC subway
December 1999	Ahmed Ressam arrested crossing from Victoria BC to US on his way to bomb Los Angeles Airport

Ahmed Ressam had been living in Montreal since 1994 and had also attempted to claim refugee status, but when his application failed and he was ordered deported in 1998, he went underground, procuring a fake ID as "Canadian citizen Beni Norris." His arrest by an American customs official owed more to chance than to good border controls or RCMP alertness. As recently as April 2005, *The Globe and Mail* carried a major story on Ressam's support group, calling it "a Montreal ring of Islamic extremists" with pictures and bios of 12 members.[36] The story points out that they were not held or tried under terrorist laws because such laws did not exist until after 9/11.

Though most of the American INS's pre-9/11 efforts were focused on the Mexican border, this Islamist threat increasingly drew the government's notice to Canada. In 1998, an INS official testified before Congress that in 1996, illegal immigrants from 118 countries tried to enter the United States from Canada. For 1995, the INS reported some

15,000 attempts to cross illegally from Canada.[37] The Canadian government made some efforts to increase border security coordination to stop smuggling, as described at the end of Chapter 2. But many commentators still wonder if Ottawa has fully appreciated and dealt with this US security concern, since Canada itself has not been targeted by the terrorists. Stewart Bell states that "through negligence and indifference, the Canadian government has permitted virtually every major terrorist organization to operate within its borders."[38] Stephen Gallagher lays much of the blame on Canada's refugee policies, particularly its "lax screening and endless judicial appeal possibilities."[39] Add to this the tendency of failed applicants such as Ressam to simply go missing, assume new identities, and stay in the country when they are ordered to depart: "The openness of Canada's system might be providing a haven and springboard for terrorism."[40] Gallagher's conclusion clearly shows the link between immigration and refugee policy, and national security.

Therefore, it has been suggested that to maintain our access to the American market, Canada must inevitably accept greater harmonization of its customs and immigration policies with the US. This coordination might involve common treatment of third-party immigrants, refugees, and tourists. At a minimum, it might entail a common "point of entry" clearance for people and goods. Efforts at greater electronic bookkeeping and prescreening of people and goods are already present. While complete harmonization of immigration and refugee policies is not likely at this point, more bilateral agreements are possible, such as the refugee "safe third country agreement" introduced in December 2004, which makes Canada and the US equivalent refugee destinations. (In other words, refugees should stay in the first refuge they land in, whether Canada or US, and not seek to move to the other country later.) But increased regulatory integration raises sovereign independence issues (see Chapter 7), and greater security through greater governmental surveillance can pose problems for civil liberties.

CONCLUSION

We can now begin to see how conflicts in various interests can arise. Sovereignty protection sits uneasily with NORAD, since the former is premised on a reduced American presence while the later opens the way to an increased American presence. For a while, in the early 1950s, American jets were officially entitled to fly into the Canadian Prairies and shoot down what they took to be hostile aircraft on the approval of an American officer.[41] As a result of NORAD agreements, American military personnel have been stationed at Goose Bay and in the Arctic. Some will argue that this American presence is reciprocated by Canadian personnel at American headquarters and now on American AWACs. But can there ever be true reciprocity between two such differently sized countries?

Yet NORAD also complements sovereignty protection. Possibly the single most important benefit to Canada of remaining in NORAD is the access it gives us to the vast array of US surveillance satellites to watch our own remote shorelines. It would be extremely costly if not impossible for Canada to duplicate this entire security asset on its own. Also, the real threat imposed by Islamist terrorism to both countries calls for at least some greater coordination of effort, as suggested by the Binational Planning Group. Since 9/11, both countries have tried on their own to reorganize, integrate, and streamline their domestic chains of command to better deal with homeland security and other emergencies. The US attempted to better integrate its own defence of North America by creating USNORTHCOM in the fall of 2002. Located at Peterson Air Force Base, it is ironically just next door to Mt. Cheyenne, the centre of NORAD, and Peterson Base itself has some NORAD administrative offices. This means the numerous Canadian officers located there have clear "Off Limit" lines for US security areas that are "not for foreign eyes." Canada is similarly attempting to better integrate its security forces through a planned Canada Command located in Ottawa. NORAD itself has expanded since 9/11 with the establishment of an air-warning centre at Mt. Cheyenne. Previously, NORAD monitored air traffic at the fringes of North America, and, as a result, received word of the airline hijackings within the US heartland too late to use its jet interceptors. With direct feeds from Canadian and American domestic flight regulators, it can now watch flight paths across the continent.

NATO, while posing fewer theoretical problems with sovereignty, in practice competes with other interests for scarce defence funding. Furthermore, it seems harder to defend on narrow national security lines, as witness the low priority Trudeau initially gave it and the Mulroney government's speedy removal of forces with the end of the cold war. Strong arguments can be made for NATO on economic, political, and cultural grounds to maintain our ties to similar Western liberal democracies across the Atlantic. Also, the military argument was made that NATO membership has given Canada "a voice at the table" for determining overall Western military strategy.

The loss of its Soviet enemy in 1991 heralded a period of existential soul-searching for NATO. Some have argued that the continued existence of NATO has in fact retarded the development of a European defence force, a step necessary for completing European integration. But now, in the twenty-first century, most European leaders have shown a surprising reluctance to let NATO die. It adapted to regional security tasks in the 1990s Balkan crises. Despite major foreign policy disagreements, such as the 2003 intervention in Iraq, riffs within the alliance seem to self-repair and NATO continues to attract new members. Indeed, a major indirect purpose of NATO may be to protect its members from each other: keeping its members locked into military cooperation has helped prevent intra-bloc rivalries from developing into arms races and military threats. The lesson of Kosovo also shows the utility (if not the necessity) of keeping the world's most advanced military power, the US, involved in European security matters. Ultimately, it may simply be the fear of the unknown, a desire not to unlink North America from Europe, and bureaucratic inertia that will keep NATO around for many years yet.

Furthermore, 9/11 has recalled the old main purpose of the alliance as a mutual defence pact under Article 5. Though the strong solidarity was soon fractured over the 2003 Iraq intervention, the major new "out-of-area" task for NATO in Afghanistan will last for years. Thus, the reports 10 years ago of NATO's imminent demise are now long forgotten.

A theme winding through all three of the past chapters is Canada's historic reliance on others for its basic security, as reflected in the NORAD and NATO memberships. In part, this stems from a chronic unwillingness by Canadian governments to spend much on national defence. During the Chrétien years, this tendency reached a new low. Clarion calls to rescue the Canadian Forces from imminent doom have been presented in Douglas Bland's *Without Armed Forces?*, J.L. Granatstein's *Who Killed the Canadian Military?*, recent hearings and reports from both houses of the Canadian Parliament, and numerous academic articles. To support the claim of underfunding, such critics point to Canadian expenditure as a percentage of GDP compared to other NATO allies. In 2002, Canada spent the equivalent of $8.2 billion (US) on defence or about 1 per cent of its GDP, and given that the US effort is 3.5 per cent and Turkey's is 5 per cent, this relatively low figure for decades has ranked Canada ahead only of Luxembourg within NATO. However, as Phillippe Lagassé points out, this statistic hides the actual amount spent and how it compares to other states and their needs. That $8.2 billion (US) in 2002 ranked Canada eighth and among other middle powers such as Spain and Turkey. He concludes, "Measured in real dollars, Canadian defence spending appears consistent with Canada's place in the alliance."[42]

Lagassé dissents from the common view that the Canadian Forces are grossly under-funded. He suggests the real problem is not the total amount of spending but its allocation between short-term spending on personnel and operations, and long-term spending on future capital investment. Since 1990, to respond to the increased demand for peacekeep-ers and to keep its internationalist credentials, "the Canadian government committed CF units and personnel to nearly every available UN and NATO operation."[43] This policy put an inordinate strain on CF personnel and training capabilities, and ran down Canada's investment in the future funds from about 30 per cent of military spending to half that share by 2003. To relieve the pressure on personnel and restore the balance,

> Ottawa must reduce the CF's operational tempo. This means fewer deployments and rotations. In the current context, this translates to choosing between a continuing Canadian role in Bosnia or Afghanistan, Haiti or the Golan Heights, and NATO's Standing Naval Force Atlantic or the Arabian Sea.[44]

The Martin government seemed to agree, and while its 2005 International Policy Statement promised to boost spending and troop levels, it has also announced cutbacks in overseas operations, as with its summer 2005 cutback on the Golan Heights, remov-ing its logistics unit and leaving only a token force of 40 behind. Assuming the Stephen Harper minority government carries out or betters the Liberal long-term commitment of an additional $12.8 billion in defence funds, then the CF do not appear in danger of immediate demise. Nonetheless, the government must weigh the tradeoffs between the numerous security commitments and objectives. Such an assessment is incomplete with-out including Canada's support of peacekeeping and international security, which we will examine in the next chapter.

Notes

1. Excellent general histories are available, including Peter Calvocoressi's *World politics, 1945-2000* (London: Longman, 2000).

2. The Warsaw Pact governments can be treated as dependents on Moscow in foreign policy, as can be seen in the total unanimity of their UN voting until the mid-1980s.

3. Only under Gorbachev in the 1980s did the Soviet government admit the major contribution of Fuchs and others spies to the Soviet nuclear program.

4. Smith, Denis (1988), p. 134.

5. *Ibid.*, p. 132.

6. Holmes (1982), p. 12.

7. Deighton (1987), p. 456. If any Western government should have been predisposed to challenge the view of the Soviets as a threat to the West, it ought to have been the British Labour government. In fact they supported a quite hawkish view, which can clearly be seen in the 1947 Labour pamphlet by Denis Healey called *Cards on the Table*.

8. Smith, Denis (1988), p. 142.

9. *Ibid.*, p. 137.

10. Deighton (1987), p. 454.

11. See Yergin (1977) for more on this interpretation of US foreign policy.

12. Goforth and Katz (1951).

13. By agreement, Canada got title, application of its laws, purchase of Canadian equipment, and greater recognition for its northern claims as part of the deal.

14. Joseph Jockel's study *No Boundaries Upstairs* (1987) shows that the American JCS and Secretary of Defence were at first unwilling to seek a formal integrated command but did so after combined pressure from the USAF and RCAF, and an invitation for such a proposal by the RCAF.

15. Defences of Diefenbaker notwithstanding, Jockel is correct in highlighting the uniqueness of this treaty. For the first time during peace, Canadian jets in Canada were put under American command.

16. Mahant and Mount (1984), p. 205.

17. Middlemiss and Sokolsky (1989), p. 156.

18. States accused of clandestine nuclear acquisitions programs typically claim they seek only peaceful uses, such as nuclear energy to generate electricity.

19. Also, see the issue debated in Charlton (2005), pp. 138-40.

20. Bush himself speculated about this during a visit to Canada in late 2004.

21. Despite elaborate security precautions, it latter emerged that Donald Maclean on the British side was a Soviet spy and probably kept Stalin informed.

22. Dawson (2003), p. 191.

23. Cotter (2005), A13.

24. Granatstein (2002, p. 427) says JTF-2 has "under 350 personnel at present."

25. LeBlanc (2005), A19.

26. Janigan (2005), F3.

27. Dawson (2003), p. 186.

28. Welsh (2004), p. 11.

29. Huntington (1993).
30. Quoted in Oziewicz (2005), A14.
31. Geddes and Gillis (2005) *Maclean's*, p. 21.
32. Molot and Hillmer (2002), p. 17.
33. Sands (2002), p. 49-73.
34. Welsh (2004), p. 59.
35. Sands (2002), p. 58-59.
36. Mickleburgh and Freeze (2005), A8.
37. Sands (2002), p. 54, 58.
38. Bell (2002), p. 174.
39. Gallagher (2002), p. 116.
40. *Ibid.*, p. 116.
41. Jockel (1987), p. 55.
42. Lagassé (2005), p. 85.
43. *Ibid.*, p. 86.
44. *Ibid.*, p. 86.

Chapter Five

International Security and Alternatives to Traditional Defence: Neutrality, Disarmament, Collective Security, and Peacekeeping

So far, we have examined security from a traditional, national perspective. There are a number of reasons for being dissatisfied with such a unilateral approach. First, the world is becoming a more interdependent place. The word *globalization* sums up the numerous economic, social, and cultural linkages that cross state boundaries. Since 1945, the introduction of nuclear weapons has made the security of even the more powerful states increasingly interdependent, given that there is ultimately no way to deter an irrational or accidental nuclear attack. Nuclear weapons have also heightened the traditional "security dilemma," which reminds us that security policy is interactive. That is, to be more secure, we build up our small military into a large military, and in response, our enemy builds up its military forces to a larger size. Hence the paradox: though we try to become more secure, in the end we are less secure than when we started.

In addition, the end of the cold war has produced a long and as yet unresolved debate about the nature of the current global power system (unipolar or multipolar), the new types of threats Canada faces, and appropriate responses. Given this profound change, radically different models of security may now be desirable. In this chapter we will consider alternative security options and Canada's past experiences with each.

NEUTRALITY

Two very different motives may justify a state's adoption of neutrality. In the first place, neutrality may grow out of isolationism or a desire not to get involved. Wars bring about tremendous loss of life and economic destruction, and simple self-interest would seem to demand that they be avoided if possible. In the second place, we could argue for neutrality as a matter of ethical principle, as many religions enjoin us to avoid violence and the taking of human lives. If we believe that war itself is immoral, we may wish to renounce it as a matter of policy and remove the instruments of conflict from our soil.

For most of Canada's history, neutrality was not considered an option. When it was discussed, advocates used predominately isolationist justifications. As Kim Nossal points out, isolationism has been a "dominant idea" in North America for large periods of the twentieth century.[1] In the United States, avoidance of "entangling alliances" and suspicion of European militarism have a long tradition, stretching back to President George

Washington's farewell address. Perhaps due to our similarities in geography, many in rural Canada and Quebec also felt a desire to turn inward to the tasks of settling and developing a vast territory and to ignore world politics. Canada was blessed in its geographic isolation: if the Americans were not perceived as a real threat, then we needed no more than a token army. As we have seen, for most of Confederation's early years, defence-spending commitments were rarely met. This sentiment is also seen in the Canadian leader Raoul Dandurand's famous observation to the League of Nations in the 1920s that "Canada is a fireproof house far from inflammable materials." There was of course the imperial tie to Great Britain, but French Canadian nationalists, feeling less attachment to any European home country, were asking early on what real Canadian interest was served by involvement in British imperial wars.

Isolationist sentiment was particularly strong after World War I, in which Canada lost nearly 1 per cent of its population and suffered the fragmenting Conscription Crisis. While Canada did not go as far as the US in staying out of the new League of Nations, Conservative and Liberal leaders fought hard to limit our military obligations to that organization. Canada's experiences from the Great War help us to understand Mackenzie King's cautious policy in World War II.

Indeed, King's "caution" may reflect a common Canadian trait, a desire not to judge hastily or take sides in foreign conflicts. In the early cold war years, King was suspicious and cautious about British and American defence schemes. He nearly prevented Canada from participating in the Berlin Airlift, and when a UN mission ran into problems in divided Korea, he demanded that the Canadian participant not take sides and withdraw at the earliest convenience. This same caution may in part explain Diefenbaker's desire to delay going to full alert in the Cuban Missile Crisis.

During the cold war and still today, many groups, particularly on the left, believe Canada should adopt neutrality on moral grounds. Whether out of religious or moral conviction, they think that the taking of human life is wrong and that war represents murder on a grand scale. As a consequence, they argue, Canada should renounce its weaponry, withdraw from NATO and NORAD, and declare itself neutral in any future conflict. But this position raises the question, would other nations respect Canada's neutrality?

Table 5.1 Types of Neutrality

Type	Example	Problem
Armed	Sweden, Switzerland	High defence expenditure
Unarmed	Belgium, Austria, Ireland	Does not always work
Dependent	Finland	Loss of political autonomy

Proponents of neutrality might cite models to serve as examples. Many nations have declared themselves neutral in the past, with varying degrees of success. Part of the problem in assessing neutrality is that, as with deterrence, we can never truly prove that it succeeded, but only show where it failed. Nonetheless, Table 5.1 compares three different types of neutrality (armed, unarmed, and dependent) based on real-world models, which we can use to assess their relevance to Canada.

In support of neutrality, Canada shares many foreign policy positions with these states, such as not developing its own nuclear weapons and, recently, treating Canadian soil as an undeclared nuclear-free zone. Canada has made a name for itself as a peace-keeper, and traditionally such troops were to be drawn from neutral states. At times, Canada has led initiatives to encourage disarmament of nuclear or conventional weapons, as Howard Green did during his term as secretary of state for external affairs. Despite that Canada was a member of NATO and NORAD, many Canadians throughout the cold war did not share the same assessment of the Soviet Bloc as our American allies and suggested we distance ourselves militarily from the US position by dropping from one or both commitments. This sentiment still seems relevant today when it appears the United States might launch a new "cold war" with China or the Arab and Islamic world.

Sweden and Switzerland are often cited as possible models of neutrality for Canada, but as examples of "armed neutrality," they spend proportionally more on defence than Canada does at present or appears willing to spend, based on history. Indeed, Stephen Clarkson argues that to establish the same degree of defence effort as Sweden, Canada would require a massive rearmament and an independent military-industrial complex.[2] Given our unwillingness to spend much on defence, unarmed neutrality, such as practiced by Belgium in the first half of the twentieth century or Ireland at present, appears a better match. The logic of unarmed neutrality seems to run as follows: if we don't make ourselves a threat, stay on good terms with everyone, and keep our heads down, no one will invade us. However, Belgium found that relying on a declaration of neutrality and the goodwill of others failed it in both world wars. Of course, the example of Belgium, as opposed to Ireland, shows the importance of having a strategic location. Until World War II, Canada's relatively isolated location might have favoured such an Irish neutrality. But the cold war made Canada's airspace too strategic to both superpowers for that model to work.

In his 1980s CBC series *In Defence of Canada*, Gwynne Dyer drew an analogy between Canada's security situation and Finland's dependent neutrality during the cold war. Both were compelled by their strategic locations to be accommodating to super-power neighbours and keep their armaments low, in part to pose no threat to those neighbours. Yet in time of war, it was assumed that the Soviets would deny Finnish airspace to the West just as the United States would try to keep the Soviets out of Canadian skies. At this point the similarities end: Finland was not in the Warsaw Pact and followed a foreign policy of strict non-alignment. By treaty with the Soviets, it had formally surrendered the option of joining any alliance hostile to the USSR. Further, Finland had just been at war with the Soviets, and as a result, lost territory at the end of World War II.

Canada differed in that it had not recently been defeated by its neighbour and joined NATO of its own free choice. Nonetheless, some would argue that the US would have no more allowed Canada to change sides to the Soviet Bloc than the USSR would have allowed Finland to join NATO. They suggest, though, that the Americans might have allowed a grudging non-alignment along Finnish lines.[3] In addition, the Canadian army could have been kept quite small: defence against the US was and is hopeless, and defence against anyone else would automatically be undertaken by the US.

While this scenario seems overly defeatist and dependent, it does have some features that recommend it. There are social, cultural, and economic benefits arising from demilitarization. Both Finland and Japan have combined low defence expenditure with rapid growth. Furthermore, Finland has benefited from being a linchpin between East and West. If Canada were a non-aligned power, it might have more diplomatic success in relations with non-Western states.

But Canada may already be enjoying some of these benefits of demilitarization, without making the concessions to national sovereignty implied by the Finnish example. By relying on its alliances, Canada has gained a fair amount of security at a fraction of the cost of defending itself. Some have claimed that Canada is a "free rider" in NATO and NORAD, enjoying security benefits without paying the full cost. Japan also has been labelled a free rider, and until the 1980s it avoided pressure from the US to raise its defence spending above 1 per cent of Gross National Product (GNP). Indeed, Japan contrasts with Finland as an example of dependent security without the loss of sovereignty. But in terms of its overall foreign policy (and especially its defence treaty with the US), Japan, like Canada, is certainly not a neutral state.

DISARMAMENT

The massive increase in the destructive capacity of warfare created by the introduction of nuclear weapons has led some people to feel that only the complete elimination of these weapons will ultimately make us all safer. Since the main security system developed to handle the nuclear threat in the West since the early cold war period was reliance on American deterrence, it behoves such an advocate to show how disarmament is superior to the deterrence status quo.

First, we must ask how the threat of nuclear weapons is to be removed. Even if we could destroy all the weapons, we cannot unlearn the secret of making them. Furthermore, deterrence theory suggests that the early stages of acquisition are the most unstable and dangerous. A government that has only a few nuclear weapons knows its enemies are sorely tempted to try a disarming strike and thus might need to fire first to avoid losing its weapons. Even if we achieved a non-nuclear world, there would be constant pressure to recreate nuclear weapons secretly in case of future conflict. In the early stages of such conflict, when governments began rearming, the likelihood of use would be very high.

Consider also the following: a single nuclear weapon submarine with multiple warheads has the capability of devastating 200 cities. Once in position in the ocean depths, such submarines are nearly impossible to detect. Thus, in any process of complete disarmament, there would be incredible incentives to cheat by hiding away one nearly undetectable sub. The leap of faith involved in trusting all other governments to disarm and remain disarmed is very great. Complete and universal disarmament without a general solution to the problem of warfare or a dramatic restructuring of the nation-state system seems unlikely to deliver compliance.

That is not to rule out the benefits of arms control and arms reduction. A strong case can be made for trying to halt the further spread of nuclear weapons among states, called for in the Nuclear Non-proliferation Treaty (NPT) of 1968. The argument here is that as more states acquire nuclear weapons, the likelihood of their use increases. Canada and a vast majority of UN members have signed this agreement. What is more, Canada is one of the few states that has had access to and involvement in nuclear weapons research and decided not to develop a strategic nuclear deterrent. For a period in the 1960s and 70s Canada possessed weapons with tactical nuclear warheads, but by the mid-1980s all of these weapons had left Canadian soil.[4] It could be argued that Canada still relies on the American and NATO nuclear deterrent, but this does not involve direct Canadian possession of the weapons.

Another argument to support non-proliferation is that a runaway nuclear arms race may prove destabilizing to deterrence; therefore, prudence suggests arms control and/or reductions to achieve a stable, basic deterrent. Since Canada does not possess nuclear weapons, our role is limited to attempting to persuade others to enter meaningful negotiations such as the Strategic Arms Limitation Talks (SALT), Anti-ballistic Missile Treaty (ABM), and Strategic Arms Reduction Treaty (START). But as Trudeau's "peace initiative" of 1983-84 shows, such a role is limited by the willingness of the major powers to listen. Overall, Canadian policy tends towards moderation, voting with its NATO allies at the United Nations as either "against" or "abstaining from" the more radical resolutions for complete disarmament. At the UN, Canada has sought instead to affirm and strengthen existing treaties to control nuclear and now other weapons of mass destruction (WMD) and occasionally propose marginal changes for further limitations. Even this moderate position sometimes puts Canada at odds with the more adventurous Republicans in the US government who propose new uses for nuclear weaponry. As we have seen, Canadian support for the ABM Treaty and the ban on the weaponization of space led to its refusal of US invitations to join its missile defence system.

Occasionally, Canadian proposals run too far ahead of even its NATO allies. When Canada proposed at the 1999 fiftieth anniversary summit that NATO end its first-use-of-nuclear-weapons policy as an outdated relic of the cold war, it was outvoted eighteen to one.[5] On the other hand, some Canadian arms-control innovations find much wider support, as in the Land Mines Treaty of 1999.

Though unsuccessful with nuclear disarmament, international organizations have in the past banned certain weapons, including chemicals and mustard gas, as too horrendous for use. Some NGOs such as the Red Cross have long argued that land mines should also be so designated due to their long-lasting threat to civilians, and in 1992 these NGOs formed the International Campaign to Ban Land Mines, with Jody Williams at its head. Ironically, Canada initially opposed the ban. Opposition to a land mine ban from the Department of National Defence was accidentally nullified through a mistake in a United Nations document that showed Canada supporting it.[6] Later on, Foreign Minister Lloyd Axworthy adopted land mines as a personal campaign, hosting a series of conferences as opposed to the slower UN channels favoured by the US, France, and other major powers. Two Ottawa conferences with NGOs in October 1998 and December 1999 resulted in the Convention on the Prohibition of the Use, Stockpiling, Production and Transfer of Anti-Personnel Mines and on their Destruction. Though US president Bill Clinton initially supported efforts to limit land mine export and use, he ultimately refused to sign the treaty due to pressure from Congress and the military over the use of land mines to defend South Korea. The George W. Bush administration adopted an even harder line.

COLLECTIVE SECURITY

The question of how to prevent war and proposals to limit it existed long before the development of nuclear weapons. After the devastation of World War I, many idealists put their faith in the newly created League of Nations and its Article 10 to revolutionize world politics. (Article 10 set up the collective security mechanism of the League, which is premised on all nations sharing responsibility for global conflict.) Thus, rather than running away from conflict into isolationism or neutrality, nations should join together in a military alliance of the whole. The League itself would investigate and if necessary label the aggressor in a given conflict. If the "world court of public opinion" failed to force the aggressor to withdraw, then collective sanctions and other unspecified steps (perhaps even a League police force) could be applied. By collective involvement and intervention, the hope was to stop wars as soon as they broke out.

As originally envisioned, collective security should take place at the highest level of global governance; hence only the "upper chamber" or Council of the League of Nations and its successor the United Nations were to be authorized to carry out the procedure outlined in Table 5.2. Idealists believed that World War I had been caused in part by the existence of large, antagonistic alliances and that under the new collective security system, states should abandon that alliance system to avoid conflict among huge blocs of states. Commentators will sometimes use the term *collective security* to refer to regional alliances such as NATO, but under the definitions used here, this should be called collective defence. For our purposes, the only alliance in collective security is an "alliance of the whole" with all members of the international community allied through the League to stop aggression.

Table 5.2 The Collective Security Procedure

1. Notification of a complaint
2. Assessment of the situation (fact-finding mission)
3. Judgment and resolution to label and condemn aggressor
4. Diplomatic and political sanctions
5. Economic sanctions
6. Military sanctions to forcibly remove the aggressor

This system of collective security seems a bit odd at first, since it may require "fighting for peace." But, the initial hope of the idealists was that it would never reach the stage where it would require a police force: the decision to label one party at fault and the threat of sanctions were believed to be sufficient deterrence to an aggressor. But the prospect of becoming involved and perhaps fighting in distant places worried both Conservative and Liberal Canadian governments in the interwar period: while Canada supported the ideal of world peace, why should Canadians die fighting in Africa and Asia? What right did Canada have to judge distant conflicts and different cultures?

Thanks to Canada's major role in fighting World War I (see Chapter 3), the United Kingdom and the other allies conceded Canada's right to have a separate seat at the League, which was created as part of the Versailles Peace Treaty of 1919. As we will see in Chapter 6, this first major independent seat at an international organization was an important step in the evolution of Canadian political autonomy. Indeed, the Canadian government's major objective throughout the 1920s (supported by both major parties) was to water down the collective security provisions of Article 10 of the League. This initial, more isolationist position, contrasts with the current perception of Canada as a long-time supporter of the United Nations and multilateralism. Governments of that day were in the process of gaining sovereignty over foreign affairs, and saw collective security as a challenge to that independence, both in the right to declare war and in the loss of control of one's own troops. Isolationism may also have played a role, especially for the Liberal party who feared another Conscription Crisis and needed support in Quebec.

Canada and the Ethiopian Crisis

The Italo-Ethiopian War of 1935-36 provides an excellent example of the Canadian government's lukewarm support for the League's collective security policy. Earlier, in 1931, the League's effectiveness had been challenged by the Japanese invasion and occupation of Manchuria. It had been caught unprepared, and by the time the League Commission arrived to establish the facts, the conquest was complete. The League did eventually verbally condemn Japan, which only resulted in Japan leaving the League in protest.

The League seemed better prepared for Mussolini's attack on Ethiopia in 1935. Ethiopia was one of the few remaining uncolonized nations in Africa, and *Il Duce* wanted an Italian empire. The League had just completed new rules on sanctions when the dictator struck. If ever there was a time for collective security to work, it was in the fall of 1935.

Canada had two major roles to play in these events: the drafting of new rules on sanctions and the attempts to apply them. For the first, Canada had an able legal representative, Dr. Walter Riddell, on the sanctions committee and thus had a major part in creating the new rules. The Conservative government of R.B. Bennett was contesting a national election at the time of crisis, but due to the persuasion of pro-League activists, such as Riddell and Lester Pearson, it allowed the Canadian delegation to vote with the majority in labelling Italy the aggressor.

The next stage was to vote for economic sanctions, and Canada again had an active role: Dr. Riddell joined a committee of 18 to draw up a list of embargoed materials. On October 19, the League Assembly voted in favour of a relatively mild list of goods not to be exported to Italy, and the newly formed government of Mackenzie King accepted the list as long as no military action was contemplated. Riddell took this as permission to press ahead, and on October 31 he called for giving the sanctions real teeth by adding oil, iron, and steel to the list of embargoed goods. This call for tougher sanctions became known as the "Canadian proposal." Italy depended heavily on imports of these goods for her war making. Mussolini declared that oil sanctions would mean war. Mackenzie King took fright and retreated to the traditional Canadian isolationist position. On December 2, the Canadian government officially repudiated the Canadian proposal, and in mid-month Riddell was called home and Lester Pearson was given clear instructions to do nothing. Pearson was quite bitter at this outcome, later saying that "this disavowal of its representative by the Canadian government played an important part in destroying any remaining hope that strong sanctions, collectively and effectively applied, would force Italy to halt its military aggression against Ethiopia."[7]

Other governments were also having second thoughts. In the secret Hoare-Laval Pact, Britain and France decided not to implement the sanctions for fear of driving Mussolini closer to Hitler. When this deal became public, Samuel Hoare (British secretary of state for foreign affairs) was forced to resign, but tougher sanctions were rapidly becoming a lost cause. In May 1936, Italian troops marched into the capital of Ethiopia, ending the conquest. Prime Minister King had a very different interpretation of events: "I am not at all sure that when the whole story comes to be told, that but for the action of the government of Canada in this particular matter [of sanctions] [...] the whole of Europe might have been aflame today."[8]

Economic sanctions have continued to be a major instrument of defence policy in the post-1945 world, though with mixed results. Boycotts against Communist nations were employed by the United States with little long-term impact in changing their governments. Indeed, scholars writing on sanctions have generally been skeptical of their effectiveness. Nonetheless, there is some evidence that United Nations-imposed sanctions on Rhodesia (Zimbabwe) and South Africa did eventually help to bring change to those governments. But in most situations of modern warfare, it seems sanctions take too long to affect the course of the war, and they often harm the wrong targets. Furthermore, in the absence of an effective police force, most international sanctions must rely on the voluntary agreement of all nations.

The United Nations and Korea

The failure in Ethiopia destroyed the League as a credible instrument of collective security. For the American president Franklin D. Roosevelt (FDR) and other supporters of global governance, it failed as a bad implementation of a good idea. The League, it was later said, had lacked the muscle and the will to stand up to the Japanese and Mussolini: with tough enforcement, perhaps World War II could have been prevented. By the end of that war, FDR and idealists throughout the Western community pushed for a new international organization to replace the League and carry on the task of collective security. Though organizationally not that different from its predecessor, the new Security Council of the United Nations was to have greater teeth, with resolutions binding on all members, the possibility of a regular UN security force (never implemented in part due to later American resistance), and, this time, the full membership and support of the biggest powers: the US and the USSR. The idealistic model of a United Nations was to be backed by the reality of a great power concert, created by giving FDR's "four policemen" (China, the UK, US, and the USSR — with the addition of France upon British insistence) permanent seats and vetoes in the Council. It was hoped such a formidable line-up of powers would create a credible deterrent to any future Mussolini. When the United Nations Security Council (UNSC) "big five" were in agreement, as in opposing the Netherlands' attempt to recolonize Indonesia, this power condominium appeared to work.

However, the Korean conflict immediately showed the impossibility of collective security during the cold war. Since 1905, Korea had been occupied by Japanese troops, and with the defeat of Japan in 1945, the US and the USSR agreed to temporarily divide the Korean peninsula into occupation zones at the 38th parallel. Both powers agreed in theory that Korea should become independent and united, but due to the same ideological issues that caused the division of Germany, they could not agree on how to achieve this goal. The Soviets suggested that they both withdraw their armies and "let the Koreans work things out," which, thanks to the efforts of the Red Army, would have allowed their more industrialized, better-armed and -organized Northern Communist zone to predominate. The US wanted national elections, which would probably have favoured the better-known nationalist (and pro-Western) Syngman Rhee. With negotiations deadlocked, the US took the matter to the UN in September of 1947 with a proposal for an impartial commission, the United Nations Temporary Commission on Korea (UNTCOK), to oversee national elections.

Despite Prime Minister King's desire not to get involved in another potential war, Canada initially served on this commission. When UNTCOK arrived at the North Korean border, they were denied entry. The United Nations General Assembly (UNGA) voted 31 to 2, with 11 abstentions, to carry out the mandated elections where it had access — in the south — though this risked permanently dividing Korea. Thus, in May 1948, in what UNTCOK supervised and called "a valid expression of the free will of the electorate," an election was held and a government of the new state of the Republic of Korea (ROK) was formed, with Syngman Rhee as leader. In August, Soviet-style elections were held in the North, confirming Stalin's choice of Kim Il-sung, a former Korean officer in the Soviet Army, as leader of the Democratic People's Republic of Korea (DPRK). Both the North and the South claimed jurisdiction over the entire peninsula. Both the US and USSR withdrew the bulk of their troops, and Korea, like Germany and later Vietnam, had become a cold war divided state.

These events provide background to the first great test of collective security for the UN and show that it already had a deep involvement in and sense of responsibility for the Republic of Korea. After the elections, UNTCOK dropped the "Temporary" to become the more permanent UNCOK. The question is not so much why the UN got involved but how it could have stayed out of the open conflict that began in 1950.

On June 25 of that year, the US, the UN, and most Western capitals were shocked by the news of a major military assault from the North across the 38th parallel. North Korea, China, the Soviet Union, and its allies all immediately claimed that this action was a North Korean defensive response to a South Korean "incursion." In fact, the opening of the Soviet archives and recent admissions by the Chinese government now show this "cover story" to be false on all counts. In any case, the Norwegian United Nations Secretary-General Trygve Halvdan Lie, the US president Truman, Prime Minister St. Laurent, his adviser, Lester Pearson, and most UN Western leaders, saw it as a clear act of aggression and a test case for the UN's collective security procedures. On June 25, the UNSC called for a cease in hostilities and withdrawal of North Korean forces. After receiving the on-the-spot report of UNCOK, the UNSC in effect labelled North Korea as the aggressor and called on all members to render assistance to the ROK in repelling the attack. On July 7, the UN created a unified command under a US leader (Truman-appointed General MacArthur) with the right to use the UN flag. Secretary-General Lie persuaded 17 nations to contribute troops, and even neutral nations such as Sweden donated supplies and medical units to the UN action. Nonetheless, the UN forces were 50 per cent South Korean and 40 per cent American, with all other members contributing only 10 per cent.

The front line see-sawed back and forth. After the initial North Korean onslaught, UN forces in Busan barely held on long enough for General MacArthur to launch a successful amphibious assault at Incheon and retake the capital Seoul, which turned the tide of fighting and caused a massive retreat of North Korean forces. Faced, then, with the decision whether to pursue the enemy back into the North, the UN voted to continue the war and fulfill the original UNCOK mandate to create a unified democratic Korea. China threatened to intervene as the battlefront approached its border, but MacArthur wrongly assured Truman that the Chinese were bluffing. The massive Chinese intervention in late 1950 produced another turn in the tide of battle, with UN forces flung into retreat. Controversy continues as to whether this new, larger, and bloodier phase of the war could have been avoided, with recent evidence suggesting that Mao Zedong had made the decision that China would intervene as soon as the North Korean offense faltered, before the UN resolution to go north. In any case, China's stated policy at that point was to "liberate" the South, and the Communist forces again took Seoul. The United States sponsored a successful United Nations motion to condemn China as an aggressor also. Eventually, the UN counter-attack recaptured Seoul, though without the leadership of General MacArthur, and dug in its troops near the original 38th parallel, where the war stalemated with protracted ceasefire negotiations from July 1951 to July 1953.

The Canadian government viewed the war as a UN collective security action and, under Prime Minister St. Laurent's leadership, supported it fully. All three parties in Parliament immediately approved the dispatch of three destroyers and the RCAF long-range transport squadron. A volunteer Canadian Army Special Force (CASF) of 10,587 was recruited (with 3,134 from Quebec, reflecting a much greater level of popular support than with World War II), and a Canadian brigade arrived in May 1951 to join a Commonwealth division with British, Australian, and New Zealand soldiers. The bloody fighting continued through the two-year negotiations, so that by the ceasefire of 1953, 20,000 Canadians had served in Korea, with 1557 casualties and 312 fatalities.

Evaluating Collective Security in Korea

The responses to and outcomes of aggression in the Korean conflict of 1950-53 and Ethiopia in 1935 were markedly different. Unlike Mussolini, Kim Il-sung and his allies did not achieve their aim of taking their target by military force. Optimists will highlight this successful defence of South Korea, which made possible the economic and democratic achievements of that country today. Pessimists will point out that the United Nations did not, in fact, achieve its stated goal of defeating the aggressors and unifying Korea. Indeed, militarily, the war is usually portrayed as a stalemate with no clear victory. Other critics claim that the collective security procedures of the UN were violated in letter and spirit, and that instead the war was fought for American interests. It is probably true that the United States would have fought to defend the South, even if the UN had voted not to.

Korea is instructive for pointing out a number of apparent problems in the collective security procedure outlined in Table 5.2. If the UN response to the Japanese invasion of Manchuria in 1931 demonstrates the danger of acting too slowly in the initial stages (ascertaining the facts and labelling the aggressor), then many believe that the reaction to Korea showed the opposite tendency: rushing through all the steps and sending in military forces in a matter of days. Of course, supporters of the action would stress the lack of time for such careful deliberation. As it was, they would argue, the UN forces only barely prevented the complete overtaking of the South. There was simply no time to try diplomacy or sanctions.

Questions have been raised about the timing, speed, and size of the American response. Outside of the ROK, the US provided by far and away the bulk of the troops and resources. The US sponsored most of the resolutions for UN action and provided the overall commander in Douglas MacArthur. At what point does "leadership" blend into "control?" These charges raise the issue of what motivates the states that contribute forces to UN collective security operations. If the United Nations is to bless a cause as "just," must all its troops have the same lofty motivations? Is an operation discredited because a member state has ulterior motives? Would any action have been possible with such a tough criterion?

Why was it so hard to defeat the aggressor with the weight of United Nations' membership backing the war? Obviously, many states in the Communist Bloc disagreed that North Korea was the aggressor and were willing to support it, in violation of UNSC and UNGA resolutions. In total, these critiques suggest that a set of assumptions limits the effectiveness of the UN collective security procedures (outlined in Table 5.3):

Table 5.3 Problematic Assumptions for Collective Security

1. Peace is indivisible.
2. An alliance of the whole replaces separate alliances.
3. States agree on a clear definition of aggression.
4. Peacemakers have the capacity and will to deploy preponderant strength.

Each assumption deserves a brief discussion:

1. *Peace is indivisible.* For collective security to work, every state must redefine peace and security in global terms. When we say, "Canada is at peace," we mean Canada is not currently involved in a war with another state. However, the indivisibility-of-peace principle suggests that if any states in the world are at war, then no state is at peace. This statement is the moral equivalent of saying "if you're not part of the solution, you're part of the problem." A war anywhere on the globe requires a response from all states.

Historically, most states have tended to calculate their interests in a more limited, "selfish" way. Why should a government commit its citizens to die in wars in which its own territory or immediate national interests are not involved? This attitude, as we have seen, was predominant in Canada and elsewhere in the first half of the twentieth century and explains much of the failure of the League of Nations.

There are two further critiques of the assumption that involvement in foreign conflicts is necessary for all states in a collective security system. The first is the question "Who are we to judge?" when dealing with peoples and cultures far from our own domestic values. This complaint seems buttressed by the awful things that often have happened in foreign interventions, even when motivated by high moral principles. Second is the idea of "preserving the status quo." It seems everyone agrees there is something wrong, unfair, or unjust about the status quo. Isn't collective security, then, merely an attempt by the great powers to keep the world as it is, serving their interests? Certainly, in the 1930s, the "aggressors" were mainly "revisionist" states (those wanting change). Can we distinguish our opposition to the means (use of force) from the ends?

2. *An alliance of the whole replaces separate alliances.* This assumption or condition is necessary to collective security for two reasons. First, identification and judgment of aggression requires impartiality on the part of all states. Ties of political alignment, past history, and cultural affinity must be laid aside. Friends must be condemned as well as enemies. Second, to coerce the aggressor into backing down, the aggressor should be isolated. The greater the number of allies the aggressor has, the greater the means the United Nations will be forced to employ, which increases the chances that it will fail.

Figure 5.1 shows how this assumption failed in Korea, when the ideal of isolating the aggressor met the reality of cold war alignments. Once it was clear that North Korea had the strength of China and the USSR, and its allies, behind it, even the Truman administration lost its taste for further fighting. It was the violation of this assumption more than any other that prevented the further use of collective security for the whole period of the cold war.

Figure 5.1 Collective Security: The Failure of Assumption Two

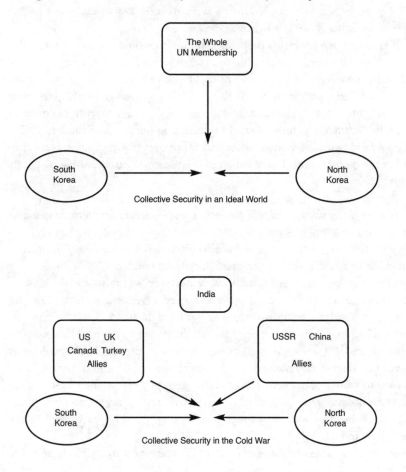

95

3. *States agree on a clear definition of aggression.* Given the huge cultural differences among states, it should not be surprising that problems might arise here. (The current debates over human rights at the UN are illustrative.) Even within our Western culture, considerable difference of opinion exists as to whether a narrow concept of aggression based on the first armed attack is enough. Even using the "first armed attack" definition, it's difficult to ignore the grey areas, such as the events that provoked the initial attack. Israel's pre-emptive attack against Egypt in 1967 and the notion that Germany was responsible for the outbreak of World War I are examples of how such a narrow definition of aggression can fail.

Furthermore, aggressors will nearly always provide a carefully constructed "cover story," justifying their attack, sometimes as a necessary defensive move. This counter-evidence greatly slows and weakens the resolve needed for collective security to work. Given that the leaders of the aggressor state may sincerely and intensely believe their version of the story (even if most impartial judges would find it based on inaccuracies and misperceptions), the task of ferreting out obvious lies and propaganda is made more difficult. To this day, many Serbs do not see their government or co-nationalists as having been the aggressor in either Bosnia or Kosovo.

Ironically, given the huge problems that this assumption would appear to present, it has not been much of a barrier in the handful of cases where collective security was used or attempted. Most observers today would probably agree that in the narrow sense, Japan (1931), Italy (1935), and even North Korea (1950) were aggressors, given their blatant attacks. All three cases featured large-scale, premeditated, conventional military assaults (unlike the North Vietnamese alleged aggression in the South in the late 1950s, which initially used aid to local-based guerrilla units). Ethiopia involved the actual extinguishing of a League member, and Korea involved the potential extinguishing of a state under UN protection.

4. *Peacemakers have the capacity and will to deploy preponderant strength.* States usually do not take recourse to military action lightly. Usually the stakes are high, and therefore the resolve on the part of the aggressor is also high, making it unlikely in practice that any sanction short of the threat or use of military force will work.

The assumption that peacemakers can and will use force was most clearly violated when the League of Nations and the great powers showed a tremendous lack of resolve in confronting Japan and Italy. Even will alone is not enough. In 1931, China passionately had the "will" to stop Japan but clearly lacked the power to do so. The situations in both China and Ethiopia involved great power aggressors that probably could only have been coerced by the military actions of other great powers. This need for predominant force is used to justify permanent seats for the great powers on the UNSC. In the case of Korea, three of these great powers (the US, the UK, and France) committed themselves to the conflict, but this was not enough to coerce a North Korea backed by the other two (the USSR and China).

This assumption also raises the issue of conflict of interest on the part of the peace enforcers. As we saw above, many critics were uncomfortable with the American leadership or even involvement in Korea. Because of its intense security interests in South Korea (defence of Japan; containment of Communism in Asia), some critics even depicted the US as "using" the UN for its own policy ends. But ruling out participation by the Americans (and probably Britain and France) for this reason would clearly weaken fulfilment of this assumption. Who but the US had the power to stop the North Korean invasion? A UN action without the US might have been morally more righteous but politically impotent. In the 1930s, could Japan or Italy have been stopped by a coalition of neutral powers? In 1991, could the UN-approved coalition have removed Saddam Hussein from Kuwait without the US, British, and French forces?

Unfortunately, there appears to be a strong relationship between power and interest. Great powers are more likely to have greater alliance commitments and greater global interests than lesser powers. And these interests are more likely to give them greater motivation and will to deploy their power, which this assumption requires that they do. As we will see, for this very reason, United Nations peacekeeping has traditionally not accepted recruits from great powers. But peacekeeping has a much less ambitious mandate than collective security, requiring much less power.

The Soviets, among others, made one final, very cogent argument against the UN involvement in Korea, namely that many of the actions taken in the war were procedurally illegal. The UNSC was able to pass the early resolutions only due to an accident: the Soviet delegation was boycotting the UNSC meeting over the issue of China's representation. Very quickly the Soviet delegates realized their mistake and returned to veto any further UN action against North Korea. But the United States and its allies switched the action to the floor of the General Assembly through the lofty sounding "uniting for peace" mechanism, which violated the spirit of the principle of permanent member consensus, enshrined in the United Nations Charter. It was this very lack of consensus that prevented collective security from being used again until after the cold war's end.

Collective Security Redux: Iraq 1990 and 2003

The ending of the cold war appeared to remove the obstacle that a divided United Nations Security Council had presented to collective security. Therefore, on August 2, 1990, when UN member-state Kuwait was attacked and quickly overrun by the armies of neighbouring Iraq, many members believed that now at last was a chance to make collective security work. Iraq, ruled at the time by Saddam Hussein, offered a justification for its attack, claiming Kuwait was an historical part of Iraq, and immediately annexed the entire country. Saddam had previously launched an attack on Iran and fought a long and bloody war from 1980-88.[9] In that war, the Kuwaiti government, also feeling threatened by the revolutionary Iranian regime, allied itself with Iraq and provided financial support. When that war ended in stalemate, friction flared between the two former allies over repayment of the war debts and a disputed oil field. World leaders expected some strong-armed threats by Iraq against the small state, but few expected the sudden invasion and annexation of Kuwait.

Peter Baehr and Leon Gordenker refer to the events that followed as "the most forceful and far-reaching enforcement actions in its history," which were closer to true collective security than Korea.[10] The following, then, is a quick, simplified review of those events, framed by the procedures given in Table 5.2 (see p. 89). Due to modern telecommunications and the global news media, and Saddam's own admission of his goal of annexing Kuwait, steps one to three occurred almost immediately after the assault. On August 2, the 15 UNSC members met and voted a motion (with the exception of Yemen "not participating"), noting a "breach of peace" and calling for the unconditional withdrawal of Iraqi military forces.

Unlike in Korea, there appeared to be no way to stop the initial military occupation of Kuwait, so the UNSC had more time to implement step four (diplomatic sanctions) and step five (economic sanctions) of the collective security procedure. On August 6, after a negative response from Iraq, the UNSC began to implement a series of sanctions, beginning with cutting aid to Iraq (by the vote of 13 in favour and 2 abstentions: Yemen and Cuba). Independent of the UN, the United States responded to Saudi requests for assistance and began to build up its forces there in order to defend its ally. On August 24, Iraq responded by surrounding various Western embassies in Baghdad and Kuwait, and then, on September 13, violating international law by invading those embassies and taking foreign personnel hostage. Prime Minister Brian Mulroney considered the illegal entry of the Iraqi army into Canadian diplomatic compounds and the seizure of some 800 Canadian hostages as acts of war justifying a military response.[11]

After numerous diplomatic efforts and the imposition of economic pressures, military action (step 6) was implemented. On November 29, 1990, UNSC Resolution 678 authorized the use of force to evict Iraqi forces from Kuwait, following a deadline for voluntary withdrawal by January 15, 1991. The vote was slightly more contentious this time, with 12 states voting in favour, Cuba and Yemen voting against, and China abstaining. This motion did not create a UN-controlled force but allowed members to take such actions as they deemed necessary. The Bush (Sr.) administration in the US and Thatcher government in the UK took the lead in forming a coalition of forces from 34 UN member states, augmenting the 400,000 American troops already in Saudi Arabia. Other UN members, including Germany and Japan, provided financial, medical, and other support instead of troops. Though Saddam Hussein attempted to portray the coalition in Western versus Arab terms, Egypt, Saudi Arabia, and Syria also provided military forces. Though the first two could possibly be labelled US allies or "friends," the same could not be said of Syria.

Canada's military role began on August 2, with the provision of two destroyers and a supply ship to assist the UN embargo in the Persian Gulf. In September, a squadron of CF-18 fighters was sent, along with a small contingent of supporting ground troops and a field hospital. The ground component was small, simply because no more troops were available. When the air-attack phase began, the CF-18s first flew support for US bombing missions and then later took on attack missions of their own. Despite that the NDP and Liberal party leaders opposed Canada's participation in the actual fighting, polls showed a majority of Canadians generally approved of the military contribution.

In the run-up to the January deadline, numerous peace missions to Baghdad were attempted, including efforts by the UN secretary-general and the USSR, Iraq's former ally. Saddam spurned all such efforts, formally annexed Kuwait, threatened missile attacks armed with chemical weapons (hinting at nuclear warheads), and conceded only the release of the diplomatic hostages.

When the deadline passed, military hostilities opened, with an air war and bombardment beginning on January 17. Saddam's response was to attempt to widen the war with Scud missile attacks on Israel. Iraq even launched the first ground assault against Saudi Arabia before the ground war began on February 24. This ground phase was surprisingly brief, lasting only five days. Though the coalition briefly crossed the Iraqi border and commander General Schwarzkopf wanted to pursue the Iraqi army to Baghdad, President Bush (Sr.) terminated the Gulf War after the liberation of Kuwait, citing the lack of UN mandate to go further. Though Saddam Hussein remained in power, he was forced to accept a series of UN conditions as part of the ceasefire. These included Resolution 660, renouncing the annexation of Kuwait, and Resolutions 686 and 687, which required a UN-supervised audit and destruction of his arsenal of missiles and chemical, biological, and nuclear programs and weapons. United Nations inspection teams were sent into Iraq to conduct this disarmament. Sanctions were to be maintained to guarantee Saddam's compliance.

However, through the following decade, the Iraqi leader used a combination of sabre-rattling (even threatening to invade Kuwait again), evasion, delay, and minimal compliance to prevent the inspectors from completing their mission. He further showed his defiance by attempting to assassinate President Bush (Sr.) while on a visit to Kuwait. After a confrontation in 1998, Saddam broke off all cooperation with the UN and refused to allow any nuclear inspectors into Iraq. A stalemate had been reached.

Soon after the terrorist attacks of September 11, 2001, George W. Bush's administration began linking Iraq to terrorism and raised again the issue of weapons of mass destruction, claiming it had evidence that Iraq still possessed them and was therefore in violation of its UN agreements, which posed a major threat to the US and the world community. Believing that sanctions and UN enforcement efforts had failed, the Bush administration began mobilizing its armed forces and sought allies for a military invasion of Iraq to effect "regime change" (to forcibly remove Saddam from power). Under this threat, Saddam agreed to allow UN inspectors to return in September 2002 and minimally complied with UN requests for information. In November, after heated debate between the hardline (US and UK) and the soft line (France, Russia, and China) permanent members, the UNSC passed Resolution 1441, agreeing that Iraq was in "material breach" of previous UNSC resolutions but disagreeing on enforcement action beyond a threat of "serious consequences."

The "soft liners" and many other governments, including Canada, disagreed with both the US position on the existence of Iraqi WMD and the need for armed intervention and regime change to solve the problem. When the United States queried Canada for support, the government of Jean Chrétien declined to join a military action that was not explicitly endorsed by the UNSC.[12] Thus, the Iraq War became a major dispute in US-Canada relations, as described in Chapter 7. Early in 2003, the United Kingdom made final efforts to get a UN resolution for military action, and Canada and others tried to find a compromise agreement, but all attempts failed.

Thus, in March 2003, the US, the UK, and a "coalition of the willing" launched a military intervention in Iraq to remove Saddam from power on the basis of his non-compliance, but without a specific UNSC endorsement of the action. The Americans and the British have claimed they had sufficient UN authority (and legal justification) for the military action through previous UNSC resolutions. However, that claim was denied by a majority of UNSC members (including veto holders China, France, and Russia) and by the UN Secretary-General Kofi Annan. Thus, it appears that efforts by Bush Sr. to revive the UNSC collective security mechanism were undone by Bush Jr.

Evaluation of Collective Security in Iraq

As stated above, Baehr and Gordenker believed the UNSC's actions in 1990-91 over the Kuwaiti conflict were close to the intentions and spirit of collective security. Certainly, on that occasion, the required consensus of the permanent members was achieved. Some supporters of collective security would have preferred that the coalition leader had carried a UN title and the UN flag (as MacArthur reluctantly did in Korea), and that the UNSC had exercised more direct control over the conduct of the war. At the time, some argued that sanctions were not given enough time to operate before the military deadline was imposed; but in hindsight, given Saddam's decade-long defiance of sanctions, it is difficult to accept this argument.

As in Korea, the issue of the role of the US in Iraq has been raised. Critics have wished that some other state could have led the military operation. But, we are immediately reminded of the fourth assumption of collective security, which requires "preponderant strength." Iraq's army at the time was rated in the world's top five: it was large, well equipped, and battle tested after the long war with Iran. Ironically, on the eve of the fighting, many critics accepted the numerous press accounts that military action would fail and agreed with Saddam's characterization of a coming "mother of all battles." Who else but the United States had the power and the will to make even a credible threat to Saddam? As with Korea (and with the events of 2003 in Iraq), the US may well have gone ahead on its own, even without a UN mandate. But the end result of removing Saddam from Kuwait was widely desired among all UN members. The huge majority of votes against Iraq in the General Assembly show how deeply isolated Saddam was at that point. It also shows how the second assumption (alliance of the whole replacing separate alliances) was less a stumbling block this time, even though Saddam tried to call up the Arab, anti-Israel "alliance" with his sudden embrace of the Palestinian Liberation Organization (PLO) and Scud attacks on Israel.

Ulterior motives were again raised over suggestions that the real issue was control of oil. Kuwait, Iraq, and Saudi Arabia sit atop a large global oil reserve and the fact that many states depend on this energy source may have influenced the motivations of many coalition members and Saddam himself. The failing of the first assumption (peace is indivisible) was demonstrated when some critics argued that either Kuwait was not worthy of defence or not worth it given the costs involved or compared to other situations in the world. And some even raised the problem of the third assumption (states agree on a definition of aggression) by accepting Saddam's argument that, in some deeper sense, Iraq had not really committed aggression.

So, if the story had ended there, and Saddam had fully complied with the UN inspectors and the sanctions been removed, the gloss might have returned to collective security as a mechanism for preserving peace. But the long, messy coda finally ending in the outright abandonment of collective security by two major UNSC members seems to have been a great setback to its future prospects. However, as we'll see below, the need for some form of global "peace enforcement" procedure is not so easily abandoned.

PEACEKEEPING: "ECONOMY-SIZED" GLOBAL SECURITY

Though both the League of Nations and the United Nations were initially created to focus on the issue of preventing war among its members, collective security was not the only available tool. The UN Charter, while not banning armies or recourse to military force, calls on its entire membership to seek first to resolve disputes peacefully. To that end, it suggests many traditional diplomatic means, including bilateral negotiations, mediation, conciliation, arbitration, and deliberation before the World Court. Some of these practices require the involvement of a third party, often a representative of the UN itself. Many UN secretary-generals have taken on an activist role in conflict mediation. Peacekeeping was to evolve out of this neutral, moderator role.

Within a few years of its creation, the UN was to play a role in negotiating a ceasefire in both the Arab-Israeli conflict of 1948-49 and the Indo-Pakistani War of 1947-49. Both agreements involved creating a special UN quasi-military team of observers to be stationed on the front line to impartially monitor any violations of the ceasefire. Due to its Commonwealth connection, Canadian participation in peacekeeping began with sending 19 military observers to the UN Military Observer Group India-Pakistan in 1949.[13]

The United Nations found a need for this sort of mediation and team of observers, given the numerous small-scale regional conflicts that dotted the cold war period. Indeed, states often find it useful to involve the UN when they tire of a conflict, often because they realize they are not able to win and want a face-saving means to withdraw from it. The third party does not have to be the UN: the International Commission for Supervision and Control in Vietnam, Laos, and Cambodia was created as part of the Geneva accords of 1954. The French army sought a face-saving exit from Indochina and, with Soviet and Chinese assistance, it was granted under the monitoring of a cold war "balanced" commission consisting of Poland, India, and Canada. Canada served on this controversy-wracked body from 1954 to 1974.

The next major stage in the evolution of peacekeeping occurred in the Suez Crisis of

1956 and prominently involved Canada's minister for external affairs, working with the UN Secretary-General Dag Hammarskjöld. The crisis began when Gamal Abdel Nasser, president of Egypt, nationalized the French- and British-owned Suez Canal, which the British government considered a key strategic asset. Egypt and Britain had a long history of semi-colonial conflict, so for Nasser, the action was a final declaration of independence. In addition to wanting to protect their shareholders, the French government would also have been happy to see Nasser overthrown because they suspected him of arming their enemies in the nearby Algerian colonial war. Likewise, the Israelis saw Nasser's hand in the armed *fedayeen* attacks against Israel from the Gaza strip. Thus, a conspiracy of the three was born. Using the pretext of these Arab *fedayeen* attacks, Israel launched a general invasion against Egypt in Gaza and the Sinai on October 29. As Israeli forces approached the canal, British and French troops parachuted onto it and again took control. The "cover story" was that they were protecting this vital commercial link from damage in the Arab-Israeli conflict. This story fooled no one, least of all US president Eisenhower, who worried publicly about double standards (the USSR was invading Hungary at the same time) and angrily demanded the British and French withdraw. This led to an unusual cold war moment in which the US and USSR sided together on a UNSC resolution calling for an Israeli withdrawal, which Britain and France, of course, vetoed.

Nonetheless, faced with opposition from their allies, their own publics, and their own stock and currency markets, the British and French were forced to seek a face-saving exit, and Prime Minister Pearson saw a way that Canada could oblige her two European "founding nations." Lunching on November 2 with Hammarskjöld, Pearson presented his ideas for a UN force. On November 6, Hammarskjöld presented his report to the UNGA, calling for the creation of a UN buffer force to replace the British and French troops in the canal zone between the Egyptian and Israeli forces. The procedures that embodied the creation of this United Nations Emergency Force (UNEF) are listed in Table 5.4 as the Guidelines for Classic Peacekeeping. This model of peacekeeping organizes a multinational force from UN members but with the following important stipulations:

Table 5.4 Guidelines for Classic Peacekeeping

1. No "great power" troops
2. Not a fighting force—use weapons only in self-defence
3. Neutral buffer zone between the combatants
4. But only after the fighting is over
5. With the full acceptance of the sovereignty of the belligerents
6. Under the control of the UN itself

1. *No "great power" troops.* Secretary-General Hammarskjöld saw this as a key condition to accepting a member's offer to contribute troops. He argued that if the UN peace-

keeping force accepted units from either superpower or their major allies, then the conflict would immediately take on cold war overtones. In fact, he saw intervention by UN peacekeepers as a way to pre-empt involvement by either the US or the USSR and prevent the transformation of small regional conflicts into global ones. (This was not always possible; for example, the 1960 Congo Crisis in part escalated into a battle between the two superpowers.) Hence, UN peacekeepers were usually selected from smaller, neutral states whose presence was less likely to antagonize either cold war bloc. The UNEF started with offers of troops from Norway and Colombia. Many future peacekeepers were drawn from Sweden, India, Ireland, and other mainly neutral states, with one important exception: Canada. Perhaps because of Pearson's early involvement in the UN, Canadian forces were eventually accepted, too, (with complications noted below), and despite its close connection with the United States, Canada has participated in every UN peacekeeping mission since.

2. *Not a fighting force—use weapons only in self-defence.* In keeping with this emphasis on impartiality and neutrality, the UN force is not to take sides or use its fire power to support either side. Ideally, UN peacekeeping missions do not use their weapons at all. "Ducking and covering" is often preferable to firing back and antagonizing either one side or the other in the conflict.

3. *Create a neutral buffer zone between the combatants.* The ideas of peacekeeping are rooted in the concepts of mediation and peaceful resolution practices, such as separating the angry parties and allowing them to cool off. Creating a buffer zone occupied by the blue helmets between the two antagonistic state armies serves this function. If it is wide enough, the zone can prevent unauthorized sniping and accidental clashes across a disputed border. More importantly, it usually creates a temporary barrier to surprise attacks or resumption of direct hostilities, though sometimes fighting resumes despite the buffer zone.

4. *Only after the fighting is over.* In its most classic form, peacekeeping comes into play when two parties, usually states and UN members, have been fighting and a ceasefire has been achieved. Given their minimal weaponry and mandate of self-defence, sending blue helmets into a raging battlefield might well be homicide. Thus, in cases of renewed fighting, the UN mission is either ordered out (Sinai 1967) or takes cover and stays out of the way of the moving armies (e.g., Cyprus 1974; Lebanon 1982). United Nations blue helmets are not expected to operate as peace activists or human shields.

5. *With the full acceptance of the sovereignty of the belligerents.* Compared to collective security's capabilities, the mandates of peacekeeping missions are extremely limited. Usually, the belligerents are sovereign states, and the United Nations, as an organization founded by sovereign state members, must respect that sovereignty. The buffer zone occupied by the blue helmets does not become a little island of UN jurisdiction like a foreign

embassy. The laws and authority of the host state still apply, and while blue-helmet patrols may ensure law and order, it is the laws of the host state that they enforce. Following the Suez Crisis and Israel's removal of its army back to the pre-Crisis border, the Egyptian government offered the land on its side of the border for the buffer zone. In 1967, when Nasser ordered the UNEF to leave (in response to his Syrian ally's taunts that he was hiding behind the UN), the peacekeepers had to comply, and the Six-Day War of 1967 followed.

6. *Under the control of the United Nations itself.* UN peacekeeping missions are created by the UNSC and directed not by a member state, but by the secretary-general, usually through a special representative who makes all military decisions to implement the UNSC's mandate. Procedures in the Charter that were never fully realized—the empowerment of the Military Staff Committee—might have placed collective security under similar direct UN control, but in practice, in Korea and Kuwait, the UNSC endorsed action by a coalition under a member's military control: the US.

The stark contrast between collective security and the passive, classic form of peacekeeping should now be evident. In the former, the UNSC passes judgment on a situation and takes action against one belligerent as the aggressor; in peacekeeping, the UN does not take sides and tries to avoid any inkling of favouring one side or the other. In collective security, the UN soldiers go to war against the aggressor; in peacekeeping, the soldiers are minimally armed for self-defence and policing only. As in any war, military action in collective security does not require the consent of the belligerent and may not respect its territory or sovereign claims; in peacekeeping, consent and sovereignty are observed, even to the point of rendering the force nearly militarily impotent. Of course, peacekeeping soon evolved and developed exceptions, so in practice it is better to think of collective security's peace enforcement and classic peacekeeping's peace observance as two ends of a continuum, with many gradations between them.

The UNEF, for all its success, shows the limits of the UN peacekeeping model. When Nasser, the host head of state after the Suez Crisis, clashed with UN authority, the former usually won. And despite Pearson's major role in the creating the UNEF, Nasser at first vetoed an active role for Canadian soldiers, believing them to be too closely allied to Britain. Ironically, at the same time, opposition leader John Diefenbaker was attacking Pearson and the Liberals for abandoning Britain. Eventually, Canadian doctors were allowed to join the UNEF, and Pearson's efforts were recognized with a Nobel Peace Prize in 1957. So one might say that Nasser, and not the UN, determined the composition of the force and the termination point for the UN mission.

Peacekeeping in Cyprus

The next best example of classic peacekeeping is the Cyprus Crisis of 1964, where Canada again played a major role. This case deviates slightly from the classic model in that the crisis began as an intra-state conflict between the majority Greek community (roughly 80 per cent of the population) and the Turkish minority, but with both sides receiving support from UN members Greece and Turkey, respectively. Having long maintained two military bases on the island of Cyprus, Britain ignored the Greek majority's wish for union with Greece when it granted Cyprus independence under a power-sharing constitution in 1960. This delicate political balance broke down in 1964 with fighting between the communities, and, under the threat of a Turkish invasion, the Greek Cypriot leader asked for help from the UNSC and Britain. Initially, Britain tried to organize a Commonwealth force to restore order, but Canadian External Minister Paul Martin Sr. diverted the plan into a more traditional UN force. Instead of a British-led Commonwealth force, Martin convinced the Swedes and the Irish to offer troops along with Canada for the core of the mission, which the UN secretary-general was forming as the United Nations Forces In Cyprus (UNFICYP). The previous peacekeeping crisis in the Congo in 1960 had shown that, unlike collective security, peacekeeping did not require the consent of all the UNSC permanent members. And so the UN blue helmets were deployed to restore peace in Cyprus, in spite of protests from the Soviet delegate, joined this time by France. For almost ten years, the UNFICYP maintained relative peace between the two communities across a provisional line of demarcation, or Green Line, that separated them.

However, the weaknesses of peacekeeping were exposed in the crisis of July 1974, when the Turkish army responded to a plot to force annexation of Cyprus to Greece by invading the northeastern, predominantly Turkish, part of the island. The UNFICYP were unable to prevent the arrival of the Turkish army or their establishment of a new Green Line that gave the Turkish community a much bigger portion of the island. The presence of peacekeepers in the buffer zone on the new, more impermeable, Green Line dividing the island has not brought a peace settlement or reunification, despite numerous negotiations. Frustrated with the long-term stalemate and its costs, Canada withdrew most of its contingent in 1993.

The Peacekeeping Expansion after the Cold War

Peacekeeping seemed to have reached the end of it usefulness about the time of the second crisis in Cyprus in 1974. As we have seen, the Trudeau government relegated peacekeeping to last place in its defence priorities, placing emphasis on needs closer to home. This low status reflected general disillusionment with the failure of peacekeeping in either the Middle East or Cyprus and the lingering controversy over its role in the Congo. Critics of peacekeeping pointed out its alleged flaws and its failure to prevent wars.

Despite these arguments, the Canadian commitment to peacekeeping has remained strong and become a defining element of Canadian foreign policy. Table 5.5 lists the major peacekeeping missions: Canada has contributed to all of them and to several missions organized outside the UN as well. In 1993, with the post-cold war peak in peacekeeping, Canada had peacekeepers in Angola, Kuwait, El Salvador, Mozambique, Cambodia, Somalia, Bosnia, Rwanda, Cyprus, and Sahara, and on the Israel-Arab borders. Canada's deployment of 4,500 troops represented about 10 per cent of all UN peacekeepers.[14] Furthermore, Canada had developed a reputation for special competence in logistics, communications, and air transport. However, critics often wonder whether, in trying to be a part of every mission, the Canadian Forces are stretched too thin and if the expense is worth the cost to Canadian taxpayers.

Table 5.5 Partial list of Canadian Involvement in Peacekeeping Operations

UNTCOK	1947–1948	UN Temporary Commission on Korea
UNTSO	1948–	UN Truce Supervision Organization, Mideast
UNMOGIP	1949–1996	UN Military Observer Group in India and Pakistan
UNCMAC	1953–	UN Command Military Armistice Commission, Korea
ICSC	1954–1974	International Commission for Supervision and Control (non-UN mission in Indochina)
UNEF	1956–1967	UN Emergency Force, Mideast
UNOGIL	1958	UN Observation Group in Lebanon
ONUC	1960–1964	UN Operation in the Congo
UNSF	1962–1963	UN Security Force in West New Guinea (West Irian)
UNFICYP	1964–	UN Peacekeeping Force in Cyprus
DOMREP	1965–1966	Mission of the Representative of UN Secretary-General, Dominican Republic
UNIPOM	1965–1966	UN India-Pakistan Observation Mission
ICCS	1973	International Commission for Control and Supervision. (non-UN)
UNEF II	1973–1979	UN Emergency Force II, Mideast
UNDOF	1974–	UN Disengagement Observer Mideast (Golan Heights)
UNIFIL	1978–	UN Interim Force in Lebanon
MFO	1986–	Multinational Force and Observers Mideast (Sinai) (non-UN)
UNGOMAP	1988–1990	UN Good Offices Mission in Afghanistan and Pakistan
UNIIMOG	1988–1991	UN Iran-Iraq Military Observer Group
UNAVEM	1989–1991	UN Angola Verification Mission
ONUCA	1989–1992	UN Observer Group in Central America
UNTAG	1989–1990	UN Transition Assistance Group, Namibia
UNAVEM II	1991–1994	UN Angola Verification Mission
ONUSAL	1991–1995	UN Observer Mission in El Salvador
UNIKOM	1991–	UN Iraq-Kuwait Observation Mission
UNSCOM	1991–	UN Special Commission for Iraq
MINURSO	1991–	UN Mission for the Referendum in the Western Sahara
UNPF	1992–1996	UN Peace Force, Balkans
UNTAC	1992–1993	UN Transitional Authority in Cambodia
ONUMOZ	1992–1995	UN Operation in Mozambique
UNOSOM	1992–1993	UN Operation in Somalia
UNOMSA	1992	UN Observer Mission in South Africa

UNOMIG	1993–	UN Observer Mission in Georgia
UN ICTY	1993–	UN International Criminal Tribunal for the former Yugoslavia
UNAMIR	1993–1996	UN Assistance Mission in Rwanda
IFOR	1996–1997	Implementation Force in Bosnia-Herzegovina (non-UN)
UNSMIH	1996–1997	UN Support Mission in Haiti
MNF	1996	Multinational Force for Eastern Zaire (non-UN)
SFOR	1997–2005	NATO's Stabilization Force in Bosnia-Herzegovina (non-UN)
MINUGUA	1997	UN Verification Mission in Guatemala
MIPONUH	1997–	UN Police Operation in Haiti
MONUC	1999–	UN Mission in the Democratic Republic of the Congo
UNMEE	2000–2002	UN Mission in Ethiopia and Eritrea
ISAF	2003–2005	International Security Assistance Force, Afghanistan
UNAMI	2004–	UN Assistance Mission for Iraq
EUFOR	2004–	European Union Force, Bosnia-Herzegovina
MINUSTAH	2004–	UN Stabilization Mission in Haiti (takes over from MIF)
AU Mission	2004–	African Union Mission to Sudan, Darfur
UNMIS	2005–	UN Mission in Sudan

Source: Data from the Department of Foreign Affairs <http://www.dfait-maeci.gc.ca/peace-keeping/missions–en.asp> and the Department of National Defence <(http://www.forces.gc.ca/-site/operations/current_ops_e.asp> (both accessed August 10, 2005).

In the early 1990s, even as the threat of cold war superpower conflict came to an end, the world seemed to explode in a rash of regional conflicts. This proliferation of fighting, along with greater UNSC cooperation on security matters, led to a similar proliferation in the number of peacekeeping missions and their objectives, as new variants to the more limited classical model developed. Increasingly, the conflicts and requests for peacekeepers involved intra-state wars, often in parallel with the collapse of centralized authority (sometimes called "failed states"). The lack of a consenting state authority raised new issues about intervention, sovereignty, and state-building. The Bosnian War of the early 1990s reflects all these problems.

Case Study: The Bosnian War

The collapse of Yugoslavia and descent into ethnic conflict began in 1991 with the relatively quiet secession of the Slovenian republic, followed three months later by the Croatian bid for independence. The Serbs contested Croatia's action, seizing substantial sections of eastern Croatia, where large Serb communities existed. In September 1991, the UNSC intervened by placing an arms embargo on the region, which unintentionally strengthened the Serbs, who had inherited most of the old Yugoslav army and weaponry. After early Serb victories and a ceasefire on Serb

---

terms, the UNSC deployed the United Nations Protection Force (UNPROFOR) into Croatia and Sarajevo, Bosnia. Already, this was a departure from classic peacekeeping because it included British and French forces in the mission.

No sooner had the Croatian conflict calmed than hostilities in neighbouring Bosnia flamed in 1992. Bosnia was ethnically split roughly equally into Muslim, Croat, and Serb communities, and the Serbs were better armed here as well. With support from the Serb republic, they were soon carving out much more than a third of the territory for their own. Economic strangulation of non-Serb communities, such as Sarajevo, and other techniques of ethnic cleansing led to a humanitarian crisis and calls for tougher foreign intervention. Gradually, the UNSC expanded the military mandate, including the creation of no-fly zones enforced by NATO jets and safe havens for the Muslims. But the UN forces on the ground had neither the fire power nor the mandate to prevent the Serb militias from turning back food and humanitarian convoys, seizing peacekeepers as hostages, capturing safe havens, and, in the case of Srebrenica, committing atrocities. As a result, in 1994, NATO military forces gradually displaced the UN peacekeepers and increasingly targeted the Serbs as the aggressors in the conflict. Thus, the mission had evolved from something like classic peacekeeping to peace enforcement or collective security. But, in order to avoid a Russian veto, much of it took place outside the UNSC's control. As the Croats and Muslims rearmed despite the UN embargo, they reclaimed territory taken by the Serbs, even in the face of UN forces. At this point, all parties were prepared for the negotiations that led to the US-brokered Dayton Accords of 1995.

This ambiguity between neutral peacekeeping and partisan collective security caught the Canadian government between its UN and NATO loyalties. The increasingly violent NATO air attacks on the Serbs directly endangered Canadian peacekeepers as the Serbs retaliated against soft, blue helmet targets. Thus, when NATO resumed peace enforcement against Serbia in Kosovo in 1999, the Chrétien government appeared a less than enthusiastic participant. This time, the UNSC was by-passed even more dramatically, due to Russian and Chinese veto threats, though Russian troops were included in the multinational policing force formed to occupy Kosovo after the fighting ended.

Table 5.6 lists the new functions that peacekeeping has adopted, whether inside or outside the United Nations. Nearly all these forms involve internal conflict within a state. These messy situations often mean sending blue helmets directly into conflict, requiring them to use lethal force. But peace enforcement raises again all the questions that plague collective security. For troop providers such as Canada, this situation has led to more disputes over mandates and "mission creep." Furthermore, Canada and other peacekeepers complain that changes in mandates are made by a small group of nations in the UNSC, without sufficient input from the states with troops on the ground. Ironically, this confused situation is made worse by a dramatic growth in demand for peacekeepers in any form (see Table 5.5, p. 106).

Table 5.6 New Variants on Classic Peacekeeping

Type	Purpose
Humanitarian Missions	Provide armed escorts for relief missions
State-building Missions (Variant: Election Monitoring)	Provide law and order; create state institutions
Peace Enforcement (Variant: Civil War)	Deter aggressors; similar to collective security
Human Rights Missions	Prevent genocides

The crisis in Rwanda provides another example of how controversy can engulf the messy reality peacekeepers must face. The UNSC began a conflict resolution mission following a long domestic civil war with ethnic overtones. The conflict had pitted the Rwandan government, favoured by the Hutu majority, against a rebel movement, the Rwandan Patriotic Front (RPF), made up mainly of refugees from the Tutsi minority. The United Nations Assistance Mission for Rwanda (UNAMIR) was established in October 1993 as a neutral force to supervise a negotiated peace accord designed to create an elected power-sharing government. This peace process ended in April 1994, when Hutu extremists in the government and the army encouraged genocide against the Tutsi minority, resulting in up to a million deaths in three months. In response, the RPF restarted its military offensive and eventually seized the capital, winning the civil war by mid-July 1994. This sudden victory caused panic in the Hutu community, with over four million people fleeing to neighbouring countries. Later, the UNSC redefined the mission as a human rights intervention to stop the genocide and endorsed Operation Turquoise, a French-run military operation in southwest Rwanda. But the tardiness of this UN action and suspicions on the part of the RPF about a pro-Hutu bias meant that the new government was soon demanding the withdrawal of all UN forces.

Canada's Roméo Dallaire was UNAMIR's force commander in Rwanda, responsible for the mission of 2549 troops, mainly from Belgium, Bangladesh, and Ghana. When the genocide began, Hutu extremists targeted Belgian troops, and on the first night of violence 10 Belgian blue helmets were killed. This forced the UN troops into a defensive posture and caused Belgium and Bangladesh to withdraw their forces, further limiting the role UNAMIR could play. General Dallaire was thus placed in the agonizing situation of being forced to observe the genocide without the mandate or the means to stop it. The Belgian government attacked him for being too aggressive (and failing to protecting the 10 soldiers who died), while others criticized the UN for being too passive.

PEACEKEEPING REFORM AND INTERNATIONAL INSTITUTION-BUILDING

The UNSC has been the major arena for dealing with peacekeeping problems. The Canadian government has focused its reform efforts there, particularly during its last term as a non-permanent member in 1999-2000. Just before this, in 1996, Canada had supported a Danish initiative to create a Standby High-Readiness Brigade (SHIRBRIG): an emergency force to fill the long implementation gap (up to six months) between the time when the UNSC creates a new mission and when that force is deployed. SHIRBRIG was intended to provide 5000 troops within 2 to 4 weeks to bridge this gap. However, in its first trial run in the Eritrean-Ethiopian War in the fall of 2000, the force of Canadians, Danes, and Dutch required three months to deploy.[15] The Canadian troops had to be sent by ship because no air transport was available, again demonstrating the neglected shape of Canadian forces.

During Canada's UNSC tenure, the 2000 *Report of the Panel on United Nations Peace Operations*, also known as the Brahimi Report, supported efforts at peacekeeping reform such as the SHIRBRIG and made many proposals to aid in conflict prevention and operations efficiency. Of particular importance to Canada was the report's proposal to increase consultation with troop providers, which was adopted in UNSC Resolution 1353 in June 2001.[16]

Canada has also been at the forefront of attempts to broaden the definition of security and to build international institutions to foster greater global security. During his tenure as foreign affairs minister, Lloyd Axworthy proposed his Human Security Initiative, which emphasized the security of the individual (over the security of the state) and broadened the scope of security from a focus on physical harm and absence of violence to long-term sources of harm such as poor economic conditions and environmental degradation. The Axworthy legacy is still prominent at the Department of Foreign Affairs (DFA) Web site, where the "Five Pillars of Human Security" are listed.[17]

The first pillar, protection of civilians, weds the new emphasis on the individual to the traditional battlefield arena of conflict. Human security begins by pointing out that the most numerous victims of conflict today are not soldiers but civilians. State security actions such as sanctions may unintentionally side-swipe civilians. While it served on the UNSC in 1999-2000, Canada supported the passage of Resolutions 1265 and 1296, which called for greater accountability for civilian harm in UNSG approved sanctions and peacekeeping missions. Indeed, the lawlessness that peacekeepers increasing find in failed states, post-conflict situations, and refugee camps are another major source of harm to individuals. Therefore Canada has added the training of local police forces to its regular peacekeeper training activities.

The second pillar, peace support operations, includes all other activities that enhance and support the basic peacekeeping function. The Lester B. Pearson Canadian International Peacekeeping Training Centre in Clementsport, Nova Scotia trains not only military personnel from around the globe but also the auxiliary civilians that make up a growing portion of peacekeeping missions. Indeed, the DFA has created an inventory of Canadian civilian experts, the CANADEM, which has led to the deployment of over 320 such civilians.

Conflict prevention, the third pillar, includes collective action by regional states and NGOs to forestall or manage conflict. Organizing group efforts to boycott "conflict diamonds"[18] or buying up the guns that fuel the conflicts are types of conflict prevention, as is Canada's support for the South Asian Small Arms Initiative (to reduce the spread of small arms in the region).

Pillar four, governance and accountability, emphasizes the crucial connection between peace and the law, along with its institutions of justice and enforcement. Many basic human rights deal directly with issues of physical harm to the individual, and genocide threatens the existence of whole communities. The International Criminal Court (ICC), which began operation in July 2002, aimed to bring to account (or end the impunity of) individuals who grossly violate human rights or commit acts of genocide or war crimes. Canadian legal expert and diplomat Philippe Kirsch contributed to this enterprise as the chair of the Preparatory Commission. Kirsch was elected first as one of the judges and then as the president of the ICC itself. Canada's support for the ICC stands in stark contrast to the Bush administration's opposition.

In part, the Bush regime's hostility derives from traditional US suspicion that international institutions have the potential to violate state sovereignty. Ironically, a majority of UN members share the US's "touchiness" on the sovereignty issue, though not enough to prevent their joining the ICC. Nonetheless, Canadian governments dating back to Mulroney have suggested that a major rethinking of attitudes about the inviolability of state sovereignty is needed. In recent years, the Canadian mission to the UN has joined with Secretary-General Kofi Annan in his attempts to give precedence to humanitarian intervention over state sovereignty. *The Responsibility to Protect* is a UN report produced in December 2001 by the Canadian-sponsored International Commission on Intervention and State Sovereignty. The report attempts to establish both a basic duty for all states to protect their citizens and a duty for the international community to intervene when any state fails to do so. These responsibilities represent a major shift for international law and the UN, which have, until now, given precedence to state sovereignty and the principle of non-intervention in domestic matters. The report suggests that when large-scale loss of life or a genocide like Rwanda is occurring, international military intervention must trump state sovereignty. Despite the unwillingness of many UN members to abandon the supremacy of state sovereignty, Canada helped ensure the adoption of this responsibility principle in the final document of the UN's World Summit of September 2005.

In its discussion of the final pillar, public safety, the DFA highlights three areas of threat to the individual: transnational organized crime, illicit drugs, and terrorism. The latter has already been discussed in the last chapter as an issue of continental security.

Here, the DFA points out the international aspects of the prevention of terrorism and how its treatment dovetails with the other two problems in such counter-measures as international action against money laundering. Canada consistently supports anti-terrorist resolutions and institutional efforts by the UN, the G8, and others.

CONCLUSION

The DFA website on human security is impressive, but current realities must be kept in mind. Indeed, those realities plague all the hopeful schemes laid out in this chapter. New students are often initially excited by the concepts of disarmament, collective security, and human security and cannot understand why such obviously efficacious institutions are not put into practice more often. But the world we inhabit lacks the global government, resources, and will to do so.

As the four assumptions of collective security demonstrate, its implementation is much more complex than the idealists expected. In addition, collective security and peace enforcement in general today suffer from the lack of an obvious constituency. Who champions its cause today? The hard-nosed nationalists and realists such as those who predominate at the Pentagon and in the Bush administration are focused tightly on traditional national defence and winning wars. Therefore, one might expect it to be a rallying call for the political left, but "fighting for peace" has no attraction for pacifists. When was the last time you heard peace activists storming Parliament Hill with demands for "more collective security"!

Critics have long pointed to problems with peacekeeping. First, there was the way "temporary" ceasefires seemed to become "permanent" once the blue helmets arrived. Peacekeeping was designed as a short-term solution to give the belligerents a "cooling down" period and to move them from the battlefield to the peace table. But in the Middle East and Cyprus, serious peace negotiations, let alone an agreement, haven't seemed to follow. This lack of progress turned peacekeeping into a long, expensive commitment for those countries providing the troops.

Some critics have argued that this happens because peacekeeping removes the incentives for the belligerents to negotiate seriously. Peacekeeping allows aggressors to avoid the consequences of their actions, including the possibility of defeat. Thus, they can use the blue helmets as a "face-saving" shield behind which they can build up their forces for the next round of fighting. Some critics have even argued it might sometimes be better to let the belligerents fight it out to a decisive result rather than allow the conflict to become frozen indefinitely. Other criticisms have arisen over the more ambitious goals and diversification of roles that peacekeeping has engaged in since the cold war ended. As peacekeeping moves along the continuum toward peace enforcement, it encounters the same problems listed in Table 5.2 (see p. 89).

Lack of resources in these times of governmental financial constraint also point to a common problem of all measures of international security: they lack a continuous domestic constituency. The main beneficiaries of peacekeeping and human security activities do not vote in Canadian elections. As with international economic aid, under tightened-dollar constraints, such activities are consigned to the realm of rhetoric, marginality, and persistent under-funding.

Notes

1. Nossal (1997), p. 138-43.

2. Clarkson (1985) p. 264-65.

3. This argument assumes fairly sinister motives on the part of Washington or that security considerations alone predominate.

4. Except perhaps nuclear sea mines.

5. Quoted in Keating (2002), p. 222.

6. John English as reported in Keating (2002), p. 220. DND dropped its opposition rather than forcing the UN and the Canadian government into an "embarrassing" correction.

7. Pearson (1972), p. 94.

8. *Ibid.*, p. 96.

9. He justified that attack by claims (supported by some facts) that the new revolutionary government there was organizing his own Shia population against him (which they evidently were). However, analysts have offered other strong motivations, including 1) a long-running territorial dispute over the Iran-Iraq border, 2) desire to solve a geostrategic problem by expanding Iraq's limited coastal access to an important gulf (a factor also in the Kuwait war), 3) a desire by Saddam to establish himself as the leader of the Arab world, and 4) a belief that the recent revolution against the Shah had weakened Iran, making it an opportune target. This last belief appeared false, as Iran soon turned the tide, threatening Iraq with invasion and defeat and indirectly threatening the smaller Sunni Gulf states, such as Kuwait. Kuwait and Iraq were thus allies in the long struggle against Iran, and Kuwaiti loans helped finance Iraq's defence.

10. Baehr and Gordenker (1994), p. 68.

11. Munton and Kirton (1992), p. 387.

12. In fact, as Barry (2005) points out, Canada did admit the possibility of military action without UNSC approval, as in Kosovo, in the case of a "capricious veto" (one veto blocking the will of a clear majority of UN members; no such clear majority emerged in this crisis).

13. Canada did eventually send personnel to the Middle East observer team, the UN Truce Supervision Organization, but not until 1954.

14. Hillmer and Granatstein (1994), p. 321.

15. Riddell-Dixon (2003), p. 265.

16. *Ibid.*, p. 263.

17. Foreign Affairs Canada, <http://www.humansecurity.gc.ca/menu-en.asp> (accessed 29 March 2006.

18. These are diamonds in Africa sold by warlords, militias and rebel groups to finance their violent campaigns.

Chapter Six
Achieving Political Autonomy

Domination, *dependency*, *puppet regime*, *imperialism* — the language of international relations is rich in terms designating the loss of political autonomy. Both Marxism and Realism issue clarion calls about the dangers of subordination. Indeed, much of the historic appeal of these approaches lies in the commonsense fear that the powerful will seek to take advantage of the less powerful.

At first glance, the need for political autonomy seems an extension of the need for security. If we define political autonomy as a state's ability to make decisions independent of foreign coercion, then it is clearly related to the fear of being conquered and forcibly colonized by an outside power. But security is usually concerned with overt military threats, whereas political autonomy encompasses many more subtle pressures and influences.

Any interaction with other states must involve some loss of independence. In the past, states most sensitive to the issue of foreign domination have attempted some form of autarky, completely sealing off their borders and prohibiting citizens from contact with foreigners. But in practice, such absolute sovereignty is nearly impossible. The very action of granting diplomatic immunity to foreign diplomats represents a symbolic concession to national sovereignty. In addition, trade relations, treaties, and alliances represent voluntary constraints on a state's ability to act independently. We see immediately how national interests can conflict with alliances: in order to enhance its security, a small state may ally and grant leadership to a larger power, thus reducing its own independence. Likewise, in pursuit of growth and prosperity, a state may enter a free trade agreement that involves a considerable sacrifice of economic regulatory power.

Political autonomy, like sovereignty, is never absolute in practice. As soon as a state is obliged to take into account the desires and objectives of outside states, at least some autonomy has been lost. Even enemy superpowers are constrained in their behaviour by the moves of their opponents. In an arms race, one state's expenditure on defence is determined in part by what the opponent spent the year before. Political autonomy must, therefore, be thought of as a continuum extending from colony or satellite state at one end to autarky or isolationism at the other. Table 6.1 labels and defines degrees of political autonomy. Yet, along that scale, all states seek to maximize their freedom to act, given their resources, conflicting interests, and outside pressures.

Table 6.1 The Continuum of Autonomy

Degree of Autonomy	Characteristics
1. Complete autarky or isolationism	Closed borders; forbids exit and entry; self-sufficiency
2. Relative independence	Links with other powers, but vulnerability is slight
3. Interdependence	Vulnerability is greater but mutual (sanctions imposed by one are costly to both)
4. Dependency	Asymmetrical vulnerability
5. Sphere of influence	Exclusive great power linkages (trade; investment)
6. Protectorate	The great power controls foreign and security matters but not domestic affairs
7. Formal colony	Domestic and foreign policy serve the interests of the great power

Accordingly, most states perceive autonomy as a tactical question: what is the best means of attaining, preserving, or enhancing independence? The state must first take into account its own size and resources. A large state with a rich resource endowment and a huge internal market can pursue a policy of autarky or at least partial isolationism (as, at times, the United States and China have). Few countries meet these requirements, and so most have adopted some variation of self-strengthening or counterbalancing, and follow the same logic for increasing military security.

States may attempt to strengthen themselves by using internal policies to compensate for dependence. For example, trade regulations may be implemented to gain the advantages of trade, while minimizing its negative impacts. Government may assist a weak industry faced with competition from imports with a retooling and re-education program, a policy to purchase only from domestic firms, or an outright tariff or quota agreement. A state might allow direct foreign investment but establish a foreign investment-monitoring agency.

A strategy of counterbalancing can be adopted even when state resources are limited. If dependence is inevitable, this tactic seeks to spread it around as much as possible. The state may need foreign oil, but it diversifies its purchases to minimize the danger of being cut off by any one state. A small nation with one large multinational corporation dominating its primary export product might invite in firms from other countries to offer competition. Faced with a security problem, a state might seek to multilateralize its alliances rather than rely on one pledge of support.

It is also important to correctly assess the nature of the threat that dependency poses to sovereignty. Dominance may be concentrated (one actor) or diffused (multiple small actors). For example, if the US National Security Council decides to intervene in the domestic affairs of a state, then the threat to that state's sovereignty is extreme. The threat is concentrated in a unitary actor with a clear and single purpose and considerable power to impose negative sanctions.

On the other hand, consider the challenge posed by having a majority of one's industry owned by foreign investors. In their totality, the owners of industry are making decisions that directly affect the economy of the state. These decisions may range from whether a new investment will be made to whether workers will be hired or fired, or whether a factory will be closed down. Yet, assessing the level of a state's dependency is very complicated: is the investment held by multiple individuals or directly run from foreign headquarters? How many competing foreign firms are there in the industry, and are their home governments likely to support them in a show down? In general it appears that the more diffuse the locus of decision-making, the less immediate the threat to sovereignty.

Nonetheless, diffuse threats may pose a significant long-term danger by gradually eroding the culture of a country. The French and Canadian governments have both raised the issue of the "Americanization" of their cultural values. An asymmetrical trade or investment relationship may flood the local market with goods and products from the larger state. With those goods, it is argued, come the dominant state's cultural values. Hence, for proponents of this view, the smaller state may become a satellite when its value system mirrors that of the larger state. By losing its unique cultural perspective, the dependent state has lost autonomy and will be more open to persuasion and influence from the dominant state.

Since no coercion or intentionality on the part of the dominant state is involved,[1] one might question whether political autonomy is really lost in this case. Even within a particular culture, there are numerous occasions for conflict, disagreement, and defiance. The dependent state will still have considerable opportunity to make independent decisions and express unique positions. But, some cultural nationalists will argue that the coercion is based on the fact that the assimilated people never chose to lose their cultural identity and that if presented with the long-term consequences, they would have chosen differently. On the other hand, one could argue that through a thousand small decisions to purchase or read or watch the foreign product, they did choose. With every purchase of a foreign book, movie, or magazine, they endorsed, or expressed interest in, the foreign culture. Furthermore, if they are aware that "cultural domination" is an issue within their state, are they not then admitting they still value the foreign good more than their own culture? Or do they believe their culture is not, in fact, harmed by the purchase? But others would ask, were they making the selection on the basis of economics (price and quality) or the long-term cultural implications? The debate goes on and on. Nonetheless, if the loss of cultural heritage is feared, then some policy of self-strengthening and counterbalancing could be adopted.

In summary, we can suggest a functional grouping of issues involving autonomy. Global scholars traditionally have made a distinction between issues of "high politics" and "low politics." The former refers to security and political issues where the stakes are high; the latter refers to economic and cultural matters where the threat is less immediate. Security and political autonomy is tested when one state attempts to coerce another towards decisions that serve its own interest. Threats could also arise when a state involves itself in the domestic politics of another state or seeks to change its government. Threats to economic and cultural autonomy are less immediate, more diffuse, and perhaps not even intended by any of the parties. This latter topic has been very important in Canadian foreign policy debates and will be treated in Chapter 8.

ACHIEVING POLITICAL AUTONOMY: CANADA AND THE UNITED KINGDOM

Unlike most European states, Canada began life as a collection of British colonies. Through a gradual process lasting over one hundred years, those colonies gained control over their domestic and, much later, their foreign affairs. In the middle of this process, they confederated into a larger state. The key players in this independence process were Canadian prime ministers and governments, usually from the Liberal Party. The final stage of gaining independence from the UK was not achieved until the repatriation of the Constitution in 1982.

Even as Canada went about gaining its autonomy, many feared that dependence on Britain would merely be replaced by dependence on its southern neighbour, the United States. There were good geopolitical grounds for this concern: in its North American regional context, Canada was and is dwarfed by the US in the size of its economy, army, and population, as we saw in the chapters on security. Much of what was said in those chapters about Canada's difficult security problem is relevant here too. Furthermore, ongoing technological and economic developments seem destined to subject the different regions of Canada to strong North-South pulls and linkages.

Thus, an historical treatment of Canadian political autonomy is necessarily a study in its relations with two states: the United Kingdom and the United States. This chapter will focus on the former, where the process was to gain autonomy. The next chapter will look at the latter, where the concern has been to preserve autonomy.

THE STRUGGLE FOR RESPONSIBLE GOVERNMENT

Like the majority of the current states in the world, Canada experienced a long period of colonial rule by a European power. The British government reacted conservatively to the

American and French revolutions by attempting to pull the remaining colonies into a tighter embrace. But the great ideals of democracy and rule by the people could not be suppressed, even with the failure of the Canadian Rebellions of 1837. In nineteenth-century British North America (BNA), this desire for domestic self-determination was called "responsible government."

In this guise, Canadians were only asking for the same democratic rights as their compatriots in the mother country. They wanted government by ministers and a cabinet accountable to an elected assembly rather than the British Crown's governor. In the 1840s, this struggle played out as a tug-of-war between British-appointed governors and local legislatures for effective control over the timing of assembly elections, the budget, and the appointment of all state officials. In effect, British North America was replaying the long constitutional struggle that Britain itself had experienced between the Crown and Parliament.

A major step forward was Lord Durham's Report, which called for greater self-government and resulted in the Union of Canada in 1840 (uniting the core of modern Quebec with the core of modern Ontario). But, Nova Scotia had the honour of being the first British colony to peacefully achieve responsible government in 1846. Most of the rest of British North America followed suit shortly thereafter.

TARIFF AUTONOMY

From the 1840s onward, the rules for responsible government had supposedly been established between Britain and BNA: the "self-governing" colonies had autonomy over their domestic or internal matters, while control over external or foreign affairs would stay with the colonial power. In the real world, such neat distinctions between domestic and foreign issues rarely exist, and conflict centred first on trade policy.

The crucial importance of tariff autonomy to attaining political independence may be missed without first placing it in a larger context. In the wave of imperialism during the second half of the nineteenth century, the European states set about subjugating the peoples of much of Asia and Africa. While they did not outright colonize the ancient states of China and Japan, they did impose severe restrictions on their political autonomy. The two main features of domination were to deny these states jurisdiction over foreign people (extraterritoriality) and over foreign goods (loss of tariff autonomy). Henceforth, the European powers set the duty rate on their own products entering these markets. Both Japan and China saw these steps as the key factors in their subjugation and made reversing them the main goal of their foreign policies for the rest of the century.

In British North America, Lord Durham's Report, reformist as it was, drew the line at granting tariff autonomy to self-governing colonies, for goods from either inside or outside the British Empire. It was felt that such a concession might lead to complete independence. In 1846, Britain unilaterally removed duties on many foreign goods entering the British market and expected her colonies to do the same. But the self-governing colonies protested, and in the 1850s, a series of events established tariff autonomy for

Canada. In 1850, the Union of Canada made a first step as if to follow Britain by granting free entry to goods from other BNA colonies, such as the Maritimes, but then imposed the Cayley-Galt Tariff of 1859, which placed tariffs on imports from Britain and the rest of the empire outside BNA. The Colonial Office roundly criticized the Canadian governor general for letting this happen. The Canadian government, in defending its action, argued that it needed tariffs for revenue and protection of its young industries, and that tariff autonomy must be considered a part of "responsible government" already granted.[2] The key point is that the British Parliament did not disallow the Canadian tariff bill. Thus, a few years later, the new Dominion of Canada inherited an important right of political autonomy.

THE DOMINION OF CANADA

We saw in Chapter 3 how Confederation in 1867 strengthened the security interests of Canada. Now, we can observe how it likewise strengthened political autonomy. With vast territories added together, the new Dominion of Canada gained greater resources and a new importance, or stature, for itself. Confederation established the Dominion as Britain's largest self-governing colony, which greatly increased the possibility that Whitehall would take it into consideration in its policy-planning. It also removed the possibility that Britain would play one BNA colony against the others in future negotiations over trade policy or military contributions.

The selection of the word *Dominion* was arbitrary, and in fact, from the viewpoint of international practice, Canada more closely resembled a British "protectorate." Through the latter half of the nineteenth century, Great Britain imposed this form of domination on foreign states (such as Kuwait) that she was not prepared to totally administer as colonies. Unlike a colony, a protectorate government continued to manage its own internal affairs but surrendered control of its foreign and defence policy to Britain. By the early twentieth century, the US briefly had established de facto protectorates over Cuba, Panama, and Nicaragua. Some critics might argue that by joining NORAD, Canada took a step towards becoming a protectorate of the United States.

In any case, the legal situation after 1867 was that the Dominion left all foreign affairs, from diplomatic representation to treaty making, in the hands of Great Britain. But this attempt to pretend that Canada had no separate foreign policy interests soon again ran afoul of domestic economic needs. After all, the Parliament of the new Dominion had already established the right to tariff autonomy, and Canada needed many things from the outside world, including immigrants and markets for its exports, especially with its southern neighbour.

Pursuit of those economic interests was hindered by the cumbersome formal communication and approval mechanism connecting the Canadian cabinet to the British cabinet and the outside world. Table 6.2 shows the tiny "window on the world" and long message channel Canada had to endure in this time period. This circuitous formal procedure was especially slow, given that communication methods of the day involved sending a dispatch by boat across the Atlantic and back.

Table 6.2 The Communication Channel from Canada to the United States under Confederation pre-1931*

Request to Great Britain from cabinet for information from US government
↓
Governor General of Canada
↓
Colonial Secretary in London
↓
British cabinet
↓
British Foreign Secretary
↓
British Embassy in Washington
↓
US State Department

*The response from the United States might then retrace this route, again crossing the Atlantic twice

Yet, informal windows or "back channel" means of negotiation were easily available, given that an informal representative of the Canadian government could be in Washington by train in a matter of hours. The British government had already granted formal recognition to some of these back channels. Consuls (see glossary) from foreign nations were being established in BNA even before Confederation. The US, for example, established its first consulate in Halifax in 1833. But in every case, before and after Confederation, Britain had retained the right to "license" these consuls in Canada and made clear that they had no official diplomatic status. Most of their activities encompassed the low politics of economics, shipping, immigration, and the treatment of their own citizens in Canada.[3]

In 1877, the British government made some attempt to accommodate Canadian needs when it granted the dominions the right to "opt out" of treaties it signed with third parties. It also sometimes allowed Canadian representatives to be part of British trade negotiating delegations, as in the Treaty of Washington of 1871. But some Canadians felt even this representation was not enough.

THE HIGH COMMISSIONER FOR CANADA

It was inevitable that any Canadian government, whether Grit or loyal, imperial Tory, would seek to open more windows on the world. By far the most important bilateral relationship at Confederation was with London. If nothing else, the Dominion needed someone at the scene of the action to represent the Canadian position during any third-party trade deals Britain was considering. As with other developments in Canada's quest for autonomy, this representation in Britain developed very gradually.

From 1869, Sir John Rose operated in London as a non-permanent, "semi-official" Canadian representative, "a gentleman possessing the confidence of the Canadian government with whom Her Majesty's government may communicate on Canadian affairs."[4] The title High Commissioner for Canada was coined in 1880 and has continued to be an important posting to this day. The duties included encouraging immigration from the British Isles to Canada, helping to raise loans for Canadian railroads and the Canadian national debt, and operating as a general public relations department for Canada. Later High Commissioners used the close proximity of the Foreign Office to gain British credentials in order to attend international conferences or participate in trade negotiations with other European states through the local British embassy.

Nonetheless, Sir John Galt, the first official High Commissioner for Canada, expressed his dissatisfaction with the limitations of the position on his retirement in 1883. He felt that without full diplomatic status, the High Commissioner lacked recognition both in Whitehall and in the London diplomatic community. Galt's suggestion of greater independent representation and autonomy triggered many Canadian Parliamentary debates in the last decades of the nineteenth century. Within English Canada, a large section of the population, in tune with the New Imperialism in the 1880s, sought expansion and closer centralization of the British Empire. The Conservative Party of John A. Macdonald tapped this constituency by producing symbols and rhetoric, though not always policy, in line with an imperialist stance.

French Canadians were more inclined to question the imperial tie, in part due to the lack of cultural identification with Britain, and in part due to the fear of imperial burdens. As the Liberal Party leader Laurier put it, *"Que devons-nous à l'Angleterre?"* ("What do we owe to England?") Thus, a uniquely Canadian nationalism first appeared in the French-Canadian community. The Federal Liberal party tended to advocate greater autonomy, in part due to an electoral strategy that relied on Quebec and rural immigrant seats, and in part based on a concern for the unity of the country.

CHAMBERLAIN IMPERIALISM

New Imperialism in the mother country was sometimes called Chamberlain Imperialism, after Joseph Chamberlain, the British Colonial Secretary at the time. He sought to implement tighter centralization in the empire, to promote greater coordination of policy and pooling of resources. In practice, this meant more support was demanded from the dominions for Britain's imperial adventures.

But even the Conservative Party in Canada was not always receptive to this change in imperial policy. In 1884, John A. Macdonald responded to British calls for help in the crisis in Sudan with, "Why should we waste money and men [...] to get Gladstone & Co. [the British government] out of the hole they have plunged themselves into by their own imbecility [sic]."[5] Symbolic demonstrations of loyalty were another matter, though, and the Conservatives were more than willing to participate with the other dominions in the first colonial conference, held in of London in 1887 and called on the occasion of Queen

Victoria's Golden Jubilee. Once the British prime minister made it clear that imperial federation was not on the agenda, the Canadian Conservatives were even willing to host a second colonial conference in 1894 (see Table 6.3).

Table 6.3 Colonial and Imperial Conferences before Commonwealth

1887 First Colonial Conference: Queen Victoria's Golden Jubilee
1894 Ottawa Colonial Conference: non-military issues
1897 Colonial Conference: Queen Victoria's Diamond Jubilee
1902 Colonial Conference: agreement to meet every four years
1907 Imperial Conference: conference title changed and secretariat established
1909 First Subsidiary Conference on Military and Naval Defence
1911 Imperial Conference: coronation of Edward
1917 Imperial War Cabinet formed: duration of World War I only
1923 Imperial Conference: Lloyd George Proposals
1926 Imperial Conference: Balfour Formula and British Commonwealth established

Similarly, Liberal prime minister Laurier stoutly resisted Chamberlain's centralizing pressure during the Queen's Diamond Jubilee and colonial conference in 1897. The outbreak of the Boer War and Britain's call for assistance from the dominions provoked a crisis in Canada two years later, dividing Laurier's cabinet. The crisis was resolved by compromising to equip volunteers for the war. At the 1902 conference, Chamberlain offered Laurier a voice in a coordinated imperial foreign policy in exchange for naval contributions. This provoked a crisis in Canada, which Laurier solved by creating a small Canadian navy. By giving Canada its own defence capability instead of contributing to a British-run battleship, he took a further step towards security autonomy.

In 1911, Robert Borden's Conservatives came to power and shifted policy back in the direction of greater coordination with Great Britain: Canada would contribute money towards the purchase of three British battleships, scrapping its own navy plans; in exchange, Canada would get a seat on a committee of imperial defence and the right to be informed on policy matters. This reintegration provoked a naval crisis in 1913 and anger from the Liberals and Quebec nationalists. Borden was forced to use unconventional tactics to push his decisions through Parliament.

WORLD WAR I AND THE CRISIS IN CONSULTATION

While Borden might have been ideologically prepared to accept the role of "faithful ally" at the beginning of World War I, domestic pressures soon forced him to exercise control over the uses of Canadian resources and manpower. The war was never popular in Quebec, in parts of the Liberal Party, or in large sections of rural English Canada. Newspaper accounts of battles that resembled slaughters fed the public perception that Canadian boys were being used as cannon fodder by incompetent British generals. Yet, the front lines demanded more soldiers, and in 1916, Borden proposed to the British government that he would introduce conscription in Canada in exchange for direct consultation in war policy. Thus, in 1917, all the dominion prime ministers gained the right to sit as equals with a smaller British cabinet on the Imperial War Cabinet.

But this idea posed a horrendous threat to domestic unity in Canada, as we will see in Chapter 9. The Conscription Crisis deeply divided French and English Canada and instilled in the Liberal party, and in the mind of Mackenzie King in particular, the conviction that after the war, greater political autonomy was of the utmost importance.

It was equally clear to Britain and the dominions that the high level of coordination required of the Imperial War Cabinet could not be sustained after the war. Thus, ironically, it was the Conservative Borden who demanded and attained separate representation for Canada at the conferences to negotiate the Versailles Treaty and a seat at the new League of Nations.

THE UNITED STATES AS COUNTERWEIGHT

Paradoxically, Canada turned to the United States to gain autonomy from Britain. After British negotiations that favoured the US at the Treaty of Washington in 1871 and the decision on the Alaska boundary in 1903, both the Conservatives and Liberals began to question the advantage of having Britain speak for Canada if Canadian interests were to be sacrificed each time. In fact, British foreign policy in the late nineteenth century inclined towards appeasement with the US. For Britain, the policy eventually paid off: there were no Anglo-American wars in the late nineteenth century, and in 1917, the US entered World War I on the British side. But, such success was purchased in part with Canadian concessions. If Canada was going to lose every time under British control, many Canadians felt perhaps it was time for Canada to negotiate with the US on her own.

Canada needed more direct representation in Washington because official channels across the Atlantic to Britain and back again to the British Embassy in Washington were extremely slow. Most of Canada's conflicts and interests involved her close southern neighbour. In 1908, Prime Minister Laurier sent Mackenzie King to Washington in a first informal (non-diplomatic) exchange of views. The Boundary Waters Treaty of 1909 was an even more important development, leading to the International Joint Commission, a permanent international body staffed solely by Americans and Canadians. The commission, which still operates today, has equal representation from both countries and settles cross-boundary water disputes. Though the treaty that created the commission had been negotiated and signed by Britain, there would be no further British input in its deliberations.

In the same year, the Liberal government took another important step in creating formal structures to deal with the outside world. The Conservatives had already taken a big institution-building step in 1892 by creating the Department for Trade and Commerce, after which trade commissioners were sent to the West Indies and Australia. The number of informal Canadian commercial representatives grew rapidly, which created jurisdictional and coordination problems with other departments in the Canadian government. The root of the problem, as diagnosed in a Royal Commission on the civil service, was the lack of an overarching department on foreign affairs. All matters dealing with external relations were being handled in an ad hoc manner by the cabinet or various departments without any record keeping or policy coordination. The solution for the Liberals was to create the Department of External Affairs (DEA) in 1909. By resolution of Parliament, it was staffed by a department head, John Pope, and a few clerks, and was to have been led by a cabinet-level secretary of state for external affairs.[6]

The new department's mission was to supervise external and foreign relations, and in practice, this meant issuing passports, dealing with the foreign consuls in Canada, and building up an archive of documents on past external communications. From its humble beginnings in an office above a barber shop, with a staff of four and an annual budget of $14,950, the department grew very slowly, moving to the East Bloc of Parliament Hill in 1914 to be closer to the governor general and the prime minister. This slow development was due in part to the fact that, beginning in 1912, each prime minister acted as his own secretary of state for external affairs. This practice was adopted partly out of the fear of raising the ire of the British Colonial Office, which initially took a dim view of Canada's new DEA.

With this new institutional capacity for conducting foreign affairs, one might have expected the Liberals to immediately pursue greater representation in Washington. But Laurier took no further steps, largely because the British ambassador in Washington, James Bryce, did such a good job of looking after Canadian interests.[7] Ironically, the next step came from the Conservatives, under the pressure of wartime cooperation. Prime Minister Borden sent a Canadian mission to the US to coordinate World War I military affairs and soon wanted more — a Canadian minister with full diplomatic powers. US president Woodrow Wilson accepted the proposal, but the British government attached so many restrictions to the new Canadian representation that the Liberals in Parliament attacked it as the "kindergarten school of diplomacy."[8]

Mackenzie King, the new Liberal prime minister of 1921, was "more continentally inclined than any prime minister before"[9] and quite prepared to continue the Liberal tactic of playing the US against the UK, except for his cautious nature. But, when King learned from the newspapers that the British government was taking support from the dominions for granted in the Chanak Affair of 1922 (which involved British intervention in a conflict between Greece and Turkey), King took an uncharacteristically resolute stand on the autonomy issue. He refused to support Britain in the crisis and was punished by not being invited to sign the British treaty with Turkey that ended the conflict. By contrast, Opposition leader Arthur Meighen uttered his imperial rally-cry, "Ready, aye, ready," indicating a policy of automatic loyalty and support for the "Mother" country.

When Britain took Canada for granted, Canadian governments often responded with a strong bid for political autonomy. Prime Minister King began the final moves towards full independence by again using the American counterweight. In 1923, he invited US president Warren Harding to Canada — the first formal visit of an American president. Canada also signed the Halibut Treaty with the US that year, regulating the North Pacific fishery. Since Canada negotiated and signed this treaty without Great Britain, it was its first clear exercise of independent treaty-making power. The British were not pleased and argued, correctly, that the action was illegal. But the legal situation was going to change rapidly in the next eight years through the institution of the Imperial Conference.

At the 1923 Imperial Conference, the British prime minister Lloyd George made one last effort at imperial control, but Canada, South Africa, and the Irish Free State defeated his proposal for a single imperial policy. The political showdown came at the 1926 Imperial Conference, where King again played the key role. The six dominions of the British Empire were split among the loyalists (Australia, New Zealand, and Newfoundland) and the autonomy-seekers (Irish Free State, South Africa, and Canada). King's allegiance with the later resulted in the Balfour Formula.[10] This political agreement changed the British Empire into the British Commonwealth and recognized the six dominions, but not the other colonies, as constitutionally equal to Great Britain and independent in foreign policy, though still "loyal" to the Crown. The 1931 Statute of Westminster then followed as the full legal realization of the political decision to grant the dominions full foreign policy autonomy. Canada had ceased being a protectorate of Britain.

The way was now cleared for Canada to exchange full diplomatic representatives with any nation. In 1927, King appointed Vincent Massey as Canada's minister to Washington under the formal title His Britannic Majesty's Envoy Extraordinary and Minister Plenipotentiary to Represent the Interests of the Dominion of Canada. The symbolism of loyalty to the Crown is still present in this title, if not the new reality of Canadian control. King followed this appointment with the first formal visit of a Canadian prime minister to Washington.

King moved steadily but cautiously in exercising Canada's new power to create foreign missions (see Table 6.4). The order of their creation shows something of the importance attached to relations with each country at that time. France followed immediately after the United States. Japan received high priority due to the issue of Asian immigration to British Columbia. By the beginning of World War II, legations had been established with the other dominions outside of Newfoundland. The countries involved usually reciprocated by establishing a legation in Ottawa. More direct British representation was established in Canada in 1928 with the arrival of a British High Commissioner.[11] This step followed a departure in the governor general's duties from being an active policy and communication link between London and Ottawa to that of a more symbolic representation of the Crown in Canada.

Table 6.4 Chronology of Canadian Diplomatic Representation Abroad

1927   United States
1928   France
1929   Japan
1939   Netherlands; Belgium; Australia
1940   Ireland; New Zealand; South Africa

FINAL STAGES TO COMPLETE INDEPENDENCE

Immediately after World War II, a number of changes further enhanced Canadian autonomy. In 1946, with the appointment of St. Laurent as King's external affairs minister, the offices of prime minister and secretary of state for external affairs were separated. Since then, with brief exceptions, the DEA has had its own cabinet-level minister to present foreign policy issues. In 1947, the Canadian governor general was given all remaining Crown prerogatives. In the same year, formal Canadian citizenship, separate from British citizenship, was established along with a distinct Canadian passport.

In 1949, Canada attained judicial autonomy with its own Supreme Court becoming the court of final appeal, rather than the Judicial Committee of the British Privy Council. However, the power to amend the Constitution remained with the British Parliament until Trudeau's 1982 Canada Act, which severed all remaining constitutional and legislative ties between the two countries.

Other moves towards autonomy were more symbolic. Through the 1950s, the word *Dominion* dropped from common usage in Canada's name, just as the word *British* dropped from the Commonwealth. In the mid-1960s, there was heated debate across the country when the Pearson government adopted today's Maple Leaf Flag. Finally, in 1993, the Chrétien government renamed the Department of External Affairs, substituting the more commonly used word *foreign* for the outdated *external* in the Department of Foreign Affairs and International Trade (DFAIT).

CONCLUSION

In this chapter, we have traced political autonomy in Canada as it developed from British colonialism to Canadian independence. By the time of the Statute of Westminster in 1931, Canada had gained virtual independence from Great Britain through a long series of small incremental steps. Most of these steps were challenged but then grudgingly accepted by the British Foreign Office. We can now summarize these steps as follows:

1. Domestic Autonomy
2. Tariff Autonomy
3. Institutional Capacity
4. Foreign Representation
5. Independent Treaty-making Power

Though there was no inevitable progression through these steps, once ideological and domestic considerations brought about the first changes, the later stages followed as the logical, next-easiest steps in the pursuit of Canadian autonomy. Pressure for greater autonomy arose from a variety of sources:

Domestic Influences. As long as the connection to Britain required few Canadian resources, there was little pressure to change the relationship. But, during the late nineteenth century, the imperial tie increasingly involved Canada in wars and their attendant demands for resources and manpower. French and rural Canadians in particular contested the prospect of soldiers dying in faraway, foreign battlefields, and these groups expressed their demands primarily through the federal Liberal party. For the Liberals, seeking political autonomy dovetailed with the interest in preserving national unity, as we will see in Chapter 9.

Divergence of Interests with Britain. Canada had no interest in following Britain into free trade in the nineteenth century. Furthermore, Canadian interests were sometimes sacrificed in Britain's appeasement policy with the US. In the long term, Britain's primary focus had shifted towards Europe. Then as now, the immediate symptom of divergent interests between Canada and Britain was a crisis of consultation and a sense that Canada was being ignored or taken for granted.

A Nascent Canadian Nationalism. For most former colonies, nationalism is the primary force driving separation, rebellion, and independence. In Canada's case, a clear sense of national uniqueness has been obscured by the reality of two distinct "founding" cultures, the interplay of dominant British and American cultures, the lack of a violent independence struggle, the cultural mosaic of an immigrant nation, and the negative example of American flag-waving patriotism. These have all contributed to a situation referred to at best as "quiet nationalism" and at worst as a confused sense of national identity. Nonetheless, by the early twentieth century, many Canadians, especially those in Quebec had a sense of identity different from the British one.

Many other factors contributed to the push for autonomy. As we've seen, the demand for democracy played a major role in gaining responsible government and domestic autonomy. O.D. Skelton, soon to be King's deputy minister for external affairs, summed up the logic for not stopping with domestic affairs in 1922. As he said in his speech to the Canadian Club, foreign policy is "an extension of domestic policy and [...] as we have gained control of the one so we must gain control of the other as to matters affecting ourselves."[12]

Whatever the respective importance of all these factors, Canada pioneered, with her sister dominions, a peaceful path from empire to independence that was to be followed by many other colonies. But as many of those former colonies have discovered, the quest for political autonomy does not end with formal independence. Dependence can take many forms. The next chapter discusses the history of maintaining autonomy from the superpower on Canada's southern border.

Notes

1. Intentionality here means the larger state may not be purposefully, as an act of policy, trying to assimilate or spread its values to the other state.

2. Mansergh (1969), p. 48.

3. Hilliker (1990), p. 6.

4. From Privy Council Proceedings (Order-in-council Privy Council 716, October 2, 1869, Privy Council Records, National Archives, series 1, vol. 17).

5. Morton (1981), p. 32.

6. The word *external* was carefully chosen instead of *foreign* so as not to imply that Britain was a foreign country to Canada. This situation was not "normalized" until 1993, when the Chrétien government changed the name to the Department of Foreign Affairs and International Trade (DFAIT). The addition of "secretary of state" had to do with civil service politics and the interests of John Pope. Even so, there already was a secretary of state since 1867, and some of Pope's earliest jurisdictional battles were with him.

7. Indeed Brebner (1966) suggests he spent 90 per cent of his time looking after Canadian interests.

8. Martin (1982), p. 89.

9. *Ibid.*, p. 90.

10. We must be careful to call it the Balfour Formula and not confuse it with the Balfour Declaration, as Pearson does in his memoirs. The Balfour Declaration of 1917 is known to students of the Middle East as the important statement of British support for a Jewish homeland in Palestine.

11. In a practice that continues today, "ambassadors" exchanged among Commonwealth countries are called High Commissioners instead.

12. Quoted in Hilliker (1990), p. 93.

Chapter Seven
Preserving Political Autonomy

Canada is at liberty to act or not act, to interfere or not interfere, to do just as she pleases.
— Wilfred Laurier[1]

The United States is so big that if we don't look independent, you Americans will take us for granted [...] I just don't want Canada to be perceived as being the 51st state of America [...] As an independent country, we should be able to have an independent view in foreign affairs.
— Jean Chrétien[2]

The fact that nearly a century separates these quotes by Liberal prime ministers is a testament to the enduring nature of political autonomy as a Canadian national interest. What *has* changed is merely the target of the statements. In Laurier's day, the main threat to the accomplishment of Canadian political autonomy was the government in Britain. Since World War II, it was been the government in Washington. In the last chapter, we examined how Canada achieved political independence from Great Britain. In this one, we will study the ongoing attempts to preserve that autonomy in the shadow of the great superpower on Canada's southern border.

Cast in terms of nation interests, the issue becomes more profound than mere anti-Americanism or ideological differences between the two states. Without political autonomy, states are stripped of the independent capacity to formulate and carry out goals related to their other national interests. Hence the high priority given to autonomy. It in many ways takes priority over the realization of the other economic and domestic interests.

Under dominion status, Canada was faced with the potential loss of important interests involving territory, economics, security policy, and domestic unity. Since World War II, a threat of similar scope has emerged with regards to its relationship with the United States. The nature of this threat does not involve direct security, such as was treated in chapters 3 and 4. Only an extreme crisis would place Canada in danger of invasion or military assault by the US. The long-undefended border stands as a reminder of the unlikelihood of attack. Nonetheless, the threat to Canadian autonomy is real as long as there is such a huge asymmetry in the power relations between the two countries. Table 7.1 outlines the disparities in population, gross domestic product, exports, and military expenditure between the two nations. Given this reality, one might think our leaders in Canada live in constant fear of American retaliation over the slightest disagreement in policy. But, our knowledge of human nature suggests this asymmetry could also provoke a backlash of resentment at the threat of subordination and a heightened sensitivity to every slight or attempt at coercion. Then again, as we will see in Chapter 8, the loss of political autonomy may not even depend on the intentions of leaders in Washington or Ottawa. Autonomy may depend on deeply embedded structures such as culture and the perceptions people share.

*Table 7.1 Disparities of Size between the United States and Canada**

	United States	Canada
Population (2005)	296 million	33 million
GDP (2004)	$11,750 billion	$1,023 billion
Exports (2004)	$795 billion	$315.6 billion
Military Expenditure (2003)	$371 billion	$10 billion

*All dollar figures are in US at purchase power parity

Source: CIA Factbook 2005, <http://www.cia.gov/cia/publication/factbook/> (Accessed Nov. 14, 2005).

Some commentators have gone so far as to charge that Canada has become a political appendage, satellite, or protectorate of the American superpower. We will examine that charge here and in the next chapter, and also attempt to assess the relative merits of policies to guard Canada's autonomy.

MACKENZIE KING IN THE AFTERMATH OF WORLD WAR II

We have seen how, prior to World War II, Prime Minister King used a counterbalancing strategy of improving ties with Washington to increase manoeuvring room in relations between Canada and Britain. Faced with the real danger that Britain might fall to the Germans in World War II, King moved Canada very close to alliance with the US with the Ogdensburg Agreement, which established stronger Canadian-American military cooperation. But the experience of wartime collaboration aroused Prime Minister King's suspicion of the United States. He attempted to minimize the presence of American troops in Canada, fretted over US forces in the northwest, and took careful steps to balance the strength of troops in Newfoundland (which was not yet a part of Canada).

Once the war was over, King appeared to be more concerned with the possibility of Canada losing its newly found autonomy to the US than with seeking a closer alliance. He abruptly called off a free trade agreement being negotiated with the United States. His government (and that of his successor, St. Laurent) steadily resisted US entreaties for a North American defence pact, despite the growing Soviet threat. Instead, as we've seen previously, the Americans were diverted into the multilateral NATO alliance.

GROWING ELITE TENSIONS UNDER ST. LAURENT

Upon his retirement, King saw his cautious policy replaced with the internationalism of St. Laurent and his very able external minister, Lester Pearson. Yet, despite the government's desire for a more active and committed foreign policy and its greater willingness to collaborate with the US in the defence of the West, bilateral relations were soon in trouble.

The growing tension in US-Canadian relations over foreign affairs had two major focal points. The first centred on relations with the Communist world. As we have seen in Chapter 4, the 1950s was a period of much consensus in the North Atlantic community regarding the Soviet and Communist threat. There was also little doubt that the United States would be the logical leader of the Western Bloc, given its size and power. What was in doubt was the quality of that leadership. Some Canadian leaders feared that the US, through inexperience or rashness, would involve its allies in costly wars, blunders, and defeats.

There *were* reasons to question the quality of United States leadership in these years. The lack of consistency in policy was one of the complaints most commonly expressed in Canadian and British accounts. The Korean War was an excellent example of this problem: at first, Korea was not worth defending; then it became the crucible of the cold war. Was it a war to defend the South? To liberate the North? Or to settle accounts with the People's Republic of China? The administration of Harry Truman did not appear to have a clear idea of its own aims. General MacArthur in particular worried the allied governments when he issued rash statements about carrying the war into China and using nuclear weapons. Did the president control him or not? Ultimately, this very issue of insubordination led Truman to sack his chief general in the middle of the fighting.

Institutional factors can explain much of the inconsistency in US policy. Unlike the Canadian or British prime ministers, the American president shares foreign policy powers with Congress. Congress in turn is more sensitive to swings in American public opinion. Indeed, Truman's slowness to deal with MacArthur's insubordination was part from his fear of domestic reaction. MacArthur returned from Korea to a hero's welcome in the United States. In the early 1950s, the Truman administration was under constant domestic attack due to the demagogic activities of Senator McCarthy, who had focused the general insecurities of the American public on the supposed threat from Communist sympathizers in the government. The ugly spectacle of Congressional committees interrogating and "purging" government officials appalled Pearson and many other Canadians.

Likewise, the large role that Congress plays makes US foreign policy more open to continuous pressure from special interests. The Israel lobby in the Democratic Party caucus was a good example of such a constraint, as is the pro-oil business leaning of many Republican senators today. Likewise, the China lobby (which favoured Taiwan) as well as McCarthyism help to explain the US government's unrealistic refusal to recognize the People's Republic of China for so many years. Canada's government, less encumbered by such domestic considerations, was more willing to raise the issue, and thus recognition of China became a minor irritant in Canadian-US relations throughout the 1950s and 1960s.[3]

The second major area of friction in relations between Canada and the United States arose over the nature of the Western alliance itself. The US often acted as if it believed that it must lead, with or without the agreement of its allies. It appeared to want from NATO only "faithful allies" or "loyal followers" automatically offering support and resources for US-defined goals. This expected denial of autonomy echoes the image of Canada as a faithful ally in the imperial era. The difference here was that Canada had no domestic constituency to support such blind faith in the United States.

While accepting the usefulness and logic of American leadership, Canada and most of the Western European allies expected the US to behave in a more multilateral or consultative manner. The more the United States blundered and acted rashly, the more the allies demanded greater input or, alternatively, greater autonomy from that alliance. The desire for greater political autonomy echoes the fears the Liberals had of being drawn into costly foreign wars. The US government was often willing to grant the importance of prior consultation and mutual decision making, but in crisis situations appeared to slip back into its old unilateral ways.[4] This failure to be a more multilateral leader has been a problem from time to time, both in NATO and the United Nations.

The Korean War brought many of these differences between Canada and the US to a head. Far from being a subservient faithful ally, Canada generated its own assessments that often differed from US policy. Sometimes, the result was a grudging acceptance of the US position, as in the decision to label China as an aggressor at the UN during the Korean War. At other times, these assessments helped to moderate US policy, as when Pearson and British prime minister Attlee succeeded in pushing Truman to publicly rule out the use of nuclear weapons in the Korean War. Careful examination of this period in history does not show American dominance, but rather pushing and hauling, considerable disagreement, and sometimes ill will between elites on both sides of the border. These were mainly Canadian Liberal elite differences with US policy, because for the general Canadian public, the Korean War was "probably the most popular war Canada ever fought."[5]

The Korean War also highlighted the differences between leadership and "followership." Even before Korea, Pearson had attempted to clarify the difference between being a faithful ally and multilateralism. Speaking to the House of Commons on November 16, 1949, he stressed (according to John English) that neither country should "'take their relations with the other too much for granted.' The United States must lead the Western democratic powers, but Canada had its own contribution to make which it could do 'most effectively as a cooperating partner but not as a camp follower.'"[6]

Pearson was greatly disillusioned by the American tendency to ignore the UN, to consult neither its allies nor other UN members, and generally to prosecute the Korean War in its own unilateral way. He therefore ordered the Rogers Report on US-Canadian relations in 1951,[7] which was very critical of US leadership, expressing many of the themes cited above. The report served as the basis for Pearson's outspoken statements to the Canadian Bar Association on March 31, 1951 and to the joint meeting of the Canadian and Empire clubs on April 10, 1951.

On the second occasion, he also criticized the US for trying to turn the United

Nations into a tool of its own policy. He asserted Canada's right to criticize US policy and suggested that "the days of relatively easy and automatic political relations with our neighbour are, I think, over."[8] The US ambassador in Ottawa characterized the speech as "a declaration of independence," thus underlining Canada's political autonomy. Given that this critique was made during Truman's controversial sacking of MacArthur, it could have been viewed by the US as unwarranted interference in a difficult domestic situation. Clearly, it showed that Pearson was not willing to be a mute "loyal ally" and could speak out critically in time of war and American difficulty. He was also willing to jeopardize good relations with the US: "after 1951, Mike's [Pearson's] relationship with the US was not the same."[9]

The 1953 change to a Republican administration in the US only made matters worse. The Liberal elites in Ottawa were ideologically more attuned to the Democratic "New Dealers" and blamed the Republicans for McCarthyism. Thus, tensions in the bilateral relationship increased, and opportunities for Canada to demonstrate its political autonomy flourished.

In 1953, Pearson twice rejected a request to let Igor Gouzenko testify before the US Senate Internal Security Subcommittee, even when the second query came from the US State Department.[10] When the new US secretary of state John F. Dulles announced his massive retaliation doctrine (which expanded the number of situations in which the US might threaten to use nuclear weapons). Pearson went public with his criticism of that policy.[11] Pearson also clashed with the US Congress and government when he protected Canadian diplomat Herbert Norman from their attempts to question him over his past links to the Communist Party.

Against the wishes of the US government, Canada was named to the International Commission for Supervision and Control for South East Asia, along with India and Poland. The Canadian government eventually sided with US policy on many occasions, as with the recognition of the Diem regime in South Vietnam. But it is also clear that Ottawa formulated that policy autonomously (as with its earlier cold war assessments of the Soviets) on the basis of its own disillusionment with North Vietnam. James Eayrs and Douglas Ross provide two Canadian accounts of this period that support this conclusion, though Eayrs places more emphasis on the secret collaborative activities of US and Canadian officers, seeing in it "the roots of complicity."[12] In any case, much later in 1965 in his Temple University speech, Pearson was to clearly and publicly distance himself from US policy on Vietnam.

Perceptions of Canadian independence may have played a role when the Soviets invited Pearson to visit in 1955.[13] The visit resulted in sales of Canadian wheat to the USSR, but also hardened Pearson's attitudes about Khrushchev's intentions. At the same time, in the UN General Assembly, representatives of Canada and the US were at odds over how to deal with a cold war stalemate over new members to the UN. Paul Martin, Sr., pushed for the "package deal" proposal that would end the deadlock created when the US and USSR vetoed each other's proposed new members. When the American UN ambassador Henry Cabot Lodge, Jr. threatened Canada with trade sanctions if it didn't drop the idea, Martin angrily rejected the crude attempt at coercion and persevered with the plan.[14]

During the Suez Crisis of 1956, Canada broke with both its founding nations, Britain and France, but Pearson also charted a course separate again from the United States. He took the initiative in formulating the peacekeeping force. Canadian voting patterns at the UN during the crisis suggest an independent policy, with Canada sometimes even voting with India and the neutral countries. Indeed, Canada was able to play the role of mediator because Pearson had built an image of the country as an independent, honest broker in the world community.

DIEFENBAKER: THE "LAMENT" VERSION

Despite the apparent record of Liberal independence, one longstanding interpretation claims that the Liberals showed a disregard for the maintenance of Canadian political autonomy throughout the post-World War II period. By this account, only the brave but doomed intervention of John Diefenbaker stood in the way of the American tide. This exultation of Diefenbaker and the Conservatives as the true Canadian nationalists fighting Liberal anti-nationalist and continentalist tendencies is quite apparent in the works of historian Donald Creighton and philosopher George Grant. Their writings (for example, Grant's *Lament for a Nation*) transform the old imperial tie to Britain into Canadian nationalism and the sole bulwark against American domination.

C.D. Howe, the Liberal "Minister of Everything," is most commonly presented as the chief villain in this piece. He is portrayed at best as colour-blind to nationality when it came to furthering economic growth and at worst as willing to sacrifice Canadian independence to US and Canadian business interests. The chief symbol of C.D. Howe's "betrayal" was the TransCanada Pipeline bill of 1956, which would have given temporary American control to this great Canadian megaproject.[15] Grant denounces "the decisions made by C.D. Howe and his men. Our traditional role — as an exporter of raw materials (particularly to Europe) with highly protected industry in central Canada — gradually lost its importance in relation to our role as a branch plant of American capitalism."[16]

But Grant also indicts the internationalism of St. Laurent and Pearson, claiming that attention to Canadian national interests suffered as a result: "for twenty years before its defeat in 1957, the Liberal Party had been pursuing policies that led inexorably to the disappearance of Canada."[17]

This interpretation of the Diefenbaker years persists in such more recent accounts as Lawrence Martin's *Pledge of Allegiance*.

[Diefenbaker's] fear of American dominance provoked bitter confrontations with John Kennedy over the Cuban Missile Crisis, the issue of nuclear warheads on Canadian soil, and other questions. In the end, his rampant nationalism alienated the entire ruling class: Bay Street, Wall Street, his civil service, and politicians from all parties, including his own [...] Grant, who readily acknowledged that the Tory leader's own foolhardiness contributed to his downfall, credited the Chief with the strongest stance against satellite status ever attempted by a Canadian.[18]

Martin portrays Diefenbaker as a nationalist in part to attack the Mulroney government for its alleged about-face from traditional Tory policy. But was Diefenbaker really the great champion of independence? Clearly, political autonomy is a vital national interest for Canada, and the threat of its erosion by the US is real. However, the quote above itself admits an alternative explanation: Diefenbaker's own incompetence as prime minister so alienated all the above groups that even an eleventh-hour, nationalist plea could not save his government. When one places the events of 1962 in the context of his whole ministry, his loud anti-Americanism looks more like an electoral tactic seasoned with personal animosity for President Kennedy.

DIEFENBAKER REASSESSED

Before examining his record, it is important to distinguish Diefenbaker's "love of Britain" from his pursuit of national autonomy. As we have seen in the previous chapter, loyalty to United Kingdom in the nineteenth century represented the opposite of political independence. Furthermore, after 1931, waving the Red Ensign (Canada's flag before the Maple Leaf and symbol of the link to Britain) could only have furthered political autonomy if it was used as part of a counterbalance strategy to the United States. In the case of both the Suez Crisis and the flag debate, in which Diefenbaker refused to accept a new Canadian flag—the two outstanding symbols of Diefenbaker's loyalty to Britain—this strategy was not relevant. He did implicitly raise the need for the trade link with Britain to counterbalance US domination in his proposal to send more Canadian exports to Britain and in his vigorous opposition to the entry of the UK into the European Community. But, in both cases, his clumsy handling of the situation worsened relations with Britain, making a counterbalance strategy virtually impossible. With Diefenbaker, the policy was so confused that intentions are often difficult to infer.

We should begin by examining Diefenbaker's attitudes towards the cold war and the United States. Numerous incidents show that Diefenbaker held very hawkish views on the cold war. Those who emphasize his differences with the US often downplay this important point. H. Basil Robinson, Diefenbaker's advisor at the Prime Minister's Office for external affairs, summarizes his views:

[H]is deep suspicion of Soviet motives, strong doubts that the Soviet leaders could ever be brought to make real concessions, concern for the plight of minorities within the Soviet perimeter, fear of the impact of Soviet economic strategy in the developing world, and conviction that strength alone would deter Soviet expansionism—all these ideas he embraced as ardently as John Foster Dulles, the leading cold war advocate of the 1950s.[19]

During elections, Diefenbaker often spoke to Ukrainians and East European constituents about the "Soviet Empire" and the "captive nations" of Eastern Europe. Indeed, an ongoing irritant in his relations with the DEA was his desire to introduce a resolution in the United Nations General Assembly (UNGA) condemning "Soviet Colonialism." Though the DEA sidetracked the motion, Diefenbaker nonetheless included the theme in his famous rebuttal speech to Khrushchev at the 1960 UNGA session. Speaking on colonialism, he said,

> I pause to ask this question: how many human beings have been liberated by the USSR? Do we forget how one of the post-war colonies of the Soviet Union sought to liberate itself four years ago [the Hungarian rebellion], and with what results?[20]

The speech was a vintage cold war polemic and placed Canada on the hawkish side of East-West relations at the United Nations. It was quite a change from the image Pearson had presented of Canada. Indeed, as late as the 1965 federal election, Diefenbaker considered attacking Pearson's alleged Communist ties,[21] a tactic from Nixon's early cold war school of campaigning. Seen from this perspective, Diefenbaker's decisions to sell wheat to the People's Republic of China and maintain ties with Cuba were exceptions only, made for pragmatic, economic reasons.

Diefenbaker shared with Dulles a serious concern about neutralism and non-alignment in the Third World. In his tour of India and Ceylon in 1958, he seemed anxious to probe whether neutralism was opening the door to Soviet influence. According to Basil Robinson, Diefenbaker took on the role of defender of the United States in these meetings, singing the praises of the Eisenhower government. In Singapore, he even extolled the virtues of US foreign investment in Canada and said it was not as bad as sometimes presented, "otherwise Canada would not have survived as an independent state, and he had no worries whatsoever about Canadian survival even with an extremely liberal policy towards foreign investment."[22] This theme also was repeated in Diefenbaker's 1960 United Nations speech and has interesting resonance with the Mulroney government.

Diefenbaker worked hard to build a strong personal bond with Eisenhower and appeared quite comfortable in his relationship with the American president. During Eisenhower's visit to Canada in May 1958, Diefenbaker "insisted on plenty of time alone," including a private fishing trip on Harrington Lake.[23] His personal loyalty to Eisenhower can be seen in how he responded to the U-2 Crisis of 1960. An American spy plane had been shot down over Soviet airspace. Initially, the American government denied any knowledge of the flight, but when Khrushchev produced the pilot, Eisenhower felt obliged to admit his personal responsibility in ordering the flight. Diefenbaker stood by Eisenhower, and when the Soviets cancelled an important summit shortly after, Diefenbaker publicly blamed Khrushchev for the dangerous turn in relations.

But most remarkable and symbolic of Diefenbaker's relationship with Eisenhower was his performance at the American president's last official duty, the signing of the Columbia River Treaty in January 1961. On that occasion, the Canadian prime minister celebrated Eisenhower's fame by telling a joke about a Canadian high school student who answered that the Canadian governor general's name was "General Eisenhower."[24] One does not expect to hear such public jokes from an ardent Canadian nationalist.

The actual accomplishments of the Diefenbaker government during the period of overlap with the Eisenhower administration were even more important, for these actions show a clear abnegation of the pursuit of political autonomy. It was Diefenbaker who bound Canada into its closest security dependence on the United States: the NORAD agreement. As we saw in Chapter 4, this 1958 agreement integrated the US and Canadian airspace defence commands. It placed Canadian forces in Canada during peacetime under a US commander. The implications of this move as a fundamental denial of sovereignty can be seen by comparing it to the situation in the European Union (EU). Most champions of a united Europe would consider integration of the military commands of its members as the last, most difficult, and therefore most meaningful step. Yet, Diefenbaker approved a partial form of this very step with a haste and informality that suggests a lack of sensitivity to political autonomy. Indeed, Diefenbaker appeared to have initially accepted the opinion of his top military man, General Foulkes, that no formal treaty was even required.[25] It was instead the DEA that raised the issue of a formal treaty to specify the political consultation and control measures. Even then, the treaty could not guarantee prevention of the problems that soon emerged in the Cuban Missile Crisis.

It was Diefenbaker who, in September 1958, suspended the AVRO *Arrow*, a potent symbol of Canadian security independence. It was also Diefenbaker who initiated the Defence Production Sharing Agreement, despite Eisenhower's lack of enthusiasm for the integration of defence procurement. Finally, it was Diefenbaker who, in accord with US nuclear policy, ordered weapon systems with nuclear components, such as the Bomarc B, the missiles for the CF-100s and F-104s, Honest Johns for NATO, and anti-submarine weapons for Canadian and US forces at Argentia, Newfoundland. In short, from 1957 to 1961, Diefenbaker brought Canada into a closer peacetime military dependence on the United States than any previous government.

THE CLASH WITH KENNEDY

Thus, there was little indication in the first years of the Diefenbaker government that a crisis in Canadian-US relations was looming. With Eisenhower in the White House, Diefenbaker seemed ready to play the "faithful ally" more completely than Pearson under St. Laurent would have ever contemplated. However, with the election of the young Democratic president John F. Kennedy (JFK), the tone of relations began to sour. Diefenbaker's dislike for Kennedy began early. Perhaps for ideological reasons or from personal affection for Eisenhower, he had preferred Nixon in the 1960 election, calling JFK an "opportunist" and doubting his leadership abilities. As early as January 18, 1961, Robinson recorded in his diary that the prime minister "has formed an irrational prejudice against Kennedy and Rusk, which could be a serious portent."[26] Numerous small negative, contributing incidents beginning with the Kennedy visit to Ottawa in 1961 can be found in the writing of Knowlton Nash and Lawrence Martin.[27]

Major issues of political autonomy soon arose, and this animosity did not help matters. First, the issue of consultation in the Cuban Missile Crisis showed clearly that the NORAD agreement, which Diefenbaker so hastily entered in 1958, had serious consequences for sovereignty. In October 1962, after discovering photographic evidence of Soviet missiles being constructed in Cuba, the Kennedy administration decided that a naval blockade was the appropriate response to force the Soviets to withdraw the weapons. On October 22, just hours before the American president went on TV with his decision, he informed his NATO allies, in Canada's case by sending a special envoy. This envoy received a cool reception from Diefenbaker because under the NORAD agreement, he expected "consultation" to mean joint decision-making and not merely to be informed beforehand. Indeed, that same evening, the Kennedy administration requested that Diefenbaker put the Canadian Forces involved in NORAD on alert, as the Soviets might respond to the Cuban blockade with a bomber attack. Diefenbaker delayed giving his consent until October 24, when pressed by Defence Minister Douglas Harkness.

Furthermore, Diefenbaker's call for a UN inquiry on the evening of October 22, along with Secretary of State for External Affairs (SSEA) Howard Green's statements in a TV interview two days later, seemed to imply that the Canadian government doubted JFK's version of events. Then, Diefenbaker appeared to reverse his position in the House of Commons on October 25, with a strong statement of support. Unfortunately for Diefenbaker, public opinion supported JKF's stand. After the Soviets' apparent retreat, JFK was the hero, but Diefenbaker "had called attention to his reputation for indecisiveness."[28]

The fact that the Canadian Forces went on an "informal" alert, cooperating with their US counterparts long before the prime minister's official agreement, highlights the reality that Canadian independence was at stake.[29] The Kennedy administration could have cogently argued that given the crisis situation, the demands of secrecy and the shortness of time had not allowed for the kind of consultation Diefenbaker had expected. But this implied that in a crisis, Canada had no effective control over some of its own forces.

This brings us to the second issue of political autonomy from this period: control over nuclear devices in Canada—the Bomarcs and other weapons ordered by Diefenbaker. Though in World War II, Canada had played a role with the United States and Britain in developing the atomic bomb, subsequent Canadian governments made clear that Canada would not develop its own nuclear weapons. Nonetheless, in his weapon procurement decisions and publicly on February 20, 1959, Diefenbaker admitted "the need in present circumstances for nuclear weapons in Canada."[30] A long joint military study on the issue of the custody and control of those nuclear components followed. Custody seemed straightforward: both sides agreed that the nuclear warheads were to be owned by the US. But if brought onto Canadian soil and placed in Canadian weapons, were they now not under Canadian jurisdiction and control? To solve this sovereignty question in Britain, the "dual-key" system was employed, by which both an American and British officer had to jointly "arm" the weapon before its use. Thus, both countries had a veto over the use of nuclear weapons and Britain could ensure that they were not pulled unwittingly into an American nuclear war through use of their own weapons. The question for Canada was whether such a system, involving joint control of the weapons, would interfere with its claim to be a non-nuclear power. In Diefenbaker's mind, the crucial factor was that the weapons not be kept on Canadian soil. Thus he liked the "shuttle" solution by which the nukes were to be kept in the US until a crisis, and then flown in to Canada. Apparently, he felt Canada would then de facto remain non-nuclear, unless a nuclear crisis occurred. The trouble was that US and Canadian military studies showed that a last minute installation of this sort was unworkable.

The third and most obvious political autonomy issue of the period was the Kennedy administration's apparent attempt to change the government of Canada. The case is bolstered by the presence of motive and Kennedy's covert operations elsewhere to influence the succession of governments in South Vietnam and the Congo. Ultimately, the charge can be answered by the question, was the Kennedy government responsible for Diefenbaker's fall, or did he "self-destruct"? The arguments on both sides of this debate are presented in following case study.

Case Study: The Nuclear Weapons Controversy

This first interpretation of the events surrounding Diefenbaker's defeat can be crudely labelled the "Kennedy pushed" conspiracy, after McGeorge Bundy's boast that he and George Ball, two officials in the Kennedy administration, "knocked over the Diefenbaker government by one incautious press release."[31] Advocates of this version claim that a series of events aroused Diefenbaker's consistent Canadian nationalism: often cited are the discovery of a "pushy" confidential memo left behind on Kennedy's visit to Ottawa and Diefenbaker's allegation that Kennedy's failed to consult him sufficiently during the Cuban Missile Crisis of October 1962. Whatever the reason, Diefenbaker stalled in his decision to acquire the nuclear components for the weapons that he had ordered, despite that both his own defence establishment and the Americans wanted him to "honour his promises." When the Liberal Party, lead by Pearson, came out in favour of accepting the nuclear parts on January 12, 1963, the Kennedy administration was given a clear motive to "destabilize" Diefenbaker's government by assisting the Liberals in the 1963 election. According to this line, they did so intentionally and systematically in a number of ways:

1. They bestowed public honour on Pearson and gave him support (for example, they held a private meeting with him at the May 1962 White House banquet to honour past Nobel Prize winners);
2. They released the president's polling expert, Lou Harris, to work on the 1962 and 1963 campaigns for Pearson;
3. General Norstad made a public statement on January 2, 1963, stating that Canada was not fulfilling its pledges to NATO; and most importantly,
4. On January 30, the US State Department issued a strongly worded rebuke of the prime minister's statements in the House of Commons. This is the press release that Bundy claims to have drafted.

Proponents of this conspiracy claim that proof is to be found in its consequence. On February 3, 1963, Defence Minister Harkness resigned from cabinet, followed shortly thereafter by other ministers. On February 5, the government lost a vote of no confidence in the House of Commons, triggering the 1963 election in which Diefenbaker was defeated, despite his attempts "to exploit public indignation about US interference."[32]

The second explanation for his downfall — the argument that Diefenbaker "self-destructed" — focuses on two key events: the appointment of Howard Green as SSEA on June 4, 1959, and the inauguration of John F. Kennedy as US president in January 1961. This version focuses on the personality clashes among three important actors: Diefenbaker, Green, and Kennedy.

The appointment of Green, as Robinson so insightfully concludes, "set in train a course of events quite different from what I think he [Diefenbaker] had envisaged ... [Green's] impact on policy proved in the end to be more than the prime minister himself could control or cope with."[33] Surrounded in cabinet by few close allies and some he still considered rivals for power, Diefenbaker valued Green's friendship and trusted his loyalty.[34] He trusted it enough to grant his SSEA considerable autonomy in determining policy on disarmament and Third World issues at the United Nations, while he himself retained pre-eminence in security and cold war issues. But this very division of interests foretold conflict. Immersed in the political controversy of the UNGA with its growing Third World majority, Green soon adopted disarmament as an area in which he could make a strong impact for himself and for Canada. Thanks to strong advocacy and skilful tactics, he was able to manoeuvre the cabinet into support for more radical positions at the UNGA and to delay further nuclear agreements with the US at home.[35]

Diefenbaker's own reaction to Green's growing disarmament offensive was ambivalent. At one point, he referred to Green's support in Canada as coming from "*Maclean's* magazine and other long hairs."[36] While cynical of the chances of real progress and distrustful of the Soviets, Diefenbaker nonetheless feared opposing what he thought were strong domestic sentiments in favour of disarmament's lofty goals. Indeed, he appears to have appointed Harkness as defence minister in October 1960 from a desire to have a stronger security advocate in cabinet, for he saw that "Green had outplayed the defence minister [Pearkes] in the cabinet and was stimulating public opposition to the acquisition or use of nuclear weapons."[37] With Harkness at the helm, the Department of National Defence (DND) now had a strong pro-nuclear advocate, and a major cabinet crisis was thus made inevitable.

Green's actions had created three strong reasons for Diefenbaker to reject the nuclear components. First, with Canada now so visibly committed to the disarmament and non-proliferation causes, it would have appeared hypocritical to accept such weapons. Second, Green's campaign had mobilized vocal domestic support in groups such as the Voice of Women. Diefenbaker, ever the politician, worried about electoral support, especially after forming a minority government in 1962. Distrusting the relatively new opinion polls, he relied too heavily on letters received from activists on the issue. In fact, an important poll in November 1962 showed that a slight majority favoured accepting the nuclear weapons, but by then too much water had gone under the bridge. Finally, with Green taking a strong stand against the weapons and Harkness a strong stand in favour, the cabinet was stalemated and Diefenbaker faced a decision that would cost him a cabinet resignation and public embarrassment either way.

The role of the United States in the "self-destruct" version of events centres on the bad personal relations that developed between Diefenbaker and JFK. Diefenbaker's barely concealed dislike of the American president clouded his judgment and made agreement with the US unlikely. It also ensured that eventually Kennedy would reciprocate the ill will.

From the US point of view, the Kennedy administration had suffered long provocation before retaliating. Diefenbaker's intentions seem absolutely unfathomable. In private conversation, he seemed personally to favour accepting the weapons, blaming his delays on Green, the DEA, and public opinion at home. The Americans granted him more time, and offered a major concession in the F-101 "swap deal" by which in exchange for purchasing US-made jets, Canada received $200 million in Pentagon procurement and control over 16 Pinetree radar stations. The Pentagon, in good faith, entered long joint investigations of Diefenbaker's shuttle or stand-by option before both military establishments rejected it. Yet, Diefenbaker did not seize obvious opportunities to advance the issue (such as the building of the Berlin Wall in 1961 or the Cuban Missile Crisis in 1962). Instead, he grasped at the weakest straws to delay the decision further with new explanations, some quite harmful to US interests.

The last such straw was on January 24, 1962, when Diefenbaker revealed confidential talks between the British prime minister and Kennedy at Nassau, which he claimed threw NATO's whole nuclear strategy into question. The advocate of consultation made this confused statement without consulting either Britain or the United States, though West Germany and other NATO allies immediately demanded an explanation. Diefenbaker's own finance minister, Donald Fleming, called the speech "without exception the most equivocal,"[38] a nice way of saying Diefenbaker lied. The State Department felt it must refute Diefenbaker's statement for the sake of NATO policy and solidarity. The harsh tone used in its press release enabled Diefenbaker to charge that it was an unwanted intervention in Canadian politics and make it a major campaign issue.

Though Diefenbaker believed in a conspiracy between Pearson and Kennedy to remove him from office, there is just as much evidence of a conspiracy within his own Conservative Party to do the same thing. What specifically caused his removal as leader of the Conservative Party was the Social Credit Party's decision to support a vote of no confidence. Evidence points to a bungled attempt by

Conservative Party members and the Social Credit Party to create a political crisis enabling a change of party leadership. Supporters of the Diefenbaker myth frequently fail to mention the long and bitter fight in the 1960s to remove him from his position.

As this case study shows, personalities played an important role in delaying the government's acceptance of the nuclear warheads. In the last years of the Diefenbaker government, a form of bureaucratic warfare existed between cabinet ministers Harkness and Green, backed by their respective ministries, the DND and DEA. Rather than choose decisively to support one minister and risk having the other very publicly resign, Diefenbaker procrastinated, seizing on one excuse after another for the delay and thus confirming his reputation for indecisiveness. In the end, his delays did not prevent the feared resignation.

Critics of the Statist model may argue that examples of such bureaucratic politics disprove its assumption of the unitary actor. But, the Statist would reply, Diefenbaker's story shows a failure to take the pursuit of clearly articulated national interests seriously. This articulation requires strong leadership, which was lacking in Diefenbaker's case. A strong leader such as FDR or Trudeau could use heated differences of opinion in their cabinet to broaden their options and safeguard against mistakes and "groupthink." A weaker leader such as US president Carter allowed cabinet divisions to confuse his policy. Diefenbaker belongs in this latter category.

In hindsight and informed by the Statist model, we could say Diefenbaker had three clear options to resolve the nuclear weapons controversy, each supportable by vital national interests. Each could have been sold to the Canadian public particularly by reference to analogous models:

1. Canada, like the UK and West Germany, is an active leader in NATO. It therefore accepts the necessity of nuclear weapons in its own and Western Europe's defence. It therefore also accepts the dual-key system as a reasonable compromise with political autonomy concerns. (This was Harkness's position and probably Diefenbaker's original intent.)
2. Canada is like Norway and Denmark. It actively supports NATO, but on principle, and because of political autonomy considerations and long-term security interests, does not accept stationing of nuclear weapons on its soil. (This is Green's apparent intention.)
3. Since Canada gave its word, and commitment is important in international relations, the government accepts nuclear weapons for now but will work for disarmament in the long run. (This is the logical compromise and Liberal policy under Pearson and Trudeau.)

True, there would have been costs to pay with either of the first two, more dramatic options. Option one might have provoked Green to resign, just as option two might have led to Harkness's resignation. The US and NATO would have been upset with option two, but in fact they accepted this position for NATO members Denmark and Norway. In terms of North American defence, the US had already admitted the Bomarcs were obsolete. And probably the Kennedy administration would have preferred an early, decisive option two to a long, delayed option one.

Thus, there is much evidence to support the "Diefenbaker as creator of his own defeat" argument. It would be easier to make the case for Diefenbaker as a national hero if he had adopted a position that contradicted US policy, such as option two above, and had then been driven from office by US machinations. But he never expressed a clear public stand. Instead, in the 1963 election, he attempted to gain sympathy for being unfairly pressured into a hasty decision. This much weaker claim was less supported by the facts and rejected by most Canadians in the election.

In contrast to Bundy's claim that the US brought down Diefenbaker's government, the Kennedy official's press release nearly provided Diefenbaker with the ammunition to get re-elected in spite of all his other failures. Indeed, at Pearson's first meeting with Kennedy just after the 1963 election, the president asked if the press release had had an effect on the election. Pearson replied yes, it had *cost* the Liberals 50 seats. In other words, due to the strength of feeling about political autonomy in Canada, anything perceived as an overt attempt to influence Canadian politics would in fact produce a backlash.

Perhaps critics have spent too much time and energy focusing on the negative events of the nuclear weapons controversy at the expenses of the more important question: what did Diefenbaker contribute to the positive enhancement of Canadian independence? This question will be examined in Chapter 8, with special regard for economic and cultural autonomy. Only then can we fully assess the claim made by Grant and others that Diefenbaker was superior to the Pearson Liberals in developing Canadian independence and nationalism.

POLITICAL CONFLICTS UNDER PEARSON

Given the strong friendship between American president JFK and newly elected prime minister Pearson, along with the Liberals' supposed preference for "quiet diplomacy" and the role of "faithful ally," one might have expected political autonomy concerns to weaken through the rest of the 1960s. In fact, just the opposite occurred, as the Canadian public and the Liberal Party became more sensitized than ever to the issue of US control of the Canadian economy. When the Merchant-Heeney report of 1965 recommended stronger institutional ties with the United States, the widespread critical reaction against it suggested a new strengthening of political autonomy concerns.

In practice, the Pearson government ignored the Merchant-Heeney report and responded with autonomy-enhancing regulations (see Chapter 8) and an unprecedented peacetime build-up of the role of the Canadian state. By strengthening the regulatory powers of the Canadian state and encouraging regional development, Pearson was in effect following a political autonomy strategy of self-strengthening. Similarly, his government's Royal Commission on Bilingualism and Biculturalism and the introduction of the new Maple Leaf Flag can be seen as encouraging a distinctively Canadian sense of identity.

Political autonomy was also reinforced at the highest level in peace and security issues. Pearson struck a compromise on the nuclear issue by honouring the previous government's commitments on specific weapons, but deciding not to acquire new nuclear weapons and in the long run to phase out any nuclear role for Canada. Thus, under Pearson and successive Liberal governments, Canada moved to the "dove" wing of NATO. Vietnam was the issue where Pearson most publicly diverged from US policy.

American involvement in Vietnam was a great watershed in US-Canada relations because it brought about a change in Canadian public attitudes towards the US. As we have seen, disillusionment, disappointment, and distrust of US leadership was not a new sentiment among Canadian elites, especially for Pearson and the DEA. The protracted stalemate and heavy media coverage of the brutality of the war eroded public support for US policy among foreign as well as American publics. For opponents of the war, the decision to begin heavy bombing of Northern military targets in 1965 became symbolic of a "hi-tech" Goliath destroying a poor, Asian David. In the United States, public opposition to the war grew steadily from 1965 to 1968, eventually leading President Lyndon Johnson to announce a bombing halt and to decide not to run for re-election.

In 1963, when Pearson met with Kennedy, he still had some reason to be hopeful about US policy. As with foreign policy liberals in the US, Kennedy was credited with showing restraint in the Cuban Missile Crisis when he chose not to launch a full invasion of Cuba in 1962, against the advice of his military. In the aftermath of that crisis, he negotiated and signed the milestone Nuclear Test Ban Treaty with the Soviets. Many believed he was moving away from the hardline rhetoric of his first years in office, becoming more distrustful of the military establishment and the military option. In his last statements, some have seen a desire to withdraw from South Vietnam after the 1964 US election. But when Kennedy died in November 1963, he was succeeded by Lyndon Johnson, a progressive on the domestic front but a hawk on cold war issues. Indeed, on issues concerning the role of the state in solving social problems, Pearson's and Johnson's agendas had much in common. Even on the Vietnam issue, Pearson had consented to allow a Canadian emissary to carry diplomatic "feelers" to Hanoi.[39] But the summit between the two leaders at Johnson's Texas ranch in January 1965 failed to produce a strong personal bond as witnessed between Diefenbaker and Eisenhower or Pearson and Kennedy. Though the meeting resulted in a political deal on sectoral trade, the Auto Pact, the Canadian delegation left Texas more concerned about US escalation of the war.

Increased US military involvement was quick in coming. After the attack in Pleiku on US advisors in February 1965, Johnson committed US forces to direct combat roles, sending larger and larger numbers of soldiers, and began steady bombing of the North. While Pearson and many in the DEA did not support the collapse of South Vietnam, they saw US military action as a misguided attempt to forestall the inevitable. Initially, Pearson appeared to prefer using "quiet diplomacy" to express these concerns. But at his Temple University speech in Philadelphia of April 1965, he broke publicly with Johnson and suggested a bombing halt to explore again the possibilities for negotiation.

Johnson reacted with rage at a private meeting at Camp David following the speech. After all, the Canadian prime minister had given the White House neither advanced warning nor the text for the speech. As Johnson saw it, the leader of Canada had come to the US and publicly sided with growing domestic opposition to the war.[40] Pearson's action appears all the more extreme for the fact that in 1965, it was well ahead of Canadian public opinion. His own foreign minister, Paul Martin, Sr., threatened to resign over it. On the other hand, Pearson may have felt his action was no different from his public criticism of Dulles's "massive retaliation" doctrine in the 1950s.

Washington's anger did not prevent both Pearson and Martin from calling for a bombing halt again in September 1967, but it lead to a marked decline in US-Canada relations.[41] Canada was excluded from US war councils on Vietnam, but given the eventual failure of the war policy, Canada's action now might appear prescient. More importantly, Canada had established for herself the autonomous position of a more neutral mediator,[42] rather than being merely a "loyal ally." In this regard, Pearson accomplished what former SSEA Green had only suggested.

ENHANCED AUTONOMY UNDER TRUDEAU

Though a new leader assumed command of the Liberal Party in 1968, strained relations with the US over the sovereignty issue continued. Pierre Trudeau was to expand the economic and cultural measures Pearson had begun to repatriate the Canadian economy. Trudeau believed Pearson's "helper-fixer" role had left Canada too subservient to the US.[43] His own focus on national interests was to assure due consideration of sovereignty and political autonomy. Certainly, Trudeau developed no personal relationship with the Republican president Nixon, which might have eased US-Canadian conflicts. These disputes were quick in coming, with the Northwest Passage dispute of 1969 and the 1971 "Nixon shock" surcharges, which included a new tariff against Canadian exports and the ending of any special economic considerations between the two states (see Chapter 8).

Mitchell Sharp, Trudeau's SSEA in Sept 1972, responded with an article entitled "Canada-US relations: Options for the Future," in which he laid out his famous Third Option for debate. He proposed three possible directions for relations with the US: that Canada 1) maintain the status quo; 2) move closer to the US, as suggested by Merchant-Heeney in 1965; or 3) seek to balance US trade with new markets and relations in Europe and Japan. Trudeau chose this Third Option, adopting yet another tactic of maintaining political autonomy: counterbalancing. Trudeau also used the self-strengthening tactic in such regulatory actions as creating the Foreign Investment Review Agency (FIRA) in 1974 and the National Energy Program (NEP) in 1981. Both institutions were to spark intense conflicts in relations during the 1980s.

After the brief interregnum of the Clark government in 1979-80, a nationalistic Liberal Party returned to power just in time to be confronted by a conservative and nationalistic US government under Ronald Reagan. Though relations with the US had improved briefly under the Democratic president Jimmy Carter (1977-80), they deteriorated dramatically, beginning with Reagan's dismissal of an agreement on the fisheries and his challenge to Canada on the FIRA and the NEP. As demonstrated in the next chapter, intense American pressure only resulted in the scrapping of tenuous future plans; FIRA and the NEP were, for the time being, largely preserved. In foreign policy matters, the Trudeau government occasionally obliged the US, as in accepting cruise missile tests in Canada, but was generally skeptical and critical of President Reagan's attempts to renew the cold war and intervene in Grenada and Central America.

The 1984 election victory of Brian Mulroney's Progressive Conservatives (PC) produced a major reversal in relations with the US. Lawrence Martin locates the beginning of the Mulroney-Reagan relationship with the Canadian prime minister's tribute to the US at the 1985 Commonwealth meeting at Nassau.[44] Faced with anti-Americanism in his audience, Mulroney acted much as Diefenbaker had done on his Asian Commonwealth tour — as self-appointed defender of the US. Martin implies that when the US president learned of this defence, it became the basis of a strong personal friendship between the two leaders, cemented at the Shamrock Summit of March 1985.

The Mulroney and Reagan governments shared much common ideological ground. Both favoured a reduction in the role of government, reliance on the market, privatization, and fiscal conservatism. Both shared a higher opinion of the military option and the Soviet threat than their predecessors. The Mulroney government admitted that Trudeau's Third Option had in ten years produced very little, and instead embraced the continentalist option with gusto. The NEP was dismantled, and FIRA's name was changed and its powers were greatly reduced. More importantly, the Mulroney government took Canada into the Free Trade Agreement (FTA) with the US, long an anathema to Canadian nationalists.

In foreign policy, the Mulroney government seemed more aligned with the American president's hawkish views, as demonstrated by its initial proposals to increase Canada's NATO commitment (as discussed in Chapter 4). However, Canadian policy on East-West matters was soon overtaken by the dramatic change in Reagan's relationship with Gorbachev after the introduction of Glasnost in the Soviet Union. Canada's relatively mild reaction to the US intervention in Panama in 1990 is a better example of accommodating the US.

Likewise, Mulroney's active support for the Bush administration's leadership in the Gulf War of 1990-91 led some critics to charge that he had completely acquiesced to US policy. However, in his account of the war, John Kirton argues that Canada made an autonomous decision to participate based on its own independent assessment of the threat Saddam Hussein posed to its allies' oil sources, collective security considerations, and the Iraqi invasion of the Canadian embassy in Kuwait City.[45]

The Mulroney government's change in policy towards the US can be explained in terms of national interest as a reordering of priorities. The PCs felt that security interests deserved more attention than the Trudeau governments gave them. They were more sensitive to charges from NATO allies that Canada was not bearing its share of defence expenditure, and while not as hard line as the Reaganites, they took a less sanguine view of the Soviet Union and Marxists in Central America.

Likewise, the PCs' decisions to reduce state intervention in the market and enter the FTA reflect greater priority for promoting economic prosperity. By the late 1980s, the intellectual trend of state economic advisers around the globe was to favour the "market solution" as the key to economic growth. But in accepting this belief, the PC governments of Brian Mulroney and Kim Campbell were willing to lower the priority given to political autonomy. The PCs were not totally insensitive to infringement on Canadian sovereignty, as seen in the renewed Northwest Passage dispute. But, even here, a vague compromise was accepted as a means to improve US-Canadian relations and not to derail the FTA (see the discussion on territorial waters in Chapter 2).

Canadian support for the FTA itself was tested in the 1988 federal election. In the TV debate just before the voting, Liberal leader John Turner argued that even though the FTA might increase the economic welfare of Canada, the loss of economic autonomy would lead to the loss of political autonomy. While the PCs won re-election, opinion polls showed the nation evenly divided on the free trade issue.

When the Liberals returned to power under Jean Chrétien in 1993, the old Liberal nationalist pattern of greater concern for political autonomy was restored. As Chrétien's quote at the beginning of the chapter shows, he wanted greater independence of policy, and he ended the practice of annual summits with the US president, established under Mulroney. Nonetheless, some agreement with the US might be expected, simply because of the Liberals' ideological similarity to the moderate-liberal Clinton administration elected about the same time. Both leaders called for and got at least minor revisions to boost Mexican labour conditions and environmental laws in the North America Free Trade Agreement (NAFTA), which superseded the FTA in 1994. However, on a visit to Mexico, Chrétien resurrected the rhetoric of counterbalancing by calling for a "united front" on trade conflicts with the US.[46]

Chrétien's interest in foreign policy appeared somewhat limited to creating domestic jobs with Team Canada business promotion missions to various regions of the globe. The initiative for foreign affairs therefore shifted in the 1990s to his foreign ministers. Two of these, Lloyd Axworthy and William Graham, gave high priority to the protection of Canadian political autonomy. Axworthy (minister of foreign affairs from 1996 to 2000) demonstrated how autonomy could be enhanced by projecting a distinctive, coherent set of ideals to the global community, as in his emphasis on human security and his achievement of the Ottawa Treaty to ban land mines. This approach clearly distinguished Canadian policy from American, due to US opposition to the land mine treaty and to Canadian support for the new International Criminal Court. A major weakness of Axworthy's strategy, as pointed out by his Liberal successor, John Manley, was the failure of the government to back these lofty internationalist ideals with hard cash.

Manley's refocus on traditional security matters and continentalism fit well with the events of the 9/11 terrorist attacks on the US. He led the prime minister in expressions of sympathy and solidarity with the US and quickly enlisted Canada in the NATO-supported war in Afghanistan against the Taliban and al Qaeda. Canadian troops were placed under US commanders, raising the issue of independence, but this was soon offset by Canada's refusal to join the US and UK in the campaign against Iraq in 2003. This operation to unseat Saddam Hussein dramatically demonstrated a clear distinction between the US and Canada on an important issue. Minister of Foreign Affairs Graham Bill (2002 to 2003) justified this distancing from US policy in a 2003 speech at the Couchiching conference:

> [W]e've seen a distinctive Canadian stand not just on Iraq but also on the Kyoto Accord, the international landmines convention, the preservation of our medicare system, and other areas where Canadians' views on social policy diverge from those prevailing in the United States — areas such as family benefits, maternity leave, gun control, and political campaign financing. In fact, we are going our way; and it is a distinctly Canadian way.[47]

In 2005, Prime Minister Paul Martin and his foreign minister, Pierre Pettigrew (known for taking on the Americans over the softwood lumber dispute), faced two major autonomy questions in the post-9/11 issues of border security and the future of NORAD (see Chapter 4). These issues also show the trade-offs among national interests, with increased security clashing with autonomy. For example, a proposed solution for border security and fast processing of people and goods would be to standardize customs and immigration procedures between the two countries, even to the extent of creating a common customs clearance on arrival in North America. But such a solution implies greater regulatory and perhaps organizational integration and begs the question of whether standardization means adopting the US model.

CONCLUSION

During the cold war, there was a strong belief that Soviet leaders instigated minor crises to test new US presidents. Supposedly, presidents who responded firmly could expect less conflict from the USSR in the following years, having demonstrated their "resolve." Perhaps new Canadian leaders should likewise be expected to respond resolutely to the first incident of American encroachment to prove the importance of political autonomy to Canada. Stephen Harper's quick retort to US claims in the Arctic within days of becoming prime minister serves as an example.

Such a demonstration would have the additional benefit of keeping political autonomy on the public agenda. Unfortunately, political autonomy can all too easily be taken for granted. Like deterrence, it is difficult to prove when it is operating. Only a clash and successful defiance on Canada's part can show its presence. But conflicts must be chosen carefully with a mind to Canada's other interests. After all, too much attention to political autonomy can leave any state isolated and without allies (e.g., North Korea).

Shared interests between states are less likely to provoke attempts at coercion than divergent interests. Thus, challenges to Canadian political autonomy tended to be greater when there was an ideological disharmony between Washington and Ottawa. For example, during the Trudeau years, more occasions of direct US pressure on Canada occurred when the Republicans were in the White House than during Carter's term. By this logic, Liberal-Democratic or Conservative-Republican match-ups should provide more harmonious relations: Diefenbaker-Eisenhower and Mulroney-Reagan/Bush fit this pattern, while Pearson-Johnson doesn't. By the same logic, the largest conflicts occurred during the following match-ups: St. Laurent/Pearson-Eisenhower, Diefenbaker-Kennedy, Trudeau-Nixon, and Trudeau-Reagan. But a clash of interests *does* provide the Canadian prime minister with an opportunity to demonstrate resolve.

Similarly, harmonious relations do not ensure the preservation of political autonomy, as the Mulroney-Reagan partnership demonstrates. Under Mulroney, the FTA was signed, which posed a double jeopardy to Canada. Not only did it tend to integrate the smaller Canadian economy into the US, but with its implicit reliance on markets, it forced some diminution of Canadian state regulatory powers. From the standpoint of political autonomy, North American free trade or even a hemispheric bloc is preferable to the FTA in that it allows counterbalancing manoeuvres, as Prime Minister Chrétien's rhetoric suggested. Indeed, if the bloc is expanded wide enough, it begins to turn into the preferred Liberal trade policy of general "global" liberalization. This solution provides the economic growth advantages of free trade without increasing bilateral dependence on the US market.

With the greater economic integration since the FTA, one can also see the need for compensation on the political side. The Canadian state, now more than ever, should maintain a vigilant watch over political autonomy. Under a self-strengthening strategy, the state could make compensating moves in areas of jurisdiction not constrained by the FTA, such as culture and education. Also, the recent displays of Canadian political independence on Iraq and Kyoto, as well as in numerous other areas cited above by Bill Graham, demonstrate to the world that Canada is not just a protectorate of the US.

Notes

1. Morton (1981), p. 32.
2. Szulc (1994), p. 4-5.
3. Under St. Laurent, SSEA Pearson raised the issue; under Diefenbaker, SSEA Sidney Smith. See English (1993) and Robinson (1989).
4. This American penchant for unilateralism, while regrettable, should not be surprising. It is the long, historical habit of US policy (no entangling alliances, isolationism), as well as the path of least resistance (less time, less resources, less compromising).
5. English (1993), p. 30.
6. As quoted in English (1993), p. 29.
7. *Ibid.*, p. 408.
8. *Ibid.*, p. 59.
9. *Ibid.*, p. 62.
10. *Ibid.*, p. 86-87.
11. Holmes (1982), p. 200-01.
12. For two different versions of Canada's role see Douglas Ross (1984) and Eayrs (1983).

13. See Molotov's questioning in English (1993), p. 96.

14. Holmes (1982), p. 342.

15. English (1993), p. 156.

16. Grant (1965), p. 8-9.

17. *Ibid.*, p. 4.

18. Martin (1993), p. 34.

19. Robinson (1989), p. 48-49.

20. UNGA Fifteenth Session, Plenary Meetings, p. 109.

21. English (1993), p. 308.

22. Robinson (1989), p. 80.

23. *Ibid.*, p. 51.

24. *Ibid.*, p. 167.

25. *Ibid.*, p. 20.

26. *Ibid.*, p. 168.

27. Nash (1990) and Martin (1982).

28. Robinson (1989), p. 294.

29. Harkness claims to have given this "unauthorized" order, though action may have begun in the forces themselves even before. Robinson (1989) suggests that Diefenbaker in fact knew about the informal alert, preferring to handle it that way.

30. House of Commons (Debates, 20 Feb. 1959, p. 1221-24).

31. As quoted in Martin (1993), p. 35. However, even from the large quote given there, it is not clear that Bundy or Ball had the intention of overthrowing Diefenbaker, that they foresaw the consequences of their action. Nor is it proof that the press release itself caused the government to collapse.

32. Robinson (1989), p. 309.

33. *Ibid.*, p. 97.

34. *Ibid.*, p. 93.

35. See for example Robinson (1989), p. 114, where Green sat on DND proposals.

36. Robinson (1989), p. 160.

37. *Ibid.*, p. 158.

38. Quoted in Robinson (1989), p. 305.

39. These were the Seaborn missions of 1964, which returned the message that North Vietnam was not interested in negotiation at that time.

40. Some accounts have Johnson saying in undiplomatic language "You don't come here and piss on my rug!" as reported in English (1993), p. 364.

41. However, as critics have pointed out, Canadian business continued to benefit from US war procurement under the Defence Production Sharing Agreement.

42. As seen in both sides in Vietnam accepting Canadian peacekeepers in 1973.

43. English (1993), p. 385.

44. Martin (1993), p. 5.

45. Munton and Kirton (1992).

46. Sallot (1994), A1.

47. Goold (2004), p. 934.

Chapter Eight
Defending Economic and Cultural Autonomy

In the last two chapters, we saw how the Canadian state has maintained itself as an independent political actor. This chapter demonstrates how the regulation of economic and cultural vulnerability also plays a role in the political autonomy of a state. In the short run, economic dependence could be used intentionally by another state to threaten or coerce a concession from Canada, particularly where the relationship is asymmetrical. In the long run, some nationalists have argued, economic and cultural dependency could imperil the autonomy of the Canadian state by weakening the people's sense of their distinctive national identity. This could occur as a gradual erosion of uniquely Canadian values and perceptions. Both threats will be examined here, along with the measures past governments have taken to forestall them. Such measures are frequently labelled as acts of Canadian economic or cultural nationalism.

ECONOMIC DEPENDENCE: TRADE

Both the realist school and radical critique of international relations have developed rich literatures on the subject of asymmetric economic dependency. Radical and Marxist approaches usually reject the methods of mainstream economic theory, and thus rely on alternative economic theories and methodologies (such as the labour theory of value). On the other hand, while objecting to some of the conclusions of efficiency economics as politically naïve, the realist, or neo-mercantilist, approach is willing to accept mainstream liberal economic methods. Nonetheless, they demand that power relations or bargaining asymmetries be included in the analysis. This chapter takes seriously the neo-mercantilist line of argument that dependence can arise through trade, foreign investment, or debt.

Chapter 10 will take an in depth look at Canada's trade policy, examining it as a vehicle for promoting Canadian economic growth and prosperity. When it comes to trade and foreign investment, autonomy as a national interest is often incompatible with that of prosperity. What leads to maximum economic growth may weaken long-term autonomy, and vice versa. In this chapter, we examine only the autonomy aspects of trade policy.

The impact of trade on autonomy can be briefly summarized. Trade dependence, with its attendant threat of coercion, arises in three ways. First, the economy of a given state may be dependent on imports of strategic raw materials such as oil or steel; energy, food, or other imports may be necessary for the direct maintenance of the population or the smooth functioning of the economy. Where such goods are turned into weapons, the state's security interests may also be dependent. Autonomy interests can be affected if the threat of embargo is used to reduce the state's freedom to act, as in the oil embargo of 1973 when Arab oil producers succeeded in shifting some oil dependent states away from their pro-Israeli policies. Japan is often cited as a state especially sensitive to raw material dependence.

Second, a state may be dependent on foreign sources for essential manufactured goods, also leaving it vulnerable to the threat of embargo. In time of war, the most obvious case is a state that must rely on weapons imports because it has no domestic arms industry. It is precisely this fear that led states such as apartheid South Africa and Israel to develop their own arms industries. More generally, the import of manufactured goods, from machine tools to consumer products and advanced technology, represents a source of potential vulnerability. In the eighteenth and nineteenth centuries, mercantilists such as the American Alexander Hamilton and the German Friedrich List argued for the promotion of domestic industry to advance autonomy as well as prosperity.

As a state that exchanges raw materials for manufactured goods, this form of trade dependence is relevant to Canada. Many authors have expressed concern that without state intervention, Canada would become (or stay) a humble "drawer of water and hewer of wood." Indeed, John A. Macdonald's national policy of 1879 introduced protectionism for manufactured goods to ensure a Canadian industrial base. Historically, Canadian trade policy has tended to favour high tariffs, even if this meant higher prices on consumer goods. As the old adage put it, the price of Canadian independence was a higher cost of living than in the neighbouring US.

Figure 8.1 Canadian Exports to the UK and the US as a Percentage of Total Exports

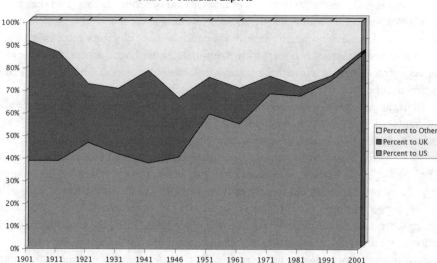

A third source of trade dependence develops when a state relies too heavily on one market for its exports. The vulnerability of selling to only one customer is particularly extreme if exports also represent a large share of overall production within the economy. Trade sanctions can be aimed at exports as easily as imports. Canada is very much subject to this form of dependency. Figure 8.1 shows Canada's exports to its two main trade partners as a per cent of its total exports. The graph demonstrates how, over the twentieth century, its main export market shifted from Great Britain to become extremely concentrated on the United States. The fact that about a third of all the goods produced in Canada are for sale outside the country highlights this dependence. Policies designed to reduce this dependency on the US have included Diefenbaker's largely rhetorical 15 per cent trade diversion toward Britain and Trudeau's Third Option.

ECONOMIC DEPENDENCE: FOREIGN INVESTMENT

Ironically, foreign investment as a form of economic dependence is often the result of a high tariff policy: foreign firms set up manufacturing plants inside a country to avoid paying those duties. For example, if an American exporter of appliances with a large share of the Canadian market is suddenly faced with a high tariff, it may decide to "leap the tariff wall" and start an appliance factory in Canada to protect its sales in the that market. While this practice does result in the creation of an industrial base in Canada, it raises concerns about high levels of foreign ownership in specific industries and the effects of the repatriation of profits from those subsidiary companies to their parent company.

Foreign capital played a crucial role in the development of Canada. In the nineteenth century, British capital, mainly in the form of loans, bonds, and portfolio investment, built the railroads and much of the infrastructure for the Canadian economy. After World War II, such large projects as the development of Labrador's iron ore mines were financed by US capital. Why didn't Canadian capitalists supply the needed capital so that Canada could avoid foreign dependence? Initially, Canadian capital was simply not adequate to the huge demand. Furthermore, as suggested by historian Blair Fraser among others, Canadian capitalists are risk-avoiders compared to Americans, and without US capital, many post-World War II projects would not have been undertaken by the private sector.

The twentieth century has seen the growth of foreign direct investment (FDI), in addition to portfolio investment. Both forms involve a financial cost, whether in the form of dividends on stocks and bonds or repatriated profits (in the case of FDI). But the latter also entails the issue of foreign ownership and control: the fear that decisions important to the future of the Canadian economy are being made by non-Canadians.

As stated in Chapter 6, this fear must be evaluated first in light of the concentration of decision-making. In the last century, it was possible for one large multinational corporation (MNC) to dominate the local economy of a small country, as the United Fruit Company did in some Central American nations. But such instances are relatively few now, and certainly in Canada, it is impossible to point to one MNC as dominating the Canadian economy. The decision-making units are diffused and independent (even competitive) rather than concentrated, though the amount of concentration varies a great deal from industry to industry.

However, one very important source of concentrated power exists in the form of the foreign investors' home governments. This situation arises in the perennial attempts by United States government to exercise jurisdiction over the Canadian affiliates of American firms. The practice is referred to as extraterritoriality, since a foreign state is attempting to exercise the authority of its laws within the jurisdiction of Canada. Usually, we expect a company incorporated in Canada to obey only Canadian laws. But, if the firm is 100 per cent owned by an American company, does it also have a duty to respect US laws? This becomes an issue when the laws of the two states disagree, as they did under during the cold war when the US passed laws limiting trading with Communist states. On numerous occasions, disputes arouse when the US government attempted to apply those rules to Canadian companies controlled by US firms, most recently in respect to Cuba, one of the few remaining Communist countries.

The huge inflow of US investments after World War II initially raised public concern over the issue of FDI in Canada. This wave, which peaked in Canada in the early 1960s, paralleled a general outward flow of US FDI around the world in the post-war years. Much of it took the form of branch plants set up in Canada not just to serve the Canadian market but also to export to other states inside the Commonwealth Bloc, thanks to Imperial Preference (see Chapter 10). In fact, US firms came to Canada for many reasons. Canada was the easiest foreign market for US business due to the common language with the English-speaking majority, and similar culture and business practices. Geographic proximity made a Canadian branch the first experience at foreign operation for many US businesses.

Whatever the reasons, public awareness of US investment slowly caught up with the phenomenon in the 1960s with a series of popular books, including Andrew Lamorie, *How They Sold Our Canada* (1964); Walter Gordon (a Liberal government member), *A Choice for Canada* (1966); Kari Levitt, *Silent Surrender* (1970); and John Redekop, *The Star Spangled Beaver* (1971). These titles themselves suggest loss of autonomy, takeover, and annexation by the US economy. Public opinion surveys on US FDI in Canada show that public concern for this issue peaked around the mid-1970s.

Various federal governments have tackled the problem but disagreed about tactics to use and how far to go in applying them. Most governments have acknowledged benefits from allowing at least some FDI. The question has been how to maximize those benefits while minimizing the negative aspects. Nearly all states engage in some form of regulation of FDI, but the wealthier high average income states (HAIS) and lower average income states (LAIS) tend to employ different laws to different degrees (see Glossary). HAIS states tend to use "national treatment" in their regulations, which means they do not discriminate between foreign and domestic firms in their laws. Extensive business regulations do exist, protecting workers through labour and safety laws, and protecting consumers through food and drug testing, product labelling, safety standards, and the like. Furthermore, HAISs protect overall state interests through laws governing the environment, competition, and fair-trading. A strong state with developed and relatively uncorrupted enforcement agencies can rely on such laws to ensure MNCs behave as "good corporate citizens."

Such conditions are not always found in the smaller LAISs. There is generally a lack of efficient bureaucratic structures for regulation and enforcement, and corruption is often a problem. Smaller size, economic and technological weakness, and past history all contribute to a greater sensitivity to foreign domination. As a result, laws often specifically discriminate in a nationalist or neo-mercantilist manner against foreign firms.

One common strategy for such dependent states has been to close certain important sectors of the economy to FDI. The oil and energy industries are often seen as key to economic development and therefore are commonly restricted. Countries that have long relied on raw material exports have put mining and agriculture off limits to foreigners. Some countries have, at times, banned or restricted foreign ownership of land, as in Mexico and China.

Many states have created foreign investment review agencies. At a minimum, such bodies merely monitor investment and collect data to analyze its impact on the overall economy. States that are more interventionist may require prior approval for all proposed FDI projects. Such agencies may then establish a list of qualifying criteria for projects.

States in which large-scale foreign ownership already exists may take more direct action to reduce foreign ownership. In the 1970s, this often meant complete nationalization of foreign assets in oil and primary industries. Some states demanded a minimum percentage of local ownership, and other states insisted that foreign investors form joint ventures with local businesses. Laws in Malaysia required MNCs to train local people to assume management positions after a specified time interval.

Finally, many governments attempt to regulate the outflow of capital and repatriate profits by controlling access to foreign exchange. Foreign exchange is controlled by the central bank, and permission may be required to change locally earned monies into foreign currencies.[1]

HAISs with strong economies tend to rely on market forces to produce economic growth and criticize the use of discriminatory state practices. LAISs argue that their disadvantaged position requires special support for their "infant industries" and that they can't be expected to compete immediately with the big MNCs of the HAISs. The HAISs and the International Monetary Fund (IMF) counter-argue that such protected infants grow into distorted, inefficient businesses that can never compete and hamper growth of the local economy. Nonetheless, it is often difficult to determine how much an HAISs complaint is based on sound economic theory, how much on an ideological commitment to markets, and how much on the desire to protect its own national MNCs and investments.

Some political economists feel that Canada is economically in between the HAIS and LAIS economies. Like the HAISs, Canada enjoys a high standard of living and a technologically advanced economy. But like the LAISs, Canada primarily exports raw materials, fears that its manufacturers cannot stand up to international competition, and worries about foreign capital and control. It should not be surprising, therefore, to see that Canadian policy has had elements of both strategies of regulation.

INVESTMENT REGULATIONS UNDER ST. LAURENT AND DIEFENBAKER

C.D. Howe's pursuit of Canadian growth required capital investment and seemed indifferent as to whether that capital was foreign or domestic. It is likely that without US FDI, some projects, such as the development of iron ore deposits in Labrador, would have occurred later or not at all.[2] Nonetheless, it was in these years that the issue of foreign control of capital was first raised in a major way. In January 1957, Walter Gordon released the preliminary report of the Royal Commission on Canada's Economic Prospects, which identified the growing level of US FDI as a matter of concern. In the final report issued in 1958, he recommended a goal of limiting FDI to 75 per cent and the appointment of more Canadians to executive positions in foreign-owned firms. However, by that time, Diefenbaker was prime minister, and he chose to ignore these recommendations.

Diefenbaker's main forays into international economic policy occurred on the areas of trade and energy. With trade, his main preoccupation was to maintain special access to the British market through the system of Imperial Preference. Despite his hasty retreat from his unrealistic proposal to divert 15 per cent of Canadian trade to Britain, he fought hard against British membership in the European Common Market (today's EU), seeing it as the end of many Canadian exports to Britain. He also used the argument that Canada would be forced into the American economic orbit as a result. However, the British government had decided that joining Europe was in its long-term economic interests. The more Diefenbaker complained, the more he soured relations with the UK and lessened the possibility of counterbalancing relations. Kennedy's GATT initiative to reduce tariffs generally drew his suspicion as a further attack on Imperial Preference.

But it should be remembered that before Kennedy came to office, Diefenbaker had actively pursued continental integration. Certainly, this was one effect of his Defence Production Sharing Agreement. Furthermore, he accepted the use of the Canadian exemption. This doctrine holds that due to a "special relationship" between the US and Canada, Ottawa could expect to be exempt from harsh measures taken by the US government against other foreign states. For example, in 1959, when Eisenhower created barriers against foreign imports of oil and a variety of minerals, Diefenbaker asked for and got an exemption for Canadian products. But exemptionism is clearly a continentalist doctrine and not what one would expect from a Canadian nationalist.

On energy policy, Diefenbaker was influenced by his minister Alvin Hamilton, who was motivated by national and specifically Western Canadian interests, and wanted protection for the West's growing oil industry. In pursuit of a national energy market and a stable exchange rate,[3] the government created the National Energy Board in 1959 to regulate oil exports. The national oil policy in 1961 restricted oil imports to east of the Ottawa River, thus reserving the Ontario market for the Western oil producers. (Unlike today, Canada was not yet self-sufficient in oil production.) In 1960, Hamilton created regulations guaranteeing that Arctic licenses for oil and gas production would only be granted to Canadian companies.

But, despite the fact that FDI peaked in these years, Diefenbaker did virtually nothing on the issue. In fact, with the Canadian dollar crisis of May and June 1962, he was eager for FDI as a short-term solution for Canada's balance of payments problems.

PEARSON AND THE FIRST ATTEMPTS TO REPATRIATE THE CANADIAN ECONOMY

Ironically, despite Pearson's 1963 election platform promising a more continentalist approach, his government was later characterized as the first to make "any substantial effort to repatriate the Canadian economy."[4] But, the growth in nationalist outlook coincided with the state's growing intervention in the economy and the rise of welfare issues in general. Under Pearson, the Canadian state became identified as a nationalist, social-welfare state.

Much of this change can be initially credited to Pearson's finance minister, the same Walter Gordon of the Gordon Report of 1958. In a nationalist vein, the first Gordon budget of June 1963 proposed the following: a 30 per cent tax on foreign takeovers of Canadian firms; a change in the tax on dividends, which would discriminate against foreign firms; and a general policy of distinguishing between debt capital and equity capital (FDI) to encourage the first and discourage the latter. Such a budget would have meant a broad repudiation of a market-oriented policy. While the Kennedy administration was restrained in its reaction, the Canadian business community howled in protest. So great was the reaction from that quarter that the budget was withdrawn and resubmitted a month later in a much watered-down form.

This temporary retreat from nationalist measures was confirmed in another act of exemptionism in July of 1963. The Kennedy administration, worried that the huge outflow of US capital was damaging investment at home, introduced an interest equalization tax that would have reduced foreigners' access to the US money markets for financing their debt. Through Pearson's good relations with Kennedy and "quiet diplomacy," a partial exemption for Canada was negotiated.

Though Johnson had replaced Kennedy by the time the Auto Pact was signed in January of 1965, that agreement represented an integration of the North American car and auto parts industries. However, the pact represented a political deal rather than a free trade agreement, since it specifically guaranteed Canada a share of North American auto production.

Nonetheless, by the end of 1965, Pearson had greatly expanded the role of the Canadian state. As part of this new social-welfare orientation, the Liberals had established the Canada Pension Plan, the Economic Council of Canada, youth allowances, student loans, job-training programs, a program of national medical care, and increased regional development funds.

Despite this incredible record of domestic achievement, the Liberals failed to win a majority government in the election of 1965. Walter Gordon, who had organized the campaign, took responsibility and resigned from cabinet. In May 1966, his book *A Choice for Canada* was published and became a rallying point for young, nationalist Liberals. Finally, in January 1967, Pearson brought him back into cabinet as a minister without portfolio and agreed to two of Gordon's nationalist objectives.

The first objective was an amendment to the Canadian Bank Act in 1967. In 1963, Citibank of New York City had purchased control of the Mercantile Bank in Montreal. Though a Dutch bank owned it at the time of purchase, Gordon, finance minister at the time, raised the issue of foreign control and proposed a 25 per cent ceiling for Canadian banks. In 1966, the US (under Johnson) protested and the matter was shelved. Now, in 1967, Gordon demanded action, despite US opposition, and the 25 per cent cap was passed (though Citibank was later given an extra eight months to comply). It is ironic that Gordon chose to fight over banking, since it was one of the least foreign-owned sectors and Canadian banks tend to be as big or even bigger than their US rivals. Nonetheless, other states have considered banking a strategic sector, as seen in President Lopez Portillo's decision in the early 1980s to nationalize all foreign banks in Mexico.

Gordon's second objective was to take another look at the overall FDI situation. As a result, in January 1967, he instigated the establishment of the Watkins Task Force to update the 1958 Gordon Report. The Watkins Report of February 1968 became an important platform for the nationalists. It proposed a foreign investment review agency, as well as an agency to watch US attempts to extend extraterritorial control over its Canadian branches, and a strong Canadian development agency.

Thus, despite wavering and false starts, the Pearson record is one of great achievement for the Canadian state. Yet, he seems to get scant credit for the state-building done under his watch from either the Diefenbaker loyalists or Trudeau nationalists that followed.

TRUDEAU AND THE NATIONALIST PEAK

The Trudeau government inherited the foreign investment issue and set about exploring further regulations. The 1970 Wahn Report of the House of Commons Standing Committee on External Affairs and National Defence (SCEAND) recommended a goal of increasing Canadian ownership to 51 per cent. The 1972 Gray Report echoed the Watkins Report, calling for a screening agency for foreign investment. In 1971, the Watkins' recommendation for a Canadian development corporation was implemented to facilitate direct government involvement in capital investment in Canada. Using a mix of private and public means, capital could be directed to projects viewed as essential for Canadian economic growth. The Canada Development Corporation (CDC) was also used to buy out some foreign companies in Canada, and by 1979 it owned mines and chemical firms.

The souring relations provoked by the *Manhattan* voyage and Northwest Passage dispute in 1969 also increased the probability of action against US FDI. The final catalyst came with the Nixon shocks of 1971. In that year, the US experienced its first trade deficit of the twentieth century; due to the declining competitiveness of its own manufactured goods, it now imported much more than it exported. American industry was taking a beating from foreign imports, and, in conjunction with its continuing balance of payments problems, the US dollar was under attack from speculators who believed it had lost value. The Nixon administration responded by trying to stem the flood of imports with a 10 per cent surcharge or tariff on imported goods and an end to the convertibility of the US dollar to gold.

As the US was Canada's most important market for exports, the surcharge was having a major negative impact on the Canadian economy. When the Trudeau government requested the standard Canadian exemption from the Nixon surcharge, it was told that the tariff was specifically aimed at nations like Canada and that the days of exemptionism were over. President Nixon seemed to formalize this position when, on his April 1972 trip to Ottawa, he said, "Mature partners must have autonomous, independent policies."[5] The Third Option was the Canadian response (discussed in Chapter 7), changing the focus of Canadian trade policy towards seeking new markets and lowering dependence on the US market.

In 1972 also, by one account, foreign ownership in Canada peaked, and public hostility to it peaked the following year.[6] A Canadian public opinion poll of that year indicated 55 per cent thought US FDI was "a bad thing."[7] Table 8.1 shows the results of a *Toronto Star* poll conducted in 1972 in which respondents were asked to give reasons why they liked or disliked US FDI. Notice that while most of the reasons in favour were economic (employment, investment, growth), only one economic reason was cited on the negative side ("profits leave Canada"). In the general public's view, most of the negative reasons had to do with guarding Canada's independence or political autonomy.

Table 8.1 Survey of Public Attitudes on US Foreign Direct Investment

Why US FDI Is Good

Creates employment	45%
Need outside investment for growth	21%
Canadian business too cautious	13%
Expands economy/higher incomes	13%
Better products/exports	2%

Why US FDI Is Bad

US taking us over	35%
Profits leave Canada	29%
Canada should be independent	12%
Canadians should invest here	8%
Discrimination/not fair	4%
Tends to Americanize us	4%

Source: A poll reported in the *Toronto Star,* 30 December 1972.

Thus, in 1974, a most important step was taken to protect Canada's political and economic autonomy: the creation of the Foreign Investment Review Agency (FIRA), another Watkins Report proposal. Initially, FIRA was established to review proposed foreign takeovers of Canadian firms or assets, but in 1975, its jurisdiction was extended to include FDI used to create new businesses as well. FIRA gave the Canadian state two new capabilities. First, it provided the state, the academic community, and the public with information about what was happening with foreign investment. By requiring these investments and takeovers to be registered, it monitored who was investing in specific Canadian industries, information considered by some businesses as confidential. Second, and more important, it gave the Canadian state the potential to say no to particular investments seen as harmful to the public good. The Canadian state was claiming the right under its normal regulatory powers to limit the play of market forces. Indeed, the Trudeau government's action implied the market was not always allocating investment in the Canadian public's best interests. Instead, the state was going to make decisions on foreign investment proposals by a set of clear guidelines reflecting the public interest. Table 8.2 lists the criteria used by FIRA to judge whether a proposal merited approval.

Table 8.2 FIRA's Criteria for FDI

FDI in Canada should
1. Increase employment
2. Represent a new investment
3. Increase resource processing or use of Canadian parts and services
4. Lead to additional exports
5. Involve participation of Canadian shareholders, directors, or managers
6. Improve productivity and efficiency
7. Enhance technology
8. Improve product variety
9. Have a beneficial impact on competition
10. Be compatibility with industrial and economic policy

Some critics claimed that FIRA did not reject enough FDI proposals. Such critics often seemed to believe that any FDI was harmful to Canada, or perhaps they looked only at the political autonomy side of the equation. But, FIRA was in fact attempting to maximize the benefits of two potentially contradictory interests: economic prosperity and political autonomy. Its challenge was to find a level of FDI that gave the country the highest "bundle" of both growth and independence. Such explicitly rational behaviour by the Canadian government deserves to be repeated more often.

FIRA provoked no significant response from the United States until the arrival of the Reagan revolution in 1981. Committed to free markets, the Reagan administration viewed the recently restored and more nationalist Trudeau government of 1980 as an ideological challenge. Complaints about FIRA from the American quarter may have scrubbed plans to strengthen FIRA, and in November 1982, the Trudeau government made the modest concession of raising the minimum size of investments to be reviewed from 100 to 200 employees. The United States also launched a challenge of FIRA with the GATT. In January 1984, the GATT determined that the Canadian state had the right to require that new investments lead to greater exports from Canada but upheld the United States' contention that requiring local sourcing (buying locally) was unfair. The Canadian minister for trade, Gerald Regan, agreed to make the necessary changes for the sourcing criterion.

Overall, the Trudeau government appears to have had some success in repatriating the Canadian economy. As Table 8.3 demonstrates, foreign ownership as a percentage of assets dropped in most industries between 1971 and the mid-1980s. The Wahn Report's target of achieving 51 per cent Canadian control was reached overall for the manufacturing industries, rising from 41 to 56 per cent, though individual industries such as tobacco, rubber, transport equipment, chemicals, and petroleum and coal remained dominated by foreign companies. Overall, for all non-financial industries, the foreign share dropped from 37 per cent in 1971 to 24 per cent in 1986, and the US share from 27 per cent in 1971 to 17 per cent in 1986.[8]

Table 8.3 Percentage of Foreign-controlled Assets by Industry

Year	1971 (%)	1986 (%)	1999 (%)	2003 (%)
Manufacturing	59	44	47	51
Oil and gas	99	53	44	49
Mining	69	31	25	35
Total for all industries	37	24	25	29

Source: Data calculated from various Statistics Canada Corporate Returns Acts.

Economists disagree about how much credit should go to FIRA for this decline. Some argue that the UK's entry into the European Community (now the EU) in 1973 was a more important factor, as it removed the incentive for countries to invest in Canada as an export platform to the UK. After 1973, US investments tended to go directly to the UK to take advantage of duty-free access to the whole European Community. Some nationalists argue that FIRA was too permissive to have had any impact on FDI levels. Conservatives argued, on the other hand, that the very existence of FIRA and government red tape inhibited many foreign investors from making proposals.[9] But, for political autonomy, some FIRA regulation was better than no FIRA at all. Chapter 10 investigates the trade-off between political autonomy and growth in greater detail.

REPATRIATING THE OIL INDUSTRY

As discussed at the beginning of this chapter, dependent states often single out energy or oil as a particularly strategic domestic industry worthy of special protection. For Canada, the 1973 Arab oil embargo (to protest Western support of Israel), which quadrupled the price of imported oil, brought home the importance of this commodity. Canadian consumers immediately felt the pinch of higher gasoline and heating oil prices, and businesses worried that the higher cost of energy would make their goods uncompetitive. The long-term effect was an increase in the inflation rate. Much of the resulting ire was focused on those members of the Organization of the Petroleum Exporting Countries (OPEC) who participated directly in the oil cartel and were obviously reaping windfall profits, though many argued that the large oil MNCs were also collecting their share of the windfall "take."

The Trudeau government reacted by establishing Petro-Canada as a Crown Corporation, or state-owned, oil company in 1975. Responding in part to public concerns about excess profits, the Canadian state's action can be viewed as a strategic move to open a window on the oil industry to allow the state its own source of information on reserves, markets, and profits for a commodity so important to the national economy. Despite the fact that Western Canada was an oil producer, Eastern Canada relied on foreign imports of oil. Petro-Canada was seen as the rallying point to begin a repatriation of that industry and to secure Canada's future supply. Furthermore, Canada was copying the actions of other oil-producing countries in forming its own national oil company to lessen reliance on the major oil MNCs.

The second round of oil cartel price increases in 1979 prompted the newly re-elected and more nationalist Trudeau government to launch the National Energy Program (NEP) in October 1980. With this second increase in oil prices, the question of equity and "windfall" profits also returned. In Canada, the conflicting interests between the Western producers and Eastern consumers of oil at the new high price threatened to tear the country apart. The Trudeau government's solution, the NEP, left oil-producing Alberta greatly alienated.

Rather than allowing Canadian-produced gas and oil prices to rise to the new "market price,"[10] the NEP created a controlled price system to keep the prices lower and to protect Canadian consumers and Canadian manufacturing exporters. The NEP also aimed to make Canada energy self-sufficiency by 1990 and thus free of future "oil shocks," through conservation, encouragement of alternatives, and an export tax on natural gas. Even at the NEP's controlled price, Alberta stood to make oil profits. The federal government adjusted its provincial revenue sharing to give Ottawa a share of those profits.

The NEP also set a target of 50 per cent Canadian ownership in the oil industry by 1990. The discriminatory Petroleum Incentives Program (PIP) took direct action towards this goal. The Trudeau government argued it had the right to show favouritism to Canadian owners when it came to exploring and producing on lands that the government owned. To lease such Crown lands under the PIP, a business must be 50 per cent Canadian owned and the Federal government reserved the right to acquire a 25 per cent interest of its own. Under another provision, the PIP could be applied to existing leases as well.

The NEP and the PIP provoked immediate and ongoing hostility from Western provinces, the oil industry generally, and the Reagan administration. Westerners argued they were entitled to the world price for oil, and if they reaped higher returns, it was only fair compensation for past under-pricing of their resource in exchange for Ontario manufactured goods.

For ideological reasons, the Reagan administration already objected to FIRA, and likewise it opposed taking the pricing of oil away from market forces. More important was the possibility that cheaper energy costs for Canadian exporters to the US could lead to an unfair trading advantages. Similarly, the GATT principle of "national treatment" or non-discrimination against foreign firms was violated by the PIP and the nationalization of the oil industry implied in the NEP. Furthermore, the American public's sense of fair play was aggravated at that time by a Canadian buying spree of American companies. Seagram of Montreal led this charge with highly public takeover bids for St. Joe Minerals and later the Conoco oil company. An asymmetry in governmental rules for raising money to finance takeovers, which favoured the Canadian businesses, further fostered a sense in the US that it was time to retaliate.

During its first year in office, the Reagan administration raised demands that Ottawa make concessions on the NEP, the PIP, and FIRA. In Finance Minister Allan MacEachern's November 1981 budget, Canada agreed to no new NEP or Canadianization programs for other industries, and no strengthening of FIRA's rules. Demands for more concrete concessions in the following month provoked a "furious" refusal from Ottawa,[11] leading the Americans to abandon their bilateral pressure tactics in 1982.

Meanwhile, a steady Canadianization of the oil industry was underway. As Table 8.4 shows, through 1981 and 1982, Petro-Canada, the government's CDC, and other Canadian actors were buying up foreign companies in Canada's oil fields and the service station market. Ironically, in 1981, Allan MacEachern expressed concern about the huge outflow of foreign investment capital and its deleterious effects on our balance of payments, but overall Canadian ownership in the oil industry rose from almost nothing (6.7 per cent) to a third (34.7 per cent).

Table 8.4 A Chronology of Increasing Canadian Ownership of Oil Industry in the 1980s

Early 1981
- Dome Canada created to get federal grants for Beaufort Sea exploration

February 1981
- Petro-Canada acquired Petrofina (Belgium) for $1.46 billion

May 1981
- NuWest Group (Calgary) acquired 7.2% of Cities Service (a US oil company)

June 1981
- Canadian Development Corporation acquired Elf Aquitanine, a French oil company, for $1.6 billion
- Dome Petro buys Conoco's stake in Hudson's Bay Oil & Gas
- Husky and Drummond Petrol (Calgary) acquired Allied Canadian operations

July 1981

- Hudson's Bay acquired Cyprus Anvil Mining (Vancouver) from Amoco, after FIRA prevented its sale to Standard of Indiana (US)
- Husky acquired most Canadian assets of Shell Explorer

October 1981

- Ontario Energy Corporation (provincially owned) acquired 25% of Suncor (US)

1982

- Petro-Canada acquired some refining and distributing assets of British Petroleum (UK) for $347.6 million

1985

- Reichman Brothers acquired Gulf Canada (US) and sold off some assets to Petro-Canada and some to Ultramar (UK)

By 1984, the NEP and FIRA represented the high point in Canadian policy toward economic autonomy: no government before or after Trudeau did as much to create regulatory tools to repatriate and protect the Canadian economy from foreign ownership. In fact, as stated earlier, US FDI had already peaked and foreign control of Canadian assets declined in the decade after 1974 as did public interest in the issue. The Trudeau government had also tried the Third Option, an honest but ultimately unsuccessful attempt to diversify Canadian export markets. But all of this was to change dramatically with the 1984 Conservative election victory.

THE MULRONEY REVOLUTION

In the fall of 1984, the Progressive Conservative Party swept the Liberals from power. The new Mulroney administration shared many ideological affinities with the conservative Reagan and Thatcher governments of Canada's most important allies. That shared neo-conservatism included a faith in the marketplace as the main locomotive for economic growth and prosperity. Given also the apparent decline in public support for state intervention, Mulroney's PCs concluded it was time for a change in priorities and a "downsizing" of state control through privatization, deregulation, and free trade.

The dismantling of the NEP began in November 1984 when Finance Minister Michael Wilson announced the removal of oil price controls within Canada. Luckily for Canadian consumers, the OPEC cartel was in disarray and the world oil price had tumbled to nearly the domestic Canadian price. On April 25, 1985, Energy Minister Patricia Carney finished off the job by removing the equalizing tax and the PIP, so despised in Western Canada.

For similar reasons, the FIRA also came under attack. Many in the Conservative Party and Canadian business community blamed FIRA for lower levels of FDI in Canada during the early 1980s. Since high value was placed on foreign investment to create jobs and growth in Canada, they believed that FIRA must be downsized to decrease the obstacles to potential foreign investors. Consequently, in December 1984, Industry Minister Sinclair Stevens changed the name of FIRA to Investment Canada and announced a series of reforms. From that point, only very large investments and acquisitions valued over $5 million were to be reviewed, estimated to be only 10 per cent of what was reviewed previously by FIRA. Furthermore, the criteria were changed so that investments in question needed to provide only a "net benefit" to Canada rather than a "significant benefit." To trumpet these changes to the investor community, the Canadian government took out ads in *The Economist* and *The Wall Street Journal* proclaiming, "Canada is open for business."

Finally, and probably most importantly, the Mulroney government concluded a free trade agreement with the US (FTA and NAFTA, discussed in greater detail in Chapter 10). The primary ideological assumption behind this move was that removing trade barriers would create greater export opportunities, leading to increased economic prosperity. The benefits of a trade agreement would include protecting Canadian access to the US market, lowering the cost of imported goods to consumers and manufacturers, and forcing Canadian businesses to become more efficient and thus more competitive in world markets. But many Canadian workers believed that "lowering costs" meant using foreign competition to force down the price of labour and break up trade unions. Other critics claimed that such justifications of free trade concealed a larger ideological goal of using international pressure to shrink the government. By committing itself to international free trade agreements, the Mulroney government knowingly invited foreign challenges to all sorts of state programs, incentives, and subsidies (such as the marketing boards) as unfair trade practices — or so this critique claimed.

Finally, the Mulroney government may well have calculated that the fundamental nature of the commitments made in these international agreements made their repeal by any succeeding government almost impossible. Though either the FTA or NAFTA may be terminated with prior notice, such a move by Canada would certainly produce a strong protectionist backlash in the US Congress. By making trade issues more salient, the Mulroney government left the additional legacy that an attempted return to the status quo would entail very high political and economic costs.

Despite the Conservative government's apparent abandonment of nationalist economic policies, informal Canadianization of the oil industry continued through the 1980s. In 1985, the Reichman brothers acquired Gulf Canada, selling off some of its assets to Petro-Canada. This brought the Canadian share of the industry to 46 per cent and close to the Liberal goal of 50 per cent by 1990. The move to privatize Petro-Canada was slowed by its poor showing in the first offering of public stock shares.

Ironically, with the signing of the FTA, public concern over the "foreign control" aspect of foreign investment dropped to a new low. Indeed, if the critics of the FTA are correct in that it will cause a massive closure of US branch plants, we may judge it as the most effective policy yet for reducing American ownership of the Canadian economy. The impact of substituting trade for investment will be examined in Chapter 10.

PROTECTING CANADIAN CULTURAL AUTONOMY

Much has been written debating the nature of Canadian culture, the threat posed to it by our dominant southern neighbour, and the correct policy response. Our discussion here cannot do justice to this wide literature and instead will focus on a few key issues and summarize some major past state policy initiatives. More questions will be raised than answered in this brief overview.

The most immediate concern is that Canadian culture is threatened with "Americanization." But in analyzing this general sentiment, we soon run into a series of open-ended and perhaps unanswerable questions. What is culture? Is it a specific country-and-western song, or singer, or style? Or is it a broad set of values that unite a community? Given either definition, many questions arise: is there a single distinctive Canadian culture or are there different subcultures? Is the difference between English Canada's culture and the American culture greater than the difference between English Canada's and Quebec's? Is the difference between a Canadian jazz musician and an American jazz musician greater than the difference between Canadian jazz and Canadian classical music? And how can a "community of communities" or a cultural mosaic have a distinctive culture anyway?

Consider just one art form: music. If someone says they have a career in music, we immediately ask what type of music—classical, pop, jazz, rap, Celtic—the possibilities seem endless. We might also ask if they are a composer or performer in that particular genre. The question of Canadian culture then would suggest there is a distinctive Canadian version of all the above. But is there?

In many of the arts, a further historical distinction exists between "high culture" and mass or pop culture. To use the example of music again, it may be hard to see how Canada is threatened by an American "high culture." There is an old joke about the three historic influences on Canada. Through our linkages to Great Britain, France, and the United States, we could have had the best of each country: British politics, French culture, and American efficiency. Instead we got the worst of each: British efficiency, French politics, and American culture. This joke suggests the very idea of American "high culture" is an oxymoron. Indeed, one recent American critic suggested that no American (or Canadian) composer ranks among the top-ten greatest classical composers (who are mainly European)—an attitude probably shared by most North American concert-goers.

Democracy places a high value on freedom of expression. Can a democratic state select or impose one style or vision of culture without being charged with censorship? In Canada, there are rules mandating Canadian content. But what if Canadians prefer watching American programs? Technological advances are making the cost of regulating our porous boundaries ever higher.

Content rules also seem to imply the need to regulate programs for the values they may instil. For example, it has been suggested that Canadians need protection from more violent American TV programming. But years of investigation by social scientists and media experts show that the question of value transmission through the media is a very complex one. How sure do we need to be before we censor the broadcasts?

One way to simplify these quandaries is to reduce the problem to economics. We can distinguish between the content of a culture and its production within a cultural industry. In practice, the Canadian state has preferred to use this method of supporting Canadian culture: Canadian culture is what Canadian citizens working full-time in a defined cultural industry produce. As such, the traditional methods of economic protectionism — tariffs and subsidies — can be used to support it. This definition also gets the government off the hook for passing judgment on the output: is it really Canadian or not?

As much as any industry, the arts and entertainment sector has been greatly influenced by technological developments. The past century has brought us new forms of communication, such as radio, cinema, television, videos, cable, and the Internet. The state seems always to be two steps behind in its attempts to regulate the new technologies. Yet, persistent attempts bespeak an underlying national interest in cultural promotion and preservation.

Going back to the 1930s, it was the Conservative Richard Bennett government that created the Canadian Broadcasting Corporation (CBC) to allow state control over the new radio broadcasting technology. After World War II, the Liberal St. Laurent government created the Canada Council to support the arts in Canada with public funds. This government also dealt for the first time with the issue of Canadian editions of *Time* and *Newsweek*. Both of these large US weekly news magazines had decided to begin publishing editions with slightly more Canadian stories, but more significantly, with large amounts of Canadian advertising. *Maclean's* and other Canadian magazines argued that this practice was unfair competition since most of the costs of producing a given issue were already covered in their large run for the American market. The lower costs of producing the Canadian editions meant that the big US publishers could offer Canadian advertising space much cheaper than publishers of indigenous Canadian magazines. All news publishers rely heavily on advertising fees to cover their costs of production. The fear was that the big US publishers would soak up most of the limited advertising dollars from Canadian businesses and force *Maclean's* and other Canadian publishers out of business.

Canadian publishers were in effect asking for trade protection, the same way any Canadian business threatened by competition from large American firms with special cost advantages might. Their special plea for protection was enhanced due to the issue of foreign control of news reporting. Many in Canada were concerned that the collapse of Canadian current affairs journals would result in the loss of a Canadian perspective on events and an indirect subversion of mass Canadian culture. The St. Laurent government responded with a form of tariff protection, placing a discriminatory tax on these Canadianized editions.

Given Diefenbaker's alleged nationalist perspective, one might have expected him to offer a strong cultural autonomy policy and support for the CBC. Instead, the Conservatives encouraged the creation of a private Canadian TV network to challenge what they perceived as the "liberal" bias of the CBC. More surprisingly, his government removed the tax on Canadian editions of US magazines. However, it did establish the O'Leary Commission in 1960 to examine the issue. Its report showed that the Canadian editions of

Time and *Newsweek* had captured 40 per cent of all Canadian magazine advertising funds. It recommended removing tax deduction for advertising in Canadian magazines from these Canadianized editions. This policy would have greatly reduced the incentive for Canadian businesses to advertise in these editions, but Diefenbaker ignored the recommendation.

It was left to the Liberal Pearson government to implement the O'Leary Commission proposal on eliminating tax deductions. But the US government protested vigorously and were granted exemptions for the big two: *Time* and *Newsweek*. Nonetheless, Pearson greatly hindered further penetration of the market by other Canadian editions of US magazines. With the creation of the Canadian Film Development Corporation in 1967, Pearson also began government support for the film industry.

The Trudeau government completed the O'Leary proposal by passing Bill C-58 in 1976, which removed the exemption for the big two. The bill also defined what consti-tuted a "Canadian" magazine: the publisher must be 75 per cent Canadian owned and the publication noticeably different in content from its foreign parent. Only publications meeting these criteria could provide tax breaks to their advertisers. The Ford administra-tion protested this bill as discriminatory and therefore a violation of international rules on "national treatment." Nonetheless, Bill C-58 soon spelled the demise of the Canadian edition of *Time*, though another major American magazine managed to qualify under the new rules. *Reader's Digest Canadian Edition* created a Canadian charity foundation with Canadian directors to hold 75 per cent of the stock of the local affiliate. Furthermore, it assured the Canadian government that material brought in from the US would be edited in Canada and that more Canadian books and articles would be used.

The idea of regulating Canadian content was also applied to broadcasting. Radio and TV were seen as crucial both as news sources for the Canadian citizenry and as formula-tors of mass culture. As early as 1961, the CBC announced its own initiative to try to devote 45 per cent of its air time to Canadian content, though much British and American material qualified under its very general guidelines. The CBC raised this quota to 55 per cent a year later.

By 1968, the growth of private TV broadcasters prompted the Liberals to create the Canadian Radio-Television Commission (CRTC) to regulate the airwaves. In 1971, this new government agency introduced Canadian radio and television content rules. Thirty per cent of all music played on Canadian radio (public and private) must be Canadian in its composition, performance, or production. This rule mainly affected economics: since production alone qualified, many American businesses simply recorded more records in Canadian studios. TV faced similar rules of 60 per cent (later reduced to 50 per cent) Canadian programming in prime time (6 p.m. to midnight) to prevent the programmers from relegating the Canadian shows to off hours. According to the CRTC's website, these basic content rules have persisted (as of 2005): at least 60 per cent Canadian con-tent overall and 50 per cent during prime time. The CBC has shown an even higher com-mitment to Canadian broadcasting: in 1995, it announced plans to phase out all US programs between 7 and 11 p.m.[12]

Two major challenges to these content rules immediately appeared in the form of cable TV and cross-border broadcasts. The latter raised the advertising revenue issue again. Canadian businesses near the US border found they could reach many Canadians who were watching American TV stations. Of course, if most businesses in Windsor can advertise on Detroit stations, it's going to detract revenue from Windsor's broadcasters. Ottawa cannot compel Windsor viewers to stop watching the Detroit channels (and thus also circumventing the content rules), but it can and did staunch the outflow of advertising funds by again using the O'Leary proposal in its 1976 Income Tax Act. Canadians advertising on American stations lost a tax exemption and thus had less incentive to go south of the border. American station owners lobbied the US Congress to retaliate against the tax discrimination on their Canadian advertisers. Congress briefly responded by removing tax deductions for American associations and businesses holding conferences in Canada, an action that potentially could have cost Canada hundreds of millions of dollars.[13]

THE CHALLENGE OF TECHNOLOGICAL ADVANCES

The rise of cable TV, video and DVD rentals, and various incarnations of satellite TV demonstrates the inevitable battle between obsolescing state regulation and technological advance. Through cable and satellite, we are offered a cornucopia of new stations and specialty channels. In addition, a Canadian equivalent direct-to-home (DTH) satellite service has become available. To enforce Canadian content policies on both cable and DTH services, the CRTC has relied on very specific instructions about which channels may be offered. For example, the CRTC informed Country Music Television (US) that as of January 1, 1995, and by prior agreement, its place on Canadian cable would be taken by the newly formed New Country Network (Calgary). American cable channels protested and demanded retaliation, but eventually a private deal was made between the two country music channels.[14]

In June of 2005, the CRTC established rules for Canadian satellite radio subscription services and licensed three Canadian pay-radio companies. Nationalists were upset by the low requirement for Canadian content: each service must offer a minimum of eight domestic channels and can add nine foreign channels for each Canadian one. However, the CRTC's rules must be realistic, given the availability of US services and the difficulties of enforcing a ban on such subscriptions. Unlike satellite TV, which requires a large and very visible "dish," the new satellite radio receivers are pocket-sized and possibly will be commonly used in future car radios. Some Canadian artists celebrated the rulings, hopeful that they would now have greater access both to Canadian and American audiences.[15]

For a while in the 1990s, the absence of a viable supply of Canadian channels to support Canadian content regulations caused a delay in the expansion of satellite TV and radio broadcasting in Canada. Indeed, the economic problems of supply and consumer choice have posed ongoing dilemmas for Canadian content policy. Without the huge market and economies of scale that the United States has, Canadian broadcasters have had to scramble to find enough Canadian songs and programs. This inadequate supply has been exacerbated by the steady drain of Canadian artists and actors to larger American centres, such as New York City and Hollywood. To increase supply, the CBC has encouraged domestic artists and producers through its broadcast fund and generous tax incentives. But critics have called the results "American clone programming," with Canadian versions of popular American TV shows. Nor can regulations force the public to watch the mandated Canadian content. Despite millions of dollars in government subsidies and tax breaks to both the Canadian TV and film industries, studies consistently show few Canadians are watching. Leaving aside news and sports, Canadian-made content is only 7.5 per cent of the average Canadian's prime-time TV viewing and 3 per cent of cinema viewing. According to a *Globe and Mail* special feature on cultural nationalism, "most Canadians can't name a TV drama made here." As this same report puts it, "the end results of 30 years of nationalist policies are disquieting."[16]

In 1993, the magazine advertising issue resurged with the appearance of a Canadian edition of *Sports Illustrated*. Though printed in Canada and, like the *Reader's Digest Canadian Edition*, qualifying as a Canadian magazine, the Canadian content this time was minimal.[17] The Liberal government responded with a tough new excise tax of 80 per cent on advertising revenues for this type of split run magazine. American businesses protested this blatant violation of the free trade principle of national treatment.[18] But, both the FTA and NAFTA give Canada the right to discriminate in favour of its own cultural industries. Of course, under the same agreements, the US claims the right to retaliate.

In 1995, *Sports Illustrated* gave up on its Canadian edition, but the US government did not give up, and in 1996, took the case to the World Trade Organization (WTO). It ruled against Canada on all counts, including the excise tax and a postal subsidy the government had been giving only to Canadian magazines. Initially, the Liberal government threatened tough new laws banning Canadian advertising from spilt runs altogether, but when the US threatened legal action and trade retaliation, the Liberals realized they must compromise. The deal reached in May 1999 featured the following: 1) a compromise allowing only partial tax deductions for Canadian ads in split runs and all foreign produced magazines; 2) US acceptance of Canadian government magazine industry subsidies through the Canadian Magazine Fund; 3) Canadian removal of a 25 per cent limit on foreign ownership; and 4) for the first time, an implied acceptance that culture was a special industry which could receive special treatment.[19] The Canadian government has since relied primarily on postal subsidies (of $49 million in 2005) through its Publications Assistance Program to protect Canadian magazines.

Shocked by its failure at the WTO, the Liberal government decided to try its old tactic of multilateralism to build a coalition of "like-minded" governments interested in creating a new international regime for cultural protection, just as it had contributed to the new principles of the Law of the Sea in 1970s (see Chapter 2). This new regime would attempt to establish the right of states to support and preserve local cultures and was linked to Canada's domestic policy of multiculturalism. This goal was initially pursued at a 1998 meeting in Sweden of culture ministers from the United Nations Educational, Scientific, and Cultural Organization (UNESCO, the UN's main culture intergovernmental organization). Two months later, Canada's minister for heritage, Sheila Copps, followed up with an invitation for 20 "like-minded" culture ministers (including France, Sweden, Greece, and South Africa, but not the US) to come to Ottawa and establish the International Network on Culture Policy (INCP). Furthermore, Canada offered space and staff to the network within its own Department of Canadian Heritage. The Canadian Conference of the Arts (CCA) helped found and house a parallel NGO to support the INCP.

In 1999, armed with these new institutions, Ottawa changed the focus of its trade policy from seeking cultural exemptions to negotiating "a new international instrument: a legally binding treaty, convention, or protocol that would allow countries to pursue their own cultural policies without facing the threat of retaliation from trading partners."[20] Also, Ottawa proclaimed it would not accept any new international trade deals involving culture before the above instrument was created, thus threatening to hold up the current Doha round of the WTO negotiations to reduce trade barriers. The INCP accepted this Canadian proposal in 2001 and by the following year had a rough draft stating in general terms the principle of government intervention and support for culture. Among the issues the INCP had to resolve were the following: 1) dispute settlement, 2) the home institution for the policy (either UNESCO, potentially ineffective, or WTO, potentially unsympathetic), 3) a clear definition of culture and acceptable policy instruments for governments to adopt, and 4) lack of support from the US. In October 2005, Canada and France succeeded in getting an endorsement of the cultural protection principle at UNESCO, despite US objections.

CONCLUSIONS: BUSINESS AND CULTURE

The issue of US ownership of Canadian businesses has virtually disappeared in the first decade of the twenty-first century. The degree of US control over Canadian non-financial industries has trended steadily downward since its peak in the late 1960s. By the end of 2002, Canadians held more in foreign investments (worth $432 billion CAD) than foreigners did in Canada ($349 billion CAD). Indeed, Canadian business leaders were more likely to complain that Canada was not getting its fair share of FDI compared to other Western economies. Investment Canada is still required to review large foreign investments, though few are refused now. But significant regulations on certain industries, including telecommunications, airlines, banking, and insurance, remain as a legacy of the 1960s and 1970s. Most of the attention now is focused on the various cultural ownership controls and regulations (e.g., publishing, broadcasting, and filmmaking) overseen by the Department of Canadian Heritage and other governmental regulators.

American businesses can be expected to continue to complain to their government that Canada is using unfair economic protectionism to shelter Canadian jobs in a variety of media, news, and arts and entertainment industries. Culture was exempted from the terms of the FTA and NAFTA by Conservative governments, but the strong Liberal reactions show that cultural autonomy continues to be viewed as an important Canadian national interest. And Canada is not alone in the world on this issue.

But what is the best route to implement a policy to protect cultural autonomy? Is economic protectionism enough, or should we do more to ensure specifically "Canadian" content? One great danger of such an approach would be to adopt an "inverse American" culture in which Canadians try to be the opposite of whatever Americans are perceived to be. If Americans are individualists, Canadians should be collectivists, and so on. Ironically, such a cultural definition would be just as dependent on the US, though in a negative way. Attempts to enforce any definition of a single Canadian culture would also face charges of indoctrination and censorship.

An alternative defence of Canadian culture (without defining its content) might lie in language policy. Certainly the long attempts to create an integrated Europe have shown how different languages can at least slow assimilation where a large population base exists. Indeed, Quebec's language laws are premised on preserving the language as a defence against absorption. Israel's adoption of Hebrew shows the use of a "new" language to foster a new national identity. And, in Canada, such an alternative is already at hand. If English Canadians could all become bilingual, it would be a simple matter to simply drop the use of English at some future time. Such a solution would probably ameliorate the national unity problems discussed in the following chapter. And it would add a clear linguistic difference between Canada and the US, since most Americans are more likely to learn Spanish, if they learn any second language at all.

Perhaps a more realistic alternative is suggested in our previous analysis of autonomy strategies. Most of Canada's cultural regulations represent efforts at self-strengthening. But counterbalancing is also an option. Instead of blocking specifically American channels, why not balance them with other foreign channels? Most Canadian cable operators now carry TV5 from France, but why not more British and French channels? In fact, Britain offers four additional English channels, and more can be found from our Commonwealth partners Australia, South Africa, and India, among others. Surely, such a solution is also more consistent with Canada's stated policy of multiculturalism. Indeed, some of the more likely scenarios presented in Table 8.5 suggest we are inevitably headed to such a multicultural future.

Table 8.5 Four Alternative Futures for Canadian Culture

1. **US Cultural Imperialism**
   This alternative assumes there is one monolithic US hegemony of mass culture and values (e.g., individualist, violent, racist, conservative) which threatens to absorb Canada, either through intentional cultural domination by US leaders or passively by existing structures (e.g., size, proximity, higher technology, as a by-product of free trade).

2. **North American Mosaic**
   The North American Mosaic disputes that there is one hegemonic US culture. Instead, the US and Canada are both cultural mosaics with significant subcultures

(in US, South versus North, Black and Hispanic ...) and increasingly fragmented lifestyles (professional, New Age, born again, etc.).

3. **Technological Imperative**

What is often mislabelled a "US cultural hegemony" is in fact the result of adopting a certain level of technology. Mass culture is embedded in the technology: with the automobile comes "drive-in" and "strip mall" society. Multimedia brings the triumph of the picture over the word. If we want the current highest standard of technology (US, German, Japanese), we are also going to get certain cultural values.

4. **Global Culture**

This refers to what Anthony Smith calls a pastiche of postmodern motifs, out of context and self-parodying. Technological advance (see above) and global diffusion produces a mass consumer fusion of styles. See World Beat music as example.

Table 8.5 can also serve as the basis for a discussion of what is happening to Canadian culture today. The most feared option of absorption by US cultural imperialism is only one of four possible interpretations. Consider, for example, what is happening in terms of popular musical styles. Which of the scenarios looks most plausible from that perspective?

Our investigation of autonomy policy has shown that it is persistent across the political, economic, and cultural issues, and across governments. It is time to stop glorifying Diefenbaker as a single nationalist champion of mythic proportions. At a minimum, we must conclude that he did no more than previous governments in guarding this national interest. Even the Mulroney government persisted in demanding an exemption for culture in the FTA and NAFTA. Though greatly scaled back, the tools the Liberals created for screening and monitoring FDI are still in place and could be strengthened again if need be. As Thomson reminded us back in Chapter 1, temporarily scaling back state control does not imply a loss of sovereignty by the state in the long term. Indeed, the Conservatives will claim they are no less nationalist but that they believe privatization and free trade will benefit Canada over time by creating greater wealth, prosperity, and competitiveness. Such claims about tactics are a matter for our national interest debate and will be examined again in Chapter 10.

Notes

1. For example, an American company operating a plant and sales office in Canada will be earning profits in Canadian dollars. If it wants to return those profits to the US for use there, it will want to exchange those Canadian dollars into US dollars at a Canadian bank. In theory, the Canadian government could do as many LAIS governments do and pass foreign currency controls regulating the amounts of US dollars and other currencies available, and thus control the outflow of such profits.

2. Fraser (1967), p. 69.

3. The Canadian dollar was weak through much of Diefenbaker's tenure, due in part to trade imbalances.

4. Mahant and Mount (1984), p. 206.

5. Quoted in Martin (1993), p. 24. Ironically, Martin refers to it as a "Declaration of Independence," despite that the larger party (US) made the declaration. Perhaps it is better called a notice of divorce.

6. Gwyn (1986), p. 79.

7. Mahant and Mount (1984), p. 225.

8. Burgess (2000), p. 104. By 1995, US control had dropped to only 11 per cent.

9. See, for example, *The Chronicle-Herald* (1982), p. 5.

10. The appropriateness of the term *market price* can be questioned, given the existence of the OPEC cartel. If the world price of oil is seen as a "cartel" or "windfall profit" price, then the issue is whether Alberta should be an informal member and reap the same profits, which come in part from Eastern Canadian consumers.

11. See Clarkson (1985), p. 42-49.

12. Harris (1995), A1.

13. The measure was removed not by Canadian concessions but by lobbying from US travel agents.

14. Fagan and McKenna (1995), A1.

15. Tuck (2005), B1.

16. *The Globe and Mail* (1998), C16.

17. Ross and Fagan (1994), A1. Also, the magazine made use of new telecommunications technology to wire its text directly from its NYC home office to its printer in Ontario. Thus, it got around existing Canadian controls on shipping magazines across the border.

18. *Ibid.*, A1.

19. Azzi and Feick (2003), p. 106, 107.

20. *Ibid.*, p. 109.

Chapter Nine
Preserving National Unity

The last three chapters traced the history of Canada's efforts to gain autonomy—political, cultural, and economic—and to maintain it. But autonomy from external forces is of little value if internal divisions are destroying the state. Civil war and domestic strife can leave a state vulnerable to foreign intervention and meddling. For these and other reasons, all states worry about preserving their internal cohesion. In the modern world, differences of religion and ethnicity have been powerful centrifugal forces in destabilizing large states from within. Witness the problems of India, with its divisions between Hindu, Muslim, and Sikh; the demand for autonomy by Chechnya and various Russian republics; and the disintegration of Yugoslavia and Somalia.

For Canada, the main historical challenge has been containing the ethnic division between the French and English communities. While it is true that as a largely immigrant nation, Canada has many different cultures, on the basis of language, size, and history, the schism between francophone Quebec and the anglophone majority in the rest of the country remains the most important. This chapter will examine this conflict, including the present likelihood of Quebec separation. While the domestic evolution of the conflict is briefly outlined, the role of third parties and external events in shaping the problem will be examined in more detail.

The Statist approach assumes that secession from the state by any of its subunits is a negative action. It lays aside the issues of self-determination and the democratic processes for shaping sovereignty. From the state's perspective, a number of costs or "disutilities" are expected to follow any secession of territory. Dividing the territory necessarily implies reduced resources and population for the seceding units. This reduction of the state leads to a decline in prestige and influence, and a diminished capability for international affairs. Secession rarely occurs without conflict and strife, which can mean losing lives and resources at home, as well as the possibility of third party intervention and loss of autonomy. Finally, the resulting states may well compete with each other economically and politically, thus heightening the prospect for regional conflict.

HISTORY OF THE TWO SOLITUDES

Canada's present dualism arose from the Seven Years' War of 1756-63, which ended in defeat for France and the English conquest of its North American possessions. For the English, the question then was how to administer a colony of alien Europeans. The perceived weakness of France and the remoteness of any French attempt to retake Canada made deportation and dispersion — as the British had done in the Acadian expulsion of 1755 — unnecessary. After several years of failed attempts at assimilation, Britain adopted a conciliatory approach in the Quebec Act of 1774, which established the basic pattern of Quebec governance for the coming century. In return for loyalty to English rule, the French colony was granted considerable cultural autonomy in retaining traditional laws, schools, and language, and in preserving of the power of the Catholic Church and traditional elites. This policy succeeded in that the attempts by the American colonies to recruit Quebec in their revolt of 1776 failed. In the long term, the policy preserved the largely rural, Church-dominated society, with the thin English business class controlling commerce in Montreal.

The arrival of thousands of English loyalists in Upper Canada, the growth of British immigration to all parts of British North America, and the Union of Canada all failed to diminish Quebec's linguistic and cultural differences. Though Quebec joined Confederation (1867) as a part of the colony of Canada, it was granted its own status as a province equal to the other founding members of New Brunswick and Nova Scotia. Furthermore, the legislature of the colony of Canada, made up of elected representatives of both Upper Canada (Ontario) and Lower Canada (Quebec), debated and passed resolutions on Confederation in the 1864-65 Confederation debates. Some interpret the fact that a majority of the French Canadian representatives from Quebec voted for Confederation as consent for joining Canada. There is nothing in the text of the British North America Act of 1867 that explicitly gives the province of Quebec special treatment or veto powers compared to the other provinces. Nonetheless, a popular corporatist idea developed in Quebec — the compact theory of Confederation — that perceived Canada as founded by two primary nations, English and French. The theory implies that the consent of each is required to make constitutional change and is the source of the idea that Quebec has an historic veto.

The revival of imperialism in the late nineteenth century highlighted a clear difference of loyalties between the two parties. Whereas most English Canadians, particularly in urban strongholds such as Toronto, favoured strong imperial connections with the mother country, French Canadians, who felt no similar bond to France at the time, favoured greater autonomy. The Conservative Party and Liberal Party differed on this issue in part due to the latter's strong political base in the province of Quebec. While Laurier accepted British sovereignty, he nonetheless defined it in a limited manner, as witness his famous remark, "*Que devons nous à l'Angleterre?*" ("What do we owe England?"). Indeed, at the time, some French Canadians in their demands for greater independence and autonomy for the whole country appeared to be the strongest proponents of what we now would call Canadian nationalism.

During World War I, this issue of divided loyalties came to a head in the Conscription Crisis of 1917. Borden's ruling Conservatives, long the party of the "imperial tie," justified the need to introduce conscription because of the crisis in manpower in the trenches of Europe and the failure of voluntary recruiting in Canada. Nonetheless, the victory of

Borden's Union government, fought in national elections on a platform of conscription and the passage of the Canadian Military Service Act of 1917, divided the country on French/-English lines. Finally, when many exemptions to military service were cancelled in 1918, the streets of Quebec City erupted in riots, leading to military occupation and five deaths.

While many English imperialists saw sedition in their French countrymen's behaviour, two important factors must be considered. First, the imposition of conscription has always been a controversial step for a democracy; in fact, Australia twice voted it down in 1916 and 1917. Forced service and the loss of individual liberty (and the potential for loss of life itself), heightens the contrast between liberal democratic individualism and national interests. Should an individual be forced to face death in a conflict that he or she does not support? Second, an urban versus rural divide exists in the support for conscription. In part to meet the increased wartime demand for agricultural products, Canadian farms were working overtime, and farm families were opposed to losing the labour of their sons to overseas service. Even in English Ontario, Borden's Conservatives faced rough treatment in rural ridings in the 1917 campaign. Quebec as a largely rural society would also oppose conscription.

Ultimately, what matters is that both communities defined the crisis symbolically as a French/English confrontation. Thus, a war that served the function of nation-building for Australia only polarized Canada along ethnic lines. The political division of Canada was most keenly felt by the Liberal Party, which literally split in two during the crisis. Mackenzie King learned the appropriate lesson, and as leader of the party in World War II, followed an extremely cautious path in introducing conscription ("Conscription if necessary but not necessarily conscription"). Later, the Liberal Party furthered symbolic harmony by adopting a practice of alternating its leadership (and thus frequently the prime-ministership) between anglophones (King, Pearson, Turner, and Martin) and francophones (Laurier, St. Laurent, Trudeau, and Chrétien).

The next major period of turmoil began in the 1960s with the Quiet Revolution. Politically, this change was symbolized by the replacement of Maurice Duplessis's rural-based government with the reformist Liberal government of Jean Lesage. Two long-term structural changes had drastically altered the outlook of French Canada. First, the long post-war boom of the 1950s and 1960s had spilled over into Quebec, eroding the traditional rural, agricultural society and bringing modernization, secularization, urbanization, and economic growth. Growing awareness of economic change made the English minority's domination of the Quebec economy a public issue. Thus, the Lesage government backed the nationalization of Hydro-Quebec from private Anglophone ownership and increasingly adopted the rhetoric of Quebec nationalism. But these actions were only the beginning in a long struggle by each succeeding provincial government to be *"maître chez nous"* (masters of our own house).

Second, the technological revolution of radio and television was profoundly transforming the cultural landscape of Canada. Isolated communities across the country were rapidly linking into a national cultural network. While these developments fostered nation-building and the gradual attenuation of regional and communal differences in the "melting pot" of the United States, in Canada, they generated apprehension and resentment. Statistics that showed a growing abandonment of the French language by the children of French Canadians across the country were particularly alarming to Quebec francophones. Their fear of losing language and heritage helped to create a "fortress Quebec" mentality and a Québécois cultural identity as never before. Thus, the Lesage government increasingly asserted the collective linguistic rights of French Canadians, and Daniel Johnson's succeeding Union Nationale government called for full provincial rights in education and culture in its party platform.

When French president Charles de Gaulle proclaimed "Vive le Québec libre!" on his visit to Montreal in July 1967, separatist sentiment in Quebec was given a vital stimulus. Two months later, René Lévesque issued his Option Québec, a political manifesto proposing sovereignty for the province, and when the provincial Liberal Party defeated his nationalist motion at its October party conference, he separated from the party and set in motion the events leading to the formation of the separatist Parti Québécois (PQ).

During this global era of "people's wars" and "national liberation fronts," it is not surprising that a radical group emerged in Quebec in 1970. On October 5, 1970, the Front de libération du Québec (FLQ) kidnapped a British diplomat and demanded radio access to broadcast their message to the people and the freeing of "political prisoners." After a second FLQ cell kidnapped Pierre Laporte, the provincial minister of labour, Prime Minister Trudeau decided upon a dramatic federal intervention: he invoked the War Measures Act, sent troops into Montreal, banned the FLQ, and arrested 260 suspected members. Shortly thereafter, the FLQ executed Laporte, but the British diplomat was eventually found and released.

The PQ defeated the Liberals in the 1976 provincial election, in part because of the public's perception that Liberal premier Henri Bourassa had been passive during the October Crisis and the general polarization of Quebec politics that occurred in its wake. Premier Lévesque moved quickly to protect the language and culture of Quebec. In spite of the federal program of bilingualism, Quebec asserted its provincial rights of control over education and language. Henceforth, French would be the language of all Quebec schoolchildren, except for those of established English-speaking parents. Thus, immigrants to Quebec had to send their children to French language schools. Bill 101 introduced a French-only language policy in the province, requiring French-only signs even in English-speaking communities.[1]

In 1980, Lévesque fulfilled his party's pledge to hold a referendum on Sovereignty-Association for Quebec, which promised autonomy for the province within the context of some form of economic association with Canada. After an emotional campaign featuring intervention by Trudeau and the federal Liberal Party, the proposal was defeated on May 20, 1980 by 59.5 per cent, including 52 per cent of the francophone population.

After this defeat, separatism slipped to the back pages in Canada for a while. Opinion polls showed declining support and public apathy on the issue through most of the 1980s, despite Lévesque's refusal to ratify the Constitution Act of 1982. With the defeat of the PQ and return of Bourassa's Liberals to power in 1985, separatism seemed a dead issue.

THE ROLE OF EXTERNAL PARTIES

In the history of international politics, domestic strife has had the tendency to attract outside intervention and support. In the first wave of separatist sentiment in Quebec (1967-80), the president of France, Charles de Gaulle, played a key role. His emotional procession through the province in July 1967, which culminated in his shouting "Vive le Québec libre!" from the Hotel de Ville in Montreal, was certainly a strong catalyst in radicalising the separatist movement. Furthermore, during his term in office, France actively supported the cause through inflammatory cultural exchanges and diplomatic actions granting recognition to Quebec.[2]

The question of provincial independence in foreign policy under Confederation has a long history involving all the provinces. The labour conventions case of 1937 seemed to grant the provinces some foreign policy capability in matters falling under their jurisdiction. Quebec began asserting some representation and treaty-making powers in the provincial areas of culture, language, and education during the Liberal Lesage government. In 1961, Lesage opened "*la maison du Quebec*" to foster cultural and economic ties with Paris and signed a cultural entente on educational exchanges with France in February 1965. Ottawa watched these developments with increasing disquietude, claiming that ultimately Ottawa should retain a monopoly on official contacts and treaty negotiations. In the case of the agreement of 1965, a "covering" treaty was negotiated after the fact between Canada and France.

Active diplomatic warfare erupted in the so-called War of the Conferences, beginning with the French education conference held in Gabon in 1968. Undoubtedly at de Gaulle's bidding, the government of Gabon sent its invitation to Quebec and not to Ottawa. Despite protests and a brief termination of diplomatic relations with Gabon, Ottawa was unable to get an invitation to this conference. But soon after, Ottawa established the precedent of sending a joint Canadian-Quebec delegation, including representation from the French Canadian communities in Ontario and New Brunswick, at a Francophonie conference in Zaire. Judicious use of Canadian foreign aid convinced most African governments in la Francophonie to accept Ottawa's joint delegation solution over protests from Paris. With de Gaulle's departure from French politics in 1969, the pressure from Paris declined. After 1976, Ottawa carefully watched attempts by the new PQ government to play the Paris card in developing an independent foreign policy. Under French president Valéry Giscard d'Estaing, Premier Lévesque was received in Paris with protocol more appropriate to a head of state. But after the 1980 referendum in Quebec and the instalment of President François Mitterand's government in France, the French Socialist prime minister Pierre Mauroy made it clear in 1983 that France would not interfere in Canada's affairs. As we will see below, this change of French attitudes did not end PQ attempts to enlist foreign support for its cause.

DOMESTIC AND CONSTITUTIONAL FACTORS

The defeat of the Sovereignty-Association referendum in 1980 gave Prime Minister Trudeau an opportunity to advance his constitutional agenda of repatriating the British

North America Acts (ending the British parliament's role) and adopting a Charter of Rights and Freedoms to enhance individual rights in Canada. After contentious federal-provincial negotiations, the Constitution Act of 1982 emerged, which all the provinces but Quebec ultimately supported. The PQ government's abstention resulted in a constitutional limbo, which the Mulroney government hoped to resolve by bringing the Liberal premier Robert Bourassa on board at a federal-provincial conference held in June 1987. The compromise constitutional package known as the Meech Lake Accord went some distance towards meeting Quebec's demands: Quebec was to be recognized as a "distinct society." One of Quebec's concerns with the Constitution Act was that its amending formula removed a traditional provincial veto on constitutional matters. Meech Lake addressed this by increasing the subjects that required unanimity, granting a greater provincial role in Supreme Court appointments, and limiting the federal role in immigration[3] and federal spending power in areas of concern to Quebec.

While support for Bourassa and Meech Lake was strong in Quebec, objections arose in the rest of the country, which ultimately led to the accord's failure to be approved by the June 1990 deadline. The Conservatives then launched a broader, more inclusive constitutional negotiation, which resulted in the Charlottetown Accord of 1992. But when this bundle of constitutional amendments was voted on in a countrywide referendum later that year, it was defeated, with six provinces including Quebec voting no. This compromise had seemed too little for Quebec and too large for the rest of Canada. The ill will engendered by these two defeats sparked the creation of a federal separatist party from Quebec, the Bloc Québécois, and a call for a second referendum by the PQ in 1995. Once again, separation from Canada was voted down, but only by a small margin of 50.6 per cent to 49.4 per cent. In 1998, the Supreme Court ruled that Quebec had no rights under either International Law or the Canadian Constitution to secede unilaterally; yet the federal government had a political obligation to negotiate such separation if a referendum showed it to be the will of a clear majority. Mobilized by the narrow defeat of the referendum and the court ruling, the government of Canada enacted the Clarity Act in 2000, which required prior federal agreement that the wording of any future referendum question was unambiguous and that a clear majority had voted in favour before negotiating separation with the province. Neither the Supreme Court nor the Clarity Act specified exactly what percentage was needed for a "clear majority." And the Quebec government immediately responded with its own legislation denying a federal role in the province's future.

Some areas of contention have been resolved by Ottawa-Quebec City bilateral negotiation. Constitutionally, immigration policy is a matter of shared jurisdiction. It is particularly important to Quebec, given its desire to preserve its distinctive society and French language. Immigration policy may be used to insure a steady flow of francophone immigrants, especially important given the province's current reproductive decline. Already in the 1970s, the province had negotiated federal agreements that recognized its special interests, and Quebec sought to have them entrenched in Meech Lake and Charlottetown. When those proposals failed, the federal Conservatives signed the 1991

Canada-Quebec Accord, which gave the later a stronger role in 1) the selection of immigrants to the province (with a preference for francophones or non-anglophones), 2) the guarantee of a steady supply of immigrants proportional to its population size within Canada (so Quebec maintains its weight within Confederation), and 3) the integration of new citizens (in particular, provisions that non-francophones be taught French).

Meanwhile, sentiment for more sovereignty in Quebec again seemed to cool, culminating in the defeat of the PQ by the Liberals under Jean Charest in 2003. Public opinion surveys show support for sovereignty had reached a low point of 40 per cent in 1999. But in 2005, it shot back up to 54 per cent with the revelations of the Gomery Commission (investigating allegations that the federal Liberal Party misused public money in Quebec in what was called the sponsorship scandal).

Is a constitutional compromise still the best way to derail separatism and preserve national unity? With the defeats of Meech Lake and Charlottetown, there has been scant effort, let alone success, in that regard. The major objections that arose during these negotiations still continue to plague constitutional compromise. There are two major attacks on the "distinct society" approach to accommodating Quebec. The first arises particularly among Western premiers who argue for the equality of all provinces and demand that any new concessions granted to Quebec also be given to all the others. Of course, behind the claim of equity lies a smouldering fire of anglophone resentment at bilingualism, recruitment of bilingual government employees, and a general sentiment that Quebec gets special treatment in Ottawa. This anti-Quebec feeling is strong at times and not only in the West.

On the other hand, criticism of the "distinct society" arises from citizens across the country who favour a strong, centralized state and who fear that any concessions to Quebec or the provinces set a dangerous precedent that weakens Ottawa. Eventually, they argue, transfer payments as well as federal standards and social programs might be jeopardized if the balance of power shifts too far to the provinces. Leading this charge were many in the federal Liberal Party, including former prime minister Trudeau. Additionally, the poorer provinces in the Maritimes and the Prairies worry about how willingly the richer provinces will support equalization payments to them in a decentralized Canada.

Indeed, many on the left came to see the entire constitutional revision process as a Trojan horse for a neo-conservative agenda emerging from the West and for the federal Tories to diminish the role of Ottawa. Hence, under the rubric of equality for the provinces and decentralization, a program that weakens the role of the government and phases out entitlement programs is being advanced. Thus, two anglophone books from opposed ideological positions, Philip Resnick on the left and David Bercuson and Barry Cooper on the right,[4] can nonetheless share the conclusion that Quebec must leave Confederation rather than adopt an unacceptable compromise.

Moreover, Meech and Charlottetown had the unique distinction of having managed to fracture every significant cleavage in Canadian society. Thus, the great irony is that a process intended to consolidate the defeat of separatism in 1980 and reconcile Quebec only unleashed further conflict.

Discussion at the 2004 PQ party conference revealed that though apparently dormant, the separatist volcano was preparing to erupt again, even before the revelations of the sponsorship scandal. Former premier Jacques Parizeau raised the suggestion that a victory for the PQ in the next provincial election would serve as grounds enough to declare the Quebec's independence. Parizeau's proposal was replaced with a simple pledge to hold another referendum after the next PQ victory.[5] Some commentators suggest that creating legal roadblocks to separation, such as the Clarity Act, simply increase the probability that a future PQ government will use such extra-constitutional means as a unilateral declaration of independence. Given the likelihood of another referendum and the apparent lack of will to continue looking for a compromise, Canadians must continue to be prepared for the possible separation of Quebec. What scenario would play out if the next referendum succeeded, and what role would foreign policy considerations play?

SEPARATION PQ-STYLE

Various Quebec groups may define sovereignty differently, but the Parti Québécois version would include an independent Quebec that would create and enforce its own laws, without reference to the Canadian Supreme Court, and collect and spend its own tax revenues. International treaties and representation would be handled exclusively by Quebec. Along with tax revenue would come the right to raise tariffs, although Quebec would likely seek a customs union with Canada and the continuation of free trade with the United States. Nonetheless, Quebec would have the right to impose tariffs against the rest of Canada, a right that would certainly be exercised if a resentful Canada refused entry of Quebec goods. Parizeau suggested that Quebec might retain use of the Canadian dollar, but only in the event that a sovereign Quebec had some representation and influence over the Bank of Canada (an unlikely concession from the Canadian side). In reality, a separate national bank with control over local interest rates and a separate currency would probably soon emerge. Defence would be another contentious area, but if the devolution of the Soviet Union serves as a model, the provincial police could undoubtedly form the core of a Quebec militia or security force.

Some on the separatist side have suggested that, as with the Sovereignty-Association proposal of 1980, an independent Quebec should renegotiate its economic relations with Canada as an equal party. Thus free trade, a customs union, and a unified currency could be maintained, similar to the European Union. However, the political landscape of "the rest of Canada" would look quite different from the European model, if recent elections are used as a guide. Most likely, a nationalist Liberal or Conservative Party government would be resentful of Quebec separation. Thus, an independent Quebec that claimed complete sovereignty in theory would probably soon be using all its sovereign rights in practice.

CANADIAN FOREIGN POLICY WITHOUT QUEBEC

Sovereignty for Quebec raises issues of foreign policy. It is interesting to note that aside from vaguely expressed fears of absorption into the US, the constitutional debate has rarely focused on external consequences. Table 9.1 provides statistics on population,

GDP, and debt in the event of an independent Quebec, assuming current boundaries. Quebec represents a quarter of Canada's population and slightly less of its GDP. In the terms of the political Realist, separation represents a major diminution of Canadian national power.

Table 9.1 Impact of Quebec Separation

	Canada at Present	Quebec Alone	Rest of Canada
Population (2001)	30,007,094	7,237,479	22,769,615
GDP (in billions)	$1,108	$233	$875
Debt and Possible Division of It (in billions)	$545	$136	$409

Source: Based on data from Statistics Canada <www.statscan.ca>.

Canadian academics, diplomats, and foreign policy decision-makers have long been concerned with defining Canada's relative position in the world community. Such a concern is not only an important Realist consideration, but it also delimits Canadian expectations in international forums and organizations. Prime Minister Mackenzie King emphasized this relationship between capacity and responsibility in his functional principle.[6] He developed this argument initially as a means to gain entry into allied decision-making during World War II and representation in the great power-planning sessions for new international organizations. Much later, Trudeau used the size of the Canadian economy to gain admittance with Italy to the annual Western economic summits and the Group of Seven (G7) meetings. After World War II, it became common practice in the Department of External Affairs to refer to Canada as a "middle power" in world affairs. Trudeau attempted to revise this expectation downward with his 1968 statement that Canada was "more the largest of the small powers than the smallest of the large powers."[7] Nonetheless, two Canadian academics writing in 1983 tried to reverse Trudeau's statement by arguing that Canada's relative star was rising.[8] According, then, to the Realist perspective or Canada's own functionalist principle, Canadian power is crucial to Canada's ability to defend its interests in the world community. A Canada without Quebec (CWQ) drops down in the ranking of nations to a fair degree. By population, CWQ drops from thirty-first to forty-first, just behind Taiwan and a few ranks ahead of Australia. By GDP, CWQ drops behind Brazil and Spain. Assuming that the Canadian economy does not fall into a long decline as a result of separation, the economic change is not overly dramatic. The key question is whether Spain would replace CWQ in the G8 and other forums. For Quebec, however, the changes are substantial. On the basis of population, Quebec goes from being part of the thirty-first largest to the eighty-seventh, just ahead of Bolivia. Indeed, Quebec would soon be passed by Haiti![9] Its reduced GDP would place it about twenty-second, near Poland, Argentina, or Norway.

The two most important foreign policy interests for CWQ and Quebec would remain security and economic issues. Ironically, events of the past decades have improved the outlook for an independent Quebec in each of these areas. In 1980, an independent Quebec would have faced a potential military threat from the USSR and protectionist threats from the US. The free trade agreements and the collapse of the USSR diminish both concerns.

Security Interests

Would a sovereign Quebec continue to be protected by the Canadian Forces, and if not, would it remain in Canada's two major defence pacts, NATO and NORAD? In the early 1980s, strategic concerns over a growing Soviet nuclear capability, the possibility of a Soviet first strike, the development of the Cruise Missile, and reports of Soviet penetration of Canadian airspace over Labrador and northern Quebec all generated a renewed cold war mentality, which heightened the importance of the NORAD agreement. However, with the rapid collapse of the Soviet military threat, the growth of US-Russian arms control, and the removal of the first strike fear, Canadian defence priorities entered a period of rapid retrenchment. Indeed, it is somewhat difficult to imagine what Quebec would do with an independent military establishment. In the absence of communal violence between anglophones and francophones, Quebec would probably need a militia for domestic disorders triggered by Aboriginal groups, such as the events at Oka and Cree hostility to Quebec separatism. It is doubtful that Quebec would desire an independent military presence in Europe through NATO, despite the past PQ statements to the contrary. What would Quebec do with an air force or navy? Some coastal patrol boats might be useful in the Gulf of the Saint Lawrence, though sovereignty protection for the Ungava Peninsula might require a new northern Quebec base. The questions of sovereignty and economics might arise in sorting out the Gulf of St Lawrence and the Magdelaine Islands, which could be further aggravated by declining fish stocks and the dispute over the Labrador border with Newfoundland. An air force for Quebec might seem an expensive and unnecessary luxury.

In order to secure defence beyond a land-based militia, a financially strapped Quebec government would be tempted to lease air and sea protection from Canada or the US. The latter option would be more likely if a resentful CWQ refuses or a future federal NDP government ends Canadian participation in NORAD. If Quebec turned to the US for defence assistance, complicated and asymmetrical three-way relations could emerge, at best, or, at worst, Washington might play Canada and Quebec off against each other.

If defence relations sour between Ottawa and Quebec, the Canadian Forces would be withdrawn to Canadian soil and Quebec bases closed with the usual local economic hardship.[10] Halifax would be happy to regain its status as the Atlantic navy's main base, and Winnipeg contractors could no longer claim Quebec favouritism on defence spending. Quebec citizens in the Canadian Forces would be faced with the tough decision of either leaving Quebec or leaving the Canadian Forces. Federalist sentiment is strong in the forces and a high percentage (90+) would probably stay with Canada, despite Quebec nationalists' efforts to woo them. The Canadian Forces in general would undoubtedly shrink in size to reflect the new population base, an additional blow for a military already reduced by neglect since the end of the cold war.

The PQ might seek separate membership in NORAD and NATO. Whether Quebec would be welcome in those organizations would depend again on how acrimonious the separation was and on Ottawa's attitude. (This assumes CWQ would automatically retain Canada's current membership in both organizations.)

Economic Relations

The negotiation of the FTA (1987) and NAFTA (1994) has opened another opportunity for separation for Quebec. The 1980 referendum was defeated in part on economic considerations: many in Quebec said they voted with their pocketbooks rather than their hearts. Faced with economic uncertainty and the worst-case scenario of being left with only a small Quebec market, the business community voiced strong objections to separation. Now, with access to all of North America, the threat of economic retaliation from Ottawa seems more unlikely and less consequential. Thus, one heard at least some Québécois business leaders endorsing separatism in the 1990s.

As with territory (see below), complications arise from dividing economic assets and liabilities. For the national debt, at least, a fixed value can be readily applied. Table 9.1 shows the 2001 level of net federal debt and one possible division based on an even split by population.[11] Because the tax base of each independent entity would be smaller and less diverse, the potential buyer of Canadian or Quebec debt would face greater risk and hence demand a higher return. Interest rates would have to go up, particularly in Quebec, which would increase the debt burden and slow down economic growth.

Sorting out assets is a vastly more difficult task. Should Ottawa's Crown Corporations and vast land holdings in the North be included in the settlement? Should Ottawa make the case, as the Soviets did initially to the Baltics, that all the years of transfer payments and investments in the province should be "repaid" in some way? Parizeau had suggested that Quebec would be satisfied with simply taking control of federal assets within the present boundaries of the province. Certainly, that solution would be much less complicated but perhaps not acceptable to an enraged CWQ.

The potential general economic health of Quebec and Canada after a division has been a matter of intense debate. The long list of imponderables makes resolution of the debate at least as difficult as predicting when the next recession will begin. Indeed, this very uncertainty led the Canadian Bond Rating Service of Montreal to place Quebec bonds on a credit alert during the last round of secession fears. More crucial will be the assessments of the big American credit rating institutions and the large Japanese brokers. Their assessments in turn depend on predictions from economists, and here the findings have been quite contradictory. For instance, a Fraser Institute study by Patrick Grady predicted for Quebec depressed property values, a new flight of corporate headquarters and anglophones from Montreal, a crisis of business confidence, a paucity of new investments, and a long-term recession.[12] On the other hand, a study by the Economic Council of Canada suggested that most of the negative economic effects would be short term. In May 2005, an economic study even suggested that after secession, Quebec would run a bigger budget surplus than it currently did as a province. Of course, that study was headed by Parti Québécois finance critic François Legault, and was quickly denounced by the Liberals as full of extremely rosy economic assumptions.[13]

What was clear was that Quebec would have to forgo a net federal/provincial transfer of as much as $4 billion,[14] a price that most separatists have long accepted. Furthermore, Ottawa would be spared the divisive process of allocating a large share of all federal contracts and concessions to Quebec. These two sources of savings (plus assumed savings on reduced bilingualism) have led some conservative anglophones to argue that Canada would be economically better off without Quebec.

Before the 1995 referendum, Ottawa suggested that Quebec should not assume economic cooperation from either Canada or the United States. It argued that Quebec would have to renegotiate admittance to NAFTA, an action that would allow the Americans to reopen contentious issues. Likewise, a hostile Canada might try to block Quebec admission to other economic forums, including the Organization for Economic Cooperation and Development (OECD), the IMF, the World Bank, and the WTO. As noted, Canada's participation in the G8 may also be jeopardized, and Quebec would certainly have no voice there. If the break were to be acrimonious, economic rivalry or trade war would be a serious possibility. Even a friendly separation may be scuttled by significant economic policy disagreements. Either Quebec or CWQ might in the future be governed by a radical nationalist party with a protectionist bent that may decide to withdraw from NAFTA. Tariff barriers would necessarily then rise between Canada and Quebec.

The Territorial Issue and the Future of Canada

Sovereign states possess internationally recognized territorial boundaries. Numerous complicating factors may come into play with Quebec if the mood of separatist negotiations turns ugly or violence breaks out. Historical questions arise as to Quebec's claim to Labrador and northern Quebec. Northern Quebec was only added to the province in 1912, and Quebec's claim to Labrador was questioned in the early 1990s by a Conservative Member of Parliament (MP). However, Premier Parizeau suggested that the PQ was content with the current provincial boundary and indeed would accept nothing less.

Still, if violence were to erupt between the anglophones and francophones, or if disorder arose from the Aboriginal communities (Mohawk, Cree, etc.), significant territorial changes could come about. If civil violence in the order of Yugoslavia broke out (though the possibility seems remote at present), boundaries might change to reflect ethnic divisions. Under such conditions, the English parts of the Eastern Townships and Montreal might seek to remain in Canada. If linguistic confrontation were to spill over provincial borders, francophones in Eastern Ontario or even (although extreme) Acadians of northeastern New Brunswick might desire to join a separate francophone entity. But, a much more likely threat to the current borders comes from the Aboriginal residents of Quebec.

Conflict with the Mohawk community at Oka in the summer of 1990 soured relations between the province of Quebec and the Aboriginal communities of Canada and raised the issue of how they would be treated within a separate Quebec. The Cree of northern Quebec have suggested that they will refuse to allow their territories to be separated from Canada. Their legal justification for separating from Quebec would be based either on the assertion that Quebec had failed to fulfil its agreement on phase I of the James Bay hydroelectric project or with a more fundamental claim to sovereignty over ancestral lands in the North. Also, the federal government would want to maintain its obligations to the First Nations, which it cannot easily turn over to Quebec.

THE EXTERNAL DIMENSION RETURNS

American attitudes towards Quebec separation are crucial to its success. Unlike France, US administrations regardless of party affiliation have tended to favour the Canadian federal position. As one US academic put it, "a 'strong and unified Canada' is what the United States favours."[15] This was the position former president Clinton took during the 1995 referendum. For the United States, the desire to maintain security and stability on its northern border have trumped incentives to exploit the short-term gains by playing Quebec against Ottawa. Nonetheless, when in power in Quebec City, the PQ has spent much effort to gain US acquiescence if not support for separation. In May 2002, Quebec opened a mission in Los Angeles, even though Ottawa already had a large consulate there. Many of the provinces have offices in the US to promote trade and tourism, but Quebec is "unique in maintaining an expensive foreign network of pseudo-embassies, which assert the province's sovereignty abroad."[16] Quebec has seven such missions scattered across the United States, as well as offices in Paris, Mexico, Brussels, London, Tokyo, and 14 other countries.

Other international forums have provoked spats reminiscent of the "war of the conferences." In December 2000, Quebec premier Lucien Bouchard received a "special invitation" to Mexican president Vicente Fox's inauguration. What was "special" was that initially Bouchard was invited to sit inside the cathedral with the other heads of state. When Ottawa requested "clarification," the Mexican foreign ministry said it made a mistake and downgraded Bouchard's seating, which provoked an angry boycott from the Premier. Likewise, Bouchard used the 2001 Summit of the Americas in Quebec to hold bilateral meetings with other Latin American heads of state.

In addition to the United States, France remains a crucial player in the sovereignty question, and the PQ found a warmer reception in Paris once President Chirac became head of state. This warmth extended even to Liberal premiers after Jean Charest set a new precedent by meeting with French leaders alone, without the presence of the Canadian ambassador, on his June 2004 trip to Paris. In another groundbreaking development in

November 2004, the Premier travelled to meet Mexican president Fox with French prime minister Jean-Pierre Raffarin, but without the usual Ottawa chaperone. The Liberal Martin government has defended such actions and Foreign Affairs Minister Pierre Pettigrew called them "in line with rules adopted in 1999 that allow premiers to meet directly with foreign heads of government."[17]

Then, in September 2005, after a provincial foreign policy review, the Charest government announced it was prepared to end 40 years of seeking an independent overseas voice in exchange for a new federal-provincial accord that would give Quebec formal representation on Canadian delegations to provincially relevant international organizations, such as UNESCO and the WTO. While in principle this sounds like a major breakthrough, as usual the devil is in the detail. So, while PQ leaders still charge the Quebec Liberals with conceding too much, federal critics wonder about this resurrection of the "war of the conferences" solution, sending mixed delegations of federal and provincial representatives. How might a future PQ government exploit it? Could the Quebec representative contradict the Canadian head of the delegation or conduct his or her own negotiations? Might Quebec delegates show a Quebec flag? Would it be "war of the conferences" all over again?

CONCLUSION

Quebec separation is not the only potential challenge to national unity. Aboriginals across Canada claimed an inherent right to sovereignty throughout the constitutional debate. If the precedent of territorial division along ethnic lines is established in Quebec, other communities may demand similar secession. In particular, the Inuit of the North might feel they have more in common with their cousins in Greenland than with the rest of Canada.

Some small threat of further secession on regional lines also exists in the English-speaking community. The West has seen the formation of small separatist parties from time to time, and there has been occasional talk of Labrador leaving Newfoundland. The physical separation of Atlantic Canada from the rest of Canada caused by Quebec's departure would pose a serious problem. Due to Atlantic Canada's economic dependency on equalization payments from Ottawa, no immediate demands for secession would be likely. Indeed, of greater concern is whether in a dramatically altered federalism, the richer provinces (e.g. Alberta) would still be willing to support transfers of wealth to the East. Loyalty to Canada is still strong in all provinces outside Quebec, but the fear is that provinces territorially fractured and plunged into a long recession might begin to consider more stable and permanent political relations with the United States.

But, all that said, Quebec remains the main source of concern, and the chief tactical threat remains a PQ-sponsored referendum. Based on a recent US study, Figure 9.1 shows the ongoing appeal of sovereignty among the young, suggesting that the PQ practice of continually holding referendums until it gets the results it wants could eventually work.[18] And if this "Big Bang" approach fails, there is also the slow, evolutionary route to independence.

Figure 9.1 Age Cohorts and Support for Separation

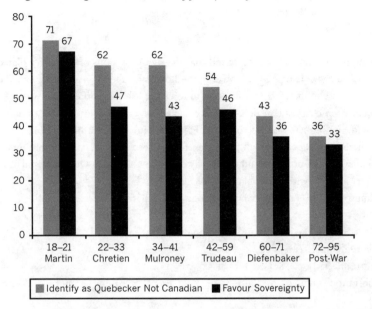

Source: 2004 Political Support in Canada Pre-election Survey, Harold D. Clarke, Allan Kornberg, John MacLeod, and Thomas Scotto, "Too Close to Call: Political Choice in Canada, 2004." *PS: Political Science & Politics* 38.2 (2005): 251.

Jean Chrétien has reported that Quebec independence partisan Claude Morin told him, "We'll separate from Canada the same way that Canada separated from England: we'll cut the links one at a time, a concession here and a concession there, and eventually there'll be nothing left."[19] We have seen in Chapter 6 exactly how this process worked. The Dominion of Canada never held a referendum to leave London's control. Instead, the Liberal party achieved independence through a long process of incremental steps that involved establishing overseas missions and agreements and demanding one legal concession from Britain after another. A foreign third party (the US) was used, even if unwittingly, to accelerate this process. With Morin's quote in mind, Quebec's diplomatic efforts take on a very different meaning.

Indeed, even "federalist" politicians in Quebec have raised the bar of minimal sovereign demands. What was unacceptable ten years ago is now seen as a minor concession. In the 1980s and early 1990s, Meech Lake and Charlottetown were defeated in part over the rest of Canada's unwillingness to make exceptions for Quebec. Yet, Premier Charest's "asymmetrical federalism" achieved just that in the special deal on health care Ottawa gave to Quebec in September 2004.[20] Perhaps it is easier for a Liberal federal government to grant a Liberal premier more foreign policy independence, as seen in Charest's independent meetings with foreign heads of state. Charest does not invest these foreign visits with the same symbolism as the PQ. But once a precedent is established, how can Ottawa prevent a future PQ government from doing the same thing, but with its own independence symbolism?

Notes

1. In 1988, the Supreme Court of Canada found that the sign provisions of Bill 101 violated the Canadian and Quebec charters of rights. However, the Bourassa Liberal government invoked the "notwithstanding" clause of the 1982 Constitution to force English signs off exterior walls.

2. There have even been charges that de Gaulle conducted a secret war in Canada, granting subsidies to the PQ and training separatist terrorists on French territory. See Bushkoff (1991).

3. Some powers here were allocated to all provinces, but Quebec's special concern that immigrants would avoid living in the province and eventually shift the Canada-to-Quebec population ratio against it was met in effect with a special quota for Quebec.

4. See Jeffery Simpson's (1991) review of David Bercuson and Barry Cooper.

5. Ha (2004), A1.

6. Not to be confused with David Mitrany's functionalism.

7. Quoted in Thordarson (1972), p. 69.

8. Dewitt and Kirton (1983), p. 38.

9. Assuming substantial numbers of Haitians or other French-speaking immigrants do not arrive.

10. The Canadian Forces currently have a headquarters in Montreal and bases in Bagotville, Valcartier, and St. Jean.

11. Similar to the analysis in Drohan (1991).

12. Freeman (1991), A1.

13. Séguin (2005), A12.

14. Patterson (1991), A17.

15. Doran (2001), p. 40.

16. Saunders (2002), A4.

17. MacKinnon (2004), A7.

18. Clarke, Kornberg, MacLeod, and Scotto (2005), p. 251.

19. Quoted in Granatstein and Bothwell (1990), p. 117.

20. Séguin (2004), A4.

Chapter Ten
Ensuring Economic Growth and Welfare

Chapter 8 examined how Canada's heavy dependence on exporting to the US market could operate as a political liability, reducing Canada's freedom of choice in relations with its southern neighbour. This chapter shifts gears and focuses on the benefits of those exports to Canadians in the form of jobs and incomes, and a positive balance of payments.

ECONOMIC POLICY TOOLS

Generally speaking, this national interest can be divided into three separate challenges: 1) maintaining economic growth, 2) keeping unemployment and inflation low, and 3) avoiding a balance of payments crisis. The first objective is often measured by increases in the Gross Domestic Product (GDP). This indicator is an attempt by government economists to give a dollar value to all the goods and services produced within the borders of Canada, whether by Canadian-owned or foreign businesses, in one year. For example, according to Statistics Canada, the GDP for Canada in 2003 was just over $1200 billion. Governments of all ideological hues would like to see this figure increase each year as a sign of economic prosperity. Indeed, the economist's definition of the word *recession* is three consecutive quarters of negative GDP growth. A growing GDP is valuable because tax revenues available to the government tend to fluctuate with GDP. More revenue allows governments to spend money and acquire more things, which can fulfill other objectives, security for example.

The second challenge involves the next two most widely reported statistics after GDP: the rate of unemployment and the rate of inflation. Most governments would like to see these two statistics remain as low as possible. In political science, there is a long tradition of linking a high or increasing unemployment rate with domestic turmoil and even the fall of government. Likewise, skyrocketing prices can cause economic hardship for the poor and elderly, and present risk for business investors. The German hyperinflation is cited as a factor in delegitimizing the Weimar government of the 1920s and 1930s. In fact, economists sometimes add the two "bads" of unemployment and inflation to create a "Misery Index." So, if in mid 2004, the Canadian unemployment rate was 7.2 per cent and inflation was 2.3 per cent (Consumer Prices), then the Canadian Misery Index was 9.5 per cent.

Unfortunately, under ordinary conditions, the solutions for unemployment and inflation are at odds. To some extent, you might argue that fighting unemployment is the same as the first goal: getting the GDP to grow. As Table 10.1 shows, the two are related, and policies that stimulate growth in the economy are usually also prescribed for lowering the unemployment rate. However, as the recent "jobless recovery" in the US shows, the relationship is not a perfect one.

Table 10.1 Policy Tools for Inflation and Unemployment

	Inflation	Unemployment
Fiscal Policy	Increase taxes	Lower taxes
	Cut government spending	Increase government spending
Monetary Policy	Cut the money supply (raise interest rates)	Expand the money supply (lower interest rates)
External Policy		
Tariffs	Lower tariffs	Raise tariffs ("export unemployment")
Currency	Appreciate: raise dollar value (foreign goods are cheaper)	Depreciate: lower dollar value (domestic goods are cheaper)
Other (Capital)		Encourage foreign investment

On the other hand, an economy that is expanding too rapidly can trigger hyperinflation. The government of China constantly worries that the miracle growth rates of its economy will overheat and trigger uncontrollable price rises. Inflation, by increasing instability and therefore economic risk, can damage future growth prospects. "Price bubbles" often burst suddenly, causing panics and dramatic recessions. Therefore, measures such as increasing taxes, cutting spending, and raising interest rates to cool down the economy are recommended. But these same policies, if applied too vigorously, could slow down the economy too much, resulting in the misery of more unemployment. Consequently, governments must usually walk a fine line in balancing these two forces.

The third challenge, avoiding balance of payments crisis, is the most complex and demonstrates the importance of trade and external transactions to the health of the economy. Exports are an obvious source of wealth and economic growth, and one sometimes hears of an "export-led boom." For resource-rich nations like Canada, Australia, and Saudi Arabia, exports have been a direct source of economic prosperity. But again, thanks to price rises, there can be too much of a good thing, so the balance of imports and exports and inward and outward flows of capital must be watched. That is, if the outward flows of money prevail too much, the country could run up a huge balance of payments deficit and run out of money to meet its international obligations (to pay all its debts). It might then have to go cap in hand to the IMF for a bailout loan with very harsh conditions attached. Most readers will recognize this scenario in the 1980s debt crises, but Third World countries such as Mexico and Jamaica are not the only economies that have had to face this humiliation, as UK, Italy, and South Korea well know.

The major policy tools for dealing with the second challenge, inflation and unemployment, are shown on Table 10.1. Since fiscal and monetary policy are domestic, we focus here on external policy, which includes trade and the currency activities of the government. Economists and public policy advisors argue about the perennial question of whether to rely on market forces or government intervention. A government could have a policy of no intervention to allow the market to find its own equilibrium. Most neoclassical economists would prefer minimal government intervention in both trade (advocating free trade) and currency pricing (supporting a free-floating exchange rate). But, in reality, most governments today still intervene in both areas by various devices. Those who advocate active government intervention in both areas of international political economy (IPE) are referred to as mercantilists and bear many resemblances to the economic nationalists we encountered in Chapter 8. Protectionism or the use of tariffs or other non-tariff barriers (NTBs) is the favoured trade policy of this group. We can think of the current debate between neo-classical economists and mercantilists as a continuum, from total government "laissez-faire" at one end to complete government control of all transactions across the border. (Hong Kong used to be cited as the best example of a "wide-open trading port." North Korea is the best example of strict government intervention.) In between these two positions are various levels of selective government regulation to achieve specific policy goals. The free-marketers would argue that the historical pattern in the last 100 years has been away from government intervention towards freer international markets, and if we track tariff levels of the major economies, the evidence seems to support this.

The neo-classical advocate would present five major benefits for moving to freer trade. First, without trade, some resources and goods would not be available. Japan is a classic example of a country poor in natural resources that must import the raw materials needed to drive its massive industrial combines. In Canada, if we want orange juice (at a reasonable price), we will have to import it. Second, an economic argument for freer trade can be made from the theory of comparative advantage, which stipulates that when two producers specialize in producing goods in which they have a relative cost advantage and then trade them for other goods, they can consume more goods than they would have been able to make on their own. Basically, the same process of specialization has been going on within our economies for some time and is the main reason for our past growth and high standard of living today.

The third benefit, economies of scale, is actually a corollary to the theory of comparative advantage (or perhaps one reason for it) but provides a special incentive for small economies to trade. Basically, it says that for most goods, big factories are beautiful: the larger the production run, the cheaper each individual unit can be produced and sold.

Figure 10.1 shows this relationship graphically. A small country trying to be self-sufficient and not rely on imports would be producing small runs at the high end of its cost curves for many different goods. The way to produce goods at a competitive price is to expand the production run by exporting into foreign markets and to specialize in a few goods, trading for the goods produced less efficiently.

Figure 10.1 An Example of Economies of Scale

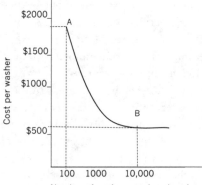

Situation A: A small local firm produces only 100 washers at a cost of $1,800 each.
Situation B: A large multinational can produce 10,000 washers at a cost of $600 each.

We have already mentioned competition and efficiency, which are so important we can treat them separately as the fourth benefit of free trade. Competition from cheaper and better quality products keeps our own producers own their toes, adopting new technologies and innovating new products and new ways of producing them. Being more efficient ensures the best quality good at the lowest price. Choice, the fifth benefit, re-emphasizes the importance of free trade in that it increases the number of products available to the consumer. Automobiles are good example: imagine buying a car in North America if your only options were GM or Ford. Or, imagine buying a pop music CD if local groups were your only choices.

Mercantilists, of course, would contest these free trade benefits and argue that in fact the costs are high. For them, the technical phrase "shifting resources to products with a comparative advantage" hides much suffering that happens when workers lose jobs or factories and farms close in the inefficient sectors that can't compete with foreign goods. (Neo-classicists do not deny these adaptation costs but see them as short-term pain for overall long-term gain. Some therefore justify various forms of government intervention, but only for re-education or social welfare for displaced workers and producers.) Mercantilists also argue that comparative advantage is often simply a matter of getting there first. Using the logic of economies of scale, they point out that starting up a new business or industry initially means a low-volume, high-cost production run. As the firm learns the ropes and expands its markets, it can move down the cost slope in step with its output increase. Early entrants to a business have a huge competitive advantage, as they are already low-cost producers once a firm in another country tries to start up. This "infant-industry" argument suggests that the young firm, out of fairness, should be protected by government-imposed tariffs until it has matured enough to take on the grown-up foreign competition. Some neo-classicists accept parts of this argument but nearly all worry that tariffs are a political instrument supported by self-interested domestic groups (management and labour in the protected industry) and are therefore difficult to remove once imposed. Hence, they cite numerous examples of "infants that never grow up" but limp along as ongoing uncompetitive drains on the public welfare.

Nationalist, as we saw in Chapter 8, also worry about the corrosive effects of more open borders on our national culture and national control and ownership of our businesses. As well, economists acknowledge that specialization and comparative advantage make economies more dependent on each other, and political scientists point out that this dependency is often asymmetric. These apparent costs to national autonomy and identity must be evaluated and then balanced against the benefits of freer trade. Finding this balance has been at the centre of a long, historic Canadian debate.

A BRIEF HISTORY OF CANADIAN TRADE POLICY

Historically, Canada has always been economically dependent on foreign markets and any early examples of "globalization." Canada has also known the mixed blessing of living off an abundant natural resource base, as many developing countries are forced to do. Yet our experience has demonstrated that such a situation can produce a very high standard of living for our population, as it has for Australia as well.

Pre-Confederation

During the long colonial period, British North America followed the trade policies of Great Britain, which evolved slowly from mercantilism to arrive at free trade liberalism in the mid-nineteenth century. Growing out of the militarized, imperial competition of European states in the seventeenth century, mercantilist doctrines emphasized the importance of colonies as strategic assets in the struggle for dominance of the great powers (Spain, Holland, France, and Great Britain). In this state of almost continual warfare, economic relations were seen as a "zero-sum game," where any advantage one state gained through trade implied a disadvantage to the trading partner. The main source of wealth and power (particular after the Spanish plunder of the Aztecs and Incas) was believed to be the gold stocks held by each great power. Since imports were paid for in gold coin, while exports boosted the gold supply coming in, the simple rule of mercantilism was this: exports good; imports bad. Therefore, the mercantilists favoured protectionism, active government promotion of export industries, and avoidance of balance of payment deficits. Indeed, an inflow of gold was considered (until David Hume showed its inflationary effects) an excellent thing.

Colonies were an integral part of this economic competition. As the Spanish had shown, colonies might be, at a minimum, loaded with gold booty. But, after French and British hopes for gold were disappointed in North America, these great powers contented themselves with using the colonies as cheap sources of raw materials that could be processed into valuable exports in the mother country. The mercantilists perceived the colonies' role as follows: 1) as a source of raw materials, 2) as a market for manufacturers, and 3) as a dumping ground for surplus population. Nineteenth-century socialists added a fourth role: as a target of investment for surplus capital. Maximizing the benefits of all these roles required complete control by the mother country over the colony's trade. In response to warfare with the Dutch, the English Navigation Acts of 1651 created a British advantage in shipping and trade with British colonies. In effect, it put an economic wall around the British Empire, excluding Dutch and foreign ships from entering British ports as trade "middlemen."

The exclusive nature of this mercantilist doctrine (the Navigation Acts) and others is demonstrated in the expulsion of the rebellious American colonies from the British trade system in the 1783 Treaty of Paris, after their war for independence. The removal of New England ships from the growing supply of export stables (furs, fish, and timber) from BNA was a boon for the Maritimes, which could now take over the trade with British ports in the Caribbean and expand their shipbuilding industry to support it. However, the geographic reality and size of the New England merchant fleet meant that by the end of the War of 1812, the closed British trading system was a leaking sieve as far as the western Atlantic was concerned. In response to this smuggling and a British desire for improved relations with the US, the Statute of 1822 allowed US merchant ships to enter certain "free ports" in the Caribbean and BNA. While a blow to Maritime shipping, an advantage was maintained by granting a tariff concession on BNA exports to Britain. The Canada Corn Act of 1843 augmented this preference for BNA exports by increasing the tariff on US corn imports into the United Kingdom. As an added concession to Canada, the act allowed grain from the US that was shipped to Canada and processed into flour there to then enter the UK as a low-duty Canadian product. Montreal business interests, who had long hoped the Saint Lawrence would become the main shipping conduit to the Great Lakes region, were ecstatic at the prospect of Canada becoming the processor and trans-shipper of North American agricultural produce. But the engineering triumph of the Erie Canal and, later, the railroad connections across New York State, along with the end of the Corn Law tariff advantage in 1846, meant that New York City and not Montreal was destined to be the premier trade port for the continent's interior.

Many factors lead to the repeal of the Corn Laws in 1846.[1] Primary among these was the ideological ascendancy of liberal doctrines, both economic and political, within Britain. It is not a coincidence that responsible government, a major goal of liberal reform, was granted to BNA about the same time. So convinced was the British government of the wisdom of free trade that within a few years most tariffs were unilaterally removed, leaving Britain open to foreign goods. Faced with an economic downturn in BNA at the same time, Canadian producers were so distraught at this loss of their privileged access to the British market that many were ready to consider joining the competition. The 1849 Montreal Annexation Manifesto expressed a desire for a "a friendly and peaceful separation from the British connection, and a union upon equitable terms with the great North American Confederacy of sovereign states."[2] However, given the general lack of enthusiasm for annexation either in Canada or the US,[3] other economic solutions were soon sought.

Instead, Canadian producers sought access to the large and growing US market as compensation for losses in the mother country. The resulting Reciprocity Treaty of 1854 was the first sectoral free trade agreement between BNA and the United States. Essentially, it removed all duties on nearly all raw materials and agricultural goods traded between the two countries. Aside from Nova Scotia's complaint that Canada had enticed the United States into the deal by granting them access to the Maritime fishery, the agreement was extremely popular because it facilitated the export of Canada's strong suits (fish, agriculture, lumber, etc.) while still protecting infant Canadian manufacturing industries. As an early act of autonomy from the colonial power, the Union of Canada enacted the 1859 Cayley-Galt Tariff, which broke London's free trade policy and charged a duty on manufactured goods, even from Britain. As Michael Hart has written, the US soon felt very aggrieved under the treaty because, despite prior understandings, Canada twice raised tariffs on their manufactured goods.[4] When further disputes arose during the US Civil War, the Americans abandoned free trade with BNA in 1865, under the terms of the agreement. But numerous attempts by later governments (especially Liberal) to revive the agreement demonstrate the ongoing popularity of this type of sectoral free trade in raw materials.

The Macdonald National Policy

Economic factors played a major role in the move to Confederation, and trade policy issues continued to be important in the nineteenth-century elections of the new Dominion of Canada. The hope was that a country linked by an east-west transcontinental railroad would create a large enough continental domestic market to encourage Canadian manufactures and producers. The federal Conservatives added the doctrine of protectionism for central Canada's infant industries to this vision by applying the old Union of Canada tariffs to the Dominion as a whole and then gradually raising them to an average duty of about 20 per cent to the value of the import by 1874.

By the 1878 federal election, which the Macdonald Conservatives chose to fight on the issue of protectionism, the trade battle lines between Tories and Liberals were well defined. Domestic groups lined up for or against free trade on the basis of their economic interests, as they did in the US, UK, and elsewhere. Agricultural producers and raw material exporters who wanted to sell to the large American market were the main supporters of free trade or, at minimum, a return to the 1854 Reciprocity Treaty. Farmers also wanted the freedom to purchase the cheaper US harvesters and other agricultural equipment. Likewise, trade unions and consumers generally liked the idea of cheaper American goods. The Liberal Party appealed to these groups by pledging to seek a renewed free trade agreement with the US. At this time, the main supporters of protection were central Canadian manufacturing firms who tended to vote for the Conservative Party. The Conservatives also pointed out that the duties associated with protectionism were the main source of government revenue at the time.

It might appear surprising, therefore, that protectionism triumphed in the election, since more domestic groups and voters seemed to support free trade. But while the benefits of free trade, such as lower prices for consumers, were widely spread across the population, they were also relatively small, at least in the short run, compared to the economic pain suffered by those industries threatened with bankruptcy resulting from foreign imports. Hence, the basic problem for free trade campaigners: diffuse benefits and concentrated costs. Even today, those who oppose free trade tend to feel more passionate about it than do its supporters, particularly if they believe their livelihood is threatened. Also, the Conservatives were able to colour the trade question with patriotism by suggesting free traders were pro-American while protectionists were loyal to Great Britain (quite ironic, given that at the time, the US government was the bastion of protectionism and Britain the champion of the free traders!).

By 1879, protectionism under the Conservatives was firmly entrenched as the national policy. National railroads brought raw materials from the Maritimes and Prairies to central Canada for processing and returned finished goods to a Canada-wide market. But given that Canada's population base was roughly one-tenth the size of its southern neighbour, protectionism worked much better for the US in the period 1873-95.[5] For Canada, the results appeared to be higher prices, a lower standard of living, a long economic slump, and emigration of Canadians to the more prosperous US. As Kenneth Norrie points out, Canada was the only new country to lose population in the period 1870-1900.[6] Even the long-term economic consequences of the national policy of protectionism were bad, according to Stephen Brooks. Maritimers and Westerners have long claimed that most of the economic benefits of protectionism went to Ontario at their expense. Brooks claims the effects were also bad at the federal level and that Canadian economists estimate the overall economic costs to have been between 4 and 10 per cent of the national GNP. As with other countries with small domestic markets that have tried import-substitution policies, the result was manufacturing infants who never grew up and who never became competitive in world markets. He claims this could still be seen in the lower performance of Canadian manufacturing after World War II.[7]

On the other hand, John Brebner and many other commentators, while acknowledging these problems, have nonetheless argued the costs were justifiable: a lower standard of living was the price Canadians paid for their separate national identity. Of course, this assumes that free trade would have resulted in the annexation of Canada to the US. And there were other costs to political autonomy, even with protectionism. As Michael Hart reports, as early as 1887, the Canadian Manufacturers' Association was noting with satisfaction that as a consequence of the national policy, American branch plants were popping up across Ontario, as American firms avoided the tariffs by setting up inside Canada.

Even the Conservatives saw the advantages of sectoral free trade as a boost for Canada's raw material exports. Thus, the 1871 Treaty of Washington, negotiated by the British with Canadian input, briefly re-established free trade in fish and some fish products. (The treaty was terminated by the US in 1885.) With the global sentiment in the late nineteenth century (especially in the US, Germany, and other European countries) turning towards greater protectionism and imperialism, it seemed even to the Liberal Party in Canada that the prospects for free trade were not good. By 1897, the Laurier government was actively trying to encourage Britain to abandon free trade in favour of imperial preference. Laurier's finance minister W.S. Fielding — "the father of modern Canadian trade policy"[8] — started enacting this preference by creating a multi-tier duty system whereby goods entering Canada from Britain or anywhere in the British Empire got a special "25 per cent off" the regular tariff as a preferential rate. The hope was that Britain would so appreciate this advantage for its goods in the Canadian market that it would want to reciprocate with a preference for Canadian goods in its own. (Of course, to do that, it would have had to introduce tariffs on all other imports to give Canada a lower rate.)

Yet, despite this growth in Canadian and global protectionism, Canada continued to be a heavily dependent on exports for its prosperity. Several related factors played a major role in the late-nineteenth-century growth of Canadian exports. First, Canada's rich endowment of raw materials included minerals for which other countries had few alternative sources. Thus, by the 1880s, Canada had become the world's leading supplier of asbestos, nickel, and cobalt. Second, abundant forests and fisheries gave Canada a low cost advantage in those sectors, even with foreign tariffs. By the end of the century, Canada was supplying 80 per cent of the huge US newsprint market. A third, more transient, advantage to export growth occurred when global industrial demand expanded again after a long global recession in the 1870s, which helped to boost the prices for Canada's raw material exports.

Into the Twentieth Century

By the turn of the century, a strong triangular trade pattern between Canada, Britain, and the US had emerged and was ongoing. Canada continued in its colonial role as a major supplier of raw materials to the mother country, so much so that it continually sold more to Britain than it bought from her. This trade surplus was useful in paying for the annual trade deficit that Canada ran up with the United States (Canadians bought more American goods than they sold to the US). As we saw previously in Chapter 8 (see Figure 8.1, p. 154), Britain was still Canada's number one trading partner, though trade with the US was growing steadily. Despite the high tariffs both ways, by 1900, the US exported raw materials such as petroleum, iron and steel, rubber, and cotton for Canadian textile mills. American machinery imports and the new technologies embodied in them were also important for Canadian manufacturing. And alongside traditional agricultural imports (oranges, for example) came a growing wave of American-made consumer products, including books and periodicals and, soon after the turn of the century, motion pictures. Despite high US tariffs, Canada managed to export many raw materials, such as nickel, asbestos, lumber, grain, fish, and meat. But, with the exception of some processed goods such as wood products, newsprint, aluminum, chemicals, and fertilizers, Canadian manufactured goods and consumer exports were not competitive in the US or elsewhere.

With the growing importance of these bilateral trade relations, it is not surprising that proposals for freer trade would again arise. In spite of their past history of support,

Laurier's Liberals showed little enthusiasm for initial overtures from the US government in 1899. But, ten years later, they changed their minds when a new proposal came direct from the US president himself. Unlike many presidents, Robert Taft, elected in 1908, actually knew something about Canada and thought freer trade would benefit both countries. What made the proposal so attractive in the eyes of many Canadians was that it was basically a return to the 1854 Reciprocity Treaty in raw materials: the Ontario manufacturers' market could be left protected. Still, the two leaders realized the political complications inherent in any such deal and secretly negotiated the Reciprocity Agreement of 1911. By enacting it as an agreement not a treaty, they avoided the required two-thirds majority in the protectionist US Senate. American politicians would have objected to the Canadian bias of removing tariffs on Canada's strong suits (raw materials), while keeping tariffs on the US strengths (manufactured goods). But, ironically, the agreement failed because Canada rejected it. Laurier decided to make it an election issue. While the Conservatives initially supported the agreement, they soon took the politically advantageous position of siding with Canadian railroads and some businesses in opposing it. As with any election, many other factors were at play in the defeat of the Liberals, such as the "unholy alliance" between Henri Bourassa's Quebec nationalists and Conservative imperialists. While it was difficult to judge levels of support in these "pre-opinion poll days," reciprocity seemed popular in the West and the Maritimes, but not to the British Imperialists in Ontario. For the Liberal Party and Mackenzie King in particular, free trade took much of the blame for the defeat and can explain his later caution towards it.

Though it cost many Canadian lives, World War I was a great boon to Canadian exports. The war in Europe destroyed much agricultural and manufacturing production and at the same time offered a huge new market for armaments and military goods, while the Canadian economy was left intact. For example, high global demand and high prices for wheat proved a huge bonanza for the Prairies. Canadian exports grew accordingly, and so by 1927, Canada had become the world's fifth-largest exporter of goods, behind the UK, the US, Germany, and France. Roughly 30 per cent of Canadian production was for export, a significant and persistently higher level of dependency on trade than in the US. Table 10.2 shows Canada's global importance in several products, with newsprint in the lead.

Table 10.2 Canada's Percentage of Total World Exports in 1930

Newsprint	63%
Wheat	32%
Aluminium	31%
Copper	14%
Lead and Zinc	12%

Source: Based on data from John Bartlet Brebner, *North Atlantic Triangle* (Toronto: McClelland and Stewart, 1966), p. 296.

For such a trading nation, the collapse of the global economy and the global trading system, beginning with the US stock market crisis of 1929, presented special challenges. As the major economies slipped into deep depression, each tried vainly to staunch rising unemployment by attacking foreign imports with high tariffs designed to "export" the problem. Retaliation served to spiral the global economy down to ever-lower levels of production. The US 1930 Hawley-Smoot Tariff, aimed in part at keeping out Canadian copper, lumber, and farm goods, is a good example of this trade hostility. In its wake came a five-year tariff war between Canada and the US, which ultimately was much more damaging to the smaller economy.

For the newly elected R.B. Bennett government, Britain seemed the salvation. Caught up by the global protectionist sentiment and under pressure from its dominions, the British government at last abandoned free trade for Imperial Preferences in 1932. A special advantage was created in the British market for imports from other Commonwealth members by setting duties against imports from all other states. Though a great boon for agricultural and other raw materials from the dominions, in the long run, as other countries retaliated, it cost Britain dearly in higher prices, lost markets, and lowered competitiveness. Britain's action divided the global economy into major currency blocs based on the primary use of the dollar, the pound, the franc, the mark, and the yen. Interestingly, despite Imperial Preference, Canada did not fully join the sterling (British pound) bloc but straddled both the dollar and the pound.

Despite the tariff wars, geographic proximity and the long undefended border made a mockery of US and Canadian trade protectionism. Higher tariffs were met with increased smuggling, especially after the US prohibition on the sale of alcohol. These factors helped convince the respective governments of the folly of ultra-high tariffs. In 1934, US president Franklin D. Roosevelt managed to get the American Reciprocal Trade Treaties Act through Congress and with it the right to negotiate tariff reductions on a reciprocal basis. When Mackenzie King's Liberals were restored to power in 1935, a deal was quickly reached that eased somewhat the entry of Canadian lumber and farm products to the US market again. This bilateral "swapping concessions" method continued to be used to lower tariffs between the two countries through World War II and the 1950s. But, when Canada and the US negotiated a more comprehensive bilateral free trade agreement in 1948, King refused the deal at the last minute when he recalled the Liberal's defeat in 1911.

THE UNITED STATES AND CANADIAN TRADE AFTER WORLD WAR II

By World War II, the Liberals had made a slight adjustment in their trade liberalism, from historic bilateral free trade to multilateral freer trade. As we saw Chapter 8, this avoidance of bilateral agreements in favour of multilateral ones was part of their post-war strategy of preserving Canadian autonomy. Thus, Canada was a major advocate of the new and open multilateral economic order created out of the allied cooperation in World War II. At the 1944 Bretton Woods Conference, where the IMF and the World Bank were founded, Prime Minister King was pleased that Canada could play an important "linchpin" role between the UK and US. In fact, according to Hart, "Canadian determination to establish a multilateral order and make it work became an enduring theme over the next 40 yrs."[9] The experience of "beggar thy neighbour" protectionism of the 1930s seemed to confirm that freer trade was the main road to economic prosperity for a trading state like Canada. When the GATT sponsored a series of trade rounds to negotiate more open borders for trade on a reciprocal basis in the 1950s, Canada was willing to bargain on half of its tariffed items, though most of the actual deals to swap concessions on tariffs were done with the US.

For Canada, the main post-World War II trade and international finance problem was Britain's rapid decline. Financially, the UK came out of the war in desperate shape. To finance the huge war effort, the UK had sold off many of its overseas investments, and with factories converted to war production and a general failure to invest and innovate, British companies found they had lost many global markets to American and other competitors. As a result, Britain found its economy in immediate need of capital. The Canadian government of course did what it could to provide loans. Nonetheless, Britain's balance of payments was in deep deficit, requiring direct government "currency controls and related QRs (Quantitative Restrictions), [which] made access to the UK market virtually a matter of state trading."[10] With access to the British market now gravely limited, the Canadian economy faced a balance of payments problem of its own, since it could no longer earn the surplus on British trade to pay for its deficit on the US trade balance. In part, this deficit problem was solved when the US government agreed to allow European countries to spend Marshall Plan American dollars on Canadian goods. (The Marshall Plan, named after Secretary of State George Marshall, was devised by the United States to aid European recovery after World War II.)

This Canadian practice of finagling a special deal out of Washington on the basis of a "neighbourly" special relationship was consolidated in the 1950s and 1960s as "exemptionism." As we have seen, Diefenbaker twice used his special friendship with President Eisenhower to get Canada exempted from US regulations. In the Defence Production Sharing Agreement, Canadian firms were granted the right to bid on US defence contracts, a sensitive national security area usually closed to foreigners. Again, in 1959, when the US put a tariff on foreign oil to stimulate domestic production, Diefenbaker gained an exemption for Western Canadian oil. Similarly, in 1963, when the Kennedy administration was concerned about the flight of American investment capital overseas (to places like Canada!), Pearson used his friendship with the US president to grant Canada a partial exemption on the Interest Equalization Tax.

This exemptionism raises the interesting question of why the US was willing to make these one-way concessions to Canada. Part of it may be explained by the proffered rhetoric of a special relationship, the undefended border, and the generally positive sentiment most of the American public seemed to have towards Canada. Given the huge size and relative wealth of the US, especially in this post-war period, there may even have been a bit of *noblesse oblige* similar to the way the US protected Japan and allowed asymmetric concessions there (some of which had very negative long-term consequences for the US). On the other hand, history points to numerous examples of American governments taking a very narrow, self-interested view and playing hardball with even its closest allies.[11]

Several explanations suggest why the smaller party can sometimes have an advantage. Since the Canadian economy is roughly one-tenth the size of the American economy, trade concessions usually have a relatively small impact on the US and a larger one on Canada. According to this argument, this dependence seems harmful to Canada at first, but it's a cloud that has a silver lining, for two reasons. First it means that for the US, concessions to Canada appear to be cheap (at least in the short-run) and thus easy to make. Second, the greater relative salience or importance of the concessions for Canada means the government has a special incentive to direct more resources at bargaining and lobbying the US for the change, and the American "checks and balances" system is more open than other types of government to this form of influence. Successful bargaining on trade treaties depends not only on bargaining chips but also on the amount of information about the situation each negotiator has. Whereas the US had many important security and economic bilateral relationships (with the USSR, China, Cuba, Mexico, the UK, Germany, Japan, etc.) all clambering for attention, the US loomed increasingly large as the most important economic relationship for Canada, according to trade statistics. As Robert Keohane and Joseph Nye have suggested,[12] this at least opens the possibility that Canadian diplomats may come to bilateral negotiations much better prepared than their American counterparts.

For many commentators, this salience factor explains Canada's success in the negotiation of the Auto Pact of 1965. Still looking for ways to reduce the chronic trade deficit with the US, the Pearson government decided to focus on auto imports. After very quick negotiations, this sectoral trade agreement created a duty-free border for autos and auto parts, but with an important production guarantee to Canada attached. For every car imported into Canada, the big three US automakers agreed to build a car in their Canadian plants. Further, to prevent this "Canadian-made car" from being merely the assembly of parts shipped in from the US, the Canadian car had to be made from at least 60 per cent Canadian produced parts. Since the effect of the agreement was to nearly double Canada's share of North American auto production (from 7 per cent in 1964 to 13 per cent in 1972) and to help turn the trade deficit with the US into a trade surplus, the Auto Pact has widely been assessed as an economic "win" for Canada.

Perhaps because of this same perception of the Auto Pact south of the border, the next US government was unwilling to grant a Canadian request for a tariff exemption. In 1971, the Nixon administration, forced at last to deal with American trade and balance of payments problems, slapped a 10 per cent surcharge on all imports. The Trudeau government's hopes that the US would again grant Canada an exemption from this tariff were firmly rebuffed, resulting in the search for alternative trade relations outlined in Mitchell Sharp's 1972 Third Option policy article (see Chapter 7). Ironically, the government's decision to seek a diversification of trade relations to Europe came just as Britain's entry into the European Community (EC; now the EU) in 1973 made that less likely. Indeed, for the traditional British market, Canada was now outside the European Community common external tariff. Despite this loss of advantage in the British market,

Trudeau sought to negotiate a "contractual link" with the EC, but the result—the July 1976 Framework Agreement for Commercial and Economic Cooperation—was more symbol than substance.

Attempts to increase markets in Europe and Japan in the late 1970s and early 1980s failed for numerous reasons, but primarily because both those regions relied on heavy protectionism. Canada's exports of timber, raw materials, and fish competed with similar sources from Scandinavia at a time when the EC was using trade concessions to woo those countries into joining it. There were numerous trade disputes between Canada and the EC, including bitter rows over the EC's allocation of Canadian cod exports to non-fish-consuming Germans and European sanctions to end the seal hunt. Japan was even more protectionist. While willing to expand their imports of natural resources from British Columbia, Japanese firms were not willing to do more processing of those raw materials in Canada, as sought with the EC in the contractual link.

The Trudeau government posted one significant institutional gain in the turbulent world economy of the 1970s. The Nixon shocks heralded the gradual abandonment of fixed exchange rates, a cornerstone of the Bretton Woods Agreement. Canada had already had some experience with "free floating" exchange rates, and thus entered the uncertain new system with more confidence than those countries more committed to the gold standard. That confidence was immediately tested in the economic turmoil generated by two oil price shocks and shortages (1973 and 1978-79) and increasingly radical demands from the developing states for a new international economic order with a redistribution of wealth from rich to poor. In addition, a global recession and hyperinflation spread like a wildfire from one economy to another. By 1975, faced with this apparent multitude of economic threats, the great powers attempted a rare "circle the wagons" manoeuvre as France issued invitations to an exclusive summit of the five top capitalist powers (France, US, Germany, Japan, and the UK) to try to form a common response. When these world leaders decided the meeting was worth repeating on an annual basis, the economic summit was born, with an agreement to rotate host countries. Though not prominently featured in DEA policy statements, Canada, as a big middle power or small big power, has long devoted much attention to seeking a place at the head table, after gaining crucial seats in international forums during World War II by claiming some special status or "functional" ability. Though disappointed at not making the French invitation list, Trudeau was able to manage an invite from President Ford when the Americans hosted the 1976 summit. The French response was then to insist that the Italians also be included, and the group known through the next decade as the G7 was born.

THE FREE TRADE AGREEMENT WITH THE UNITED STATES

The apparent failure of Third Option trade diversification led the Mulroney government to reconsider a free trade deal with the US. Some authors[13] have portrayed this decision as a dramatic reversal of historic Conservative opposition to free trade with the US, and certainly it is the antithesis of nineteenth-century Macdonald protectionism. However, with the right president, even the Conservative Diefenbaker was willing to embrace greater economic integration with the US (the Defence Production Sharing Agreement). Ideologically, the neo-Conservative wing of the Progressive Conservative (PC) party in the 1980s accepted neo-classical arguments in favour of free trade, and the ideological and personal compatibilities of Prime Minister Mulroney and President Reagan certainly facilitated matters. Finally, the party's long historical constituency in the Ontario business community indicated that once most members of that group endorsed free trade, the party was likely to concur.

Drawing on the neo-classical benefits outlined at the beginning of this chapter, the Mulroney government argued that Canadian economic conditions in the 1980s required a free trade agreement with the United States. Canada had always been a trading nation, and its dependence on foreign markets, especially the US, had grown. One-third of all goods produced in Canada were for export, and over a third of those consumed here were imported. Canada's relatively small domestic market meant economies of scale worked against its manufacturers based here. This factor, along with historic protectionism, appeared (on the basis of the few manufacturing exports outside the Auto sector) to make Canadian manufactured goods overpriced and uncompetitive. By this time period, the up and coming growth model was the Asian tiger economy, which favoured aggressive manufacturing exports as the road to success. Economic and business elites in Canada broadly agreed that free trade would help Canadian businesses become more efficient, both through greater competition and greater economies of scale for production, once our "niches" (our comparative advantages) in the global economy were found. The Liberals agreed in part but since 1945 had tended to argue for a multilateral solution to freer trade and market access. The PCs, on the other hand, argued that in light of the loss of access to the British market in the 1970s, the difficulties of multilateral negotiation leading up to the Uruguay Round (1986-94) of global trade talks, and the growing use of protectionism and non-tariff barriers by the EU, Japan, and others, only a bilateral free trade treaty with the US would guarantee Canadian access to this most important market. Indeed, the increase in trade wars among the US and its partners was causing a "sideswiping problem" for Canada, as protectionist actions taken by the US Congress (such as Omnibus Trade Act) aimed at other states (Japan, the EU, Brazil) were inadvertently harming Canadian exports.

Another major issue in the debate over the Mulroney government proposal for the Free Trade Agreement (FTA) was its potential impact on FDI in Canada. The PCs cited evidence that by the 1980s, Canada was not getting its relative share of global investment due to the small size of its economy and the disincentives posed by the Liberal Party's FIRA. The Conservatives were already reducing the regulatory powers of FIRA, but they argued that unless FDI based in Canada had export access to the US market, foreign business would have little incentive to build plants here. In opposition, the NDP and the Liberals argued that removal of the tariff walls between Canada and the US would instead lead to a net outflow of FDI as American businesses closed up their Canadian branch plants. With no duties to worry about, these businesses would rationalize their production in their larger US-based factories. The PCs and many economists agreed rationalization would occur, but given some Canadian advantages (worker health care provided by the government, etc.) at least some would favour Canada.

Armed with these arguments and polls showing at least some public acceptance of the idea, the Mulroney government proceeded with trade proposals to the US at the Quebec City Summit (Shamrock) with President Reagan on March 17-18, 1985. It was agreed to begin talks, and Canada immediately appointed seasoned economic negotiator Simon Reisman to lead the well-organized Canadian team in discussions with Peter Murphy and the smaller American negotiating team. Through two years of slow progress, the American team seemed constantly to be unprepared, disorganized, and less committed to reaching a deal, indicating the salience factor was a hindrance in this case. Both sides believed there were mutual benefits to free trade, but these economic benefits would represent a smaller proportion of the US total GDP, and so perhaps the Reagan administration gave the talks a lower priority than Canada. With the negotiation deadline approaching in the fall of 1987, Reisman decided on the dramatic public tactic of walking out of the negotiations. The move had the desired effect of galvanizing James Baker, a high Reagan administration official, to assert more executive authority over the US team and assure a deal was reached in time.

Critics and supporters agree the resulting Free Trade Agreement (FTA) signed in January 1988 by the US and Canada represented an historic and dramatic milestone in bilateral trade relations. Whereas past nineteenth-century trade agreements and the Auto Pact had opened only limited sectors to free trade, this agreement has a wide, across the board application. Basically, over a ten-year period, the agreement reduced to the point of elimination all tariffs between the two economies and provided for easier access to government procurement on both sides. Service industries receive non-discriminatory treatment: Americans in Canada are to be treated by the same rules applied to Canadians and vice versa for Canadians in the US. While consistent with global GATT rules on national treatment, this agreement ruled out Trudeau-like policies such as the NEP, which favoured Canadian over American businesses. The agreement also attempted to standardize rules in the agricultural sector and allow more access for US farm goods, though Canadian marketing boards remained. Crucially, for the Canadian side, cultural policies and the Auto Pact were left off the bargaining table, and national discrimination could continue for them. Also, Canada sought but was unable to change the American internal process for handling unfair trade disputes (more on this below) but did get a new appeals process to such American decisions through the creation of binational panels with equal representation.

Many critics have argued that this last point was a grave failure of the deal, as the numerous "trade harassing" cases against Canadian exports in the years following seem to demonstrate. The Mulroney government argued that the binational panels were better than the status quo, which gave Canada much less ability to redress these widely condemned US practices. Many Liberal and NDP opponents also claimed that the national treatment measures of the FTA greatly reduced the regulatory powers of the Canadian government, but the PCs could claim in return that Canada was already a party to these non-discriminatory principles through its commitment to the GATT. Furthermore, given the PCs ideological distaste for government economic intervention, the loss or curtailment of these powers would be counted as another "win" for Canada.

In fact, the Mulroney government claimed the FTA had achieved two essential goals, which overruled all other failings of the deal. First, it had guaranteed access to Canada's most important export market at a time when such access was under threat of greater protectionism. Thus, Canada's future economic prosperity was ensured. Second, the FTA finally lay to rest the long legacy of protectionism and the national policy. It would force Canadian entrepreneurs into competition with the world's leading business community, which the Mulroney government hoped would make Canadian business more efficient and productive. As the party most sensitive to overall interests of the business community, the PCs can point to the FTA as a strong sign of their confidence in Canadian entrepreneurs.

Mulroney decided to contest the 1988 election over the FTA due to complications in the ratification of the agreement. In nationally televised debates, Mulroney again stressed the main benefit of the FTA as ensuring the future economic prosperity of the country. Liberal leader John Turner forcefully raised the concern about the potential loss of political sovereignty. As in the election of 1911, free trade with the US was raised as a major issue, but, as in that case, some have argued the election was actually determined by many other factors. But the result this time was clearly different because the free trade government was returned with a majority and the agreement was assured.

Scarcely had the dust settled on this fight when a new trade challenge arose in 1990, in the form of discussions between the United States and Mexico for another free trade agreement. What eventually emerged was the three-way North America Free Trade Agreement, reached in August 1992 and taking effect January 1, 1994. Canada's decision to join the opening round of formal talks in June 1991 was largely defensive. The Mulroney government's initial predisposition not to join the talks was overwhelmed by fears of the consequences of staying out. In particular, the Canadian government was afraid crucial aspects of the FTA might be eroded (such as protection of culture industries) and that the US would gain the lion's share of benefits by becoming the "hub" or centre in a series of "spoke" bilateral agreements.[14]

Given these fears, the PC government was pleased with the 1992 deal, which basically extended the FTA to include Mexico while exempting the Auto Pact, culture, agriculture, and government health care programs. Opposition parties and critics in both the US and Canada fought more fiercely against this agreement, largely because of the low incomes that characterized the Mexican economy. Unlike Canada and the US, Mexico was seen as a developing economy that possessed an unfair trade advantage in its low wages and low standards for labour and the environment. As American presidential candidate Ross Perot famously put it in 1992, there would be "a great sucking sound" as US (and Canadian) companies rushed to relocate factories in Mexico in order to exploit the work force and pollute the environment there. In successful election campaigns in 1992 and 1993, the Democrats and Liberals demanded some form of "side agreements" to NAFTA specifically on these issues before they ultimately accepted the agreement.

THE PROBLEM OF TRADE REMEDY DISPUTES

Before assessing the impact of NAFTA, it is necessary to examine one of the areas of greatest concern and disappointment for Canada: the ongoing American interference with Canadian exports such as softwood lumber through the use of trade remedy laws. Table 10.3 represents a quick primer on how states can deal with the issue of "damaging" imports. All of these trade remedy measures aid the government in protecting domestic producers from low-priced foreign imports. In two categories, this price advantage is alleged to come from unfair, market distorting practices. Countervail is used when the foreign government allegedly subsidizes its firms' exports, for example by giving a direct payment to them to lower their costs or perhaps a tax break for selling a certain number of goods abroad. Anti-dumping remedies are used when foreign firms are allegedly selling ("dumping") a product below the cost it sells for in its own home market or below the cost of production. For example, the European Union might operate an agricultural price-support scheme that involves buying up excess butter within Europe when the price falls below a given threshold. If the EU were to then sell off this surplus butter in the US market at half price, the US could charge the EU with dumping.

Table 10.3 Trade Remedy Measures (used when low-priced imports cause "serious" or "material injury" to domestic producers)

Name	Description of Cause	Comment	Compensation
Countervail allowed	"unfair" government subsidies	can be applied only against "guilty" firms	no retaliation
Anti-dumping	"unfair" prices cheaper than in own market or below production cost	can be applied only against "guilty" firms	no retaliation allowed
Safeguards	"General escape clause" sudden "surge" causing serious injury	applied universally to all firms and countries	exporting country may retaliate often only temporary

Finally, there is an all-purpose safety-net provision for allowing states to protect domestic industries even when an unfair practice is not involved. A few industries may be "permanently exempted" (or protected) even under free trade, such as national security or culture. The use of a temporary safeguard is invoked when an unexpected surge of imports does serious injury to domestic producers, and those domestic firms need a breather to respond. However, under GATT and later WTO rules, when safeguards of this sort are used, the exporting country (the one hit by the safeguard duties) can retaliate by charging duties on a similar value of imports from the "safeguarding" country. Canada pioneered these measures in the early twentieth century and the United States fully developed them. Today these measures are adopted and fully exploited for their protectionist value by virtually everyone. They may appear to contradict the very idea of free trade, but they can also be seen as a compromise to complete free trade by allowing the state some sovereign measure of regulating and protecting its own economy.

The Canadian and US governments have both developed bureaucratic regulatory mechanisms for handling complaints of unfair trade practices, usually voiced by domestic firms who claim to be hurt by cheaper imports. In the US, a complaint or petition about subsidies or dumping can arise from private firms, trade unions, or an agency of the US government itself and immediately generates a two-track investigation involving the International Trade Administration (ITA), a branch of the US Commerce Department, and the International Trade Commission (ITC), an independent US government agency.[15] For either type of complaint, the ITA then investigates the foreign source of the imports and asks, for example, if there is evidence of a foreign subsidy or dumping. The ITC investigates the impact of the imports on domestic producers and determines whether they are causing "material" or "serious" injury. Both tracks of investigation involve preliminary and final hearings, and if the ITA finds evidence of a subsidy or dumping, it can impose a penalty duty on the imports. All of this is legal under GATT procedures, which nonetheless allow the country hit with a penalty duty to demand the creation of a five-person GATT trade expert panel to review the procedures used in the investigation and determine if they followed common trade practices. A major gain of the FTA and NAFTA was the creation of an additional mechanism for Canada (or its partners) to appeal trade remedy decisions through binational panels whose decisions can be appealed to an Extraordinary Challenge Committee. Since their creation, all of these trade remedy procedures and their various WTO, GATT, or NAFTA appeal mechanisms have been used extensively.

These developments in trade remedy procedures and appeals in the past two decades could result in the gradual expansion of international trade law and institution-building. As various state government and international appeal bodies issue their findings, the grey areas about what is or is not a subsidy or an example of dumping should be clarified because a series of precedents and common practice is built up. However, if we adopt a Realist perspective, we can see that states have different and conflicting interests depending on the amount of economic power they possess. Since international law ignores power differences and treats all plaintiffs as equal before the law, weaker states have a greater interest in binding their more powerful trade partners with laws and rules.

For example, during the free trade debate in Canada, arguments were made for trying to limit the US freedom to use trade remedies, even if it meant Canada might lose this freedom as well. One major concession was the agreement to limit the use of safeguard protection by both parties.

Even though they may have "lofty-minded" moments where they appreciate the long-term benefit of having an orderly trade system, powerful states are nonetheless constantly tempted to use their greater clout to extract a few more concessions from their weaker trade partners. These are usually arranged outside the court in political compromises or bilaterally negotiated deals. While sometimes accepting that when the stakes are very high, such agreements may be necessary, the weaker party nonetheless regrets the fact that too many such deals weaken the greater project of international law and norm-building. These features can be seen clearly in the softwood lumber dispute presented in the following case study.

Case Study: Softwood Lumber

Canadian softwood lumber exports to the US are an ongoing dispute. Round one began in 1982 before the FTA and was an example of the kind of trade dispute supporters of the free trade hoped would be fixed by the agreement. We are currently still in round four, which began in April 2001 (see Table 10.4). The stakes are high: in recent years, newspapers regularly attribute 6 to 10 billion Canadian dollars of softwood lumber exports to the US. Given the huge size of Canadian forests and the long history of the industry, economists might suspect that Canada has a natural comparative advantage over the US in lumber, and by 2002 Canadian exports had grown to make up 35 per cent of the US lumber market.[16] No surprise then that the US lumber producers feel threatened and have sought protection.

The basis for their legal complaint is a charge that Canadian federal and provincial governments in effect subsidize Canadian lumber through a variety of programs. In fact, the pricing systems for lumber are different in the two countries. In Canada, much lumber outside the Maritimes comes from provincially owned Crown land. The price is set by government-determined stumpage fees, which Canadian firms pay to harvest the timber. US producers harvest their lumber mainly from private land, and since the price of such wood is set by public auction, they claim to be paying a truer market price than the lower Canadian stumpage fee. By letting its timber go too cheaply, Canadian provincial governments are alleged to be giving an unfair price advantage or subsidy to Canadian firms. Since firms in the Maritimes use more private lumber, they were exempted from the latest US countervail duties. Many of the possible settlements considered in the 2003 and 2004 discussions involved the provinces accepting auctions to determine the price of some portion of their timber. However, many Canadian nationalist and Canadian lumber lobbyists have bridled at such a surrender of Canadian sovereignty.

The US lumber industry has used the stumpage fee to make a subsidy claim through all four rounds of dispute, as Table 10.4 shows. The general pattern of the last three rounds has been as follows:

1. A complaint based on stumpage fees as subsidies is initiated.
2. US ITA launches an investigation, which favours the US industry.
3. Canada appeals the finding.
4. The binational panel (or WTO panel) agrees with Canada.
5. The US appeals the decision and drags out the legal process as long as possible.
6. The US pressures Canada for an extralegal "political settlement."

Step 5 involves not only the American government's use of appeals, delaying tactics, and minimal compliance but also the threat or actual collection of penalty duties (in effect, a tariff on Canadian exports) as a financial cost to Canadian producers. In theory, these collected duties are to be returned to the Canadian producers when the Canadian government wins its legal case before NAFTA or the WTO (as it usually does). But the economic costs of the sustained legal battle, the penalty duties, and the uncertainties for customers all harm the Canadian industry. Thus, the producers are themselves sometimes as eager as the government to bow to US pressure and accept a deal. Round two ended when the Canadian government agreed in the Memorandum of Understanding (MOU) of December 1986 to collect an export tax roughly equal to the threatened US penalty duty. When Canada legally terminated this agreement in 1991 and the US applied penalty duties, round three began. Even though Canada won most of the appeals, a US threat to withhold the collected duties forced Canada to accept the 1996 Softwood Lumber Agreement, which restricted Canadian exports to a fixed level for five years.

This pattern fits with the realist analysis discussed above: since the US cannot win in the legal arena, it uses penalty duties and delaying tactics to "harass" Canadian exports and force the Canadian industry and government into accepting a suboptimal political compromise. Critics of the NAFTA cite this case as proof of the agreement's failure to protect Canada from US bullying. It would appear that the US government agencies, which dismissed the lumber industry's complaint in the first round, have shifted their stance from that of long-term free trade supporters or impartial legal umpires to partisans or protectors of the US industry. Furthermore, they appear ready to implement with little resistance the shocking US congressional proposal (the controversial Byrd Amendment) to give the penalty duties collected from Canadian firms to the American producers even if they lose the case. This action would give the US firms even more incentive to launch trade-harassing suits in the future.

In August 2005, the NAFTA Extraordinary Challenge Committee rendered its final decision unanimously in favour of Canada and demanded that the US tariffs be removed and all collected duties returned to Canada. In a final act of partisanship, the US government announced it would simply ignore the ruling and demanded Canada reopen negotiations for a compromise solution (as had happened in the past). This blatant disregard for the NAFTA agreement provoked a firestorm of protest across the political spectrum in Canada as even supporters of free trade worried that the Bush administration was now jeopardizing the entire agreement. In 2006, the Harper government negotiated a political settlement with the major Canadian concession of allowing the US to keep 20 per cent of the collected duties.

Some supporters of NAFTA, while admitting trade remedy procedures need reform, stress how much worse the situation would be with no binational panels. They argue that even negotiated compromises are better than duties, and Canadian victories on these panels strengthen the government's bargaining position for such agreements. Furthermore, as Greg Anderson shows, Canada itself is a major user of trade remedy measures. He cites WTO data that "between 1995 and 2002, Canada initiated 11 (from a total of 106) anti-dumping cases against the US, compared with 9 American cases against Canadian products (from a global total of 279)."[17]

Table 10.4 A Brief Chronology of the Softwood Lumber Dispute

Round One: October 1982–1983

Oct. 1982	US industry initiates complaint about stumpage fees
May 1983	US ITA rules stumpage not a government subsidy

Round Two: May 1986 to December 1986 and Memorandum of Understanding (MOU)

May 1986	another similar US industry petition
Oct. 1986	preliminary determination of ITA agrees it is a subsidy worth 15%
Dec. 1986	Canada and the US negotiate MOU; Canadian government collects 15% export tax on exports
1991	Ottawa terminates agreement under MOU provisions

Round Three: October 1991 to 1996 Canada US Softwood Lumber Agreement (SFA)

Oct. 1991	ITA responds with a new subsidy investigation
May 1992	ITA final determination against four Canadian provinces
July 1992	ITC final determination on injury supports US industry; final countervailing duties (CVD) of 6.5% imposed except on Atlantic Canada; Canada appeals both findings under FTA
Aug. 1992	Binational panel established agrees with Canadian government; US government gets creation of Extraordinary Challenge Committee (ECC); ECC also finds for Canada
Aug. 1994	US government removes tariff but would not refund $800 million duties

May 1996	Canada US Softwood Lumber Agreement (SFA); quota and tax at fixed level for five years; US returns the collected duties

Round Four: April 2001–present

April 2001	SFA expires; Canadian government does not renegotiate; US industry files countervailing (CVD) and anti-dumping (AD) duty petitions; ITA investigates subsidy, and ITC investigates dumping
July 2001	ITA exempts Atlantic Canada from CVD but not dumping investigation
March 2002	ITA CVD final determination finds 19.34% subsidy rate but exempts Atlantic Canada and 20 companies; ITC dumping final determination sets various individual rates for 6 companies from 15.83% to 5.96% and all other 9.67% (applies across Canada)
April 2002	Canada requests NAFTA Ch. 19 Review Panel of both above
May 2002	Canada also starts challenge to US Final determ at WTO; US customs begin collecting cash duties; 4 big provinces pay on average 27% = 18.8 CVD + 8.4 AD duty; Atlantic Canadian provinces only pay AD duty
Feb. 2003	talks nearing a deal break down
May 2003	WTO interim decision on US CVD favours Canada
June 2003	WTO rules against Byrd Amendment
July 2003	talks resume
Sept. 2003	NAFTA panel ruling against US duties
Dec. 2003	new deal considered but rejected by some provinces
Dec. 2003 & May 2004	more WTO rulings favourable to Canada
April 2004	NAFTA panel again rules for Canada
Sept. 2004	third and final NAFTA panel ruling against US
Nov. 2004	US files for ECC appeal
Dec. 2004	US review leads to only small reduction in duties
Feb. 2005	Canada asks WTO for right to retaliate on softwood duties; granted right to retaliate on Byrd Amendment in Fall 2004
Aug. 2005	NAFTA ECC panel rules unanimously against US; US announces it will not comply; requests Canada negotiate a compromise; Canada refuses negotiations; considers retaliation
Jan. 2006	US Congress to remove Byrd Amendment by Oct. 2007
July 2006	Canadian government offers new concessions

Source: Based in part on the International Trade Canada website <www.dfait-maeci.gc.ca/eicb/-softwood/menu-en.asp> and the author's survey of various *Globe and Mail* news stories.

MEANWHILE ... THE GLOBAL ECONOMY

During the debate on the FTA in 1988, the Liberal Party agreed that while there were many benefits to free trade, it preferred to seek them in global, multilateral agreements rather than in the bilateral FTA because of the political dangers of increased economic integration with the United States. Since the Liberal Party's return to power in 1993, we might therefore expect greater Canadian support for multilateral trade deals in line with Canada's earlier post-World War II role in setting up the Bretton Woods system. While the Liberals, like the US Democrats, did accept NAFTA with side deals, we can see the ghost of the Third Option in the Liberal quest for new freer trade deals with the EU and others. While to some EU members, political counterbalancing of the US with other Western Hemisphere trade deals makes some strategic sense, EU economic protectionism has so far proved too great a barrier. The Liberals therefore had to content themselves with a free trade agreement with Chile only.

This deal with Chile shows the Liberals had a similar desire for diversifying trade partners in the Western Hemisphere. Though Canada long avoided full membership in the Organization of American States (OAS), in part for fear of coming into conflict with the US over its interventionist policies there, the Mulroney government took the plunge and joined in 1990. Since then both Liberals and Conservatives have seen the economic and political advantages in more pan-hemispheric links, by supporting both a clause for further members in the NAFTA agreement and the Free Trade Agreement for the Americas (FTAA) project. Also for the first time, Canada hosted a Summit of the Americas conference in April 2001 in Quebec City, which discussed the FTAA. In the 1990s, Canada also joined another even broader regional trade initiative, the Asia-Pacific Economic Cooperation (APEC), to facilitate trade around the entire Pacific basin. So far, both of these large organizations have seemingly fallen victim to the old dictum: the bigger the party, the bigger the rhetoric and the smaller the concrete results. Perhaps the Chrétien government accomplished more for trade bilaterally, through a series of trade promotion missions in the 1990s that sent the prime minister and various provincial premiers abroad to drum up sales of Canadian products in Latin America and Asia.

Taking a dim view of regional trade blocs, neo-classical economists would say that if countries want free trade, they should seek it at the global level instead. This universality was the dream of Bretton Woods, and since World War II, the GATT has sponsored a series of large trade negotiation rounds. The last such completed agreement was the Uruguay Round, which was barely able to reach a deal after complex and contentious negotiations among over 100 states. Whereas past trade rounds focused on lowering tariff rates, Uruguay tackled the growing use of non-tariff barriers and protectionist domestic policies. For example, Canada initially joined with a group of agricultural-exporting states to form the Cairns Group in order to lobby against restrictive agricultural practices and state subsidies used by the EU, Japan, and the US, which damaged their exports. However, domestic resistance within Canada to proposals that might change our own marketing boards forced the government to backtrack and distance itself from its Cairns Group allies.

A much more successful Canadian contribution to the Uruguay Round was the trade minister's proposal in 1990 for a new international trade organization. Eventually, a compromise was reached in 1995 with the creation of the World Trade Organization (WTO) to give a formal institutional base to international trade governance and to at last provide the third pillar (with the World Bank and IMF) of the global economy envisioned by Bretton Woods.

The future of large economic agreements looks dim in the early years of the twenty-first century. Economic discord and disharmony of interests nearly sank the Uruguay Round and have hampered the new Doha Round, scuttled the Multilateral Agreement on Investment (MAI), weakened the FTA's prospects, and stalemated the G7s attempts at financial reform, known as the Halifax Initiative. In part, these initiatives were all the victims of past trade agreements that have succeeded in expanding global trade levels and further integrating the global economy in a process sometimes referred to as globalization. The very success of freer trade provides the evidence that feeds the anti-globalist critique, building on the arguments of mercantilists and nationalists discussed at the beginning of the chapter. Just as freer trade creates winners, it also creates losers who mobilize against it, aided by the principle of "concentrated costs, diffuse benefits." This brings us to a final examination of the overall benefits and costs of free trade for Canada.

ASSESSING NAFTA AND CANADIAN ECONOMIC GROWTH IN THE TWENTY-FIRST CENTURY

Chapter 8 examined the dangers economic openness presented for autonomy. We now focus on the economic costs or benefits of the same. It appears that judged merely on economic criteria, most mainstream economists today believe that the benefits of free trade outweigh the costs. Opponents of NAFTA and globalization would disagree. Supporters of NAFTA will cite examples of Canadian exporters expanding their production and hiring more workers, and detractors will cite news stories about bankruptcies, firms moving abroad, and workers being laid off. However, judging the overall effect on a few anecdotes is never a satisfactory procedure. In order to see the overall picture, we need to examine the Canadian balance of payments statement.

As stated back at the beginning of this chapter, "avoiding a balance of payments crisis" was one of the three great economic objectives of all states. Fear of too much debt motivated the mercantilist's desire to hoard gold and to have more exports than imports (a positive balance of trade). The annual Canadian balance of payments represents a financial accounting of all the transactions across Canadian borders, including, among others, the trade balance (exports minus imports), tourism balance (foreign guests' purchases minus purchases by Canadians abroad), the profit/interest balance (foreign earnings by Canadians minus earnings taken out of Canada by foreigners), and the investment balance (foreigners investing in Canada minus Canadians investing abroad). These items are summarized in Table 10.5. For each balance, the items in the "credits" column have a positive impact on the balance of payments and the items in the "debits" side have a negative impact. The overall balance becomes a policy issue for the government if the economy runs a high negative balance (also called "living beyond its means"), as when a US deficit forced the Nixon shock measures of 1971. For many smaller states, negative balances mean economic disruption, currency rationing by the government, and trips to the IMF for currency loans given with tough conditions.

Table 10.5 The Balance of Payments Ledger

Credits (Selling)	Debits (Buying)
Trade Balance Trade exports from Canada to other countries.	Trade imports into Canada from other countries.
Tourism Balance Money spent by foreign tourists visiting Canada.	Money spent by Canada visiting other countries.
Investment Balance Foreign investments by other countries in Canada	Foreign investments by Canada. in other countries.
Profit/Interest Balance Profits returned (repatriated) to Canada from its investments in other countries	Profits returned (repatriated) to other countries from their investments in Canada.
New Government Debt (Bonds) sold externally.	Paying the interest and principal on debt.
	Foreign aid sent by Canada to other countries.
	Military expenditures by Canada to support Canadian Forces in other countries.
Plus Creates demand for Cdn $	**Minus** Reduces demand for Cdn $

For Canada, trade balancing in the late nineteenth and early twentieth century is demonstrated in the way the Canadian trade surplus with the UK helped to pay for the deficit in trade with the US. However, as the UK declined as a trade partner in the second half of the twentieth century, Canada came to rely on other balance mechanisms. By increasing exports to the US over imports, the trade balance with that major partner was swung to a positive balance. But the major concern after World War II was the effect of the large amount of foreign (particularly US) investment in Canada. By playing host to so much FDI, Canada has and still does experience a large outflow of repatriated profits each year. That outflow in fact was so large in the post-World War II decades that it overwhelmed any trade surplus. Traditionally, the overall balance of payments was then kept out of the red by large, new FDI and portfolio investments in Canada by foreign investors. But this insured a future negative stream of capital flow out of Canada in the form of profits and interest payments. This situation strikes many Canadians, not just mercantilists, as a bit of a vicious circle in which we make our current interest payments by taking on more debt. This situation was exacerbated in the 1970s and 1980s when government budget deficits at all levels were financed by further foreign borrowing (e.g. selling Canadian bonds to the Japanese). This latter problem was only improved in the 1990s, as federal and some provincial budgets were brought more into balance.

What effect does NAFTA have on the Canadian balance of payments? Given that full implementation of the agreement is relatively recent, any evidence provided here must still be seen as tentative. The FTA, signed in January 1988, called for the gradual reduction of all tariffs over a 10-year period, and the NAFTA agreement, which brought in Mexico, likewise involved a gradual 10-year elimination of tariffs with Mexico (going into effect in 1994). Therefore, in the past decade, supporters of freer trade would predict an overall increase in trade volumes and increased prosperity for Canada. Critics would predict an export downturn coming from the closing of US branch plants and the bankruptcy of Canadian firms unable to meet the foreign competition from US and Mexican products.

Figure 10.2 tracks Canadian exports by volume from 1980 to 2004 and shows a dramatic increase (doubling) of Canadian exports for the 1990s, as has been reported elsewhere.[18] Expressed in more constant terms, exports as a per cent of GDP have risen from 21.5 per cent in 1991 to 40 per cent in 2000. Imports also rose dramatically, but not faster than exports. As a result, the trade surplus as a proportion of GDP grew through the 1990s to a high of 7.5 per cent in 2000 (according to the mercantilist, a very good thing). All of this took place in the context of the great economic boom of the 1990s for the US and Canadian economies, which free trade either abetted or, at a minimum, did not choke off.

Figure 10.2 Growth in Canadian Exports of Goods

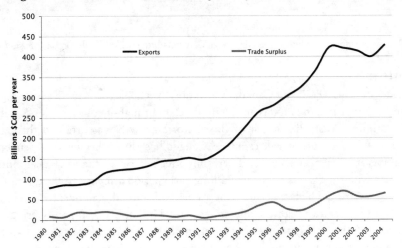

Source: Data from Statistics Canada retrieved through CanSim, <http://dc2.chass.utoronto.ca/cansim/>.

Figure 10.3 shows the behaviour of foreign investors in terms of the changes they made in their FDI based in Canada. The first line in the legend shows the inflow of new FDI investments. The second line represents divestment or the selling off of foreign-owned investments in Canada, and third line shows the resulting balance of these two. It is here specifically in the divestment line that we should look for evidence of branch plants being closed as a result of free trade. Had the trend line continued downward at the rate of the 1984-85 sell-off, then there would be great reason for concern. The year 2000 showed another divestment spike, but it was more than offset by a huge inward flow of FDI in the same year. Indeed, the overall balance of these two flows has been positive and generally rising over the whole time span (1980-2004). This trend suggests that free trade has not made Canada less attractive for foreign investors.

Figure 10.3 Changes to the Stock of FDI in Canada

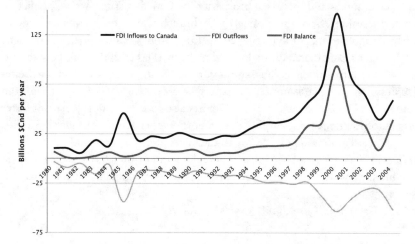

Source: Data from Statistics Canada retrieved through CanSim, <http://dc2.chass.utoronto.ca/cansim/>.

CONCLUSION

Since Confederation in 1867, the Canadian economy has achieved growth levels high enough to ensure that it stands today in the upper class of high-income states. As with her sister dominion, Australia, much of this historic growth was attained through the export of raw or semi-processed resources. Canada has always been very dependent on selling goods in foreign markets and certainly much more so than her neighbour to the south. As with the US, Canada spent a long early period attached to the doctrines of protectionism, during which time she built a fairly substantial manufacturing sector. But as with all the wealthy high-income states (UK, Holland, US, Japan, Germany, etc.), industrialization appears to have been only a phase of that growth. Recent glob-alization is moving the heavy manufacturing to lower-income states, but all the wealthy economies are finding ways to maintain their high standards of living and continue to grow in part by reliance on service industries and advanced technology.

Both of Canada's main federal parties now have accepted a relatively open trade policy; they only disagree on tactics, with the Liberals (and the NDP) more suspicious of over-reliance on the US market. And it is hard to see how even a socialist government could at this point untangle the Canadian economy from its global linkages without a major fall in overall Canadian standards of living. Figure 10.3 seems to show no dramatic loss of foreign investor interest in Canada, but NAFTA is still young and this trend needs watching. Figure 10.2 shows a dramatic growth in exports, which also implies more dependence on foreign markets and raises the issues of power and autonomy discussed in Chapter 8. This is especially true, given the US government's ongoing tendency to play hardball with trade remedy procedures. The winning policy lies in carefully balancing liberal growth and political autonomy concerns.

Notes

1. Such factors include the triumph of British manufacturing over agricultural interests, factional politics within Peel's Tory party, and the superior competitiveness of British exports at the time.

2. Quoted in Brebner (1966), p. 53.

3. Due to the precarious political balance between northern and southern (pro-slavery) states in the US Senate, it was difficult enough for Washington to compromise on new states entering from the West at this time. The South would never have allowed so many "Canadian" anti-slavery states to join the Union.

4. Hart (2002), p. 51.

5. See Brebner (1966), p. 209, 227, and 228.

6. Norrie (1991), p. 296.

7. Brooks (1989), Chapter Four.

8. Hart (2002), p. 75.

9. *Ibid.*, p. 141.

10. *Ibid.*, p. 150. He means government approval of each trade, a form usually associated with the USSR at the time. This would have been a great hindrance on the amount of trade Canada could have with Britain.

11. For example, World War I war debts, Nixon shocks, and more recently over Iraq and the International Criminal Court.

12. In Keohane and Nye (1977).

13. For example, Lawrence Martin, *Pledge of Allegiance: The Americanization of Canada in the Mulroney Years* (Toronto: McClelland and Stewart, 1993).

14. An easy way to imagine this benefit is to think an MNC manager planning to build one factory to export its product to the largest possible market. If there is no free trade between Canada and Mexico, then which of the countries is the best place to locate? Only from the US could the factory send its products to all three markets duty free.

15. The current US procedure was established in US Trade Act of 1974. The Canadian trade

remedy procedure mirrors the US, with the Department of National Revenue taking the role of the ITA and the Canadian Import Tribunal carrying out the functions of the ITC.

16. Kennedy (2002), B10.

17. Anderson (2003), p. 92.

18. The Industry Canada ministry of the Canadian Federal government provides its own analysis of recent trends through its web publication The Trade and Investment Monitor of Fall-Winter 1999-2000. This paper can be downloaded from the web at <http://strategis.ic.gc.ca/sc_ecnmy/-mera/engdoc/08.html>.

Chapter Eleven
The Projection of Canadian Identity as a National Interest

In 1995, the Department of Foreign Affairs and International Trade (DFAIT) issued the final product of its 1995 foreign policy review, *Canada in the World*, which lists the third major objective of Canadian foreign policy as "the projection of Canadian values and culture." Of all the national interests discussed so far, this one is the most amorphous, covering a broad range of potential factors: political, social, economic, and cultural. The report itself mentions political values (human rights and democracy), economic goals (sustainable development), and the more general topic of Canadian "culture and education."

Taken together, these values and culture amount to a collective Canadian identity. But unpacking the specific elements of this concept must lead us to controversy. Is there one common Canadian culture? What should it include or exclude? Is the resulting profile significantly different from other national cultures, such as Britain or the United States?

Indeed, most of the values discussed in *Canada in the World* are not unique but shared values that locate Canada as a member of a Western or North Atlantic regional community, or what the report calls "the open, advanced societies."[1] In its broadest sense, we could enumerate the members of this community as Western Europe, Canada, the US, Australia, and New Zealand, and debate whether also to include the rest of Europe, Japan, Israel, and Latin America. Many of Canada's political values, such as democracy and respect for human rights, grew out of shared political institutions that originated in European and North American liberalism. When Canada expresses concerns about civil liberties in international forums, it is usually as part of a broader "Western" initiative. Canada also shares economic institutions and ideas with this community of post-industrial, hi-tech, high-income states. The group is also defined economically by common memberships (Organisation for Economic Cooperation and Development [OECD], the G7) and common economic policies (Keynesianism, social-welfarism, and development aid to poorer nations). Even where these common policies conflict, they seem to shift in the community with synchronicity. Thus, in the 1980s, there was a common "return to the market" and, as if on cue, most governments in this wealthy group reduced their aid-giving in the 1990s.

Sociologically, more shared values probably exist within this community than outside it, for example, about the division between the religious and the secular, the public and private, and the status of women and civil liberties. A common European origin also links most of the community's arts, literature, language, and "high" culture.

While granting this common cultural heritage, *Canada in the World* goes on to attempt to distinguish a uniquely "Canadian" identity. "Canada's history as a non-colonizing power, champion of constructive multilateralism, and effective international mediator underpins an important and distinctive role among nations."[2] Specifically, our status as a Western state that never possessed colonies (along with some smaller European states), and in recent decades, our position as a strong multilateralist help to distinguish Canada from our closest cultural relative, the United States. Though both the nations were founders and developers of the leading multilateral international organizations, such as the OECD, the UN, and its vast array of specialized agencies (the Food and Agriculture Organization [FAO], World Bank, and WTO), US support for them in recent years has been far weaker than Canadian support. Similar sharp contrasts are evident in our differing responses to multilateral treaties on land mines and the International Criminal Court.

The Canadian government frequently heralds multiculturalism as a defining characteristic, but again it is not one that distinguishes us from the US or UK, unless our unique English and French bilingualism and biculturalism is stressed. *Canada in the World* summarizes the role of Canadian cultural identity this way: "Only Canadian culture can express the uniqueness of our country, which is bilingual, multicultural, and deeply influenced by its Aboriginal roots, the North, the oceans, and its own vastness."[3]

Yet, the question remains as to how much importance this subject deserves in our discussion of "weighty" national interests. The 1995 report spends much time presenting justifications for cultural policies and showing their links to other key interests. For example, in the security arena, as already noted, much of this same common cultural community is also bound together by the NATO alliance. Highlighting the shared values of that alliance's membership can only strengthen the cohesion and solidarity of the security community in the face of common problems and threats. The report itself emphasizes that multilateralism and support for international norms lead to more international "law and order" for the global community. Furthermore, promoting democracy and economic development may help to reduce the causes of violence in conflict-prone areas, such as the Balkans, the Middle East, and Africa.

In addition to ameliorating conflict, economic aid and trade can support other Canadian domestic economic objectives. General openness and growth in the global economy provides more opportunities for Canadian-based exporters. Promoting Canadian culture specifically aids producers of that culture to sell their wares, whether films, books, or works of art.

The report also makes an interesting domestic link to the unity issue: "In countries like Canada, unity springs from pride in the civic nationality — based on shared values and tolerance, respect for rule of law, and thoughtful compromise — that its citizens share." This seems self-evident: values that shape a common Canadian identity would seem to weaken separatism in Quebec and elsewhere. But the report goes further: "Our values and rights will not be safeguarded if they are not enshrined throughout the international environment. Canada is not an island: if the rights of people abroad are not protected, Canadians will ultimately feel the effects at home."[4] It's a bit tricky to sort out all the implications of this more aggressive statement. Are they justifying cultural imperialism? At a minimum, this statement suggests greater legitimacy for our domestic institutions and values if we are consistent in projecting the same values abroad. This principle can be seen in the critic's charge of hypocrisy when the US, the leader of democracy, supports dictatorships abroad.

Even hard-nosed Realists must concede some importance to cultural promotion through its indirect effects. After all, most definitions of power include the concept of "influence." Indeed, using the power of influence can involve fewer resources and less risk, and thus be more efficient than coercive military power in many situations. Joseph Nye used the concept of "soft power" to deal with many of the cultural elements discussed in this chapter. He argued the positive feelings about Hollywood, Coca-Cola, and other American products generated a low-cost form of influence for the US. Ironically, American cultural icons are just as likely today to provoke strong anti-American reactions and thus neutralize their own influence. Canada, with much fewer negative associations, is therefore more likely to be able to use such soft power. For example, when Canada negotiates in an international forum or launches diplomatic initiatives, positive images of Canada held by foreign governments can only enhance the likelihood of success.

Canada in the World gives us a long list of Canadian values and images to chose from, perhaps too many. Therefore, for the rest of this chapter, we will focus on one particular image far removed from traditional national interests: the view that Canada gives generous aid to poorer nations.

CANADIAN AID POLICY: THE LONG ROAD TO SUSTAINABLE DEVELOPMENT AND BEYOND

Under the title "International Assistance," *Canada in the World* devotes the entire sixth section of its report to the topic of Canada's Official Development Aid (ODA) policy. It links this policy area as a subfield of the broader third foreign policy goal of "projecting Canadian values and culture" by placing the stress on philanthropy or altruism.

> Finally, it [ODA] is one of the clearest international expressions of Canadian values and culture — of Canadians' desire to help the less fortunate and of their strong sense of social justice — and an effective means of sharing these values with the rest of the world.[5]

This sharing of values is clearly laid out in the description of the sustainable development that Canada promotes:

> An effective development assistance program begins with the recognition that development is a complex process and that many conditions must be met before it takes permanent root. Individuals must have *equitable access to basic social services*, to productive assets and to employment opportunities. *Women* must be able to participate fully and equally in development. Respect for *human rights* is essential, as are a *healthy civil society and political systems* that

inspire confidence and trust. The basic infrastructure that underpins society must be in place, along with policies that *promote sustainable economic growth with equity*. And, in today's interdependent world, a society's long-term prosperity depends increasingly on access to international markets and finance. Finally, development does not last if it is not *environmentally sustainable* [my emphasis].[6]

This passage summarizes all the values (equity, gender, human rights, civil society, and the environment) that have recently been added to the basic, original philanthropic intent of Canada's aid program, dating from the founding post-war years. This basic altruistic motive is never spelt out, perhaps because it is taken for granted. But it is alluded to in expressions such as "a desire to help the less fortunate" and "social justice." In the interests of clarity, Table 11.1 spells out three possible characterizations of the humanitarian motive that are not always carefully enumerated in studies of Canadian aid policy. In practice, a mix of these ethics-based motives influences the actions of governments, charitable organizations, and individuals.

Table 11.1 Ethics-based Motives for Aid

1. Traditional/Religious
- Supported by most major religions through the values of charity, alms giving, tithing
- Shows compassion/worthiness of being among God's elect
- Requirement for a good afterlife/entry into heaven
- Affects the believer/donor

2. Opposition to Inequality (as morally unacceptable, unfair, unjust)
- Involves redistribution of wealth as government policy
- Is attached to class divisions or discourses of exploitation in its leftist form
- Shows solidarity with the recipients

3. Empathy and Human Suffering
- Stresses pity as reaction to suffering and unhappiness of others
- Appeals to liberal notion that one's own happiness is in part determined by the happiness of others
- Involves emergency aid and famine relief without the requirement of long-term equality

Andrew Cooper refers to these humanitarian motives as the "missionary strain,"[7] beginning with Canadian aid policy under the Liberal governments of St. Laurent and Pearson in the 1950s and 1960s, and cites Mitchell Sharp's 1961 call for "a return to the simple principles of Christian charity" as an example. Likewise, Alain Noël and Jean-Philippe Thérien have found a common liberal ideological motive underpinning the

ODA—the externalization of the Pearsonian social-welfare model. They point to the more than doubling of Canadian external aid from 1964 to 1967, the same years as the large domestic expansion of welfare spending.[8] Similar sentiments can even be found in the conservative Mulroney years in the 1987 Winegard Report of the House of Commons Standing Committee on External Affairs and International Trade.[9]

Of course, many other motives exist, and *Canada in the World* mentions humanitarian aims only after economic and security objectives. The economic policy linkage is easy to see: ODA "connects the Canadian economy to some of the world's fastest growing markets in the developing world."[10] The most direct way to make this connection is through the practice of tied aid: the requirement that the aid recipient spend the aid funds on donor-country produced goods and services. It directly increases exports from the donor economy and helps to promote "market development" for suppliers in the donor country in the future.

Tied aid is not popular among low average income states (LAIS) and has long been criticized by Canadian commentators, despite its extensive use by the Canadian government. Economists condemn the inefficiency of not allowing the purchaser to buy the cheapest product on the market. Conservatives criticize it as a form of government subsidy to domestic groups, and liberals point out how much further the aid would go if spent freely. According to Gerald Helleiner, it "raises administrative costs and slows disbursements [...] biases techniques in favour of imported inputs and technologies, distorts overall priorities, and makes it extremely difficult to employ aid for direct poverty-alleviating projects."[11]

Of course, there must be advantages to tied aid, or the Canadian government would not have used it so often. Canadian jobs and exports and the allure of future business all beckon. Furthermore, with its *quid pro quo* aspect of reciprocity, it fits better with the rhetoric of partnership and equality. Certainly, the government believes that by showing a material benefit to Canadians, tied aid makes ODA spending, which otherwise has no direct domestic client or beneficiary, more palatable to the public.

Security is also given as a justification for aid, under several guises. In the Lloyd Axworthy sense, it helps reduce "many key threats to human security, such as the abuse of human rights, disease, environmental degradation, population growth, and the widening gap between rich and poor."[12] This gap between the "haves" and the "have-nots" was commonly cited as a source of global conflict before the Second World War. Envious, resentful, poor states may challenge richer states militarily, perhaps on the model of North Korea when it launched a missile over Japan. Cranford Pratt attacks this older concept as "fear of the poor."[13] Nonetheless, fear of Communism or of Communist in-roads in poorer regions was often directly cited to justify Canadian and American foreign aid in the cold war era. The end of the Soviet threat is often cited to explain the dramatic decline in ODA among Western nations in the 1990s. In more general terms, in many states, poor economic conditions have been linked with conflict, ethnic violence, and political instability, and these are in turn linked with regional and global insecurity.

Finally, Andrew Cooper reminds us of the political objectives served by generous

ODA as "a tool to win 'goodwill,' 'a voice,' or 'institutional access.'"[14] Both he and Kim Richard Nossal point to the Canadian government's tendency to spread its aid too thinly over too many countries as an indication of political factors at work. As we saw in Chapter 9, during the war of the conferences, the Trudeau government used ODA to francophone African states to thwart Quebec separatist ambitions. Likewise, Trudeau attempted to portray Canada as the friend of the Third World, for example, at the Cancun North-South conference, which he chaired in 1981. Whether these attempts at influence actually succeeded or not, they nonetheless tell us something about the motivation behind giving aid.

Conditionality refers to the direct attempt to influence the policy of the aid recipient. In the last two decades, there have been frequent calls for Canada to attach certain conditions to its ODA: respect for human rights, improved status for women, and better treatment of the environment. Since the debt crisis of the 1980s, the IMF, the World Bank, and other OECD governments have set economic conditions for loans and other transfers. Though the impact of all of these forms of conditionality has been hotly debated, they clearly demonstrate the attempt to use aid as a means of influencing the recipient government.

GENERAL ASPECTS OF OFFICIAL DEVELOPMENT AID

Before examining specific Canadian ODA policies further, we should discuss a few general aid issues. One is the international effort to set targets for government aid. Just as the use of the tithe in the Christian faith suggests giving of a set proportion of income to the poor, benchmarks of both 1 per cent and 0.7 per cent have been suggested for the aid efforts of wealthier states, particularly for members of the Development Aid Committee (DAC) of the OECD. For example, the World Council of Churches suggested a 1 per cent target in 1958. The UN General Assembly later adopted this principle, recommending that its richer members seek a total outflow of capital (public and private) equal to 1 per cent of their collective annual national incomes. Because of the problem of comparing national income statistics when assessing individual efforts, the United Nations Conference on Trade and Development (UNCTAD) conferences of the 1960s shifted to a GNP measure, usually a more generous target than national income, with the stipulation that it be applied to donor states individually rather than collectively. Unlike later internationally proclaimed goals, this was "the only target to have been endorsed by all DAC Members."[15] But this 1 per cent of GNP measure included all capital flows both public (ODA) and private (e.g., business investment), and the latter tended to go up and down a good deal from year to year and was usually not under the donor country's control.

Enter the 1969 Report of the Pearson Commission, *Partners in Development*. As one of his last public acts, Lester Pearson chaired the commission, which at last suggested the "definitive" target. Each high average income state (HAIS) should provide a yearly ODA equivalent of 0.7 per cent of its GNP. With various plans for phasing it in, this target was soon widely adopted by many HAISs and is now commonly cited by aid IGOs and the development literature. The problem has been that, despite promises and pledges, only a handful of OECD members ever reached this goal and two of the richest, the US and Switzerland, never adopted it.

Another issue is bilateral versus multilateral aid. Donor states generally tend to favour the former because it allows them to attach strings (such as tied aid), to exert greater oversight on how the money is spent, and to claim more direct credit for successful ventures with their home publics. Donors may feel that supervision is necessary due to poorly developed accountancy or outright corruption on the part of officials in the recipient state. The fiasco of missing aid to the Palestinian Authority in 1998 was a *cause célèbre* in this regard.

On the other hand, multilaterally processed aid is preferred by the LAISs and international organizations because it is delivered by way of a third-party organization. In the case of the UN, this makes the imposition of conditions much more unlikely. Many development economists and humanitarian organizations have also campaigned for this form, as it is less subject to distortion from non-developmental aims.

The type and the purpose of the aid is another question that has evolved over time. In the 1950s and 1960s, the focus for aid was on building industrial capacity and infrastructure, particularly aimed at modernizing the LAIS's economy. Development theory at the time viewed the problem as one of insufficient investment and lack of up-to-date production methods, which required the transfer of capital and technology from the more advanced economies. This transfer usually came in the form of large mega projects, often planned and supervised by the donor state(s) under the guise of "project aid." The common parable used at the time was "Give a man a fish and he can eat today, but give him a fishing rod and he can eat tomorrow."

This approach did not rule out commodity aid, especially in the form of surplus food stocks, which was popular with farmers in wealthier agriculture exporting states like Canada and the US. Governments justified it for humanitarian reasons and because it removed a surplus that might depress domestic food prices. Technical cooperation was offered with OECD university scholarships for Third World students and HAIS experts sent to advise LAIS governments and to work directly with them on aid projects.

Despite at least some initial evidence that this approach succeeded in boosting the average economic growth rate, a major shift from "economic" to "social investment" aid occurred in the 1970s. It was argued that the rise of private investment flows (FDI and private bank lending) and the success of the "green revolution" (e.g., new and more productive strains of grains) had reduced the need for large industrial and agricultural projects. Many OECD states believed ODA should focus on goods not available from the private marketplace, for example, health, education, clean water, and other forms of social infrastructure. Along with a greater awareness of ongoing poverty, there was a shift in focus toward providing basic needs and alleviating that poverty. The main aim of ODA shifted to immediate humanitarian goals, such as providing basic food and shelter, and raising people out of poverty. In the 1970s, the emphasis was back on giving the man (and woman) a daily fish.

This shift was caused in part by large natural disasters requiring immediate relief in the form of emergency aid. A series of large regional famines (such as the African Sahel drought of the 1970s and the Ethiopian famine beginning in 1985) and refugee problems arising from conflict in the Middle East, Africa, and the Balkans, among others, led to an expansion of emergency aid that peaked in 1994 at over 9 per cent of total bilateral ODA.[16] The focus on poverty also meant a shift in targets of the ODA from the fast growing and relatively better off LAISs to the poorest and often smallest economies. Since opportunities for donor "market development" were less available in smaller and poorer LAISs, this shift of focus could also be seen as a triumph of humanitarian motives over economic self-interest.

Since the 1970s, there has also been a decline in technical cooperation as a form of ODA. With growing Third World radicalism in the 1970s, using Western training, experts, and technology for aid was attacked as resulting in "inappropriate technology transfer," which led to local cultural erosion. The modernization model underlying earlier development theories was seen as a Western straightjacket, insensitive to local cultures and needs. The new emphasis was to be on "partnership," local solutions, and local expertise. As a result, the technical component dropped from around half of the bilateral ODA in the 1960s to as low as a quarter more recently.

In the 1980s and 1990s, many LAISs became caught in a debt trap, so the ODA was dominated by that debt crisis.[17] Beginning with the Mexican government's financial crisis and near default in 1982, many Latin American governments were forced to turn to the IMF for emergency bailout loans. The IMF and later the World Bank made such loans conditional on the adoption of austerity programs aimed at correcting the economic policies that had caused the financial and foreign exchange shortfall. Though many mainstream economists justified these Structural Adjustment Programs (SAPs) as an unavoidable "short-term pain for long-term gain," critics attacked the SAPs as unjustifiable violations of national sovereignty and solutions that placed the costs of adjustment on the poorest sectors of the low-income economy. Indeed "adjustment lending" soon crowded out the 1970s focus on poverty. While the policies of the IMF did save the world economy and banking system from collapse, for many LAISs, the 1980s and 1990s became the "lost decades of development," as their growth rates slowed or turned negative.

In terms of ODA, the debt crisis shifted the aid-giving priority to debt relief and then debt forgiveness. In the 1980s, private flows of capital in the form of new bank loans and FDI to the LAISs were greatly curtailed by fears of economic collapse. ODA might have been expected to pick up the slack. But with the emphasis on dealing with past loans, there seemed to be much less money for new investment, and many LAISs showed a net outflow of capital in this period. On top of this, HAISs as a group seemed to suffer from a net "aid fatigue" in the 1990s, as average ODA levels declined to new lows.

A BRIEF HISTORY OF CANADIAN ODA: THE EARLY YEARS

The Colombo Plan in 1950 is usually considered the starting point of Canada's own ODA activity. Named for its venue in the capital city of the newly independent Ceylon (now Sri Lanka), the meeting adopted a plan in which the wealthier members of the British Commonwealth would direct assistance to the new states created from the former colony of India. Though motivated in part by security issues and the fear of Asian Communist expansion after the 1949 victory of Mao in China and the 1950 Korean War, the plan did address the real humanitarian needs of South Asia in a manner that, from Canada's perspective, bolstered the Indian and Commonwealth connections.

Multilateralism was a recurring theme for Canada in these immediate post-war years in which the country played a major role in founding the economic development institutions of the new Bretton Woods system. Primary among these was the World Bank, which in 1960 took on a more direct role in LAIS assistance with the creation of the International Development Agency (IDA). In that same year, the OECD established its Development Assistance Committee as the main coordinator and advocate for ODA for the wealthy countries. By 1970, the LAISs had responded with their own organization, the UN Development Program (UNDP), which partially made up for the failure of the more ambitious UN forum, the 1951 special UN fund for soft loans (SUNFED). But, as with the other Western donors, Canadian governments preferred to use the World Bank's IDA and the OECD's DAC, where membership and voting rules favoured the wealthier states.

With the rapid increase in newly independent low-income states and favourable global economic conditions, the 1960s soon became a true "decade of development." Parallel with the expansion of the UN development system was the creation of a series of regional development banks. Again, Canada became an active participant on each of these organizations: the Asian Bank in 1965, the Caribbean in 1970, the Inter-American in 1972, and the African in 1982.

Except for a few voluntary groups, such as the Canadian University Service Overseas (CUSO), the Canadian aid effort in this period tended to be highly centralized, not just in the federal government but also in the hands of a small DEA elite. For Pearson, Escott Reid, and other Canadian statesmen of this diplomatic "golden age," international assistance was a further demonstration of Canadian internationalism and good global citizenship. Even when Pearson became prime minister, policy tended to be ad hoc and ODA lacked a bureaucratic base until the 1966 creation of an external aid office in the DEA.

ODA PROFESSIONALIZATION UNDER TRUDEAU

Given the more self-interested, hard-headed rhetoric of the new Trudeau government, one might have expected a lower profile for ODA, a Pearsonian internationalist endeavour. But the 1970 foreign policy review *Foreign Policy for Canadians* praised ODA as a distinctly Canadian activity. Though a tough-minded realist, Trudeau still saw the merits of ODA in enhancing Canadian prestige and influence. In 1968, ODA received a new bureaucratic home, independent of DEA, in the Canadian International Development Agency (CIDA). Given the Trudeau government's interest in reforming the bureaucracy according to the latest business management practices, CIDA soon became a "model of rational management."[18]

Another major innovation was the Trudeau government's desire to bring the private sector into the assistance process, both business leaders and development Non-governmental Organizations (NGOs) such as Care and Oxfam. In 1968, a special program branch was created in CIDA to provide funding to these NGOs in the form of matching grants for worthy Third World projects. CIDA also sought greater business involvement in the development process by establishing an industrial cooperation division in 1978 and a business cooperation branch in 1984.

Other changes of policy reflected the larger international trends of the 1970s mentioned above. Robert McNamara used his appointment as president of the World Bank in 1972 to guide that organization in the direction of "poverty alleviation," and this approach along with "basic needs" was, by 1975, mirrored in the ODA policy statements of the UK, the US, and Canada. Since some of the poorest LAISs were in Africa, this dovetailed nicely with the Trudeau government's desire, for unity reasons, to increase ODA spending in francophone Africa. But more generally, Canadian ODA policy adopted the poverty and basic needs approaches as Trudeau attempted to cement the image of Canada as a friend of the Third World and develop links to "like-minded" countries there.

ODA IN THE CONSERVATIVE YEARS: 1984 TO 1993

In terms of the global ODA situation, the Mulroney government arrived at the height of concerns about the debt crisis and its ramifications for overextended Canadian banks and the global financial system at large. Thus, ideologically, the Canadian government was predisposed to support the IMF's SAPs and restructuring polices as conditions for new loans. Just as the Conservatives favoured privatization at home, so they called for greater reliance on the market in development efforts abroad. Furthermore, the head of CIDA under the Conservatives, Marcel Masse, had a more direct link, having been Canada's representative to the IMF when the SAP policy was formulated.

Ironically, the Conservatives' ideological inclinations allowed them to support a Liberal innovation and increase funding through NGOs as a means of relying on the private sector. Likewise, the government's initial response to the Ethiopian famines beginning in 1984 was to allow private efforts to take the lead in providing emergency aid. Similarly, the government was able to support and adopt other current ideas as expressed in the Winegard Report of the House of Commons and CIDA's 1987 report *Sharing Our Future*. These ideas included reliance on decentralization and "civil society" (in this context, the private sector), greater "partnership" with LAISs, IOs, and NGOs (implying less direct Canadian government responsibility and expense), and "sustainable development," which seemed to mean, among other things, fewer large, environmentally intrusive, and expensive projects.

Indeed, expense was a growing concern as Canada faced the same fiscal crunch as nearly all the HAISs by the 1990s. Growing deficits appeared to necessitate budget cutbacks, and this shortfall, along with general "aid fatigue" by the end of the Conservative's tenure, led to significantly lower levels of ODA.

THE LIBERALS RETURN: 1993 TO 2005

During the 1993 election campaign, the incoming Chrétien government had tried to clearly distinguish itself from the Conservatives on a number of policies. As the 1995 review *Canada in the World* shows, there were at least rhetorical differences. Resembling to some extend a return to the Trudeauvian 1970s, the report put the emphasis back on poverty and basic needs. This in turn justified softening the support for conditionality and the IMF's austere SAPs, though the World Bank, responding to criticism, had already begun to modify its policy. Its 1990 development report suggested a "return to poverty" and more careful monitoring of the social costs of adjustment. Likewise, consistent with the early Trudeau period, the government called for greater public access to the foreign and ODA policy process, and to this end created the National Forum on Canada's International Relations and established a special joint committee in Parliament. The NGOs initially welcomed this effort at greater consultation but soon wondered if Liberal "partnership" meant co-option and control by the government. Elements of the 1970s commercial emphasis re-emerged under the Chrétien "Team Canada" missions, and bureaucratic efficiency reappeared as new attempts at reunifying and "rationalizing" CIDA and ODA under DFAIT control. But continuities with the deposed Conservatives can also be seen in the response to the deficit and Finance Minister Paul Martin's 1994 cutback of ODA. Funding for ODA declined through the 1990s, calling into question the Liberals' and Canada's special interest in this endeavour.

EVALUATING ODA POLICIES

The Canadian government has received much criticism about ODA over the years. Despite attempts of various governments to portray Canada as a generous friend of the world's poor, critics argue that we have grossly underfunded our promises. As with our military commitments, it is a case of our rhetorical bark not matching our resource allocation bite. In particular, the decline in Canadian foreign aid over the last ten years is cited as proof of our hypocrisy. But in fairness, such complaints must be viewed in relative terms. Just as the famous 0.7 per cent target is a relative measure of effort, Canadian ODA should be seen in light of the efforts of other HAISs and the general global context. How has the 0.7 per cent target faired since its adoption by the UNGA in 1970?

Table 11.2 shows that, as of 2003, only a few smaller HAISs have achieved the 0.7 per cent goal. The total effort—the combined ODA of the DAC members (the wealthiest OECD states) divided by their total Gross National Incomes—stood at 0.25 per cent in 2003. That figure had peaked in the 1980s at 0.33 per cent, then fell back steadily to only 0.22 per cent in the late 1990s. Most spectacular has of course been the declining effort of the United States, which fell from providing half of the total ODA in the 1960s to only an eighth at present. This amounts in 1998 to 0.1 per cent of the US GNP, but the US government might respond that it never accepted the target, and so at worst it can be charged as a miser but not a hypocrite.

Table 11.2 Some OECD Members' ODA Effort in 2003

	ODA/GNI %*
Norway	0.92
Denmark	0.84
Luxembourg	0.81
Netherlands	0.80
Sweden	0.79
Belgium	0.60
France	0.41
Ireland	0.39
Switzerland	0.39
Finland	0.35
United Kingdom	0.34
Germany	0.28
Australia	0.25
Canada	0.24
New Zealand	0.23
Spain	0.23
Portugal	0.22
Greece	0.21
Austria	0.20
Japan	0.20
Italy	0.17
United States	0.15
Total DAC	0.25
Average Country Effort	0.41

* GNI (Gross National Income) is similar to GDP as a measure of total wealth.
Source: Organization for Economic Cooperation and Development, <www.oecd.org/dataoecd/-19/52/34352584.pdf>.

Two other very wealthy HAISs with much lighter defence budgets, Japan and Germany, have accepted the target but not accomplished it. Germany came the closest in 1982 at 0.48 per cent, and Japan reached only 0.34 per cent in 1984. With such lacklustre performance on the part of close allies, the Canadian failure doesn't stand out as much. The Canadian ODA effort peaked in 1988 at 0.50 per cent, before declining rapidly to 0.28 ten years later and 0.22 in 2001.

Two causes for this general decline in ODA stand out. First, the end of the cold war and the collapse of the USSR in 1991 removed much of the political and security competition for Third World allies, which motivated at least some previous aid-giving. Ironically though, the same event that caused the supply of ODA to shrink also enhanced the demand for ODA as the Soviet Bloc itself shifted from aid-provider to aid-recipient. Canada followed the trend to fund reconstruction efforts in Eastern Europe, which in effect "crowded out" ODA for Africa (see table 11.3).

Second, the common fiscal crisis of expanding budget deficits reduced the levels of HAIS ODA, as elected governments found foreign aid the least painful (in terms of domestic political consequences) expenditure to cut. In Europe, this problem was compounded by the Maastricht Treaty requirements that EU members joining the new euro currency keep their deficits within tight common limits for sound economic reasons. At one time in the early 1990s, Canada was one of the worst aid-cutting "offenders" among economies such as Belgium and Italy with huge deficits. This funding crunch was a key part of the aid fatigue that grew out of the alleged refusal of voters to fund higher tax levels and their belief (right or wrong) that governments were not using tax revenues wisely or efficiently.[19]

A third cause may lie in an intellectual form of aid fatigue. In the last two decades, ODA itself has been widely criticized as being at best useless and at worst harmful. Part of this idea comes from a "what have we to show for it after fifty years" mentality. The original economic theories of development are widely disputed now, and the main economic institutions such as the World Bank are frequently under attack. The latter is condemned for every past project failure and labelled as the builder of dams that destroy the environment and poor Aboriginal communities. The NGOs alone seem to maintain their public legitimacy, which has led, ironically, to a common cause between the far left and the far right to "get the state out of ODA."

Table 11.3 Top-10 Recipients of Canadian Bilateral ODA* **

Rank	1999-2000		2003-2004	
1	Ex-Yugoslavia	80.82	Iraq	115.86
2	Bangladesh	56.06	Afghanistan	99.38
3	China	47.05	Ethiopia	66.69
4	Indonesia	42.94	Bangladesh	66.31
5	Haiti	38.79	China	46.07
6	Ghana	28.51	Ghana	43.93
7	Vietnam	26.99	Mali	40.86
8	Mali	24.32	Tanzania	36.61
9	Senegal	22.10	Mozambique	33.81
10	Pakistan	22.00	Vietnam	31.31

* Not including debt relief
** In millions of dollars
Source: CIDA, Statistical Report on ODA, 1999-2000 and 2003-2004.

Modernization theory has become a dirty word on many college campuses. One relatively mild recent critique of foreign aid attacks the heavy dominance of HAISs in the main ODA organizations and the resulting "modernist ideological stance of donors: they tend to believe there is a single model of development based on a particular conception of Western liberal democracy."[20] Also, critics charge that "development objectives [...] have been distorted by the use of aid for donor commercial and political advantage."[21] As we have seen, Helleiner and others have attacked the Canadian government preference for tied aid. OECD figures show that the Canadian share of untied aid in bilateral ODA rose from only 18 per cent in 1981 to 62 per cent in 1993, but fell under the Liberals to 33 per cent in 1997. This was worse than the US at 37 per cent in 1993 and far below the OECD members' average of 87 per cent. A preference for tied aid implies also a preference for bilateral instead of multilateral channels, also criticized by many commentators.

Some social constructivist writers attack the entire notion of development. Post-modernists charge that "development is a disabling and archly Western discourse."[22] By again stressing the hierarchy latent in any act of charity between a rich donor and a poor recipient, this attack reawakens the sense of humiliation and past grievance of many in the Third World and continues to dovetail with nationalism and now fundamentalism. The very act of receiving charity can imply subordination. This anger is made worse when linked to memories of past imperialism and current cultural intrusion. "Third World education projects" become "a form of cultural defoliation."[23] Faced with such trenchant attacks, is it any wonder that Sylvia Maxfield, in her recent overview of the field, agrees with James Caporaso, Paul Krugman, and others that "development studies, as a coherent social science, is dead."[24] If we don't know what we are doing, how do we know our money isn't doing more harm than good?

On the other hand, as the DAC notes, before we give up on ODA altogether, we should note that "every country which has achieved a substantial rise in per capita income over the last thirty years was a substantial recipient of ODA."[25] Do the people of Japan, the fast-growing Asian tigers (e.g., South Korea and Taiwan), and the rising middle classes of India and China renounce their current wealth because it relied in part on Western capital? And what of the huge enormity of global hunger and suffering? Are we after all a patchwork of resentful autonomous solitudes or a global community?

SUMMARY OF CANADIAN IDENTITY

Our discussion of Canada's role in ODA has served to highlight one important area of the image Canada tries to project to the world. Our ODA serves a number of goals: to present Canada as charitable society concerned with the plight of the global poor; to show Canada as a good citizen doing its part along with other wealthy OECD states to bridge the gulf between the high and low income states; and to build specific political, economic, and cultural ties between Canada and states in South Asia, Africa, and Latin America.

We recounted a number of other values and images at the beginning of this chapter. Many of them dovetail or give additional justification to national interests discussed in previous chapters. In brief, we can inventory some of these again under a few headings.

Peacekeeping

In Chapter 5, Canadian peacekeeping was justified as part of the pursuit of global security. Over the years, Canada's active participation in international security activities has built a reputation, which is now a key part of our image overseas as well as a source of domestic pride. Among other states, this reputation creates an expectation of and openness to further participation and initiatives from Canada in this field.

Multilateralism

As we saw in the chapters on security and economics, Canada has traditionally sought its objectives in these areas in partnerships or coalitions. In part, this behaviour is a concession to reality; Canada often does not have the size, power, or resources to play a leadership or even independent role in many security or economic matters. However, it has also become attached to our reputation, whether as the traditional "faithful ally" or as a reliable "team-player," in multilateral forums such as NATO and the G8. As a practical matter, reciprocity helps to ensure aid from allies in time of need, a lesson the current Bush administration has not entirely learned. It also reinforces good global citizenship.

Good Global Citizenship

As a founding member of most institutions in the current UN system, Canada, unlike the United States, has been consistent in its support for the strengthening of those institutions. For example, on the numerous occasions when Canada has served on the UN Security Council, it has used those opportunities to initiate proposals to strengthen and reform that body. In NATO and elsewhere, Canada's ambitious proposals have not always been successful (such as the failure to fully utilize Article 2 and develop more political and economic links within NATO), but the land mine treaty shows the importance of persistence. International institutions include International Law, and with the exception of the 1970s Arctic Waters Act, Canada is usually in the forefront of efforts to expand its jurisdiction and use (such as the creation of the ICC).

Bilingualism and Biculturalism

As we saw in Chapter 9, the source of bilingual and bicultural policy was concern for domestic unity, particularly in regard to Quebec. As *Canada in the World* suggested, the values a society projects abroad may have implications for domestic unity. Under the Trudeau governments, the DEA promoted the bilingual and bicultural image of Canada and thus expanded relations and aid connections to francophone Africa. This expansion of aid served both strategically to reinforce the French connection and tactically to thwart Quebec separatist attempts at international recognition. Furthermore, in the post-cold war era of rising ethnicity, successful Canadian biculturalism and multiculturalism provides a hopeful counter-model. Indeed, overseas promotion of our English, French, and Aboriginal heritage emphasizes that which is unique in Canada's contribution to global culture.

North American Society and "Canada the Good"

Ultimately, for good or ill, most foreigners perceive Canadian culture as a variant of North American culture. Despite our many policy disagreements, the US remains our "most similar" culture. This is particularly true for the majority of Canadians who share in the huge anglophone media pool (TV, film, magazines, etc.) of North America. On the positive side, it must be noted that even the most anti-American foreigners often show some ambivalence to certain aspects of North American culture. Among the positive associations for North America are the vast and beautiful natural environment; the bountiful resourcefulness of the land and its people; the high levels of wealth and personal freedoms most enjoy; the liberal traditions of tolerance, classlessness, and equality; the volunteer- and community-oriented civil society; and the technological innovation and creativity of what is still, comparatively speaking, an "achieving society."

Most of these factors lie behind Canada's consistent high rankings on international indicators of "social development" or simply "best places to live." Fortunately, for Canada, we differ from the US today in precisely those characteristics least admired by other nations. And most of those characteristics grow out of the post-1945 role of the United States as the Western superpower. Canada, though sharing much of the security benefits, nonetheless was able to avoid direct association with the more negative aspects of the cold war: the vastly expanded military sector, the growth of national security institutions such as the CIA, the Third World interventionism, political unilateralism (justified as a necessity of "leadership"), the Vietnam War, and the reliance on bombing campaigns in general. Indeed, the Vietnam War shows dramatically how this global role also distracted the US from the pressing domestic issues of economic inequality, racial antagonism, and the urban and industrial decay of the 1960s. Canada shared fewer of these "downsides" of the North American experience due to its more modest international pretensions.

Ironically, aside from the English/French historical differences, Canada today represents a more positive fulfillment of the "American Dream" than the US itself. Certainly, post-1945 Canadian foreign policy (and perhaps government policy more generally) reflects the ideals of former presidents Woodrow Wilson and FDR better than policy in their own homeland. Thus, for most of the world, Canada today reflects what, on a better historical trajectory, the US might have been.

Notes

1. Canada, *Canada In the World* (1995), p. i.
2. *Ibid.*, p. i.
3. *Ibid.*, p. 37.
4. *Ibid.*, p. 34.
5. *Ibid.*, p. 40.
6. *Ibid.*, p. 40.
7. Cooper (1997), p. 211.

8. As quoted in Cooper (1997), p. 212.

9. The full title is Standing Committee on External Affairs and International Trade. *For Whose Benefit?* House of Commons, 1987.

10. Canada, *Canada In the World* (1995), p. 40.

11. As quoted in Cooper (1997), p. 224.

12. Canada, *Canada In the World* (1995), p. 40.

13. Pratt (1999), p. 306-23.

14. Cooper (1997), p. 222.

15. Organisation for Economic Cooperation and Development (OECD) (2003), p. 45.

16. *Ibid.*, p. 48.

17. The oil crisis of 1973 pushed up oil prices to four times their previous value. The resulting windfall of "petro dollars" piling up in relatively few hands (the wealthier oil exporters of the Persian Gulf) caused many economists to worry about a global crash with so much cash out of circulation (and there was a global recession in 1974-75). Many of these petro dollars wound up in private Western banks, which were encouraged for this reason to lend the money out quickly, especially to the governments of LAISs. But as a result of hasty loans to bad projects and the sudden skyrocketing of interest rates in the early 1980s, many of these LAIS borrowers found they were too deep in debt and unable to pay back the loans.

18. Cooper (1997), p. 218.

19. My own survey results show that 60 to 70 per cent of incoming college students from year to year agree with the statement that the government "misspends our taxes."

20. Hjertholm and White (2002), p. 80.

21. *Ibid.*, p. 80.

22. Corbridge (1998), 138-39.

23. Maxwell (2002), p. 472.

24. *Ibid.*

25. Organisation for Economic Cooperation and Development (OECD) (2003), p. 57.

Chapter Twelve
Canadian National Interests: From the Realm of Ideas to the Realm of Practices

This book has attempted to show the usefulness of a National Interest Perspective (NIP) for framing the main issues of Canadian foreign policy today. It has demonstrated how past governments have been guided by the handful of national interests — either implicitly through their decisions and actions or explicitly through foreign policy reviews and priorities listed in department reports. In broad terms, these interests were divided into security (territorial sovereignty, national defence, and international security), autonomy (political, economic, and cultural), economic prosperity, national unity, and national identity. This list of national interests could be deduced from either Statist or Realist principles, suggesting they are broadly the same for any government. The uniqueness of Canada's foreign policy derives from our distinctive historical experience and bundle of attributes (resources, size, location, etc.). In dealing with these constraints while pursuing its national interests, Canadian governments have developed their own sets of tactics to attempt to implement their objectives.

So far we have dealt with national interests as abstract principles: issues teased from history to be debated by academic historians and the general public. Now, we seek to move from the realm of ideas to the realm of practice. The next section briefly surveys the process by which national interests are accepted as foreign policy goals and implemented through government policies and diplomatic action.

THE PROCESS OF CANADIAN FOREIGN POLICY

From the Statist perspective, the obvious place to look for the autonomous formulation of state policies is in the state itself. And the obvious agents would be the top government employees in the bureaucracies that have authority over foreign affairs and national defence. In Canada, the two main ministries for these matters would be the Department of Foreign Affairs and the Department of National Defence. Their reviews and reports often list government objectives and goals very similar to the national interests found here. Constitutionally, the authority to set the objectives of the state lies with the elected political executive (the prime minister and cabinet) of a government enjoying the confidence of Parliament and not with these civil servants in DFA and DND. Legally, they are merely non-partisan "servants" carrying out the wishes of their politically elected "masters," the prime minister and the ministers heading up their departments.

However, there has long been a debate about how truly "disinterested" are these top civil servants (also known as mandarins). As portrayed in the BBC series *Yes, Minister*, the mandarins are career professionals, whereas ministers tend to be generalists with limited tenure, mainly focused on political issues affecting their chance of winning the next election. If we are looking for state agents who can rise above partisan loyalties and specific societal or regional interests, these mandarins would seem to have the most capacity and motivation to formulate what is in the long-term interests of the whole state.

Indeed, most textbooks on Canadian politics present the civil servants as having three acknowledged sources of influence on government policy. First, the ministers depend heavily on their departments for information about their area of jurisdiction. This is particularly true of international affairs, where the state must rely on an extensive diplomatic service to be its eyes and ears through overseas embassies and consulates. In addition, the complexity of the subject and most politicians' lack of specific training in international relations give the mandarins "a virtual monopoly over information and the analysis of that information."[1] Analysis and options constitute the second source of influence. Beyond providing information, deputy ministers are typically asked to assess the problems, lay out alternative policy options with the costs and benefits of each, and even suggest preferences among those options. Ultimately, the minister must approve the policy (after taking more important decisions to the prime minister and/or the cabinet). After that, a third source of influence appears when the minister must rely on the bureaucracy to implement the policy.

Thus, the political executive retrains legal authority to select policy, even if it is merely choosing among options or approving the preference of the department. For foreign affairs and security, that power makes the prime minister and a handful of cabinet ministers the key players. These positions include the minister for foreign affairs, the minister for national defence, and the minister for international trade. Most recent commentators in Canadian politics have focused on the paramount position of the prime minister. First, as formal "head of government" and chair of the cabinet, the prime minister is *primus inter pares* (first among equals). Second, the Canadian prime minister is leader of a political party both as head of the parliamentary caucus and as leader of the broader party outside Ottawa. The strong party discipline of the Canadian system can give a prime minister with a clear majority nearly "dictatorial" power over governmental policy. Third, the prime minister has extensive powers of appointment, selecting the members of cabinet (including the ministers mentioned above), the Canadian ambassadors, the Clerk of the Privy Council, and the other top civil servants, including the deputy ministers. Thus, for a politically strong prime minister, the main constraint over foreign affairs is only his or her interest in the subject.

Unlike the American system, in Canada there is little constitutional sharing of foreign policy authority with the legislative branch. Unlike Congress, the Canadian political executive holds the powers of treaty making and foreign policy appointments. Nonetheless, Parliament has a limited role to play when it is called upon to legitimize important government decisions, such as declaring war in 1939 or joining NATO in 1949. Also, Parliament serves as an important link to the citizenry when individuals or groups raise issues, make demands, or support government policies. Occasionally, this pressure may result in policy changes, such as the 1975 decision to not allow the PLO to enter Canada to attend a UN Conference scheduled in Toronto due to pressure from Jewish groups on Ontario members of parliament. Likewise, Parliament has an oversight function by which government foreign policy might be challenged during Question Period, or debates in the House, or hearings in Committee, when government bills are under consideration. The chief committee in the House of Commons to consider such matters is the Standing Committee on Foreign Affairs, Trade, and Defence, and the weaker Senate has its own committees. Sometimes, special joint committees of both houses are formed at the government's request, such as the 1994 Special Joint Committee Reviewing Canadian Foreign Policy. In 2004, due to the international terrorist challenges discussed in Chapter 4, a standing committee on national security was created in the House of Commons. But the majority party will control the operations of these committees, and so with party discipline, opposition to government policies is rarely effective. The situation is different under minority governments where the threat of a vote of no confidence forces the party in power to be more cautious. Thus, foreign policy was a factor in the defeat of Diefenbaker's government in 1963, as we saw in Chapter 7. But unless Canada changes its voting system, such governments will remain rare.

Even beyond the lack of constitutional authority, Parliament seems to lack interest in influencing foreign policy. In part, this lack of interest arose from the incremental way in which Canada gained its political autonomy from Britain. As we saw in Chapter 6, the Dominion of Canada experienced the long period from Confederation to the Statute of Westminster, when Parliament existed and developed procedures for handling domestic matters, but, constitutionally, foreign policy remained under the control of Britain. Even after the legal achievement of full diplomatic powers, Prime Minister King was slow to exercise it at least in so far as appointing diplomats. By that point, parliamentary habits were well established, and so deference to executive authority continued and was reinforced by the strong leadership in the DEA of this period.

Furthermore, members of parliament (MPs) receive little urging from the voters: their constituents back home rarely show much interest or willingness to express themselves on foreign affairs. Most average Canadians find international events difficult to understand or follow. To them, foreign affairs lack the immediate interest and salience of domestic "bread and butter" issues such as unemployment, prices, pensions, and health care. Parochialism abounds as most Canadians focus on their families, their local community, and their provinces or region first. Only then, it seems, do they have time for Ottawa (or the United States), let alone the larger world. Finally, MPs come under little pressure from organized interest groups. The American Congress is notorious for its penetration by lobbyists and special interests, reflecting the greater chance that this more open (or less disciplined) body might serve or harm their interests. Since political outcomes depend less on individual votes by MPs and decisions are being made elsewhere, Canadian lobbyist must make what effort they can with other elites in the government.

A complex society such as Canada rarely is able to speak with one voice when it does speak up. When societal groups organize to lobby the government on foreign affairs, one group's voice is often offset by another group. A classic example is the Israel-Palestine conflict in which a growing Arab community within Canada is increasingly counteracting the interests of the Jewish community. Likewise, during the US free trade debate, opposition to the deal by most Canadian trade unions was offset by the support of many business groups. Even within the business sector, there were offsetting balances between exporters and importers. Agricultural interests were split, with the Canadian Cattlemen's Association and wheat growers seeking access to the US market but Canadian wine growers seeking to keep US wines out. In such situations, the government can legitimately feel its choices are unconstrained because public opinion is evenly divided.

Overall, most commentators on the Canadian foreign policy process conclude that it has been a fairly elitist activity. This elitism sits poorly with our vision of Canada as a democratic society. Governments of the day are aware of this dilemma and, going back to Trudeau's *Foreign Policy for Canadians*, have tried to increase public involvement through open reviews, public forums, opinion surveys, and hearings. Clearly, interest and education are the keys to greater public participation, and they can be enhanced by generating a larger awareness about the goals of Canada's foreign policy. At this point, we could broaden our National Interest Perspective away from its Statist roots and propose it as a vehicle for stimulating a larger open public discourse. If you don't agree with the national interests or the "objectives" examined here, what would you propose instead? If you don't agree with the rankings, how would you prioritize them? All that is required for a broader National Interest Perspective is that the debaters justify their proposals in a larger, longer-term frame, encompassing the good of the whole state.

A FINELY BALANCED MOBILE

A major strength of the NIP is that it helps us spell out goals for our foreign policy and make explicit the assumptions and arguments that lie behind those objectives. However, as a guide to policy-makers, it is not complete. Even if we reach consensus about certain vital Canadian interests, debate and controversy will remain about the best means to achieve those ends. Is economic growth best fostered by reliance on free markets or state intervention? What is the best policy to protect an independent Canadian film industry?

This task of executing our goals is further complicated by the intricate way that national interests interact with each other. Since the funds necessary for their implementation must be allocated from the same limited budgetary pot, an immediate fiscal trade-off exists. Furthermore, the goals often directly contradict each other in their application. As we saw, increasing security by military integration with the US raises political autonomy issues. Fortunately, the interests are not discrete, on/off, either/or categories but graduated scales of more versus less. Economic growth develops at various rates. Security interests are not measured as either a zero or fully complete, but as more or less adequate. Balances can be struck at some optimum value. In its totality, Canadian foreign policy is not a single balance or scale but a web of multiple balances linked in complex ways. Hence, the best visualization is that of a free-hanging mobile constantly in motion with changing environmental circumstances. Each main beam represents a finely tuned balance between major national interests, but adjustments in any one beam will affect other balances elsewhere in the whole. Some beams (such as security) are more fundamental with a higher priority, and thus are nearer the top and bear more weight. But even shifts on small balances further down the suspension may require compensatory adjustments at the top.

For most states, basic security must be located near the top. As observed in recent Canadian defence reviews, national defence is given pride of place, with sovereignty protection and international security now located much further down. Legal sovereign claims are given low priority in part due to the lack of burning border disputes. True, in 2004 Denmark again planted a flag on Hans Island to renew its claim to that disputed Arctic land. Canada also continues to have minor border disputes with the United States over Alaska's maritime border at both ends. But compared with the terrible conflicts that non-contiguous states typically have over borders (e.g., the Polish corridor, Armenia, and Azerbaijan), these are minor disputes. Periodic revisiting of US icebreakers to the Northwest Passage, most recently in 2003, are necessary legal exercises to maintain the claim of innocent passage under international law, and these require only routine legal responses from Ottawa. Disputes with European Union members over the Grand Banks fishery pose much more serious complications for other interests. When Canada takes unilateral enforcement action, such as arresting Iberian ships on the high seas during the Turbot War, it may serve to protect vital resources but damages Canada's image as a multilateralist, law-abiding global citizen. In damaging our relations with the EU, we also harm potential economic ties long sought for the economic growth potential they represent and as a counterbalance to dependence on the US market. Luckily, the current compromise agreement, flawed as it may be, allows Canada to step back inside international legal boundaries, and yet permits us a sort of "inspection harassment" to achieve some protection of the fish stocks.

This book has also demonstrated the value of separating political autonomy concerns from matters of straight legal sovereignty. This distinction is still missed by politicians: when the United States asked for passenger lists on Canadian domestic flights in 2005, Transport Minister Jean Lapierre labelled the request "a question of sovereignty."[2] However, since the planes fly through US sovereign territory, Washington was within its legal rights to make such demands. (At a cost, the airlines could have avoided US airspace.) Retaliation, in the form of reciprocal demands on US flights across Canadian territory, would only reaffirm the US practice. In fact, the political autonomy issue at stake here is whether we must adopt all aspects of Washington's policy on counterterrorism.

In the larger historical frame, the interest of national defence has long clashed with the political autonomy issue. In Canada, the logics of geography, technology, and military efficiency create a constant pressure for greater continent-wide military cooperation. That pressure intensifies at the start of each new US security era (e.g., the cold war and now the threats of Islamist terror and WMD). Given our memberships in NORAD and NATO, a certain amount of interoperability between the Canadian Forces with our major military ally is inevitable. Acquiring compatible equipment cuts costs and allows easy cooperation on agreed joint military operations, such the 2001 naval deployments to the Arabian Sea (Operation Apollo). Yet, as Michael Byers points out, what happens when Ottawa does not completely subscribe to the goals of the US mission and wishes to untangle its troops? Can Canada go it alone if its forces depend upon being plugged into US units to operate effectively? A striking example of this dependence is the recent acquisition of vertical launch missiles (SM-2MR) for Canada's Iroquois-class destroyers, which to be fully operational are best plugged into the Aegis radar systems installed on US destroyers. This fact implies that the main use for these missiles will be when the Canadian ships are assigned to US naval task forces and can thus electronically link up to the US system. Since the Americans are extending the use of Aegis into short-range missile defence systems, it might create a back door from which Canada can enter a larger missile defence system unnoticed.[3]

Michael Byers also points to fundamental differences of doctrine and treaty obligations that should block more extensive military integration between the two states. In April 2002, when the US created the Northern Command to be its primary military structure for an integrated defence of North America, it hoped that Canada would sign on, placing Canadian units permanently under US command. While Canadian units have served temporarily under American commanders in the past (Operation Apollo, for one), long-term integration would cause legal conflicts for Canadian troops, since Canada has accepted treaty obligations that the US has not. For example, Canada has ratified Protocol I to the Geneva Conventions of 1949, which entails much tighter standards on the protection of civilians in such matters as targeting for bombing. This treaty also prohibits use of "weapons that cause unnecessary suffering," which could include weapons used by the US, such as depleted uranium shells and land mines. Canada and the US differ over nuclear policy and interpretation of the Nuclear Non-proliferation Treaty. Canada's own Charter of Rights and Freedoms was "probably violated in January 2002 when Canadian Forces in Afghanistan transferred Taliban or al Qaeda suspects to the US without obtaining assurances that the death penalty would not be applied."[4] Finally, Canada has accepted the International Criminal Court, which the US opposes and which therefore holds Canadian troops to more restrictive standards of war criminality than American troops. All of these examples point to very different moral stands on the conduct of war and suggest Canadian troops are confronted with legal jeopardy when they operate in American units.

Sometimes the foretold tradeoffs do not emerge in practice. In both the Persian Gulf War and the US intervention in Afghanistan, critics warned that Canadian participation would harm Canada's peacekeeping reputation. In fact, neither war had much impact in that regard. As observed, Canada was long able to participate in classic peacekeeping in spite of not being a neutral country. What is more, both operations had wide support at the UN, unlike the 2003 US intervention in Iraq. By refusing to participate in the latter, Canada's UN and internationalist credentials were significantly reaffirmed. This case also shows that not all connections in our complex mobile are contradictory. Playing up one interest often spills over to strengthen others. Refusing certain US requests (i.e., to stay out of the ICC) can strengthen Canada's political autonomy and international reputation at the same time. Such "dual-use" policies should be sought out and exploited, but only when don't come with "dual oppositions." Indeed, with the current Bush administration, it seems political autonomy and the image of Canadian internationalism are often allied with, but also facing off against, the tag-team of domestic security and economic prosperity. This desire to exploit dual-use policies is most evident among continentalists, who argue our future lies in greater economic and military integration with the US in missile defence and currency union. Sometimes even this alignment is less than perfect, as acquiescence on US demands for tighter border security could threaten the Canadian economy, as we observed.

Furthermore, it serves no one's interest to follow an ally blindly into policies we know are wrong-headed. Historically, "ready, aye, ready" was not Canada's response to the UK in Sudan, Chanak, or the Boer War, or to the US in Vietnam. At this point, it is hard to imagine a conclusion to the Iraqi intervention that would justify the costs and suffering for either Iraq or the United States. Many of Bush's strategies, whether on the fiscal deficit or foreign policy, are simply unsustainable and will have to be reversed by future US governments.

ECONOMIC PROSPERITY

One of the most fundamental dictums of political science is the hallowed trade-off of "guns versus butter." Nineteenth-century Japan did try to reconcile them with the slogan "Strong Army, Rich Country," until the militarist leadership crashed their country disastrously in World War II. Since then, Japan has prospered like Canada, while spending only 1 per cent of GDP on defence.

Differing methods for achieving economic growth appear equally irreconcilable. Since Macdonald's National Plan, Canadians have debated the merits of liberal openness and nationalist protectionism. Over the decades, the structure and size of the Canadian economy have insured that Canada has become a "trading nation," exporting a much larger portion of its domestic production than its large southern neighbour. This need for access to foreign markets, and the requirement of reciprocity that accompanies it, has tended to gradually wean Canada off protectionism. By the 1970s and 1980s, the issue was less about "freer trade or not" and more about "trade with whom?" Eventually, the growing importance of the US market was formally recognized in Canadian acceptance of the FTA and NAFTA. However, concerns throughout the free trade debate about loss of political autonomy show that this trade-off, acknowledged in the nineteenth-century trade debates, is still with us. It is clearly visible in the demonstrations of anti-globalists and nationalist warnings against further integration. No sooner had the Martin government proposed a free trade agreement with South Korea in its April 2005 foreign policy report than domestic interest groups from the beef, auto, and shipbuilding industries loudly opposed it.[5] Nonetheless, enduring concerns about political autonomy motivate the ongoing search for trade counterweights, also highlighted in the Martin foreign policy report.

On the other side, continentalist commentators who advocate today for greater economic integration with the US are motivated by the interest of economic prosperity. To preserve and increase prosperity, they seek to follow the EU's path towards a total common market. Such a policy would add a common external tariff, remove remaining restrictions on the movement of labour and capital, introduce greater harmonization of tax and regulatory policy, and perhaps even adopt the US dollar. Even if it can be guaranteed that such policies would remove the existing income gap and allow both economies to flourish, the losses to Canadian identity and political autonomy mean this proposal is viewed as an imbalanced option in the eyes of most citizens.

CRITIQUE OF THE NATIONAL INTEREST PERSPECTIVE

Historically, Canadian policies used to implement the interest of economic autonomy seem to open a major critique of the whole NIP. In no other arena has governmental policy swung so dramatically in the past 50 years. One can look back in wonder at the economic nationalism of the Pearson and Trudeau eras. Where have FIRA and the NEP, and the interests that created them, gone? Why are Canadians unconcerned about levels of US FDI or control over Canadian capital any more? Indeed, I have found it impossible to update public opinion statistics on the FDI issue: pollsters are not asking the question because it's a non-issue now. This reality seems much better explained by the liberal model of the democratic state than by the Statist model, with its enduring national interests. Policy on FDI has shifted dramatically and appears best explained by competition between political parties, interest groups, and shifting public attitudes.

In part, the change in attitudes about US branch plants may be explained by the intervention of the debate on the FTA in the late 1980s. As a strategy for opposing that agreement, trade unions and left-wing organizations argued that free trade would cause these American-owned factories to close, with job losses and other deleterious effects to the Canadian economy. Thus, the constituency most likely to have condemned branch plants shifted their position to embrace and even defend them.

But, by relying on domestic politics and shifting ideas, this explanation does nothing to help out the NIP. Is economic autonomy important enough to be considered a national interest or not? One defence is to argue that economic autonomy was never anything more than an adjunct and a means to achieve the actual national interest of political autonomy. As stated before, national interests are constant, but their means of attainment vary over time. Furthermore, returning to the analogy of human needs, as they are fulfilled, their salience declines. Satisfied interests may even disappear temporarily from the public agenda. In fact, the state's retreat in this policy area is by no means complete. FIRA and the NEP may be gone, but Canadian regulations on business and culture are much more extensive today than 50 years ago. The legacy of economic nationalism endures, even if it has a low profile in public discourse today.

The parallel between economic prosperity and national unity is instructive. As

Quebec nationalism rose again in the 1960s and 1970s, the provincial government enacted defensive regulations, and ironically (from the separatist's viewpoint), these successful attempts to repatriate the Quebec economy and protect French language and culture blunted the drive for full independence. In effect, Quebec Bill 101 may have been a better defence against separatism than any plan Ottawa could have come up with.

Similarly, Canadians today perhaps feel that experience has shown that political autonomy is sufficiently protected. Initially, the growth in American ownership of Canadian assets in the 1950s and the growing dependence on the US market in the 1980s sparked uncertainty about the state of Canadian autonomy. But the Canadian identity proved more resilient and in less need of protection than previously thought. Identity and nationalism look much different now in the light of post-cold war events. Given the apparent intractability of ethnic and religious identity, cultures generally look more robust than they did then. The recent rejection of the European Constitution by the publics of France and Holland (and indirectly Britain) shows this to be true, even in the hotbed of European integration. Canadians have learned that despite depending on the US to buy 80 per cent of their exports, their government can still say no to missile defence and intervention in Iraq.

This reference to identity brings us to a last criticism of the NIP: that it does not give enough emphasis to the impact of Canadian values and identity. There is a long tradition in the Canadian foreign policy literature (based on the even longer tradition in the study of international relations) of dividing commentators into Realist or Idealist camps. The clash between the foreign policies of Pearson's internationalism and Trudeau's political nationalism is but one Canadian example. Idealists tend to be universalists, focusing on the global community rather than parochial self-interests. They often seek to place ideas, or ethical principles, at the forefront of policy discussions. They would argue that the NIP, due to its association with Realist assumptions, has an inherent bias against the inclusion of such principles. Indeed, the premise of constant all-embracing national interests may be nothing more than a subterfuge to privilege certain values (security and economics) by wrapping them in the flag of loyalty to the state. Idealists would argue that insufficient space is allocated to non-Realist issues: multilateralism, human rights, good governance, the role of women, the environment, NGOs, and so on.

I accept to some extent that such is the cost of adopting a Statist national interest approach. However, Chapter 11 attempted to show that the NIP can be modified to include issues of principle and identity as basic needs all states attempt to fulfill for their publics. Many Realists accept culture, values, and prestige as important sources of influence. Bush, with his reliance on unilateral military force, has much to learn from Axworthy's emphasis on soft power. Realists and Idealists meet again when we try to sort out the motivations for humanitarian intervention and discover how rare are totally disinterested acts. "Altruism" polishes up our self-image, and tied aid helps our exports. But, perhaps we should call it "dual-use" rather than "hypocrisy."

Finally, the NIP provides a forum for debating the fundamental objectives of our country's foreign policy. If we share a belief in democracy, then we share a desire to find consensus on our policies. This means looking beyond partisan, regional, and societal interests and thinking at least occasionally about the welfare of the whole. In this sense, a Canadian National Interest Perspective retains its value as a guiding force in our foreign policy debates.

Notes

1. Nossal (1997), p. 254.
2. Ibbitson (2003), A4.
3. Byers (2004), A19.
4. Byers (2003), p. 105.
5. Chase and Keenan (2005), B1.

Appendix: Canadian and US Leaders since 1861

CANADIAN PRIME MINISTERS	TERM	AMERICAN PRESIDENTS
	1861–1865	Abraham Lincoln (Republican)
	1865–1869	Andrew Johnson (Democratic)
Sir John A. Macdonald (Conservative)	1867–1873	
	1869–1877	Ulysses S. Grant (Republican)
Alexander Mackenzie (Liberal)	1873–1878	
	1877–1881	Rutherford B. Hayes (Republican)
Sir John A. Macdonald (Conservative)	1878–1891	
	1881–1881	James Abram Garfield (Republican)
	1881–1885	Chester Alan Arthur (Republican)
	1885–1889	Grover Cleveland (Democratic)
	1889–1893	Benjamin Harrison (Republican)
Sir John Abbott (Conservative)	1891–1892	
Sir John S.D. Thompson (Conservative)	1892–1894	
	1893–1897	Grover Cleveland (Democratic)
Sir Mackenzie Bowell (Conservative)	1894–1896	
Sir Charles Tupper (Conservative)	1896–1896	
Sir Wilfrid Laurier (Liberal)	1896–1911	
	1897–1901	William McKinley (Republican)
	1901–1909	Theodore Roosevelt (Republican)
	1909–1913	William Howard Taft (Republican)
Sir Robert Borden (Conservative)	1911–1917	
	1913–1921	Woodrow Wilson (Democratic)
Sir Robert Borden (Conservative-Unionist)	1917–1920	
Arthur Meighen (Conservative-Unionist)	1920–1921	
	1921–1923	Warren G. Harding (Republican)
W.L. Mackenzie King (Liberal)	1921–1926	
	1923–1929	Calvin Coolidge (Republican)
Arthur Meighen (Conservative)	1926–1926	
W.L. Mackenzie King (Liberal)	1926–1930	
	1929–1933	Herbert Clark Hoover (Republican)
Richard B. Bennett (Conservative)	1930–1935	

	1933–1945	Franklin Delano Roosevelt (Democratic)
W.L. Mackenzie King (Liberal)	1935–1948	
	1945–1953	Harry S. Truman (Democratic)
Louis St. Laurent (Liberal)	1948–1957	
	1953–1961	Dwight David Eisenhower (Republican)
John Diefenbaker (Progressive Conservative)	1957–1963	
	1961–1963	John Fitzgerald Kennedy (Democratic)
	1963–1969	Lyndon Baines Johnson (Democratic)
Lester B. Pearson (Liberal)	1963–1968	
Pierre E. Trudeau (Liberal)	1968–1979	
	1969–1974	Richard Milhous Nixon (Republican)
	1974–1977	Gerald R. Ford (Republican)
	1977–1981	James Earl Carter, Jr. (Democratic)
Joseph Clark (Progressive Conservative)	1979–1980	
Pierre E. Trudeau (Liberal)	1980–1984	
	1981–1989	Ronald Reagan (Republican)
John Turner (Liberal)	1984–1984	
Brian Mulroney (Progressive Conservative)	1984–1993	
	1989–1993	George Herbert Walker Bush (Republican)
	1993–2001	William Jefferson Clinton (Democratic)
Kim Campbell (Progressive Conservative)	1993–1993	
Jean Chrétien (Liberal)	1993–2003	
	2001–	George Walker Bush (Republican)
Paul Martin (Liberal)	2003–2006	
Stephen Harper (Conservative)	2006–	

Glossary

Authority The right to rule; the right to intervene coercively (to monopolize the means of coercion or force); the right to decide what is public and what is private.

Baselines Used to determine a state's territorial sea boundary; the point at low tide on the shore from which you measure. The adoption of straight baselines was a way of smoothing out jagged shorelines by drawing a baseline from one coastline point or peninsula to another.

Battalion See Military Formations.

Bretton Woods Agreements/System Named after the town in New Hampshire where they were negotiated, these agreements created the post-World War II international financial system, including fixed exchange rates supervised by the IMF (International Monetary Fund). They also established the World Bank and what eventually became the World Trade Organization (WTO).

Brigade See Military Formations.

Consulate The location of a foreign consul (a non-diplomatic representative from a foreign government) and his or her staff. Deals with the less important relations between the countries, such as immigration and trade promotion. Whereas a state has only one embassy in another state, it may have multiple consulates. For example, Canada has one embassy for the US in Washington but has consulates in New York City, Los Angeles, Chicago, and other major cities.

Continentalist In Canadian foreign policy, a continentalist is one who focuses on relations with the US. It can sometimes also mean one who favours greater Canadian cooperation or even integration with the US on economic and/or security matters.

Deterrence This word is used in several ways in international relations. In a general sense, it means getting an opponent *not* to take some action, such as launching a military attack. It is assumed that most would-be aggressors are rational in that they will not start a war they cannot win. Therefore, a traditional method of deterring an attack would be to demonstrate that you and your allies possess forces equal or superior to your opponent.

Deterrence theory The development of nuclear weapons produced a body of literature called deterrence theory. Here the issue is not so much "winning" or "losing" as it is the ability to inflict unacceptable losses (or even annihilation) on an opponent to deter a nuclear attack. Nuclear deterrence is considered most likely when Mutually

253

Assured Destruction (MAD) is achieved; that is, both opponents have weapons systems capable of surviving even a surprise attack and retaliating to destroy the assailant.

Department of External Affairs (DEA) See Department of Foreign Affairs.

Department of Foreign Affairs (DFA) Canada's governmental ministry in charge of diplomatic relations with foreign governments and international organizations. Created in 1909 as the Department of External Affairs (the word *external* was used because at the time Britain was still in charge of foreign affairs and it included relations with Britain and the empire, who were not "foreign" to Canada). In the early 1980s, the words *International Trade* were added but then dropped in 2005. In 1993, as an act of modernization, the word *Foreign* was substituted for *External*.

Department of Foreign Affairs and International Trade (DFAIT) See Department of Foreign Affairs.

Department of National Defence (DND) Canada's main agency for national security. Oversees the Canadian Forces (CF).

Doha Round The current round of international trade talks. Named for its opening meetings held in Doha, Qatar, in late 2001.

Division See Military Formations.

Embassy

1. A team of diplomats and their staff (usually led by an ambassador) that a state sends ("accredits") to a foreign government to represent it for diplomatic purposes.
2. The building or compound that they occupy in the receiving country's capital. Legally treated as a small sovereign territory of the foreign state.
3. Any diplomatic mission undertaken by an ambassador.

European Community (EC) Both EC and EEC (European Economic Community) are older terms for the European Union (EU).

European Union (EU) An organization of European states seeking closer economic and political integration, which has grown from its six founding members in 1957 to cover most of the continent.

Extraterritoriality For a person with extraterritorial status (a diplomat; a European citizen in late-nineteenth-century China), the local and/or national laws do not apply.

General Agreement on Tariffs and Trade (GATT) A 1947 international agreement to promote freer trade among its members. It has sponsored a series of trade negotiation rounds. See Uruguay and Doha.

Government A bureaucratic apparatus that allocates values for a given community (i.e., it makes an authoritative decision about who gets access to which "valued things" in a given society).

Gross Domestic Product (GDP) The value of all goods and services produced in a year within the boundaries of a given country.

Gross National Product (GNP) The value of all goods and services produced in a year by the "nationals" (citizens) of a given country. So, for example, in the Canadian GNP, the production of foreign-owned factories in Ontario would be excluded but a Canadian-owned mine in Latin America would be included.

High Average Income State (HAIS) Used in this book to denote the wealthier states in the global system. Synonymous with Advanced Industrial States (AIS), Organization for Economic Cooperation and Development (OECD) members, and the so-called First World.

Imperial Preference A form of common external tariff adopted by the Commonwealth in the 1930s. In effect, it turned the British Empire into a Customs Union (the next step beyond a Free Trade Area).

Irredentist As in "irredentist nation," which means a state that believes some part of its territory has been wrongly taken by another state and must be "redeemed," or liberated and returned.

International Atomic Energy Agency (IAEA) Among its tasks is the overseeing of safeguards meant to stop the spread of nuclear weapons technology.

Low Average Income State (LAIS) Used in this book to denote the poorer states in the global system. Replaces the terms *less developed country* (LDC), *developing nation,* and the so-called Third World.

Legation

1. (Previous usage) Before 1945, diplomatic protocol distinguished between great powers and lesser powers. Whereas great powers established "embassies" with each other, minor powers only had "legations" with them (a sort of second-class embassy in terms of status). Thus, when Canada first began establishing diplomatic relations with other great powers in the 1930s (such as France and Japan), it opened legations and not full embassies. After 1945, newly independent countries refused to accept any second-class status in their diplomacy and established only embassies. Canada's legations were soon "upgraded" to embassies as this usage fell out of fashion.

2. (Current usage) The office of an ambassador. Interchangeable with the term *embassy.*

Legitimacy

Internally, the sense of being justly ruled; acceptance of the government's authority, the withdrawal of which may lead to rebellion and revolution.

Externally, the recognition by other states of a state's existence and the understanding that that state's particular government is appropriately empowered to speak for it.

Mercantilism A nationalist approach to international economic relations that favours intervention by the state to protect domestic producers against imports and to ensure a positive balance of payments (among other things). Contrasted with neo-classical economics.

Military units and formations

A Platoon (or troop) contains 30-40 soldiers headed by a Lieutenant.

A Company (100-200 soldiers) is 3-4 Platoons headed by a Captain.

A Battalion or regiment (up to 1000 soldiers) is 2-6 Companies led by a Lieutenant Colonel.

A Brigade (3,000-6,000 soldiers) is 2-4 Battalions led by a Brigadier (General) or Colonel.

A Division (10,000-20,000 soldiers) is 2-4 Brigades led by a Major-General.
A Corps (about 60,000 soldiers) is 3 Divisions led by a Lieutenant -General.
An Army (200,000-400,000 soldiers) is 1 or more Corps led by a General.

Nation

1. (Weak definition) A community of people sharing a common history, territory, symbols, political system, mass public culture, and enemies.

2. (Strong definition) A community of people sharing the above, plus a common language, ethnicity, and, potentially, a common genealogy.

3. (Subjective definition) A group of people who perceive themselves to be one.

National interests (primarily external)

1. Inductive: Principles of the foreign policy of a state that possess the following components: they are objectives related to general societal goals; they persist over time; and they have a consistent ranking of importance. See Krasner (1978).

2. Deductive: Very broad common principles of foreign policy of any state that can be deduced from the nature of the current international system. Given the present global structure, what maximizes utility for the state defined minimally as survival. Appropriate application for a given state in a given context may vary considerably.

3. Normative: The focus of a potentially country-wide debate about the just purposes of state authority in international affairs, which is constrained both by the historical practice of the state, especially as to foreign affairs (inductive), and what is realistically possible given the current structure of the global system (deductive).

National self-determination The belief that all nations (defined in the strong sense) should possess a state (in the sense of the first definition given below).

National treatment A principle of the General Agreement on Tariffs and Trade (GATT) and now the World Trade Organization (WTO) that foreign firms in a given country should be legally treated the same way as domestic firms.

Neo-classical economics An approach to international economic relations that favours reliance on free markets rather than state intervention. Contrasted with mercantilism.

Non-governmental Organization (NGO) Any private association not organized by a government. Commonly used for international groups (INGOs) that have activities that cross international borders, such as the Red Cross, the Catholic Church, and multinational corporations (MNCs).

Organization for Economic Cooperation and Development (OECD) An intergovernmental organization (IGO) for high-income states created in 1961 to promote their economic cooperation.

Oil embargo of 1973 In the midst of the Arab-Israeli October War, Saudi Arabia, to support the Arab cause, cut back its overall oil production and refused exports to the US and Holland. The result was a quadrupling of oil prices and a major shock to the global economy.

Organization of Petroleum Exporting Countries (OPEC) An international organization of oil exporting states seeking to control the global price of oil.

Realism In international relations, an approach to world affairs that emphasizes power, anarchy, state-interests and "the way the world is," as opposed to an idealized global community founded on legal (or other) principles.

Realpolitik The German word for Realism.

Secretary of State In the United States, the designation for the cabinet member responsible for foreign affairs.

Secretary of State for External (Foreign) Affairs The Canadian cabinet minister responsible for foreign affairs. For the usage of *external* versus *foreign*, see Department of Foreign Affairs.

State
1. International definition: A political entity possessing a) a defined territory, b) a defined citizenry, c) a government that is d) sovereign.
2. Stephen Krasner's definition: A unified and autonomous actor pursuing aims understood in terms of the national interest despite internal and external resistance.
3. Definition used in the book: A generally unified and relatively autonomous institution that claims sovereignty over a given territory and people and pursues on their behalf objectives understood in terms of the national interest, though it may involve internal and external resistance.

Sovereignty The right to exclusive authority within a territory or jurisdiction that has been legitimized by external and internal actors.

Terrorism Any action intended to cause death or serious bodily harm to civilians or non-combatants with the purpose of intimidating a population or compelling a government or an international organization to do or abstain from doing any act (definition proposed by UN Secretary-General Kofi Annan).

United Nations Educational, Scientific, and Cultural Organization (UNESCO) A specialized agency of the UN system that seeks to foster cooperation and exchange in the cultural, scientific, and educational arenas.

Uruguay Round One of a series of global trade negotiations held since World War II to determine trade rules and set tariff rates. This round was negotiated from 1986 to 1994 and, among other things, created the World Trade Organization (WTO).

Utility Used by economists as a measure of the "usefulness" of a good.

Versailles Conference and Treaty of Versailles 1919 The diplomatic summit and agreements that ended World War I, which took place at the Versailles Palace near Paris, France.

World Trade Organization (WTO) A permanent international organization that took over from the General Agreement on Tariffs and Trade (GATT) in 1994 for the promotion of international trade and the resolution of trade disputes.

Bibliography

Anderson, Greg. "The Compromise of Embedded Liberalism, American Trade Remedy Law, and Canadian Softwood Lumber: Can't We All Just Get Along?" *Canadian Foreign Policy* 10.2 (2003): 87-108.

Azzi, Stephen, and Tamara Feick. "Coping with the Cultural Colossus: Canada and the International Instrument on Cultural Diversity." In David Carment, Fen Osler Hampson, and Norman Hillmer, eds., *Canada Among Nations 2003: Coping with the American Colossus*. Don Mills: Oxford University Press, 2003, 100-20.

Baehr, Peter, and Leon Gordenker. *The United Nations in the 1990s*, 2nd edition. New York: St. Martin's Press, 1994, 68.

Barry, Donald. "Chrétien, Bush, and the War in Iraq." *The American Review of Canadian Studies* 35.2 (2005): 215-45.

Beauchesne, Eric. "Foreigners' Corporate Slice Remains Same." *Chronicle-Herald* (31 December 1988): 13.

Bell, Stewart. "Blood Money: International Terrorist Fundraising in Canada." In Norman Hillmer and Maureen Appel Molot, eds., *Canada Among Nations 2002: A Fading Power*. Don Mills: Oxford University Press, 2002, 172-190.

Bercuson, David, and Barry Cooper. *Deconfederation: Canada Without Quebec*. Toronto: Key Porter, 2002.

Brebner, John Bartlet. *Canada: A Modern History*. Ann Arbour: University of Michigan Press, 1960.
————. *North Atlantic Triangle*. Toronto: McClelland and Stewart, 1966.

Brooks, Stephen. *Public Policy in Canada*. Toronto: McClelland and Stewart, 1989.

Burgess, Bill. "Foreign Direct Investment: Facts and Perceptions about Canada." *Canadian Geographer* 44.2 (2000): 104.

Bushkoff, Leonard. "Did France Wage a Secret War?" *The Globe and Mail* (5 January 1991): D5.

Byers, Michael. "Canadian Armed Forces under United States Command." *International Journal* 58.2 (2003): 89-114.
————. "The High Price of Getting Too Cozy." *The Globe and Mail* (7 December 2004): A19.

Canada. Department of Foreign Affairs and International Trade. 1995. *Canada in the World: Government Statement*. Canada Communications Group.

Canada. Industry Canada. *Trade and Investment Monitor, Fall-Winter 1999-2000*. <strategis.ic. gc.ca/sc_ecnmy/mera/engdoc/08.html>.

Canada. Standing Committee on External Affairs and International Trade. 1987. *For Whose Benefit?* House of Commons.

Canadian Press. "Europe Sets Fish Quotas at 12 Times Allocation." *The Globe and Mail* (13 December 1988): A1.

Carment, David, Fen Osler Hampson, and Norman Hillmer, eds. *Canada Among Nations 2004: Setting Priorities Straight*. Montreal: McGill-Queen's University Press, 2005.

———. *Canada Among Nations 2003: Coping with the American Colossus*. Don Mills: Oxford University Press, 2003.

Charlton, Mark. "Will a Ballistic Defence System Undermine Global Security?" In Mark Charlton, *Crosscurrents: International Relations*. Toronto: Thomson-Nelson, 2005, 138-140.

Chase, Steven, and Greg Keenan. "South Korea Free Trade Talks Face Opposition." *The Globe and Mail* (1 June 2005): B1.

Chronicle-Herald. "Liberal Nationalism Driving away Investment—Clark." 2 October 1982, 5.

Clarke, Harold D., Allan Kornberg, John MacLeod, and Thomas Scotto. "Too Close to Call: Political Choice in Canada, 2004." *PS: Political Science & Politics* 38.2 (2005): 247-254.

Clarkson, Stephen. *Canada and the Reagan Challenge: Crisis and Adjustment, 1981-85*. Toronto: James Lorimer & Company, 1985.

Cooper, Andrew F. *Canadian Foreign Policy: Old Habits and New Directions*. Scarborough: Prentice-Hall, 1997.

Corbridge, Stuart. "Beneath the Pavement Only Soil: The Poverty of Post Development." *Journal of Development Studies* 34.6 (1998): 138-39.

Cotter, John. "Canadians Hone Skills for Next Mission." *The Globe and Mail* (28 September 2005): A13.

Cox, Kevin. "Chasing North Atlantic's 'Modern-day Pirates.'" *The Globe and Mail* (2 August 2004): A5.

Dawson, Grant. "'A Special Case': Canada, Operation Apollo, and Multilateralism." In David Carment, Fen Osler Hampson, and Norman Hillmer, eds., *Canada Among Nations 2003: Coping with the American Colossus*. Don Mills: Oxford University Press, 2003, 180-99.

Deighton, Anne. "The 'Frozen Front:' The Labour Government, the Division of Germany, and the Origins of the Cold War, 1945-7." *International Affairs* 63.3 (1987): 449-65.

Dewitt, David, and John Kirton. *Canada as Principal Power: A Study of Foreign Policy and International Relations*. Toronto: John Wiley and Sons, 1983.

Dimbleby, David, and David Reynolds. *An Ocean Apart: The Relationship Between Britain and America in the Twentieth Century*. London: BBC Books, 1988.

Doran, Charles R. *Why Canadian Unity Matters and Why Americans Care: Democratic Pluralism at Risk*. Toronto: University of Toronto Press, 2001.

Drohan, Madelaine. "Breaking Up Is Hard to Do." *The Globe and Mail* (26 March 1991): B1.

Dunleavy, Patrick, and Brendan O'Leary. *Theories of the State*. London: Macmillan, 1987.

Eayrs, James. *In Defence of Canada: Indochina*. Toronto: University of Toronto Press, 1983.

———. *In Defence of Canada: Peacemaking and Deterrence*. Toronto: University of Toronto Press, 1972.

English, John. *The Worldly Years: The Life of Lester Pearson, 1949-1972*. Toronto: Vintage, 1993.

Evans, Peter, Dietrich Rueschemeyer, and Theda Skocpol, eds. *Bringing the State Back In*. New York and Cambridge: Cambridge University Press, 1985.

Fagan, Drew and Barrie McKenna. "US Channel Wins Cable Fight." *The Globe and Mail* (22 June 1995): A1.

Frankel, Joseph. *National Interest*. London: Pall Mall, 1970.

Fraser, Blair. *The Search for Identity: Canada: Postwar to Present*. Toronto: Doubleday Canada, 1967.

Freeman, Alan. "Separation Spells Gloom." *The Globe and Mail* (23 September 1991): A1.

Gallagher, Stephen. "The Open Door Beyond the Moat: Canadian Refugee Policy from a Comparative Perspective." In Norman Hillmer and Maureen Appel Molot, eds., *Canada Among Nations 2002: A Fading Power*. Don Mills: Oxford University Press, 2002, 97-121.

Galloway, Gloria. "Allies Quitting Goose Bay." *The Globe and Mail* (9 August 2004): A2.

———. "National Security in Peril, Report Says." *The Globe and Mail* (9 December 2004): A6.

The Globe and Mail. "Is the flag only flapping in the wind?" 31 October 1998, C16.

Geddes, John and Charlie Gillis. "How Safe Are We?" *Maclean's* (18 July 2005): 20-24.

Goforth, Colonel W., and S. Katz. "If the Russians Attack Canada." *Maclean's* (15 June 1951).

Goold, Douglas. "Bill Graham, Pierre Pettigrew, Jim Peterson." *International Journal* 59.4 (2004): 929-42.

Gordon, Walter L. *A Choice for Canada: Independence or Colonial Status*. Toronto: McClelland and Stewart, 1966.

Granatstein, J.L. *Canada's Army: Waging War and Keeping the Peace*. Toronto: University of Toronto Press, 2002.

Granatstein, J.L., and Robert Bothwell. *Pirouette: Pierre Trudeau and Canadian Foreign Policy*. Toronto: University of Toronto Press, 1990.

Grant, George. *Lament for a Nation: The Defeat of Canadian Nationalism*. Toronto: McClelland and Stewart, 1965.

Gwyn, Richard. *The 49th Paradox: Canada in North America*. Toronto: Totem, 1986.

Ha, Tu Thanh. "Parizeau Says Declaration Could Be Issued without a Referendum." *The Globe and Mail* (17 August 2004): A1.

Hampson, Fen Osler, Norman Hillmer, and Maureen Appel Molot, eds. *Canada Among Nations 2001: The Axworthy Legacy*. Don Mills: Oxford University Press, 2001.

Harris, Christopher. "CBC Vows No US Shows in Prime Time." *The Globe and Mail* (24 November 1995): A1.

Hart, Michael. *A Trading Nation: Canadian Trade Policy from Colonialism to Globalization*. Vancouver: University of British Columbia Press, 2002.

Helleiner, Gerald K. "Canada, the Developing Countries and the International Economy: What Next?" Department of Economics, University of Toronto. Working Paper No. B.5, September 1984.

Hilliker, John. *Canada's Department of External Affairs*. Montreal: McGill-Queen's University, 1990.

Hillmer, Norman, and J.L. Granatstein. *Empire to Umpire: Canada and the World to the 1990s*. Toronto: Copp Clark Longman, 1994.

Hillmer, Norman, and Maureen Appel Molot, eds. *Canada Among Nations 2002: A Fading Power*. Don Mills: Oxford University Press, 2002.

Hjertholm, Peter, and Howard White. "Foreign Aid in Historical Perspective," In Finn Tarp, ed., *Foreign Aid and Development: Lessons Learned and Directions for the Future*. London: Routledge, 2002, 80-102.

Holmes, John. *The Shaping of Peace, Volume 2*. Toronto: University of Toronto Press, 1982.

Howard, Ross. "54:40 or Fight!" *The Globe and Mail* (30 August 1986): A8.

Huntington, Samuel. "The Clash of Civilizations." *Foreign Affairs* (Summer 1993).

Ibbitson, John. "US No-fly Roster May Swat Canadians." *The Globe and Mail* (3 June 2003): A4.

Jockel, Joseph. *No Boundaries Upstairs*. Vancouver: University of British Columbia Press, 1987.

Janigan, Mary. "Why Are We in Afghanistan?" *The Globe and Mail* (17 September 2005): F3.

Keating, Tom. *Canada and World Order: The Multilateralist Tradition in Canadian Foreign Policy.* Don Mills: Oxford University Press, 2002.

Kennedy, Peter. "Weak Loonie Seen to Offset Lumber Duties." *The Globe and Mail* (29 January 2002): B10.

Keohane, Robert, and Joseph Nye. *Power and Independence*. Boston: Little, Brown and Company, 1977.

Krasner, Stephen D. *Defending the National Interest: Raw Materials Investments and US Foreign Policy*. Princeton: Princeton University Press, 1978.

Lagassé, Philippe. "Matching Ends and Means in Canadian Defence." In David Carmet, Fen Osler Hampson, and Norman Hillmer, *Canada Among Nations 2004: Setting Priorities Straight.* Montreal: McGill-Queen's University Press, 2005, 73-92.

Lamorie, Andrew. *How They Sold Our Canada to the USA*. Toronto: NC Press, 1976.

LeBlanc, Daniel. "Canadian Forces Offers First Peek at JTF2 Mission Underway in Afghanistan." *The Globe and Mail* (21 September 2005): A19.

Levitt, Kair. *Silent Surrender: The Multinational Corporation in Canada*. New York: St. Martin's Press, 1970.

MacKinnon, Mark. "No Confusion Created by Mission to Mexico with French PM, Martin asserts." *The Globe and Mail* (15 October 2004): A7.

Mahant, Edelgard, and Graeme Mount. *An Introduction to Canadian-American Relations*. Toronto: Methuen, 1984.

Mansergh, Nicholas. *The Commonwealth Experience*. New York: Praeger, 1969.

Martin, Lawrence. *Pledge of Allegiance: The Americanization of Canada in the Mulroney Years*. Toronto: McClelland and Stewart, 1993.

Martin, Lawrence. *The Presidents and The Prime Ministers*. Toronto: Doubleday Canada Ltd., 1982.

Maxwell, Sylvia. "International Development." In Walter Carlsnaes, Thomas Risse, and Beth A. Simmons, *Handbook of International Relations*. London: Sage, 2002, 462-79.

McNaught, Kenneth. *The Penguin History of Canada*. London: Penguin Books, 1969.

Meek, Jim. "Nova Scotia 'Holding Own' in 200-Mile Fishery Zone." *Chronicle-Herald* (8 December 1983): 3.

Mickleburgh, Rod and Colin Freeze. "Ressam Sentencing Today in Millennium Plot." *The Globe and Mail* (27 April 2005): A8.

Middlemiss, D.W., and J.J. Sokolsky. *Canadian Defence: Decisions and Determinants*. Toronto: Harcourt Brace Jovanoviach, 1989.

Miller, John D.B. *World of States*. New York: St. Martin's Press, 1981.

Molot, Maureen Appel, and Fen Osler Hampson, eds. *Canada Among Nations 2000: Vanishing Borders*. Don Mills: Oxford University Press, 2000.

Molot, Maureen Appel, and Norman Hillmer. "The Diplomacy of Decline." In Norman Hillmer and

Maureen Appel Molot, eds., *Canada Among Nations 2002: A Fading Power*. Don Mills: Oxford University Press, 2002, 1-33.

Morgenthau, Hans. *Politics Among Nations, 5th Edition*. New York: Alfred A. Knopf, 1978.

Morton, Desmond. *Canada and War*. Toronto: Butterworths, 1981.

Munton, Donald, and John Kirton, eds. *Canadian Foreign Policy: Selected Cases*. Scarborough: Prentice-Hall Canada, 1992.

Nash, Knowlton. *Kennedy and Diefenbaker: Fear and Loathing across the Undefended Border*. Toronto: McClelland & Stewart, 1990.

Nicholson, Patrick. *Vision and Indecision*. Don Mills: Longmans Canada, 1968.

Noël, Alain, and Jean-Philippe Thérien. "From Domestic to International Justice: The Welfare State and Foreign Aid." *International Organization* 49.3 (1995): 523-54.

Norrie, Kenneth, and Douglas Owram. *A History of the Canadian Economy*. Toronto: Harcourt Brace & Company, 1991.

Nossal, Kim Richard. *The Politics of Canadian Foreign Policy*. Scarborough: Prentice-Hall Canada, 1997.

Organisation for Economic Cooperation and Development (OECD), "DAC Development Co-operation 2002 Report." *DAC Journal* 4.1 (2003): 45.

Oziewicz, Estanislao. "Annan Proposes Definition of Terrorism." *The Globe and Mail* (22 March 2005): A14.

Patterson, Robert. "Can Losing Quebec Be Everyone's Gain?" *The Globe and Mail* (14 January 1991): A17.

Pearson, Lester B. *Mike*. Toronto: University of Toronto Press, 1972.

Pratt, Cranford "Competing Rationales for Canadian Development Assistance: Reducing Global Poverty, Enhancing Canadian Prosperity and Security, or Advancing Global Human Security." *International Journal* 54.2 (1999): 306-23.

Riddell-Dixon, Elizabeth. "Canada at the United Nations in the New Millennium." In David Carment, Fen Osler Hampson, and Norman Hillmer, eds., *Canada Among Nations 2003: Coping with the American Colossus*. Don Mills: Oxford University Press, 2003, 256-86.

Robinson, H. Basil. *Diefenbaker's World*. Toronto: University of Toronto, 1989.

Resnick, Philip. *Toward a Canada-Quebec Union*. Montreal: McGill-Queen's University Press, 2003.

Redekop, John H., ed. *The Star Spangled Beaver*. Toronto: Peter Martin Associates, 1971.

Ross, Douglas. *In the Interests of Peace*. Toronto: University of Toronto Press, 1984.

Ross, Val and Drew Fagan. "Magazine Tax Brings US Threat." *The Globe and Mail* (23 December 1994): A1.

Roussel, Stéphane. *The North American Democratic Peace*. Montreal: McGill-Queen's University Press, 2004.

Sallot, Jeff. "PM Calls for United Front with Mexico." *The Globe and Mail* (26 March 1994): A1.

Sands, Christopher. "Fading Power or Rising Power: 11 September and Lessons from the Section 110 Experience." In Norman Hillmer and Maureen Appel Molot, eds., *Canada Among Nations: A Fading Power*. Don Mills: Oxford University Press, 2002, 49-73.

Saunders, Doug. "Quebec Expanding Missions in the US" *The Globe and Mail* (20 May 2002): A4.

Séguin, Rhéal. "Quebec Liberal Decry Study Promoting Sovereignty." *The Globe and Mail* (6 May 2005): A12.

————. "Quebec seeking special deal on foreign affairs." *The Globe and Mail* (29 September 2004): A4.

————. "Quebec 'a nation,' National Assembly declares in vote." *The Globe and Mail* (31 October 2003): A8.

Simpson, Jeffery. "Deconfederation: Canada without Quebec." *The Globe and Mail* (24 August 1991): C8.

Smith, Anthony D. *National Identity*. London: Penguin Books, 1991.

Smith, Denis. *Diplomacy of Fear: Canada and the Cold War 1941-1948*. Toronto: University of Toronto Press, 1988.

Stairs, Denis. *In the National Interest: Canadian Foreign Policy in an Insecure World*. Canadian Defence and Foreign Affairs Institute. 2003. <www.cdfai.org/currentpublications. htm>.

Szulc, Tad. "Don't Take Canada for Granted." *Parade Magazine* (20 Feb 1994): 4-7.

Tarp, Finn, ed. *Foreign Aid and Development: Lessons Learned and Directions for the Future*. London: Routledge, 2002.

Thomson, Janice E. "State Sovereignty in International Relations." *International Studies Quarterly* 39.2 (1995): 214.

Thordarson, Bruce. *Trudeau and Foreign Policy: A Study in Decision-Making*. Toronto: Oxford University Press, 1972.

Triska, Jan, ed. *Dominant Powers and Subordinate States: The US in Latin America and the Soviet Union in Eastern Europe*. Durham: Duke University Press, 1986.

Tuck, Simon. "Regulator Grants First 3 Licences." *The Globe and Mail* (17 June 2005): B1.

Vital, David. *The Making of British Foreign Policy*. London: Allen Unwin, 1968.

Welsh, Jennifer. *At Home in the World: Canada's Global Vision for the 21st Century*. Toronto: Harper Collins, 2004.

Yergin, Daniel. *Shattered Peace: The Origins of the Cold War and the National Security State*. Boston: Houghton Mifflin, 1977.

Index